The Correspondence of
Hannah Arendt
and
Gershom Scholem

The Correspondence of **HANNAH ARENDT** and **GERSHOM SCHOLEM**

Edited by Marie Luise Knott
Translated by Anthony David

The University of Chicago Press
Chicago and London

The University of Chicago Press, Chicago 60637
The University of Chicago Press, Ltd., London

Published 2017
Printed in the United States of America

26 25 24 23 22 21 20 19 18 17   1 2 3 4 5

ISBN-13: 978-0-226-92451-9 (cloth)
ISBN-13: 978-0-226-48761-8 (e-book)
DOI: 10.7208/chicago/9780226487618.001.0001

Originally published as Hannah Arendt/Gershom Scholem, *Der Briefwechsel* Jüdischer Verlag im Suhrkamp Verlag Berlin 2011.

Library of Congress Cataloging-in-Publication Data
Names: Arendt, Hannah, 1906–1975, author. | Scholem, Gershom, 1897–1982, author. | Knott, Marie Luise, editor, writer of introduction. | David, Anthony (Translator), translator.
Title: The correspondence of Hannah Arendt and Gershom Scholem / edited by Marie Luise Knott ; translated by Anthony David.
Description: Chicago ; London : The University of Chicago Press, 2017. | Includes bibliographical references and index.
Identifiers: LCCN 2017012490 | ISBN 9780226924519 (cloth : alk. paper) | ISBN 9780226487618 (e-book)
Subjects: LCSH: Arendt, Hannah, 1906–1975—Correspondence. | Scholem, Gershom, 1897–1982—Correspondence. | Intellectuals—Correspondence. | Jews—Correspondence. | Judaism and politics. | Holocaust, Jewish (1939–1945)—Influence. | Jews, German—Intellectual life—20th century. | Jewish Cultural Reconstruction, Inc. (New York, N.Y.) | Jewish property—Germany. | Cultural property—Repatriation—Germany.
Classification: LCC JC263.A69 A7313 2017 | DDC 320.5092/2—dc23
LC record available at https://lccn.loc.gov/2017012490

∞ This paper meets the requirements of ANSI/NISO Z39.48-1992 (Permanence of Paper).

CONTENTS

INTRODUCTION

"Why Have We Been Spared?"

Marie Luise Knott

It has long been known that Gershom Scholem, who pioneered the academic field of Kabbalah, and Hannah Arendt, who in her work *The Human Condition* pioneered the realm of politics and action, were friends and carried on an extensive correspondence. The differences between them—differences in character, in political convictions, and in the focus of their scholarly work—seemed so deep that for a long time it was difficult to imagine the very close nature of their relationship. The few letters that were published on different occasions mostly focused on the political disputes that separated these two important thinkers: mainly the harsh debate over Arendt's article "Zionism Reconsidered" in 1946, and seventeen years later the dispute that broke out between them over her *Eichmann in Jerusalem*. Only now, after all of their letters have been brought together from various archives, transcribed, and annotated, does a fuller portrait of their friendship emerge.

Gerhard Scholem, born in 1897 in Berlin, rebelled against his deeply acculturated family, and as a young man moved to Jerusalem in 1923, where he—"the living embodiment of Judaism," according to Walter Benjamin—took on the name Gershom and lived and taught until his death in 1982. Hannah Arendt, born in Hanover in 1906, grew up in Königsberg in East Prussia; in 1933 she fled from Berlin for Paris, and in 1940 she continued on to New York, where she lived until her death in 1975. An obituary in the *New Yorker* described her as "a counterweight to all the world's unreason and corruption."

Under normal conditions Arendt and Scholem would probably never have met, let alone have become friends. After all, when in 1924, at the age of eighteen, Arendt began studying philosophy and theology with Martin

Heidegger and Rudolf Bultmann in Marburg, Scholem was already twenty-seven and living in Palestine, where he was "fascinated by the apocalyptic, attracted to the anarchic, and drawn to the subversive," as the Hebrew University historian Steven Aschheim has noted.[1] While in 1927 Arendt still felt "hopelessly assimilated,"[2] the mounting tide of anti-Semitism in Germany brought her in contact with Zionism. Arendt, who wrote her dissertation on St. Augustine and who viewed Judaism through the prism of a European intellectual history deeply molded by Christianity, identified with the fight against the oppression of her people, claiming that the Jews were the first people against whom Hitler had declared war. Scholem, by contrast, made a deliberate break from the Christian European tradition through his work on heterodox and mystical streams within Judaism, the goal of his work being disassimilation. To do so, he came up with a historiography that broke from the apologetic approach to Jewish tradition typically taken by German Jewish scholars, and this freed him up to approach Jewish fate with different tools.

At the start of their correspondence in the early 1930s, both Arendt and Scholem, confronting the end of the era of Jewish emancipation and assimilation, sought to revolutionize Jewish historiography with a fundamentally new reading of Jewish tradition coupled with a sense of "Tikkun Olam," or "healing of the world." Scholem uncovered an "invisible stream" within mysticism, while Arendt, adopting an existential conception of Judaism, uncovered a "hidden tradition" within the consciousness of the pariah. Scholem lived in Jerusalem, where at the Hebrew University and in the spirit of the cultural Zionist Achad Ha'am he hoped to revive the spiritual center of Judaism free of persecution and prejudice. He attempted to convince friends, acquaintances, and important scholars, including Walter Benjamin, Leo Strauss, Hans Jonas, and Shalom Spiegel, to immigrate to Jerusalem. After 1933 Arendt, too, supported immigration efforts to Palestine and the building up of a Jewish homeland. That said, in contrast to Zionist ideals, she set out to conceptualize the future of Judaism, politically and culturally, from the perspective of the entire Jewish people, not just those in Palestine.

The Beginnings

The correspondence between Arendt and Scholem began in 1939 with Arendt's letter from Paris, and as far as we know Scholem wrote the final letter in their correspondence from Jerusalem in 1964. "Jews are dying in Europe and are being buried like dogs," Arendt wrote to Scholem in her second letter, from October 1940, to announce the suicide of their common friend Walter Benjamin. Over the decades the Arendt and Scholem letters demonstrate a joint grief over the dead. "Why have we been spared?" Scholem asks in one of his letters. And the correspondence reveals an answer: They felt they had been "spared" for the task of saving Jewish cultural treasures and renewing Jewish thought after the Holocaust.

Arendt and Scholem met face-to-face fewer than ten times, and their friendship was not free of conflicts. On November 27, 1946, Arendt wrote the following lines from her office in New York:

> My heart goes out to you—and for this no passport is required, no money, and no "vacation time." My heart got a ticket and is sailing peacefully, in tourist class, to Palestine. You will then be at the port in Haifa to make sure that my heart isn't allowed to land.

This imagery of the heart crossing oceans and frontiers and yet not being in the condition to be received mirrors the intense tension of their friendship, a tension composed of intimacy and distance, of mutual attraction and mutual dissociation. Both the tension and the magic of their relationship arose out of the particular dilemma of their time—the impossibility of German Jewish life.

In 1946, triggered by Arendt's article "Zionism Reconsidered," the two debated the principles of Jewish political reorganization and the future of Palestine (Letters 19 and 20). "Zionism Reconsidered" disappointed and even embittered Scholem, who in a letter to an American Zionist friend had described Arendt in 1941 as a "wonderful woman and an outstanding Zionist."[3] Given the threats to the survival of Jewish life in Palestine, he considered her criticism akin to mockery.

According to Hannah Arendt, the future of Judaism—and this was one of her central points in "Zionism Reconsidered"—ought to be shaped politically as well as culturally by all Jews, that is, not only by the Zionists who had decided to live in Palestine. In many of their political assessments, Scholem and Arendt were not far apart. Like Arendt, he recognized what she criticized as the tendencies of uniformity within Zionism; similarly to her, Scholem complained about the "debasement of ethical Zionism into the accustomed practice of political realism." And in his response to Arendt's critique of Zionism, he emphasized that he had always advocated coming to terms with the Arab neighbors and for the creation of a binational commonwealth. "As an old Brit Shalom follower," he wrote to her, referring to an organization in Jerusalem that called for a joint Arab-Jewish confederation, "I myself have once belonged to the opposite camp."

However much he supported the right to criticize Zionism, given the Holocaust and the Arab attacks that posed a threat to Jewish life in postwar Palestine, he waved off Arendt's criticism and postulated an unconditional and unconditioned yes to the founding of a Jewish state in Palestine, arguing that any different, more accommodating policy adopted by the Jews would not have made any difference. At the end of the day, he felt, the Arabs "are mainly interested not in our morality or political convictions, but in whether or not we are here in Palestine at all."[4] Setting aside his own political disappointments in light of the threats to the state's sheer existence, he criticized Arendt's essay for putting to question the absolute priority of Jewish solidarity and a collective sense of belonging.

If in 1946 what united Arendt and Scholem remained stronger than the centrifugal forces driving them apart, their second dispute, over Arendt's *Eichmann in Jerusalem* (1963), culminated in a final rupture. In contrast to Scholem, in her book Arendt came out in support of the Israeli court's decision to impose the death penalty on Adolf Eichmann, a key figure in the destruction of European Jewry. That said, she was not in agreement with the court proceedings. She criticized the role of the Jewish Councils (Jüdische Räte) during the Holocaust, and she questioned the human capacity for freedom of action under totalitarian conditions. The shock she felt at confronting Eichmann in person, at seeing this "mass murderer [who killed] without any motives," a man who just murdered "because it was part of his career," and her horror at the devastation brought on by Eichmann's "thoughtlessness" (that a person could act without imagining the implications of his actions)—all this led at the very end of her book to the notion of the "banality of evil."[5] Scholem condemned her depiction of the Eichmann trial because in his eyes Arendt trivialized the German policy of extermination. Moreover, he detected an insolent attack against the Jewish representatives, who after all, as he argued, had found themselves after 1941 in a deadly situation with no escape. Unless you have been in their shoes, was his message to her, you have no right to judge.

Thin, Strong Ties

Scholem once described the act of writing letters as a two-way adventure in inter-human disclosure: letters are simultaneously the place of both deferred and expected encounters. In the "messianic moment"—the time horizon of the letter—the individual's existence transforms into script. Although in Scholem's recollection he met Arendt in the early 1930s in Berlin, and although Hans Jonas, their mutual friend, always claimed to have brought them together during Arendt's first trip to Palestine in 1935, judging by their correspondence, their dialogue and friendship began in 1938. Scholem stopped on his way from Jerusalem to New York in Paris to see his old friend Walter Benjamin. It was there he came into closer contact with Arendt and Heinrich Blücher, her second husband.

In Paris, Scholem and Arendt discussed, among other things, Scholem's research into mysticism, Arendt's biography of Rahel Varnhagen, the threatening political situation, the endangered position of Jews in Paris and Palestine, and their common concern regarding the dire financial position of Walter Benjamin.

The letters Arendt and Scholem exchanged between 1939 and 1948 (Letters 1–50) concentrate on Jewish concerns, the war in Europe, the fate of their people, the situation in Palestine, and the future of Jewish politics. Above all, through their missives one follows a shared grief over the death of Benjamin along with a common desire to save their friend's literary estate, and to make public his work for future generations in Germany, Israel, and the United States.

From autumn 1949 to the beginning of 1952 (Letters 51–98), the correspondence intensifies with their joint efforts on behalf of Jewish Cultural Reconstruction, Inc. (JCR). Taking up key roles within this New York–based institution, Arendt and Scholem struggled to salvage the remains of Jewish cultural heritage in Europe. On behalf of JCR, both traveled back to war-ravaged Europe.

Many people at the time asked how a German Jew could even step foot on the soil of the country that had spearheaded the extermination of Jewry. The dilemma of many Jews from Germany can be detected in a letter Arendt received from a close friend, the American exile Hilde Fränkel, who wished to hear from Arendt "that it isn't worth it [to go back], that we live in God's own country."[6] The letters Arendt sent back to her friends in far-off New York during her visit to Germany in 1949 speak of stale air, intrigues, hectic work, of destroyed lives and destroyed cities; and yet there is also a sense of happiness that suddenly breaks through the alienation: "After all, there is the German language and the inexpressibly lovely German landscape of our homeland, a familiarity that has and will never exist for us anywhere else."

As in her private letters from Germany, Arendt rarely mentions her frenetic work for JCR; the second part of her correspondence with Scholem reveals a completely new dimension of her life.

In the final period of their correspondence (1952–1964), after the end of their mutual work for JCR, the frequency of their exchange of letters slows down. Until the controversy over the Eichmann trial in 1963, the letters are essentially friendly, even if they lack any strong commitments; there is little emotion bridging the geographical distance. Historians have long assumed that Scholem broke off all contact with Arendt in the wake of her book on the trial. Yet his letter from July 1964 (Letter 141) shows him once more suggesting that they meet. In the archives, there is no evidence that the two former friends ever did.

Rahel Varnhagen: Retrieval of Honor

In the fall of 1938, following their discussions in Paris, what launched their friendship was Scholem's keen interest in Arendt's Rahel book project, a theme that "seen from a Jewish perspective involves a rather sensitive issue." The reason for this, Scholem claimed, was that in the 1930s, given the final failure of Jewish emancipation, "figures such as Rahel can be seen in an entirely new light."[7] Arendt wrote this biography, in fact, as a critique on assimilation, whose champions had fervently believed in the bright prospects of emancipation, even if emancipation didn't turn out the way its purveyors had anticipated. Arendt's study shows Rahel, who had always been considered a successful protagonist of a German-Jewish cultural dialogue, in all her factual desolation. Arendt shared Scholem's lack of illusion about life in a non-Jewish environment and asserted that he who wants to assimilate must (also) assimilate into anti-Semitism. There was no getting around the Jew's rootedness in Judaism. "There is no escape from Judaism."[8]

A few months after Arendt and Scholem met in Paris, Benjamin described in a letter to Scholem the "powerful impression" the Rahel manuscript had made on him, arguing that Arendt was "swimming against the current of an edifying and apologetic Judaic studies. You know best of all that everything one can read about 'the Jews in German literature' up to now has allowed itself to be swept up in this current."[9] Arendt, influenced by her reading of the German philosopher Johann Gottfried von Herder (1744–1803), developed the notion of a "hidden tradition" of the pariah. Unlike the previous approaches to Jewish history, hers was not, as Walter Benjamin noted, "edifying" or "apologetic." The same can be said for Scholem's rediscovery of the often-concealed, rejected, and forgotten Jewish mystics and sects, figures who during the period of emancipation were considered embarrassing remnants of the past from which Jews had happily liberated themselves on their way west, or so they thought.

What joined Arendt's study of the "hidden tradition" with Scholem's research into the "submerged heritage" was, to quote Benjamin, their mutual desire to "wrest tradition away from a conformism that is about to overpower it," and above all to strip away the illusion of there being an inexorable progress of Jewish emancipation. The fresh approaches Arendt and Scholem took to tradition offered a chance of "fanning the spark of hope in the past."[10] As Scholem writes, "The Bible and the apocalyptic writers know of no progress in history leading to the redemption. The redemption is not the product of immanent developments such as we find in modern Western reinterpretations of Messianism since the Enlightenment where, secularized as the belief in progress, Messianism still displayed unbroken and immense vigor."[11]

In his first letter to Arendt (a letter that has been lost), Scholem apparently told her how he had read her Rahel manuscript and suggested that she should publish it with the Tel Aviv publishing house Schocken Books. In her reply from May 1939 (Letter 1), she cautioned Scholem against a possible misinterpretation of her work: while she indeed wanted to describe a catastrophe, the final two chapters in the book also were a kind of "vindication." This was in particular important "these days . . . because every ignorant upstart thinks he can heap scorn onto assimilated Judaism."

She "wrangled" with Rahel Varnhagen as if they were contemporaries, Arendt wrote in a letter to Karl Jaspers, and at the same time she wrote the book using "categories that were available to [Varnhagen] at the time and which she herself somehow would have considered valid."[12] Arendt's act of "vindication" did not honor just Rahel as an individual but extended to the political status of Jewry as a whole by shedding fresh light on the dilemma of Jewish life during the upheavals of the early nineteenth century.

Scholem, by contrast, with his polemical critique of attempts at assimilation, considered the story of Rahel, as it had been transmitted, to rest on a sham bargain, namely on the "assumption that everything had to come from one side," in other words from the Germans, "while the other side, forever on the receiving end, had always to be self-denying (in the most precise sense)."[13] He realized that a hyphenated relationship such as the "German-Jewish" one, because it was based on a sham, was doomed for disaster.

He later conceded, however:

> Looking back today, I am more firmly convinced now than I could have been in my youth, when I was swept away by the passions of protest, that for many of these people illusions merged with utopia, and the anticipation of feeling at home gave them a happiness which was genuine to the extent that every utopia must be credited with an element of genuineness.[14]

The Varnhagen project, which launched their dialogue, soon took on a new meaning for both Arendt and Scholem due to the ghastly reports coming out of Europe. The "world has become so torn apart," Scholem remarked. Arendt's reply (Letter 6) was that "it is real comfort to still be hearing from friends. Such letters are like minutely thin, strong threads. We'd like to convince ourselves that these threads are able to hold together what remains of our world." Given the situation in Palestine, caught between utopia and terror, these "threads" were being put to the test.

Arendt captured the danger of a friendship shorn of a shared place by using a simile she took from the Czech antiwar novel *The Good Soldier Schweik*: "I'm angry at you," she writes to Scholem, alluding to their plans to meet after the war ended, "for not holding your end of the bargain and meeting with me in a cafe at five o'clock, right after the end of the World War. But I'll have to admit, somehow, that the cafe no longer exists."[15]

Walter Benjamin: On Translatability

Scholem, during his first trip to postwar Paris, sent Arendt a colored greeting card from the Bibliothèque Nationale. The picture, a caricature from late eighteenth-century revolutionary France, hints at the central hope of Walter Benjamin to prevent the ultimate failure of the revolutionary dream.

"Mes chers amis—what a melancholic sight to be again in Paris and be reminded of the past days," Scholem wrote from the same spot from which the two of them, in their conversations, had once battled the world together. Arendt replied: "The sadness of Paris must have been nightmarish. I wish I could have been there with you. Even if it wouldn't have helped at all, sometimes a witness from earlier times can at least help a person snap out of the unreality of melancholy." She knew that the presence of another person didn't wipe away the sadness of loss, though—perhaps—it did help overcome the "irreality of melancholy," which is to say, the danger brought on by the melancholy of losing the ground under one's feet.

The 141 surviving letters between Arendt and Scholem begin and end with Walter Benjamin, a man whose fate had tied them together since their first encounter in Paris. Benjamin's desperate need to find ways to express the devastations of his time was a constant intellectual challenge to both Arendt and Scholem. His death destroyed all his possible future intellectual attempts, everything that this radical thinker, "on the spoors of a number of new things" (Letter 4), could have written, every spiritual path he could have pursued. Both Arendt and Scholem mourned this destruction of a future, and both found ways of integrating his "new things" into their own work.

In 1946, following Scholem's fierce eruption against "Zionism Reconsidered," Arendt began her letter of reconciliation by mentioning plans for a joint edition of Benjamin's works (Letter 20); and in 1964, when in the wake of the Eichmann controversy Scholem wanted to meet up with Arendt in New York, he mentioned his "Benjamin lecture" at the Leo Baeck Institute (Letter 140). Their sadness led to joint efforts at salvaging Benjamin's literary estate from disappearance and obscurity, and then bringing his work to print.

One can follow in the correspondence several failed attempts at rescuing Benjamin's literary estate. Their first hope was an edition of Benjamin's writings through Schocken Books in Palestine. In 1946 Arendt discussed the possibility of getting Benjamin's "Conversations with Brecht" published in the *Kenyon Review*; and she tried to get the journal *View* to publish Benjamin's essay on epic theater in Brecht. She failed when the magazine folded. Equally unsuccessful was her effort, also in 1946, to sign a contract with Benjamin's son, Stefan, to permit the publication of an English translation of Benjamin's essays at Schocken Books in New York. Nothing came of it because of changes Salman Schocken, the owner of the publishing house, made in his publishing policy.

On Scholem's initiative, after 1945 he and Arendt began corresponding with Benjamin's friends and family with the aim of saving as many of his letters and writings as possible, and to present to postwar Europe a German-language edition of Benjamin's writings.

But Benjamin mostly vanished from the correspondence after Scholem's announcement, in a fragmentary letter from 1950 (Letter 84), of his and the philosopher Theodor Wiesengrund Adorno's agreement to collaborate in editing two volumes of Benjamin's letters. It was only in 1959 that Arendt and Scholem took up the subject of Benjamin again. Arthur A. Cohen of Meridian Books wanted their help in editing an English volume of Benjamin's essays. Similarly, Albert Salomon, also with the agreement of Arendt and Scholem, planned to bring out a volume of Benjamin's writings as part of the Leo Baeck Publication Series. Even if none of these plans got off the ground, their determined efforts—the sending back and forth of manuscripts, pictures, and letters, the gathering of and sifting through papers, as well as their coordinated contact of Benjamin's friends, all of which one can follow in part in the correspondence—paved the way for the eventual appearance of Benjamin's collected letters and writings. Arendt and Scholem's dedication, their "duty to the dead," saved letters and manuscripts from being forgotten or lost. Together, they secured invaluable materials for posterity and paved the way for the later editions of his work.

Between 1938 and 1964, neither Arendt nor Scholem ever spoke in public about their mutual friend Benjamin. Scholem gave his first public lecture on Benjamin in 1964, and in 1967 Arendt edited *Illuminations*, the first English edition of Benjamin's essays. From a variety of angles, both Scholem's lecture and the postscript Arendt wrote for *Illuminations* paid tribute to Benjamin's anti-utopianism. Scholem sees in Benjamin's life, "threatened" as it was by the "dread of loneliness" and a "longing" for community, a seeking of an "apocalyptic" community of "revolution" rather than a utopian community.

In a similar vein, Arendt stressed that Benjamin wasn't drawn to the positive aspects of Zionist or Marxist ideology; what interested him instead, she wrote, was a "negative force of criticism." He knew, in fact, that "all solutions were not only objectively false and inappropriate to reality, but would lead him personally to a false salvation, no matter whether that salvation was labeled Moscow or Jerusalem. He felt that he would deprive himself of the positive cognitive chances of his own position."[16]

What Arendt writes in her essay on Benjamin shows that she and Scholem shared Benjamin's critique of the teleological conception of history, along with the insight that there is an apocalyptic dimension at work within the very heart of time, and indeed within existence itself. "For every second of time was the strait gate through which Messiah might enter."[17]

A Jewish Cultural Atmosphere

In a letter to the publisher Salman Schocken, Scholem described a conversation he once had as a youth with a pious Orthodox Jew. What came to his mind after the conversation was how the world of the Kabbalah, reaching beyond "the experiences of my generation, addresses our experiences as human beings." The Kabbalists "know something we don't," he suspected. In Scholem's search to revive Jewish cultural traditions, mysticism and the Kabbalah moved to the center of his research; and in his quest for a "higher order of things," he found himself reverently hunched over musty documents. He was studying and reviving sects and movements that had hitherto been dismissed as obscure and unimportant, phenomena that scholars hadn't researched and whose language they hadn't even deciphered.

What drew Scholem to Jewish mysticism was not the emanations of the divine commonly associated with the Kabbalah; quite the contrary, his passions were stirred far more by the images of catastrophe that appear in the works of the Kabbalists Cordovero, Luria, and Nathan of Gaza. He devoted his scholarly life to investigating the "development and decay of images and symbols, of ideas and ideologies" within Jewish mysticism, a line of study that took on particular relevance for Scholem during a time in which contemporary life had become so questionable for much of humanity.

Scholem sought to anchor Jewish figures like Moses Maimonides, Sabbatai Zvi, and Jakob Frank into general intellectual history, just as Germans had done with the eighteenth-century Enlightenment writers Georg Christof Lichtenberg, Gotthold Lessing, and Friedrich Schlegel. Similarly, Arendt sought a way out of the ruins following the "death end of German Jewry." She recognized as well as Scholem the need of Jewry to escape from the well-known historical models, both the modern ones insofar as they implied assimilation, as well as traditional religious models to the extent that they meant clinging to religious laws or evasion into folklore. What Arendt strove for in the middle of the 1940s was a "new amalgamation of older traditions with new impulses and awareness without which a specifically Jewish cultural atmosphere is hardly conceivable."[18] For this reason she was committed, as an editor at Schocken Books in New York, to publishing radical Jewish intellectuals such as Bernhard Lazare, Baruch Spinoza, Heinrich Heine, and Walter Benjamin.

In New York she eagerly awaited a copy of Scholem's first edition of *Major Trends in Jewish Mysticism* (Tel Aviv: Schocken, 1941), and after reading it she sent Scholem her notes. "Scholem's new presentation and appreciation of Jewish mysticism not only fills a gap, but actually changes the whole picture of Jewish history."[19] Arendt was fascinated by his hypothesis that the movement for Jewish reform, which had always been considered to be part and parcel of Jewish emancipation, could be seen as the "outgrowth of the debacle of the last great Jewish political activity, the Sabbatian movement, of the loss of messianic hope, and of the despair about the ultimate destiny of the people."[20] The mystic, in short, had blazed the trail for the movement of reform and assimilation.

Besides the obvious parallels between the national awakening in the seventeenth century through the Sabbatians and the contemporary Zionist movement, there was something else she found compelling in Scholem's observations: it was his notion of the "treasure" of messianic freedom. The mystics, in spite of the very real external afflictions they faced, preserved a place of inner freedom from which they could defend what was left in them of what was essentially human.

In 1947 Arendt called for a cultural renewal of Judaism, for a fresh reading of biblical texts, the post-biblical religious and metaphysical canon, and medieval Hebrew poetry. These were the writings that through repetition had preserved secrets in danger of disappearing through the process of secularization. Pieces and fragments of this sacred tradition, transformed by new impulses, could now inform the present-day secular culture.

Jewish Cultural Reconstruction: An Unknown Research into Looted Art

Letters 22 and 23 in this collection, and again beginning with Letter 51, take readers into a little-known international undertaking made necessary by Nazi efforts at the extermination of the Jewish people. Parallel to the attempt at extermination, the Nazis tried "to destroy or else pervert every monument of Jewish culture, all evidence of Jewish history, and every object of Jewish art."[21] Through their work with Jewish Cultural Reconstruction (JCR), Arendt and Scholem strove with great energy and passion to gather what was left after the war of the scattered, fragmentary history and culture of European Jewry.[22] The letters show Arendt in New York and Scholem in Jerusalem working closely for two years in this transcontinental salvage operation.

JCR, a consortium of Jewish organizations from America, Palestine, and England, acted as a Jewish trust responsible for rescuing and reconstituting Jewish archives, libraries, artworks, and ceremonial artifacts robbed by the Nazis, including Torah scrolls and precious medieval manuscripts.[23] Their mission was to recover these treasures and hand them over to a living "Jewish cultural atmosphere," which in practice meant to institutions in Palestine (and, after 1948, Israel), the United States, and other countries with thriving Jewish communities.

The extensive annotations in the JCR letters—mainly carried out by David Heredia—and Arendt's various Field Reports included in this volume offer details on the mission, structure, and work of this joint American-, British-, Jewish-Palestinian-Israeli-, and New York–based organization. Arendt wrote her reports as well as her letters pertaining to the JCR in English, the common language of the organization.

Following the victory of the Allies, the bulk of Jewish cultural artifacts looted by the Nazis were found in the American zone. At the time of the founding of the Federal Republic of Germany in 1949, the American occupation authorities, in order to empty what they called their "Collection Points"—storehouses of rescued books and art—entrusted the JCR to distribute those cultural artifacts whose original owners could not be identified. But the JCR's ambitions went well beyond this. They expended great effort at locating and securing the remains of large collections once owned by destroyed Jewish communities, rabbinical seminaries, and other scholarly institutions. They tried to locate private libraries left behind by German Jews who had fled Germany or were deported to death camps. And beyond this, the JCR also tried to locate art and other artifacts formerly belonging to Jews that German museums and archives had absorbed into their own collections during or even after the war.

Although their common language was German, Arendt and Scholem wrote most of their JCR correspondence in English. Their JCR letters were businesslike in tone and content, concerning technical details such as microfilming, lists of books, transportation costs, and negotiations with librarians and German government officials. The letters, with their nearly eerie mood of professional activity, mostly do not show the pain and sorrow Arendt and Scholem must have felt when they came across people's names handwritten into books and Ex Libris labels while rooting through the mountains of books and old manuscripts in the depots in Wiesbaden and Offenbach, or among the tattered volumes of the Talmud, with a long list of ancient owners, packed in crates.

Arendt and Scholem mourned through action. They knew how much their work was a race against time, and they shared the fear that much of what survived could disappear forever. They both were well aware that in times of transition claims are accepted or rejected; objects of value tend to get lost, expropriated by the state, or whisked off by individuals; losses are incurred and new property relations get sanctioned by law. The urgent tone of their letters is animated by this awareness that during times of upheaval, if there are no owners alive to claim rare objects, they tend to disappear: they are sold or spirited away as if by the hands of a ghost. The longer the Jewish manuscripts remained in cellars, bunkers, and depots, the greater the likelihood that greedy eyes and hands, people with an appreciation of their value, would seize them.

Scholem and JCR

The reason for Scholem's work with JCR is self-evident. For years in his youth he frequented the Berlin Jewish community's library, and during his years at the university in Munich he studied the Kabbalistic texts belonging to the large Hebraica collection of the municipal library. Already by 1943 Scholem, who taught the history of religion in Jerusalem, was working to rescue the Jewish cultural heritage in Germany and Eastern Europe, and to bring whatever he could to Palestine, where the survivors lived. Jewish Palestine, growing in size and number, needed ceremonial objects for the newly established communities.

Dispersed throughout Europe, the archival sources of the history of Judaism that had survived the devastation by the Nazis were to be gathered and rescued. However skeptical he was becoming about the political realities of the Zionist project, Scholem believed that in Palestine books, archives, and printed materials would be professionally preserved and, free from anti-Semitism, future generations of scholars would have open access to these sources.

When Scholem traveled for the first time to postwar Europe in 1946 on behalf of the Hebrew University to salvage Jewish cultural heritage, he sat in Paris on tenterhooks because he didn't get permission to enter the American zone in Germany. So instead, he decided to make his way first to Prague, where he examined boxes the Nazis had stored during the war in castles and in the concentration camp of Theresienstadt. What he discovered were remains from the Berlin libraries of the Jewish community, the rabbinical seminary in Berlin, and the once world-famous Higher Institute for the Wissenschaft des Judentums, books he himself had once studied.

In Offenbach, too, he worked as the Hebrew University's designated expert to go through what the Americans had in their depot. In his excavations, he came across remains of old collections that as a young scholar he had once used in his research. In his writings and letters Scholem left many traces of his sadness and growing sense of impotence.

It bears repeating that his decisive advocacy for transporting Jewish materials to Palestine was far less motivated by politics than by a desire for a Jewish spiritual unity and renewal. "I couldn't care less about the problem of the state," he announced to Arendt, "because I do not believe that the renewal of the Jewish people depends on the question of their political or *even* social structure."

Arendt and JCR

Arendt cared about the question of the Jewish people's political structure. In 1941 in New York, she met the Galician-born rabbi and historian Salo Baron, who would later become one of the founders of JCR and act as its presiding spirit. In 1941 he was the copublisher of the journal *Jewish Social Studies* and wanted Arendt to write an essay on the Dreyfus Affair.

In 1942 Arendt was commissioned by the Institute of Jewish Affairs to do a short study on the Nazis' manic policies of pillaging and destroying Jewish culture. In this study she also examined the international angle: in Poland the Nazis looted the library of the Warsaw Theological Seminary attached to the Tlomackie synagogue, as well as the library of the Warsaw-based YIVO, a Jewish research institute. With the fall of France, the Nazis also had their hands on the library of the Alliance Israélite Universelle in Paris, which was not just the leading Judaica library in Europe; it was the only such library.

Two years later, with the end of the war in sight, Arendt began advocating a trans-European Jewish nationality. Together with the Jewish national home in Palestine, she supported the formation of a transnational Jewish representative body set up to guarantee the survival of Jewish culture within a federalized postwar Europe. But with postwar Europe falling back into national states, this renewed nationalism eliminated the possibility of an independent transnational Jewish participation within the postwar order.

Between 1944 and 1946, Arendt worked for the Commission on European Jewish Cultural Reconstruction (CEJCR), an organization led by Salo Baron. As head of research, her task was to come up with a list of Jewish cultural institutions that had existed before 1938 (the "Tentative List of Jewish Cultural Treasures in Axis-Occupied Countries"), along with the properties they had owned (Letter 22).

In 1946, upon completing most of her inventory work of destroyed Jewish culture, she left CEJCR. By this point she was well aware that if the organization wanted to function as a trustee operating within postwar European legal structures, and therefore to sift through, rescue, and preserve Jewish cultural treasures, it needed "first-class American administrators," along with historians, curators, and scholars of religion such as Scholem. She quit CEJCR because, she explained in a letter to Salo Baron, she was neither an administrator, nor a historian, nor a curator.

By 1949, when Baron hired Arendt to work as his executive secretary at JCR (the CEJCR's successor organization), JCR had established itself as the trustee for European Jewish properties and the "experts" were already hard at work.

Arendt was probably the only female scholar in a male-dominated organization; and unlike the other scholars working for JCR—men who appear frequently in her letters and Field Reports, men such as Salo Baron, Isaac Kiev, Stephen Wise, Shlomo Shunami, and of course Gershom Scholem—she wasn't trained in Jewish theology. Arendt scholars have yet to examine adequately how this close collaboration with rabbis, scholars of religion, and Jewish historians influenced her later work.

But through her own research on Rahel Varnhagen and her study of anti-Semitism in Paris, Arendt knew of the vital importance that archives, manuscripts, memoirs, and other artifacts would play in future history books and historical revisions. As Benjamin would say, archives were needed if writers were to "salvage" the past from the grips of a traditional historiography whose interpretations had always been, for the most part, in the service of the victorious.

With all her criticism of the Israeli state, Arendt never distanced herself from JCR and its main priority, which was to make Israeli libraries and archives the main recipients of the valuable materials rescued from Europe. That said, whether out of habit or conviction, until 1950 she stubbornly addressed her letters to Scholem to "Jerusalem, Palestine."

For her, the conviction that the theological and cultural artifacts from Germany and Eastern Europe should end up mainly in Israel was not based on Zionist convictions but was a matter of cultural politics combined with political realism. Testaments of Jewish religion, culture, and history, together with material evidence of anti-Semitism, assimilation, rebellion, and emancipation, should be gathered in a place with a vibrant Jewish life, a place where people were prepared to conserve the materials and conduct ongoing research.

Another factor was the fact that in the United States the documents, many of which were in Hebrew, would be used and read by only a handful of experts in Jewish theology or by rabbis, whereas in Israel, where Hebrew was the everyday language, many more people could read and care for them with the requisite expertise. In this way, she hoped, when the time was ripe, manuscripts, archives, and incunabula could one day become the raw material for a new secular, antinomian reading of Jewish history that Scholem was conducting with such exemplary skill.

Arendt and Scholem's calculations worked: today, researchers from all over the globe have access in Israel to an extraordinary collection of archival materials that once were spread throughout the Jewish world.

Arendt executed the day-to-day work of JCR in New York. During her trips back to Germany, she proved herself to be a highly able negotiator. What she brought into negotiations was her background: solid information, knowledge of people, highly refined instincts, deep experience with German libraries, a grasp of German intellectual history, and a deft approach to German bureaucratic structures and their mechanics. She did research and chased down leads, however small, and came up with effective strategies in negotiating with institutions.

In the course of her work, she even met former Nazis who were helpful to her mission on behalf of JCR. She also came across Jewish communities whose records survived because rabbis had hidden them from the Nazis. "With most of the people I still have a good relationship; they trust me, I still speak their language," she wrote to her husband, Heinrich Blücher.[24] To Scholem, she urged speed of action. "Without question, the power of those who are trustworthy has never been very great, and at the moment it is constantly dwindling as the de-Nazified people stream back" into West German institutions (Letter 63).

Arendt championed a universal point of view alongside a particular Jewish one. In Germany she wanted to help anchor a system of law as a socially binding norm. Rather than merely appealing to the goodwill of the Germans, the question she raised was how best to accustom Germans to the idea that Jews had rights, that is, that the German institutions had the duty to report former Jewish property in their possession, and to return it. During the Nazi regime, Jewish property had traded hands over and over; people from throughout German society had for years been beneficiaries of expropriation and destruction.

In her letters to Scholem, one can follow Arendt chasing down leads and finding people who might give her a clue, however slight, to the whereabouts of books and ceremonial artifacts. The picture that emerges is that of a woman later attacked vehemently by Jewish organizations, someone the Israeli historian Amos Elon said had been "excommunicated" from the Jewish fold, doing more for the future of Jewish culture than most of her critics.

Rescue and Recover

The urgent need to rescue and recover elements from the Jewish cultural heritage characterizes both Scholem's monumental philological-critical scholarship and Arendt's years of studying what she titled a collection of her essays, the *Dubious Remnants of Tradition in Contemporary Political Thought*.[25] Already in Scholem's youth Benjamin had given him numerous manuscripts for safekeeping, and then in 1939 Scholem rescued Arendt's manuscript on Rahel Varnhagen, which she had dispatched to him from Paris and which he had luckily kept in Jerusalem rather than sending it back to her in Paris. "Because all copies of my unfortunate Rahel have gone missing, I've asked my relatives to pick up the copy from you and to send it to me. Kurt Blumenfeld will transfer the necessary money for this through his wife" (Letter 4). For a time Arendt gave Scholem copies of everything she published. In March 1945 he wrote, "I'm making a small collection of your writings, and I'd like you to keep honoring me with your work so the 'archive' stays up to date" (Letter 14). Months later he added, "Please indulge my bibliographic urges and kindly send me whatever you write" (Letter 16). In view of the Nazi regime's absolute determination to uproot Jewish life in its entirety, the postwar rescue operation spearheaded by the two friends was an existential task that secured survival through salvaging looted artifacts.

Clearly, the stability of the postwar status quo eroded away what had joined Arendt and Scholem during the time of upheaval, turmoil, and threat. Following their debate over Zionist politics in 1946, their letters increasingly steered away from discussing Jewish politics, the political constitution of Jewish society, or the Israeli state-in-becoming. By 1950 there was also no longer any trace of their shared "duty for the dead" for Walter Benjamin. In 1951 their joint work for JCR came to an end.

Arendt's letters from the 1950s reveal how compelling she found aspects of Scholem's work, above all its anti-ideological slant, his attention to details, his power of storytelling, furthermore his thesis about mystical religion and its attempt at taking God from being an object of a dogmatic credo and turning Him into a living experience: Arendt asked Scholem for an extensive article on the "Revolt of the Images" (Letter 108). Arendt asserted in a research proposal: "The experiences lurking behind the most worn-out concepts remain valid and must be conquered afresh and newly actualized."[26] Little wonder she was so enthusiastic by Scholem's aphoristic "Ten Unhistorical Sentences," which she called "among the loveliest things you've ever written" (Letter 121).[27] Similarly, she described the pleasure of reading his essay "The Golem": "It is so enormously enjoyable to get both history *and* essence without the modernistic nonsense and the superficial fantasies of the Master Interpreters" (Letter 110).

What attracted and excited Arendt about Scholem's work was how he permitted contemporary readers, freed from the dictates of traditional interpretations thanks to his research, to experience stories and pictures from the past as a living part of the present.

The correspondence shows that Arendt and Scholem read each other's work carefully and carried on discussions about "God's dwelling place," the "Revolt of the Images," and the role of labor in the Garden of Eden. In the final letter before the Eichmann controversy, Scholem wrote:

> You made me so happy by sending me your Between Past and Future. When the book first appeared, I read some of your spiritual exercises in political thinking, but now I am taking them in as a whole, relishing the way you fit them together. I'm hoping to be able to match your gift of six exercises with six of my own, as soon as the Rhein-Verlag publishes my book on some, to wit six, central concepts of the Kabbalah. They won't be forgotten. The book is now being sent into production. (Letter 131)

A year later the dispute over *Eichmann in Jerusalem* ended their friendship. And yet, even in one of the last letters Scholem wrote to her, he included an essay signed with the dedication "Many thanks for this little bit of Jewish theology." But in the end, their common interest in the revival of Jewish thought was not strong enough to keep their friendship afloat.

From the beginning their relationship had been a tenuous one. After Scholem's return from Germany at the end of 1946, he described his pain at what he had experienced ("I left behind in Europe all my hopes" [Letter 26]), but also his "dismay of just how far apart the two of us are.... It's really a shame for both of us," he continued, referring to their disagreements over her "Zionism Reconsidered," that her "tone ... shuts off discussion."

In her reply of November 27, 1946, Arendt offered him a new aspect of the image of Noah's ark. This image can, in fact, serve as a motto for their entire correspondence:

> Now here we sit, the two of us survivors (and we can't really help it that we are still alive, we don't need to be happy about it, just accept the fact), and like Noah on his ark, we haven't been able to salvage even the most necessary things. Even worse is that the two of us Noahs also seem to be dogged by the additional problem of being so bad at steering our arks that we pass by one another without meeting. (Letter 28)

The rather common image of Noah and the ark was useful for Arendt, and she made her own, new use of the traditional image. After the rupture with tradition, there was no longer for her one single and common "ark" in which people could gather the commonly shared view of history; there was no longer a common view and understanding of the present, in word or image; in short, there was neither a single ark nor a single Noah capable of gathering everything together. Instead, Arendt spoke of many small boats drifting around in the world's oceans struggling against the currents of the sea, including the inner current of human contempt and despair.

Whoever is drifting in a boat in the ocean, abandoned by God and all on his own, is receptive to siren songs and chimeras and receptive to all the world's "isms" that provide a "screen against reality" (Letter 20). But, continuing with Arendt's image of the modern man lost at sea, the person who does not respond to the appeal of the siren song can listen all the more keenly for distant human voices. And by hearing one another's voices, these "Noahs" are the ones able to spin new threads and rebuild the world.

PART ONE

The Letters

LETTER 1 From Arendt

68 rue Brancion, Vaugirard 38-07
May 29, 1939

Dear Scholems,
It's become almost a scandal that I'm just today getting around to replying to your two letters that were such a delight for me.[1] Since receiving them, first of all my mother arrived; second came my furniture; and third my library. The fourth, fifth, and sixth things that have happened here is that the good Lord in heaven, in the form of the Central Bureau, has blessed me with a profession; and as everyone knows, every gift from heaven has its shadow side.[2] This shadow side, for me, is that I'm not managing to get a bit of work done.

As regards Rahel, I've naturally given wide berth to any sort of hagiography.[3] I wanted to describe bankruptcy, though admittedly a bankruptcy that was historically necessary, and possibly even redemptive. I would like it if, with all their criticism, readers would glean out of the final two chapters a kind of vindication.[4] These days this is especially important because every ignorant upstart thinks he can heap scorn onto assimilated Judaism. The book was written before Hitler. The final two chapters, which I wrote here, hardly change the book at all.

If I had only known the kind of material Schocken has in his collection![5] It was terribly annoying for me to be dependent on my excerpts from so many years ago. If there is any chance at all to get it published, I would be very grateful if you could make the connection for me. Naturally, you can keep the manuscript.[6] And, of course, I would be thrilled if you want to stir Schocken's interest in the book.

I'm really worried about Benji.[7] I tried to line up something for him here but failed miserably.[8] At the same time, I'm more than ever convinced how vital it is to put him on secure footing so he can continue his work. As I see it, his work has changed, down to his style. Everything strikes me as far more emphatic, less hesitant. It often seems to me as if he is only now making progress on the questions most decisive for him. It would be awful if he were to be prevented from continuing.

One can hardly imagine what's going on back in Germany. For most of us here, it goes without saying that things are really lousy here, in particular as well as in general. How is your work coming along? What's Fanja up to? I would be elated if the two of you could find some reason to make another trip to Europe, because I don't see much chance for me to be a tour leader over there.[9]

Blücher sends his warmest greetings. Please don't be annoyed at my tardy reply, and don't be such a stranger. I'd like to hear from you again soon.

Yours,
Hannah

LETTER 2 From Arendt

Montauban
October 21, 1940

Dear Scholem,
Walter Benjamin took his own life on September 29 in Portbou on the Spanish frontier. He had an American visa, but on the twenty-third the only people the Spanish allowed to pass the border were those with "national" passports.[1] I don't know if this letter will reach you. In the past weeks and months I had seen Walter several times, the last time being on September 20 in Marseilles. The report of his death took nearly four weeks to reach both his sister and us.[2]

Jews are dying in Europe and are being buried like dogs.

Yours,
Hannah Arendt

LETTER 3 From Fanja and Gershom Scholem

July 17, 1941
Jerusalem

Dear Hannah Arendt,
I'm so glad you are finally able to breathe freely again, and I hope to hear from you very soon. In your last letter you wrote about Benjamin's death.

I hardly need to tell you how Gerhard took the news. Do you remember the conversation we had about the relationship between Walter and Gerhard? I recall every word. It breaks my heart to think that I never saw the man.[1]

It was so lovely in Paris, and the memories of this wonderful city are bound up with memories of you. You were so kind to us. We are still living well here, and we hope for victory. Your friend Jonas, now with an artillery unit, is busy shooting down enemy airplanes. He is so proud of being a soldier, and he's a bit more childish than he was when he was occupied with Gnosticism.[2] Gerhard still wants to write to you today, so I will sign off. Take care of yourself and think about us.

Your Fanja Scholem
And greetings to Kurt Blumenfeld.[3]

My dear friend,
Mrs. Zittau tells us you've arrived safely in New York—at last one piece of good news amid all the gloom.[4] Oh, the two of us have so much to talk about, and yet who knows when we'll get the chance! We'll just have to hack our way through this mountain of darkness, if I can say so. One senses the meaning of apocalyptic prospects in one's own flesh and blood. Please write soon—it took three weeks for your letter to arrive from last October. It was the first report I received of Walter's death. I wish you had given me a return address: I wasn't able to reply without one. Please pay a visit to my friend Shalom Spiegel[5] at the Jewish Institute of Religion (New York, 309 West 93rd Street). Tell him I sent you. He's a fantastic fellow, and both Blücher and you should become friendly with him.[6]

Warmest greetings, from your Gerhard Scholem
Forgive me for this awfully bad ink!

LETTER 4 From Arendt

317 West 95th Street, New York
October 17, 1941

Dear Scholem,
Miriam Lichtheim gave me your address and relayed your greetings. While I hope that even without her I would have gotten around to writing you, I have to admit she gave me a useful nudge.

Wiesengrund tells me that he had sent to you a detailed report of Benjamin's death.[1] Here in New York I've heard some not unimportant details for the first time. It may be that I'm not all that qualified to give an account of his death because I had considered such a possibility so far-fetched that for weeks after he died I dismissed the entire business as being no more than immigrants' gossip. All this despite the fact that especially in the last few years and months we were very close friends and saw one another on a regular basis.

With the outbreak of war we were all together for a summer break in a small French village near Paris. Benji was in excellent shape. He had finished part of his work on Baudelaire and was prepared, justifiably I think, to do some extraordinary things.[2] The outbreak of war immediately terrified him beyond all measure. Fearing bombardments from the air, on the first day of the general mobilization he left Paris for Meaux. Meaux was a well-known center for the mobilization, with a militarily very important airport and train station, which made it a hub for the entire deployment of forces. Of course, the result was that from the start one air-raid alarm followed the next; rather aghast, Benjamin at once made his way back to Paris. He came back just in time to get himself duly rounded up. In the temporary camp at Colombes, where my husband[3] talked to him at length, he was rather depressed, and for good reason, of course. At once he entered into a kind of asceticism. He stopped smoking, gave away all his chocolate, refused to wash himself or shave, and more or less refused to move a limb. Upon arrival in the final camp he wasn't feeling all that bad. He had a bevy of young boys around him; they liked him a lot, and were keen to learn from him and swallowed every word he said.[4] By the time he returned in the middle or end of November, he was more or less glad to have had the experience. His initial panic was gone entirely. In the months that followed he wrote his historical-philosophical theses, of which I have been told he sent you a copy, too.[5] As you have seen, he was on the spoors of a number of new things, though at the same time he was undeniably fearful of the opinion of those at the Institute.[6] You surely know that before the war he received word from the Institute that his stipend was no longer secure and that he should look around for something else.[7] That caused him a lot of anxiety, even if he wasn't all that convinced of the seriousness of the Institute's suggestion. Which didn't improve things, and if anything it made the matter all the more disagreeable for him. The outbreak of war took care of that anxiety. Still, he wasn't all that comfortable with the reaction of his most recent, downright unorthodox theories. In January one of his new young friends from the camp, who happened to have been a student of my husband's, killed himself, mostly for personal reasons.[8] This suicide preoccupied Benjamin to an extraordinary extent; and in all the discussions about it, with a truly passionate vehemence, he stood with those who defended the young man's decision. In spring 1940, with heavy hearts, we all made our way to the American consulate. Even though we heard the same thing, that we would have to wait between two and ten years before our quota number came up, the three of us took English lessons.[9] None of us took it all that seriously. Benjamin had just one wish: to learn enough of English to say that he absolutely didn't like the language. And he succeeded. His horror at America was indescribable, and apparently already then he told friends that he preferred a shorter life in France to a longer one in America.

This all came to a quick end. From the middle of April, those of us under the age of 48 who had been released from internment were examined for our suitability for military fatigue duty. Fatigue duty was really just another word for internment with forced labor; and measured against the first round of internment, in most cases it was worse. Everyone—that is, everyone but Benji—had no doubt he would be declared unfit for service. In those days he was awfully agitated, and on a number of occasions he told me he wouldn't be able to play along once again. Of course, he was declared unfit. Independent of all of this, in the middle of May the second and far more systematic internment took place. You must know about this. As if a miracle, of the three people spared the internment, Benji was one. Due to administrative chaos, he nevertheless could never know whether, or for how long, the police would accept an order from the Interior Ministry. Would the police simply arrest him? Personally, I had no contact with him at the time because I was interned.[10] Friends told me, however, that he didn't dare venture out on the streets any longer, and he was living in constant panic. He managed to get on the last train leaving Paris. He took only a small suitcase with two shirts and a toothbrush. As you know, he traveled to Lourdes. As soon as I got out of Gurs in the middle of June, by chance I, too, headed to Lourdes, where I stayed for a few weeks at his instigation. This was the time of defeat, and after a few days the trains stopped running. No one knew what had happened to families, husbands, children, and friends. Benji and I played chess from morning to evening, and between games we read newspapers, to the extent we could get our hands on them. Everything was as fine as could be—until the ceasefire terms were published, along with the infamous extradition clause.[11] But even then I can't say that Benjamin fell into a full-blown panic, even if we were both feeling anxious. Mind you, when news reached us of the first suicide among those in internment fleeing from the Germans, Benjamin began for the first time to talk repeatedly to me about suicide:

there was always "that" way out. In response to my energetic and emphatic objections that there was still plenty of time before the situation became that desperate, he predictably repeated that you could never know, and under no circumstances should you wait too long. At the same time, we talked about America, a prospect to which he seemed more reconciled than before. He took seriously a letter from the Institute in which they informed him that they were making every effort to bring him over; less convincing for him was their declaration that he would belong to the editorial team of the journal and would receive a regular salary.[12] This he considered a phony contract in order to secure him a visa. What he feared greatly, wrongly, it seems, was that the minute he got here they would turn their backs on him.

At the beginning of July, I left Lourdes *á la recherche de mon mari perdu*. Benji was hardly thrilled, and I vacillated back and forth if I should take him with me. But that would have been simply impossible. In regards to the officials (thanks to a letter of recommendation from the Foreign Ministry), he was safer staying put than he ever would have been somewhere else. Until September, my only contact with him was through letters. In the meantime, the Gestapo had been at his apartment and confiscated everything. Judging by his letters, he was very depressed. His manuscripts had been saved, but back then he had every reason to fear he had lost everything.[13] In September we made our way to Marseilles because our visas had arrived. Benji had already been there since August, as his visa had already arrived in the middle of the month.[14] He had the famous transit passes from Spain and, naturally, Portugal. When I saw him, the Spanish visa was valid for another eight to ten days. Getting that sort of visa in those days was completely impossible. He asked me, in a fit of despair, what he should do and whether we, too, could get a Spanish visa, as quickly as possible, so we could cross the border together. I told him how hopeless that would be, and that by the same token he had to leave soon because Spanish visas were not being extended. Moreover, I said he shouldn't take the risk of allowing his visa to lapse because it was highly uncertain how long such visas would be available. Of course, we would prefer to go together, all three of us, I said. In that case he could come with us to Montauban. But no one could take the responsibility for this. Rather on the spur of the moment, he decided to leave. The Dominicans had given him a letter of introduction to some Spanish abbot. At the time, Benjamin made a forceful impression on us all, but at the same time the situation was completely absurd. In those days in Marseilles he spoke again about his suicidal intentions. You know the rest of the story: that he had to leave in the company of complete strangers; that they chose to take the long route that required a seven-hour journey by foot through the mountains; that for entirely mysterious reasons they destroyed their French residency papers and thus cut off the possibility of returning to France; that they arrived at the frontiers exactly twenty-four hours after the closing of the Spanish border to people without national passports—the only papers we had were from the American consulate; that Benji had already completely broken down a number of times on the way to the border; that the group was supposed to report to the Spanish border the next morning; and that that night they were allowed to stay, and he took his life. Months later, when we arrived at Portbou, we searched in vain for his grave. It was nowhere to be found. His name was nowhere. The cemetery looks off at a small bay, directly onto the Mediterranean. It is composed of terraces carved out of stone. The coffins are shoved into these stone walls. It is by far one of the most fantastically beautiful places I've ever seen.

The Institute has his literary estate, though for the time being they hesitate to publish anything in the German language.[15] I wonder if one couldn't bring out Benjamin's historical-philosophical theses independently with Schocken.[16] Benjamin gave me the manuscript, and the Institute got it first through me.

Dear Scholem, that's all I can tell you, and I've told the story as precisely and without comment as possible.

Greetings to you and your wife from the monsieur and me,
Your Hannah Arendt

P.S. Because all copies of my unfortunate Rahel have gone missing, I've asked my relatives to pick up the copy from you and to send it to me. Kurt Blumenfeld will transfer the necessary money for this through his wife.[17]

Merci d'avance!

LETTER 5 From Scholem

Abarbanel Rd. 28, Rehavia, Jerusalem
February 6, 1942

Dear Hannah Blücher,
I can't describe to you the kinds of contradictory feelings your long letter from last fall stirred in me. On the one hand, I was overjoyed to get a sign of life from you, and to know that you and your husband, after everything you have no doubt gone through, are in America. I would have welcomed learning more concrete details about you and how you are doing. On the other hand, naturally I was deeply stricken by what you wrote about Walter and his death. A year ago I received similar reports from Wiesengrund, to whom I then wrote a number of times concerning Benjamin's literary estate.[1] And to my greatest astonishment, I received no answer from him. Perhaps you could give the dear fellow a little bit of hell; I thought he would have an interest in remaining in contact with me.[2] Could you inquire what's behind this strange silence? I would be just as grateful if you could give me information on whether papers and manuscripts of his were rescued from Paris and taken to New York, and if so, which ones.[3] I have a large number of things here, beyond an almost complete collection of his printed works.

It was for me a great pleasure to be of service to you, at least regarding your Rahel manuscript. What a stroke of luck that I didn't send it back to you in France but instead stowed it away here. I handed it over to your cousin Dr. Fürst, and I hope you get it in time to make good use of it. Write to me in detail about your plans, your life, and your goings-on in the great seaside city of New York. Without a doubt you will be meeting people right and left, and you'll be boiling over when you think about Walter's demise and then see the sort of people with stronger nerves who are still around.

I've just read here that Mr. Koestler, for instance, is over there alive and kicking, and continues to write.[4] Admittedly, we are all also forging ahead and continuing to write, and until now without being able to do our duty vis-à-vis the dead. What shall I tell you about us here? Fanja and I are doing tolerably well. The war in turns approaches us, and then backs away again. If things remain this way, we can consider ourselves lucky. The moral atmosphere here in this country is calamitous, giving rise to the gloomiest thoughts regarding the fate of our local work here. I fear that over there you've heard enough about this, and you might well say that the atmosphere of life, the events and experiences in Zion, have proven the impossibility of Zionism to exist in haughty-aristocratic isolation from the squalor of the diaspora. We are by no means worse than those elsewhere, though it would be too much to say, as people still like to do, that we are any better. The most that can be said about us is that we are simply here.

I've continued my work during this entire time. Meanwhile, three months ago my large book on the Kabbalah, *Major Trends in Jewish Mysticism*, which grew out of my 1938 lectures in New York, has appeared in Schocken's publishing house.[5] Nearly the entire print run was sent to America. It'll surely take a couple months until it arrives there. I dedicated the book to Walter, and I would gladly give you a copy once you give me a set address and I'm sure that, even with a change in address, the book will reach you.[6] Without being presumptuous, I believe that it'll be a read that will give your Jewish heart a great lift. In any event, I would be most interested in hearing your thoughtful critique of the book (critique not as an expert but as someone with a reflective mind). It's a terrible shame we can't be together now to debate this and so many other things. For the broad public of English-reading intelligent Jews, bishops, and monks, I've done enough for now. For the present, I prefer—after examining a major theme with requisite exalted repose—to withdraw in order to compose, with exquisite dryness, dullness, and erudition, what I hope will be a few brilliant articles and studies. Just in the last few days, the Jewish Publication Society has asked if I could come up with a book for them on my specialty products. Given the local prices for food, the prospect of earning a decent honorarium, in dollars, could certainly lure me directly from the noble paths of science and onto far more enticing avenues!

I'd like to ask you in New York to reach out to my friend Shalom Spiegel. During my time in New York we became very close. He is a professor at the Jewish Institute of Religion headed by Stephen Wise. It would mean a lot to me if the two of you could come together. Please head over to the Institute (40 West 68th Street) and ask for him at the library. Tell him I sent you and that I want you to become his friend. You'll know better than I how best to phrase this frank wish of mine. It may well be that he can be of some help to you. He is an exceedingly good person, and one not at all lacking in insight. I'll write to him about you directly as well, and I'll ask him to get to know you. But as you know, there is no guarantee that a particular letter will arrive. You will therefore by no means be wasting your time by showing up with my "calling card" in Spiegel's study. That Spiegel thinks the world of me, as it were, my "calling card" isn't a bad thing to have. In New York if you should run into Paul Tillich[7] or his wife you should likewise give them my greetings.

And don't disdain writing to me about your daily goings-on. The world has become so torn apart that each and every detailed report from a different country is cause for great joy, especially when it comes from you. I wish you and Blücher the warmest wishes and greetings in hopes that we see one another again, and in a world that at least hasn't completely gone to the devil.

Always yours,
Gerhard Scholem

LETTER 6 From Arendt

317 West 95th Street, New York
April 25, 1942

Dear friends,
We were very, very happy to get both of your letters, the first of which Marianne Zittau sent me and which crossed paths with my report, and the second one from February. It is a real comfort to still be hearing from friends. Such letters are like minutely thin, strong threads. We'd like to convince ourselves that these threads are able to hold together what remains of our world.

Send me a copy of your Kabbalah, if you can.[1] The first copies have arrived here—this I've heard by chance—but until now I haven't managed to nab one. I'm very happy you've dedicated the book to Benjamin. And I'm also equally concerned about what's going on with his manuscripts: I can't get a word out of Wiesengrund. I talked to him when he was here, but after he left for California he hasn't mentioned it again. You know what I think about these gentlemen, and I must confess that I scarcely have reason to revise my opinion after everything I've seen and heard since being here.[2] The only thing of Benjamin's I have is his final manuscript. I don't even know what's been rescued.

I met Spiegel when one evening he invited me to join a small gathering at his place. I liked him a lot, though I haven't yet decided to contact him again. You can't imagine how foreign and strange this social life is for us here. (Just to be on the safe side, I left Monsieur at home because of the goy thing.)[3] These people talk about everything that concerns us Jews and about everything that has happened, and they do so with the kind of aloof despair a person can only have if he's not directly involved. This is, pardon me for saying, an awful mistake. You can see the same thing among Zionists of all shades and all backgrounds who got out of Europe before the catastrophe. And all the others are only too happy to forget their experiences and assimilate into the common attitudes here.

With all that, we're doing well. Monsieur works as a sort of expert on all possible book and research projects.[4] I'm writing my things on anti-Semitism and publishing them piecemeal in Jewish publications. A major study on the Dreyfus Affair came out in *Jewish Social Studies*, and at present I'm busy with racial anti-Semitism.[5] On the side, I'm a rather regular contributor to *Aufbau*. I've amicably established myself there as America's most minor columnist.[6]

In France with a lot of luck we managed quite well all the way to our departure. I was in Gurs[7] for only four weeks, which in the summer was no big deal. Afterward, very quickly and purely by chance I chased down Monsieur, and the two of us played at being homeless.

With regard to the atmosphere in Palestine, I've learned a thing or two here. I never believed in the Two World Theory: that of Zion and the Diaspora.[8] The events of the past few years have really proven that Jews are one people. For the best parts of this Jewish nation, it is extraordinarily important that you all are there, much more so than if you were an arrogant aristocracy only wanting to stick a feather in your cap. Much worse is the situation with the Zionist organization, an organization whose so-called radical wing is fixated on transforming notions straight out of the nineteenth century into fixed ideas. Meanwhile, the majority is trying to liquidate all ideas, and as quickly as humanly possible. In its quixotic otherworldliness, there is something grandiose about the "clash" between these two camps.

Send me your book on the Kabbalah. We are very conservative folk and won't change our address until we're forced to; even then, everything will be forwarded. And be certain to write, and in detail. Until we see each other again, we don't want these thin threads to tear.

Best wishes to you and Fanja.

Cordially yours,
Hannah
And warm greetings from Heinrich Blücher.

LETTER 7 From Arendt

317 West 95th Street, New York, NY
June 21, 1942
Prof. Gerhard Scholem
Jerusalem
Abarbanel Rd. 28

Dear friends,
I hope you got my last letter, which if I remember correctly was quite lengthy. Today I'm writing in a rush just to let you know that the Institute has published a mimeographed volume in memory of Benjamin, which wasn't even bound when they send it out.[1] The only thing you'll find in it from his literary estate is his "Historical-Philosophical Theses," which I had brought with me. What I very much fear is that this will be it, and all the rest of his work they'll bury away in the archives. It was a little more difficult for them to do with the "Theses" because so many people knew about it, and because I was the one who gave it to them in the first place. As for the rest of the volume, there is an essay by Horkheimer and one by Adorno. I assume that in a few months' time you'll be getting a copy. It would certainly help if you could expressly inquire what's happening with the rest of the estate, while coolly mentioning that you own copies of everything, so far as you know.

Here we are very worried about you,[2] which is to be expected. We are doing quite well. Monsieur has work in his field: he's busy with interesting and sensible stuff. I'm writing, and when I get a chance I'll be sending you things from time to time.

Warmest greetings to you and Fanja,
Your Hannah

LETTER 8 From Scholem

Abarbanel Rd. 28, Jerusalem
November 12, 1942

Dear friends,
I don't know if you received my response to your last letter; a lot of time has passed. I told you about what's happening with us and asked you, among other things, to send the memorial volume to Benjamin.[1] I haven't received it from *anyone*. What I did get was a complete mystery to me: a letter I wrote to Wiesengrund came back as "no such address" (which was what people at the Institute wrote in forwarding it). Please do me a great service! I still don't have a copy of the "Theses" that was published in the memorial volume (you mentioned it in your letter, but it seems that the letter pertaining to it went missing).

My English opus has apparently arrived in New York. My friend Spiegel has your name and I asked him to send you over a copy. If you still don't have it, please turn to him and mention this letter. I'm counting a lot on you as a reader, and I'll be looking forward to a letter on my book. Hopefully you won't hide your impressions behind "lack of competence." Since "competent" people in this field simply don't exist, what am I to do?

Today I read something beautiful you wrote in *Aufbau* (which I otherwise never read but came across by pure chance) about Mr. Emil Ludwig. My congratulations to you and Paul Tillich for your bit of humanity, which I admit I need to drag out of me from time to time against powerful inner resistance.[2] (With this impossible syntax I'm saying that it isn't easy for me to repress the very feelings you are fighting against.) The upshot is that by reading your article I said to myself, You really have to start thinking about this woman again! And could there be a better day for this than today, a turning point in the war, a day when all of us look to you in America with endless relief? Over time we've lived through some quite anxious days, and now it appears as if the miracle indeed has happened and Palestine will be spared.[3]

I'm carefully keeping all of Benjamin's writings together. Who knows where his own collections are? Is there any news on the whereabouts of his literary estate? I don't know a thing. I may be the only one from among all those who, in 1914–15, got copies of his important unprinted essays (such as the work on Hölderlin and the Metaphysics of Youth), and who still has them. I had copies made of them all and sent them to Wiesengrund at the beginning of this year. This package, too, seems to have been *lost*. Perhaps at some point you'll have the means, ways, and addresses to see if this is true or not.

I'm now writing a lot of things of scholarly interest for me, and I'm about to launch a major book on the Sabbatian movement.[4] As for our health, both of us, Fanja and I are so-so healthy. These days, that's about all you can expect from yours truly.

Warmest greetings to you and Blücher,
Gerhard Scholem

LETTER 9 From Arendt

317 West 95th Street, New York, NY
November 4, 1943

Dear friend,
Don't be sour! I've written you many "love" letters since reading your book[1]—after finally getting my hands on a copy in the spring I've read it several times, and since then I keep browsing through it. Initially I wanted to write down my notes, and then to read the first reviews. And now since so much time has passed, I'm sending you my notes in a separate letter.[2] The reviews, of course, are all full of the highest praise, though as far as I have been able to tell, the reviewers understand less than nothing about what they're writing. At one point I began getting terribly riled because there has been absolutely no promotion for the book, and because I learned that your noble Mr. Schocken, in spite of his love, only printed up 250 copies or so. He should have sent that amount alone to journals, universities, institutes, and experts in the field. After the war you really must put out another edition and send it out to the world with a lot of racket.

I'm sending you Benjamin's "Theses," my only copy. Negotiating with Wiesengrund is worse than pointless. What they have undertaken to do with the estate, or have in mind to do with it, I haven't the foggiest idea. I spoke with Horkheimer when he was here in the summer, but nothing came of it. He maintains that the crate is in a safe (which is certainly a lie), and he hasn't even opened it, and as such he doesn't even know which of Benjamin's writings are there, and which are missing. I am entirely on my own here, without any support, and in dealing with this gang I am out of my element. Please trust me that this is no exaggeration. For two years I've been going out of my mind trying to find a sensible way to threaten them—threat is the only language these gentlemen understand. But as you can imagine, threats can't work because they received the estate in a perfectly legal manner. There is no journal that would take up this matter. So what is one to do? Benjamin, it seems, never had the slightest illusions about the morality of his breadgivers, and yet he was depending on Wiesengrund, who intellectually owes him nothing less than everything. That was a huge mistake. Added to this is that the Institute itself is about to go under. They still have money, but they are more and more of the opinion that they must use the money to spend their sunset years in comfort. The journal has stopped coming out: its reputation here is hardly stellar—for those who even know it exists, that is. Wiesengrund and Horkheimer are living it up in California. The Institute here is purely administrative, and what is being administered, besides money, no one knows. Through agents and intrigues, they managed to relieve the American Jewish Committee of $10,000 for the purposes of a study on anti-Semitism.[3] The two poor souls are working on this because, despite the Boom, they haven't managed to rustle up a normal job. I know these people personally. They are just your average guys who don't want to go hungry, and no one should blame them for this. They complained to me that they had never been interested in Jews and their enemies, and now they have to waste their time with such crazy and "marginal" issues. Wiesengrund and his cohorts meanwhile are writing the "Message in the Bottle for the Future." I'm assuming that for this they're getting some inspiration from the contents of the "safe."

If one could get Schocken interested in publishing the literary estate, one could perhaps do something. One could, for instance, turn to Thomas Mann and ask him to intervene, which might help.[4] But Schocken is a very difficult fellow with a strong aversion against spending large sums of money. Maybe you can write to him at some point. He still loves you above everything and everyone. If you wrote first, I wouldn't have any problem going to him myself. I don't know him personally. Here he had a mountain of trouble with his Friends of the Hebrew University. Perhaps . . .

Marianne Zittau talked about you with great cheer and animation. I'm delighted that she amused you.

I've been working a lot. If I ever write my book on anti-Semitism, it'll have to include plenty of very strange things.[5] At present, I'm still writing and publishing parts of it in local journals. Monsieur has become a "visiting professor" at Princeton. For the first time in many years, I'm not in the least worried about money.

In this country one gets very lonely chiefly because people have so many things to do that, after a certain point, the need for leisure is quite simply no longer there. The result of this is a certain absence (by which I mean absentmindedness) that makes the contact between people so difficult. It is out of this general feeling of loneliness (which seen from the outside doesn't exist at all) that I've resolved to write you. I am fully aware of how unforgivable this is given your great book. For this reason, I ask you once again, don't quibble with me.

Warmest greetings to Fanja. I'm really looking forward to your book on the Sabbatai Zvi movement. What you write in your book concerning the consequences that its failure had for Jewish history over the centuries was the first truly convincing thing I've ever read on the subject.[6] This is one of your most essential discoveries, especially for modern history and for many of the questions I've been grappling with.

Monsieur sends his greetings.
In old friendship,
Hannah

LETTER 10 From Scholem

Abarbanel Rd. 28, Jerusalem
December 21, 1943

Dear Hannah,
Your letter from November 4 arrived today, and while the other items you mentioned haven't yet come (your notes on my book and Benjamin's "Theses"), I want to dash off a few words to you now. I'm suffering from a poor line of communication with the USA, and what you wrote about "public isolation" appears to be turning all of my friends and acquaintances mute—and I regret to say you are no exception. From my friend Mr. Schocken, believe it or not, I've received just one letter in three years, and that was two years ago. The publication of my book, notwithstanding his songs of praise, hasn't made him any more loquacious. The same goes for Spiegel, Wiesengrund, and the others. When he was in New York, Wiesengrund responded

to my book, quite strangely, with a few lines from his wife. Two years have passed since then, and not a single line from him has reached me.[1] Admittedly, a lot of mail *really* does get lost, though it is supposed to be better *now*.

A few comments on your letter: You are mistaken when you say that "despite his love" Schocken printed up only 250 copies of my book. The first printing run is 1,100 copies, of which more than half was sent to (and reached) New York. You are naturally correct that almost nothing has been done in the way of promotion. I'm personally painfully aware of the fact that no one there, with the exception of Spiegel (who really did make some effort), has any special interest in the book. The problems with the book are: A.) It is seemingly too lofty for the public, not watered-down enough (the Jewish Publication Society bluntly wanted me to come up with a straightforward book filled with twaddle for readers with a *moderate interest* in Jewish history or religion!!!). B.) The book doesn't fit so well into their established conceptual schemes. C) No one really understands a thing about the subject; and since they don't want to invest any time into the matter, so far as I can tell, people are happy with gibberish. By the way, Spiegel sent me a few reviews (only those that came out before April), but I probably haven't even read most of them. I'd owe you a favor if you could send me notes about or from the reviews. Schocken Publishing, which has absolutely no organization in place over there, doesn't do anything of the kind.

I've been holding out hope for someone—Leo Strauss,[2] A. Heschel,[3] Tillich, or Wiesengrund—to make purely *philosophical* connections using intellectual reflection rather than knowledge of the materials (which absolutely no one has, and this is the accursed *circulus vitiosus* of my scholarly position). In this I was also speculating a bit about someone with a philosophical head like yours. But all of these horses—every one of them—remained in the stalls; and those who ended up writing something about my book were never asked to do so. What can be done? The Institute was prepared to send copies everywhere imaginable.[4] I'm thinking about a second edition as soon as the war is over. (I would add about one hundred extra pages, including materials on the symbolism of the number 10, and—which is a must—the missing tenth chapter on the development and beginnings of the Kabbalah. This would be the new Chapter Four.)[5] Anyway, not a single copy, more or less, from the original edition has reached England.

I'm still fiddling around with my Sabbatianism; I don't have the proper concentration for it yet. Meanwhile, I'm writing all sorts of scholarly stuff both to soothe my conscience and because there is so much in this field one has to write in order to refer back to it, one of these days, with a clean conscience. If you get the chance you may gladly do some "public relations" on my behalf. I'm hoping that with some more luck I'll get the chance to spend a year or maximum two over there. This would be more of a treat for my own education than for the Jewish youth. Hence I am working untiringly on coming up with the right formula to get myself over there.

I see that you think the worst about Walter's heirs over there. I don't dare offer an opinion about the current state of affairs. My first (and I think last) encounter with Horkheimer left me with a great deal of antipathy. I'm no objective observer, but I assume the antipathy was shared. His article on the Jewish Question in the *Journal* is an impudent, arrogant, and repulsive load of nonsense without a shred of intelligence or substance. In my final letter to Benjamin, which I'm certain Horkheimer has, I vehemently and openly discussed this.[6] I'd have a good laugh if this unambiguous correspondence with Benjamin ended up among his literary estate, especially given the way I assessed, while I was in America, what was going on at the Institute and their attitude toward W. B. Those people would really be the best audience for my letters! I had a much better opinion than you of Wiesengrund, an opinion I would change only very reluctantly under the pressure of facts. His attachment to W. B. seemed too authentic for me to have anticipated a plundering of this great legacy as a tribute to the dead. In any case, with regard to Benjamin's papers I have with me here, *rebus sic stantibus*, as we used to say as small children.[7] I will maintain a certain reserve and caution until it is clear which way the wind is blowing. All along I have naturally assumed that once the war is over the opportunity would arise for a complete edition of this great body of work. There is no point in writing to Schocken about this. He doesn't read letters, and even when he does, he never comes to a decision. He suffers from a catastrophic inability to come to a decision. You can only get through to him face to face, and in that moment you either make the necessary impression on him, or—mostly even with the best of coaxing—you don't. When W. B. was still alive, I told Schocken more than three times what, in my opinion, the right course of action should be for an intelligent millionaire with his mind set on amusement. And among the unread letters in New York there should be the one in which, following Benjamin's death, I dished out for him the old theme, *feriuntque summos fulgura montes*.[8] As an aside, you'd be doing me a great service if, one of these days, you could provide me with the sort of report, according to the local custom there, detailing the unpleasantries Schocken encountered with our so-called "friends."[9]

I have no precise information on this here. I would be grateful for some illumination, which could also be important for us.

What else is there to report? We are preparing ourselves for the final stage of the war, and with considerable anticipation we are looking forward to the opportunities this will open up. We don't know what sort of revelations we will encounter about the state of the Jewish people in Europe, though one gets ill just thinking about what we already know. It finally seems as good as certain that the direct fury of the fighting won't reach us in this corner of the world, of all places. This produces an indescribable feeling. Why have we been spared? With this said, we have plenty of seething and hissing here to go around.

Fanja sends her greetings. She just left for a few days of vacation with her brother the soldier. She doesn't have it easy running our household given the high rate of inflation and the awful side effects this has for professors and others on a fixed income. Added to this is her fear that we will be caught up in the new great flu epidemic, whose ghostly march will apparently sweep through the nations toward the end of the war once again, and reach us. (Which when you come to think about it, would only be just!)

Please write or rather send me your article on anti-Semitism, if you have some extra copies at your disposal. Give my best to Mr. Blücher, and publish your book on Rahel (you didn't write a word about it in your letter!!). All the best from the Kabbalist from Jerusalem,

Gerhard Scholem

LETTER 11 From Arendt

317 West 95th Street, New York, NY
May 20, 1944
For months now this missive has been on my mind: I've been thinking about it since I received your long, lovely letter in December. I was by chance with Oko in an editorial meeting yesterday when he showed me your warm letter of recommendation, which made both of us happy.[1] This gave me the impetus to write.

I've been thinking much about you lately, and not just because I've spoken with a lot of people about your book. The real reason is that I can't get your book out of my mind because it tacitly (please don't think I'm saying "unconsciously") accompanies me in all of my own work. The same should happen to anyone who is in any way involved in Jewish affairs. As regards to your unanswered challenge about which you wrote to Oko, unfortunately most people these days don't even know the book contains a challenge, and this goes as well for your numerous fans. The others have already decided to live out their days without giving any response.[2] You shouldn't be discouraged by this, though, or only to the extent to which the situation our people finds themselves in, a nation whose intellectuals make up merely a distinctive fraction, lends itself to discouragement. When you think about it, you'd expect that what European Jewry has gone through over the past few years would have woken up even the leaders of Jewish organizations from their factional slumber. This, however, didn't happen.

Moving on to the reviews. I don't know what Spiegel sent you. I am not in contact with Leo Strauss. (I haven't been very pleased with some of his more recent articles.) You can't count on Tillich. I know that he has the absolute highest regard for the book, but he is too caught up in political shenanigans to find the time to reflect on such matters.[3] Wiesengrund is over in California and doesn't write for any of the local journals here. The Institute's journal has apparently passed away peacefully; in any event, it is no longer appearing. Yesterday I told Oko, and in no uncertain terms, what I think of Hans Kohn. My comments on the book, which I really wrote only for you, I sent to *Menorah*. I didn't do so because I considered my comments to be an adequate review (most emphatically not) but because it seemed to me that the other reviews are even less adequate. I still haven't heard back from *Menorah*.[4] Of course, they already have another reviewer.

Since Oko took over as editor, the *Contemporary Record* has vastly improved. By all means, you should submit an article.[5] It is read also in non-Jewish circles due to its subscription exchange program with a few general-interest magazines. You can naturally write in German. I've done so, and I've had only good experiences with Oko. He is an outstanding translator, doesn't shy away from spending money, and for the final editing work he has an extraordinary sense for language. In sum, he's one of the more pleasant figures over here.

Over the coming days I'll be sending you, with regular mail, some reprints of articles that have appeared here. Until now I've held off from doing so, partly because of the uncertain postal connection and partly because I'm easily intimidated by the very thought of customs declaration. I've become more cautious because here, of all places, they often make a huge fuss over nothing.

I have nothing more to say about the Institute and your illusions regarding Wiesengrund. You're better off clinging to your opinions about Horkheimer: there you are on firmer ground. With Schocken, out of pure caution and anxiety about the proper use of his money and about his posthumous fame, he's sitting on his hands. At the end of the day, he's going to end up with the ideal shared by all millionaires: namely, ensuring that his expensive offspring have millionaire standards. Based on the meager bits I've been able to glean, his difficulties with the Friends of the Hebrew University arose from the normal conflicts between natives who don't like "refugees" telling them what to do.

Monsieur sends his greetings. For a while he was teaching at Princeton, and he had lots of fun and success. For the time being, what he's doing is a lot less enjoyable than Princeton: he's a commentator for a radio station; and since it's a short-wave station, it's very difficult to measure success.[6] I too would like to earn a regular income, though at first I was really happy at last to get back to serious academic work. I'd like to give Monsieur a break so he could return to his own work. But here I don't have many options: the Jews don't want me, and I have a deeply rooted aversion against other potential jobs. This basically goes along with my ideas: people love to print them up, a relatively safe thing to do, but they are very hesitant to give them any influence. Another factor, of course, is that I live in a mixed marriage, which for local standards is a capital offense.

Recently, Jenny Blumenfeld turned up and had some interesting things to report. It is so difficult to form a picture of what's going on over there that one clutches at every straw. I don't take her to be much more than straw. Kurt and I are as close as ever, regardless of our many arguments.[7] He introduced me to Klatzkin,[8] the "philosopher"—now that's a strange bird for you!

Send Fanja my best. I very much back the idea of you coming here for a few years, and as soon as possible. What are the chances? For purely egotistical reasons I am doing everything I can to promote your fame. Anyway, people over here are completely convinced of your importance and your uniqueness. They are also afraid of this.

I'm enclosing an entirely true comment from your censor.[9]

Sincerely,
Your Hannah

LETTER 12 From Scholem

Abarbanel Rd. 28, Jerusalem
July 18, 1944

Dear friend,
Many thanks for your letter from May 20 and also for the three offprints that arrived safe and sound the day before yesterday.[1] Please send me everything you've written: I'm *very* interested in your work. Don't be angry if at the moment I can't engage in a discussion of your work. I am so extraordinarily exhausted that it takes great effort to write a thing. I'm not at my best now, and I have to reserve what little energy I have for the work I should have finished two years ago!! So I'm not even sure I can do the amusing—light—little essay I promised Oko, who just wrote me. I'm really sapped of energy. I'd really like to lead off with a discussion of your thesis of the pariah, as I have my reservations on your *very-well*-formulated interpretation of both Heine and Kafka. To my inner "Rashi" the texts speak a different language, and in my opinion in order to squeeze them into the concepts you employ you end up leaving many things out that don't fit.[2] (I'd say that your approach can't make any sense of Kafka's *Castle*, for instance.)[3] But like I said, I really can't write with any depth now.

We'd really like to head over for some time (to stay for too long isn't healthy for anyone), and I'd gladly do it if I could swing another invitation as guest professor for a year or so. It doesn't depend on me. If you want to know the truth, I already have a "theme": should the occasion arise, I've made up my mind to reveal Hasidism to the public, through my eyes. By doing so, any reasonable person will easily see what was also emphasized throughout my book, and something the final chapter points out, partly quietly and partly under the guise of neighborly love. ("Love thy Buber as thyself.")[4]

Spiegel tells me that Stephen Wise would very much like to do something with me again, but until now no one has said anything to me.[5] I would much rather go to Schechter's seminar, where my two friends Spiegel and Lieberman[6] are now.[7] But the people there would probably find too many flies in the ointment that I give them. The poet writing in dialect would sum up the situation this way, short but sweet: "This tefillin here, y' put it on? Ah, Gerhard, he doesn't go along."[8] I'd like you to take to heart this religious verse!

If you have an hour or so, please write us—and include your impressions on the Jewish dialect-philosopher Klatzkin.

Warmest greetings to you and Blücher from Fanja and yours truly.

LETTER 13 From Arendt-Blücher

317 West 95th Street, New York, NY
January 14, 1945
For almost six months now I've been once again marching around with your letter from July. I've wanted to write so many times. Of course you know that Oko died—those people on the Committee annoyed him to death.[1] He was like a child lost in the woods. Somehow he was too noble for these chaps, and naturally too innocent in matters of politics. I was very saddened because I felt somewhat more secure with him than I do with the rest of the editors. One of the reasons for his agitation pertained to an article I wrote that he wanted to publish far and wide but the other Sirs deemed too "Zionist."[2] *De facto*, the article had a dreadful objectivity to it.

Meanwhile, the Committee has charged Mr. Horkheimer with the task of battling anti-Semitism.[3] Putting the fox in charge of the henhouse is only one of the many amusing aspects of the story. Incidentally, aside from his repulsiveness, Horkheimer is even more half-witted than even I had thought possible. For the time being, Clement Greenberg is taking Oko's place.[4] He has certainly already written you. With great impatience we are all looking forward to your article. Oko is the one who discovered Greenberg: a young, radical, talented Jewish lad who knows a few things about literature and absolutely nothing about things Jewish. He seems to be as convinced as Horkheimer that Jews in general, and himself in particular, are the chosen people, which fully qualifies him for the position. In contrast to Horkheimer, at least he's a truly intelligent and nice fellow.

I've sent you some offprints, the discussions of which we'll likely have to table until after the war is over—the only question now is in which cafe we'll meet. In any event, like Schwejk,[5] it'll be five o'clock sharp. This is gallows humor, for the question of when we'll see one another again is beginning to play an ever-greater role for me personally—the Greeks rightly located the dramatic heart of tragedy to be the scene in which people recognize each other again. There are simply not many people I earnestly want to see again, but for those few I have powerful desires. It goes without saying that you are among them.

Please, can't you at least tell me how you see the situation in Palestine? Over here, at least until a few weeks ago, there has been such an idiotic optimism that one can almost describe as euphoric. What I heard from Siegfried Moses didn't exactly brighten up my mood.[6] At the same time, he's such an old-school liberal, with the attendant inability to judge things political, that I began to have my doubts again. What do you think about Alijah Hadasha?[7] Are you a member? And what about the League for Arab-Jewish Cooperation?[8] You don't have to answer if you don't want.

The reason I haven't been writing is that I've been working an awful lot. Among other things, I've come up with a fundamental reconsideration of Zionism because I seriously believe that we're going to lose everything if we continue on our present course. Then again, what I've written will cost me my last Zionist friends, that is, if they are fanatics.[9] It's been a rather heartbreaking affair, and *Menorah* is going to press with it. (Osiris said to Isis: "You have no idea how awful my life has become." Isis said to Osiris: "You have no idea how awful I am.") Recently I've returned to my work—which is innocuous only on the surface—on imperialism and race.[10] I'm constantly being pestered by requests for articles, requests that in no way can I afford to turn down.

I am really eager to undertake something to get you an invitation here. I just don't know what I can do because I have no contact with the relevant decision-makers. Sadly, besides being a woman, I'm also an epicurean with a lot more going against me than just not laying tefillin.

Write soon—letters are a kind of surrogate. And don't forget: after the war, five o'clock sharp!

Warmest greets to you and Fanja from Monsieur and me.
Your Hannah

LETTER 14 From Scholem

Abarbanel Rd. 28, Jerusalem
March 6, 1945

Dear friend,
Your letter from January 14 arrived last week, and I'm being a good role model for you by replying at once. I had been wondering if one of your letters wound up in the depths of the sea but now I see that what's been keeping you

from writing has been your long strolls along the promenade on Riverside Drive. Meanwhile, the day before yesterday your article on Kafka came out in the latest edition of *Partisan Review*.[1] Many thanks for this. I'm making a small collection of your writings, and I'd like you to keep honoring me with your work so the "archive" stays up to date. Incidentally, I should note here that all the literary venues describe you as the author of *Love and Saint Augustine*, though I don't know anything about this book. Is it supposed to be an obscure dissertation along the lines of "The Problem of Freedom in Augustine," or is it a more humble act of Gnostic expectoration? Whichever it is, the fact remains that the book is not in my library. If you have a copy you can send it over (even if, as I naturally assume, by now you consider everything in the book to be nonsense). I am so proud to have saved your manuscript on Rahel Varnhagen. Where is the book's final resting spot? At a publisher's? On your desk? I haven't heard a peep from you about the book.

My article for the *Jewish Record* still hasn't materialized. Every time I feel obliged to do something, the psychological pressure builds, and in the end I come up with something completely different. (Recently I've churned out five other articles, none being of any interest to anyone besides true scholars of the Kabbalah and myself!) And at the very moment I'm about to say something clever, I naturally want to express it as beautifully as I can, and then nothing whatsoever comes of it. But slowly, slowly, I'm getting around to writing the article. I received a very nice letter from Mr. Greenberg. Oko did a really great job of editing the journal; I have no idea what's going to happen now. Whatever became of the article that was supposed to appear in the journal but was declared "too Zionist"? And has *Menorah* managed to bring to print your comments on my book?

That the assimilated Americans picked Horkheimer to fight anti-Semitism is for me more astounding than you can imagine. The short article he wrote for the Institute's journal, on the Jewish Question in Europe, was unfathomable in its mixture of outspoken impudence and ignorance, and besides having been proven wrong by events, the article should have disqualified him as an author on the subject. The Committee[2] recently sent me its *Bulletin* in which, next to his heroic photo, H[orkheimer]'s importance is praised to the high heavens. Very strange indeed. Meanwhile, I'm puzzled that I've not heard a word from Wiesengrund. The last thing I got, and to my great amazement, was a thank-you note he had his wife send me for my "highly important" book. This was the last I heard from him, though only the devil knows how many letters have been lost. For instance, he sent me the edition the Institute put out on Benjamin but it never arrived, like so many other things. I'm counting on you to save me a copy in a corner of your room. Once the war is over you can send it over to me.

You asked me about the situation in Palestine. In my opinion, there is no longer an active Jewish political position that isn't mere empty babble and pussyfooting. The English aren't going to leave Palestine, no matter if they control it by way of a partition (I have a running bet about this) or as a continuation of the so-called international status.[3] With deference to the censor, I can't give you my true opinion of English and Jewish politics in this corner of the world. At the same time, one can't discount the possibility that situations could arise—for which Jewish leaders admittedly haven't done a thing to encourage—that could substantially increase the chances for a Jewish politics here. Politics of this sort would require a large dose of independent judgment and lots of cool, both of which Zionist political culture sadly lacks most. You asked me what I think about Alijah Hadasha and whether I'm a member. To this I can only say: not much, and by no means. The mistake these very-well-meaning gentlemen make, as you can probably guess, arises from their antediluvian, or in this case postdiluvian, liberalism. Instead of coming up with solutions that people actually believe in, such as partition, and then with intelligence and conviction taking these solutions to the Palestinian public, they are too concerned with popularity and just end up hiding behind Weltsch's articles.[4] A dialectical reader is stricken with a kind of horror by these articles. The immeasurable flexibility of the Jewish personality can be seen in the fact that the manifest bankruptcy of official policy here,[5] of which even the people behind it are convinced, in no way translates into the strengthening of parties such as Alijah Hadasha. People have utterly wrong expectations. Jews don't take the apocalypse so seriously, and now after they've been officially fed with the apocalypse for three years, they accept its end with the greatest calm as if nothing has really changed at all. People like to blame Ben-Gurion by saying, Now that you've stirred up the youth, what's going to happen if all their hopes aren't fulfilled? The answer is very simple: nothing at all. Like I said, I'd rather take up these matters with you after the military scraps its censorship—which in this country can take on the strangest forms. I presently believe, in any event, that a lot of things here will end up being much-ado-about-nothing, that is to say, things won't be nearly as exciting as we imagine.

If you have one, you can honor me with a copy of your discussion on the principles of Zionism from the perspective of the New World. With regard to the prospect you raise of a postwar meeting, at precisely at 5 o'clock PM, we'll be able to come to terms. I'll then take the opportunity to profess myself as an adherent to the theological reading of Kafka's writings that you wrongly, in my humble opinion, shove to one side.[6] Until then, take care of yourself and give me a detailed account in case you happen to meet Schocken. He told me he was going to extend an invitation to you. Convince him not only to do something to support research into the Kabbalah but also for Walter Benjamin's literary estate. That fellow is very susceptible to hints and whispers!!

For now, Fanja and I send our warmest greetings to you and Blücher

---

LETTER 15 From Arendt

317 West 95th Street, New York, NY
March 31, 1945

Dear friend,
Because good examples sometimes work, I'm sending you a prompt response. I got a good laugh from the line about the "archive." You see how I am sending you things, even when I'm certain you're not going to agree with me, as with Kafka. Soon enough I'll feel as if I'm writing behind your back if I don't send you something. I can't get *Love and Saint Augustine* to you because, sadly, I just have one (stolen) copy; otherwise, it's nowhere to be found.[1] This I heard from some university librarians who've been looking for a copy for years. It may be that Little Hans Jonas still has one, and if so I authorize you to filch it. The book is a really amusing piece of work because, first, it was written in a non-existent language, which neither the author nor the critics noticed; and second, despite all due respect to the saint, I treated him not only as a contemporary but almost as a peer—and this is something critics picked up on.

What about the *Record*?[2] What have you managed to write until now?? You told me once that there are but a handful of "true scholars of the Kabbalah" (this I accept without reserve after having read some of the reviews of your book). You're going to have to make up for not writing the article by communicating to the non-scholars of the Kabbalah what is involved in researching the truth. I'm almost getting furious. The *Record* will most certainly go to the dogs, but Greenberg isn't to blame, who is really nice, knows English well, has a good nose for standards—and hasn't the foggiest idea of Jewish matters. The problem is rather that the people on top have decided that its standards are too high (sic!) and have to be sunk to the level of a larger circle of readers. That'll happen this coming fall under the direction of a Mr. Cohen (for good reason, his first name has slipped my mind).[3] In his heyday this man was supposedly coeditor of *Menorah* and then worked for a Jewish welfare organization as the PR man or the like. The journal will be a monthly; but in order to influence the "masses," there is just one thing missing: a political position capable of having any such influence.

I recently spoke with Horkheimer and let myself endure an hour of his droning on about what he is doing and what he intends to do. I can't recount what he said—in its absolute idiocy, it was simply too grotesque to repeat. I'll try once again to get my hands on the edition with Benjamin's "Thesis" and send it to you. I'm not entirely convinced by this tale of packages sinking to the bottom of the ocean.[4]

Schocken is telling everyone that he wants to get to know me, and then he does nothing about it.[5] He seems, though, to be edging closer to it after he ran across my name in reviews printed in non-Jewish journals. Of course you know how, with Max Strauss,[6] he wants to reopen his publishing house and launch it by publishing (or reprinting) your book. Through Strauss I suggested that Schocken create a decent Jewish journal, which would really be timely. As soon as I see him, I'll naturally begin pestering him about publishing Benjamin's estate. Most likely, the publishing house will mainly be English translations from the Schocken Series, which might really be a contribution.[7] Hurvitz still hasn't printed up the review in *Menorah*. One reason for this is that the journal is only coming out sporadically; another reason is that Hurvitz regards the review to be "important," important but incomprehensible. I'd prefer it this way because I know that a new edition of your book will be coming out. For the sake of publicity, it's better to hold off on the reviews until future readers can buy the book.

Your comments on Palestine were by far the sanest things I've heard or read in ages. I don't think partition will change very much; and in other subjects I believe we're more of one mind than I had dared hope. I can't tell you what a relief it was to hear that you don't belong to Alijah Hadasha. Weltsch has become so utterly banal. Though I'd never had a very high opinion of the fellow, these days he's really overdoing it. This doesn't mean that the others are any better. I had the honor and pleasure, in a small gathering, to hear some remarks by Bentov.[8] The upshot was that even the Hashomer people no longer believe in a binational state and, to put it mildly, are not exactly keeping up-to-date on world events.[9]

People are saying that Weizmann is heading here in order to get a Haluz movement off the ground, the success of which will naturally depend on "American skill," and nor can there be any other way *rebus sic stantibus*.[10] Anti-Semitism, which without doubt is on the rise, is being completely misunderstood in terms of its influence on American Jewry and elsewhere. Everyone here is more or less pro-Zionist, and they are so accustomed to anti-Semitism that they consider it a natural life form for the goyim, a life form, moreover, that one deals with through an equally natural suspicion against Gentiles. But no one, not even in his wildest dreams, thinks about emigrating, which after all was the very same attitude people had in Europe before Hitler. If tomorrow a tourist agency launched itself with the slogan "Everyone should visit Palestine," I think half of American Jews would end up there for some rest and relaxation. They have more than enough money for it. The younger generation, which I know quite well, politically is better than we were in Central Europe because, at least in part, a little of the American tradition of freedom has rubbed off on them. Still, they generally behave according to the old pattern: that is, they are radical in all questions of a general nature and, when it comes to Jewish politics, are staunchly conservative and full of fear. It's a little like the attack on the Jewish welfare machinery: ("Now really, what would happen if everyone had his hand out?").[11] You'll get "Zionism Reconsidered" as soon as it comes out. Did I ever send you the "Minorities" article? (Not important. I was just so furious that the World Congress once again made a big fuss about minority rights. This was the Congress's way of convincing the Jews that there could be a restoration of the status quo.)[12]

If you've gotten this letter it means, perhaps, that what one could scarcely call "peace" has broken out in Europe. Despite this, for the time being I'm prepared to breathe a sigh of relief for five minutes. One can hardly imagine no longer living under the pressure we've had for twelve years now. And, I fear, we're not going to have much of a chance to get used to it.

All the best, and warmest greetings to both you and Fanja from Monsieur and me.

As always,
Your Hannah.

P.S. If I hear from Schocken, I'll write at once.

LETTER 16 From Scholem

Abarbanel Rd. 28, Jerusalem
August 6, 1945

Dear Hannah,
It seems the good example we determined to give one another has quickly come to a terrible standstill. I've had your letter from March 31 for a long time now, and it sits around still unanswered, weighing heavily on my conscience. The reasons for not replying are many: health, commitments, and a whole host of other delays. But there is no excuse. Meanwhile, Kurt Blumenfeld has turned up and, insofar as his disjointed manner of speech permits, he told me many enchanting things about you and passed along all kinds of greetings from you. I tried to listen carefully to everything he said, which isn't so easy, as you well know. He is still a very charming fellow, and occasionally he comes out with things of astounding intuition and intellectual force, but between these moments stands a total ruin of a man who has collapsed from within, is centered on himself, and analyzes contemporary world events with a few too many tears. That said, he still remains above the standard of his friends, which makes you wonder. He was completely taken by you and your husband. The other things he said about America were not cheerful.

I received your article on minorities, though not the essay on the revision of Zionist theory, which has perhaps not yet appeared. Please indulge my bibliographic urges and kindly send me whatever you write, now that I can read English, thank God, better than you do Hebrew. We'll have to wait and see if I can steal a copy of your dissertation from Jonas. He's still a sergeant with the Brigade, but he'll be demobilized within the next six weeks and will settle back in Jerusalem from Italy.[1] I got a letter from him gushing forth with heroic sentiments. After five years of fruitless effort, instead of dying in the struggle against Hitler he managed to survive. The one who died, suddenly, fourteen days ago, was his and my friend, the philologist Hans Lewy, whom you must know. Absolutely no one, and himself least of all, thought he was a candidate for death. A terrible blow for all of us.[2] No one knows what will become of the university here when gradually all the good people die away (Lewy was excellent), and because the salaries here are so bad that we can't even appoint third-rate people from Anglo-Saxon countries, let alone recruit the academic stars we're always looking for. Currently a full professor makes, including all cost-of-living bonuses, $3,600 per annum. Just calculate how many thousands of dollars Zionism has to be worth in order for someone who is age forty or fifty to come here for such a salary. Yours truly had it easy as a twenty-five-year-old idealist, having the time of his life on 15 pounds a month. You'll be doing something for the Jewish people if you inculcate enough of a sense of Zion into the minds of three promising youngsters that they resolve, irrespective of the money, to come to the university and from here to make their world reputation. One has to think that somewhere there really are people of such caliber who could be won over. What do you or Blücher, who must know him, honestly think about Dr. Lerner from the New School?[3] We'd really like to have him as a professor for political economics. If you happen to know the man, perhaps you can put in a good word for us. I've heard he's apparently very talented. Four weeks ago I got the Institute's volume on Benjamin, with a laconic dedication from Wiesengrund. Thanks so much for this. I credit you and your efforts for the book. For years now I haven't heard a thing from Wiesengrund, and why this is so, I can't say. At first there was no end to his declarations of friendship; then, suddenly, total silence. I wrote him shortly after I received the volume. His article on George[4] is really interesting, but it is also endlessly snotty and also partly malicious in its misinterpretation and obvious ignorance of precisely the thing Benjamin had: a sense for poetry. In general, the technical jargon used by all the issue's contributors turned my stomach. What will happen to Benjamin's estate, I can't say. With the war over, serious thought should be given to this. Has anyone in Paris looked into what has become of his papers that his sister had with her?[5] (She's died in the meantime.) Meanwhile, I spoke to Arthur Koestler. He may be a supremely talented writer, yet as a person he's such a *mauvais sujet* and so repulsive that, after our first renewed contact, I dropped the idea of inviting him to my home. I've met with him twice to discuss Benjamin. You know the two of them lived in the same building. But his unbearable ridicule of Benjamin's character showed me right off that I was dealing with someone completely infatuated by his own greatness, someone who can only appreciate the importance of others as a springboard for self-promotion. At that point I gave up. With one fell swoop my wife managed to insult him deeply. He apparently knows nothing about the literary estate. He said Benjamin gave him half of his morphine. It's a pity Benjamin wasn't more generous, for in Lisbon his friend Koestler swallowed whatever he had and vomited it up again. A healthy young man! His book on the Moscow trials is the only good thing I can say about him.[6]

You ask about my writing. I'm in the middle of a number of interesting things in Hebrew, things that will advance scholarship but won't do you any good. Besides this, over the coming summer I'll have to stay here and work on the second edition of *Major Trends*, which will probably come out next year in America in expanded form, most likely in two volumes.[7] I'm completely preoccupied with this, and I'm trying to concentrate enough on the book that I can have it behind me by the beginning of the semester. For this reason, not much will come out of the "profound" article destined for the *Record* (whose new look I don't like much anyway). I got the new program from Mr. Cohen. Without your comments I wouldn't have known what's so fishy about it.[8] In any event, with the new *Major Trends* you'll be able to read in English—and with more or less amusement—what else I want to tell the world about my research. I'm writing a couple new chapters and fluffing up a few others so that I can roughly summarize what I'd like the historians of religion and other thoughtful people of the next generation to at least take into account. Admittedly, the materials I'm adding contain more concrete historical information and other kinds of analysis than intimations I've smuggled surreptitiously into the text. I'm writing it in Hebrew. Hope to God that the new translator does a decent job.[9] I'll be looking over his shoulder: my English is good enough for this. Of course, it'll take plenty of time before the book gets printed. If your review comes out earlier, make me a happy man by sending me a copy. Otherwise, you can store it away for later. Once I'm finished with the book, and before returning again to dry scholarship and digging through manuscripts, I'm not at all against whipping together a few articles.

As you can see, our plan to meet five minutes after the end of the war must be postponed, even though the war is already over in Europe. Detailed reports from Europe are now arriving here. Much worse, of course, than the widespread knowledge of mass murder is the concrete effect this will have on people. The destructive impact of this information on people's minds and souls is incredibly strong; but there is no way to avoid facing the facts, even if everyone says he'd prefer ignorance in such cases.

Apparently Schocken has left America for good. I have no idea if you have seen him, as I've not heard a word from him since the beginning of the year. For the time being he's in England. It's impossible that the various meetings he had there worked out well for him. I would have wished for a more graceful exit for him. It's not likely he'll be coming here before the fall. What's actually going on with Max Strauss? Is he still smug and fat or has he begun revealing his better self, which I first discovered twenty-eight years ago?[10] It's not that he's dumb, he's just gone completely to seed.

My wife sends you many greetings. For the last ten days she's been in bed with a nasty case of rheumatism, or something of the sort. But it really cheered us up to hear from Blumenfeld that it's not beyond the realm of possibility that we'll see you here before you see us there. If you make the decision to come, you can be sure to get a very warm welcome. Meanwhile, you should repay evil with good by quickly replying to this—long-winded—letter.

All the best to you both,
Gerhard Scholem

LETTER 17 From Arendt

317 West 95th Street, New York, NY
September 22, 1945

Dear Gerhard,
I had wanted to write you immediately following the death of Hans Lewy[1] ... and in the end I didn't do it. You must surely know that, because the telegram from Jerusalem mentioned nothing about his having a brother around, it was left to Gruenewald and me to go to the family and deliver the news, a very unpleasant task. A couple weeks ago we were all there: Prinz, Gruenewald, and Tischel, and me.[2] It was a rather spooky scene with the highbrow brother, who owns a movie theater and stood there with his wife; and then the mother, who seemed physically lively and alert and yet somehow didn't know what was happening around her. Perhaps I'm mistaken, but among older people this often happens. (God spare us from old people's lethargy of the heart.) I barely knew Levy.[3] I first met him in Jerusalem and really liked him, but it was painful to be around his family.

Be nice to Kurt B. Just as you said, he's head and shoulders above the level of all his friends, people he's forever quarreling with. I adore the man. With all his flaws, he's not a ghost but is made of real flesh and blood. His judgments about America are completely one-sided. While he doesn't understand this country, he has caught a glimpse of some of its fundamental vices. You are wrong about relatively low salaries being behind the university's inability to recruit people to Jerusalem. Money isn't hobbling your efforts, language is. Don't forget that for you learning Hebrew was a part of your field.

This doesn't apply in the least to an economist or a historian or a physicist, for whom learning the language demands additional effort. I know out of bitter personal experience what kind of difference there is between picking up one of the European languages, English or French, say, and Hebrew. Learning Hebrew requires an adult, who is already chronically busy, to sacrifice years of his own work. And this kind of sacrifice is a lot more difficult to make than taking a cut in salary. This might be different with much younger people. After a certain age, and *nolens volens* after having already been forced to learn other languages, such an undertaking presses the panic button. I know you don't want to hear this, but believe me when I say you're wrong about both the "world reputation" and the financial side of things. I don't know Lerner from the New School. I only hope he's not the journalist Lerner who writes for *Partisan Review* and the *Republic*, and who gives the occasional lecture.[4] I know this Lerner, and I don't want to see his face again. He's a classic Jewish journalist straight from Vienna or somewhere else.

I don't really understand your comments on Benjamin's estate. As far as I know, his sister is quite ill but still alive living in Switzerland. We had someone from Switzerland here a couple weeks ago who saw her recently, and he spoke with her. Georg, on the other hand, was murdered at some point (I think it was five years ago) in a concentration camp.[5] The sister never had the literary estate. In his final letter he expressively gave it to the Institute. While no one has seen it, the estate arrived in New York and consists mainly of the boxes that he stored at the Bibliothèque Nationale and which someone from Paris smuggled here.[6] Horkheimer says he's stored the estate in a safe. Where this safe is, no one can say. Like I wrote, I'm no match for these fellows. I had had a glimmer of hope that Schocken would perhaps decide to publish the works, which would allow me to apply some pressure on them. Schocken, as you know, is interested exclusively in the "eternal values" of Judaism, and he doesn't consider Benjamin to fall into this category. He even went so far as to declare to me, I quote, that even Kafka was a borderline case. His assistant is Strauss,[7] who first of all can't do much, and second he's not very interested in the few important things Schocken should and could do.

You are naturally right on the money with Koestler. Even so, he's written a good reportage, *Scum of the Earth*.[8] Broadly speaking, with his prim and proper Hungarian manners and shoddy education, he's a good barometer for the general spiritual atmosphere. He also lived on 10 rue Dombasle, together with the psychiatrist Fritz Fraenkel, who later died.

We're all eagerly awaiting the new expanded edition of *Major Trends*. I'll sit on my review until then because it makes no sense to bring it out now. *Menorah*, which is to say Hurwitz, is still holding on to it; from time to time, he complains that he can't make heads or tails of it. Hurwitz is a genius in the art of not publishing manuscripts but also not letting them out of his grip. My essay "Zionism Reconsidered" will at long last be in the October or November edition. Sadly, sadly, the essay is neither obsolete nor irrelevant.

As for the terrifying reports from Europe, what has shocked me most is the way people are reacting to it, or how they don't react at all. You might have read a few lines in *Aufbau* from Jaspers's inaugural lecture at Heidelberg University. By chance I got my hands on it in a German newspaper.[9] Until now he is the first person, irrespective of nationality, who seems to have experienced the kind of metaphysical shock without which it is really pointless to continue agonizing over what has happened. Monsieur and I are both a tad relieved because we no longer feel so isolated, Monsieur naturally more than I because he is, after all, a German, which presently really isn't a lot of fun. German social democracy, which here is amply represented by Jews and non-Jews, is blowing the old nationalistic horn, which would be amusing if it weren't so endlessly outrageous. You can get a clear glimpse into the catastrophe with the claim among local Jews of "Thank God, I'm not like that." (I've sent you two articles about this, one from *Jewish Frontier* that came out at the beginning of the year. The article made a bit of a stir here and had to be reprinted. Did you get them? I *always* send you a specimen copy. My God, who should I send them to if not you?)[10]

Happily, the war has ended with atom bombs, just what we always needed. There is no flush of victory here, though there would be ample justification for it. Instead, there is an unspoken sense of panic due to the specter of unemployment, and within industry of a massive eruption of working-class warfare. I have the impression that, as in Europe, it is no longer war but unemployment that people consider the real hell, and that people now are more and more prepared to do whatever it takes, to prepare for war, go to war, exterminate nations, and so on, just to not be unemployed. We've learned how many possible forms of "employment" there are.

Give Fanja my warmest greetings. I hope her rheumatism is better. I know from experience that rheumatism is no joke. It's now five minutes after war's end and we still haven't managed to make a date at the cafe around the corner.

Sincerely,
Your Hannah

LETTER 18 From Scholem

Abarbanel Rd. 28, Jerusalem
December 16, 1945

Dear friend,
Your letter from September 22 arrived with considerable delay, and since receiving it I was remiss by allowing several weeks to pass before sending you a response. I'll make this up to you with a friendly gift I'm including with this letter: two articles by Benjamin, one on Hölderlin's poems "Dichtermut" and "Bloedigkeit," and the other on Franz Kafka.[1] For the time being they are for your eyes only, but if the opportunity arises, you can see about publishing them. I've decided to send them to you first and not to the Institute because of Wiesengrund's bizarre behavior—that for almost four years he didn't bother writing me a single line and then, a few months ago, sent me a copy of the Institute's memorial issue, and without even an accompanying letter. Another factor was your own friendly remarks about the mysterious way in which the Institute is sitting on the literary estate, to the extent it's in the Institute's possession. As a novice in such matters, I would be most grateful if you could brief me on the legal status: who has the power of disposition over those of Benjamin's unpublished writings that are not in the possession of the Institute but rather are with me, you, or whoever? Now that the war is over, we should be able to find out what his [former] wife has, what was left with Gustav Glück[2] in Berlin, or with Ernst Schoen,[3] etc. It seems impossible that the Institute would have the power of disposition over such documents. Of the two essays I'm sending to you, I know for certain that they cannot be with the Institute. Recently I got a letter from Walter's sister in Zurich. In a strangely abstract manner she asked me, without giving any details, if I'd be willing to work on a memorial volume a French newspaper is bringing out for Walter. I replied to her that, for me, it seems more important that Walter's own work finally see the light of day than for us to write essays about him, regardless of how clever they are. I said that she'd be better off investing her effort in making this happen. Now that we are on the theme of his literary estate, I'd like to mention how important it is, I feel, for there to be a volume of his correspondence. A large number of letters must still be around, and there must be several people who know with whom he maintained an extensive correspondence. His former wife would know best about the time

before 1930. And I can hardly imagine that the people on the receiving end of his letters would have tossed them into a corner. With his letters, admittedly, there are the same linguistic problems as with the rest of his writings. The stylistic charm of the originals can't be translated, and this goes especially for his letters.

Last week I dispatched to America the manuscript for the second edition of my book, that is to say, an improved version of the first edition with about fifteen lengthy addenda.[4] The biggest disappointment and loss for me came after I had worked the entire summer on expanding a new chapter, and had finished writing everything in Hebrew, only to discover that the only translator, someone I had in mind when I was writing the book and who was qualified to do the work, left me in the lurch. I tried everything possible but failed in all my desperate attempts at coming up with a decent translation of a difficult text into comprehensible English. Can you imagine that in Palestine translations from Hebrew into English are only to be had for short works and political propaganda? Schocken declared that in America he only has translators from German to English. I've been completely worn down by all this, and I can't even bear the sight of my own work. And now I would have to put everyone to one side and, all over again, to write the bit about the development of the Kabbalah from 1150 to 1250 (about 120–140 pages) in German. What I decided to do instead is to leave the book in its so-called present "classic" form, and all the missing materials can come out in a separate special publication. Next year I'm hoping to take my work from this summer and publish it as a small volume in Hebrew.[5] Perhaps then, if one has the patience to wait, a decent English translator will show up. Schocken would gladly publish the book in such a separate format. I've also been pointlessly holding you and the others back because the new edition, as it now exists, could have come out a year ago. But at least you won't have to rewrite your review. By the way, the final sentence imputes to me an opinion on the process of history that, in all seriousness, I have to reject.[6] In my stirring final comments you failed to find adequate evidence for this opinion.[7] But that doesn't matter, and nothing is worse than an author trying to influence his reviewer.

Being so preoccupied by the book and by this damned business with the translation, I've yet to write my essay for your friend Clement Greenberg. From this coming March to November I will take my so-called sabbatical. Originally I had planned on going to England to wind up my work with original manuscripts. After some serious reflection, however, I've decided it's far more vital that I use this precious time to get in as much productive writing as possible. In particular, it's more important that I finally complete my major, long-overdue study of Sabbatianism than to wade through fifty more manuscripts, which at the end of the day probably won't yield anything very revolutionary anyway. So I'm looking forward to a productive period, either here or (in case it proves better for my concentration) on Cyprus. Of course there's no telling whether at the last moment politics, a topic about which you and I are probably in tearful agreement, will kill these noble plans with a roar of cannon fire and a hail of bullets. Still, for the time being things are much quieter than many people were predicting given the prevailing mood of boundless bitterness against England.[8] I think I predicted something of the sort in an earlier letter.[9] If the English don't do anything too terribly provocative—and naturally no one can know with any certainty whose hands are really pulling the strings behind the scenes—my bet is that the winter will pass without any major incidents. What contributes a lot to the quiet, I believe, is the general feeling that the country isn't even capable of absorbing the very masses we shout about in our resolutions. We'd be facing a catastrophe if Mr. Truman's 100,000 Jews legally poured into the country tomorrow.[10] While such considerations naturally do nothing to satisfy the lust for action among our young people, they do play a considerable role in many people's thinking.

Schocken has arrived and has been sitting around for a couple months without making any decisions. After two months of negotiations and discussions with me, he still hasn't made up his mind to guarantee five more years of financing for my Kabbalah institute. He comes out with a lot of high-flown nonsense. All things considered, he's not stupid, but nothing can be done to help the man. My complaints to him on matters pertaining to Hannah Blücher must have reached you all the way over to New York. But someone so molded by the world of Zwickau is beyond reform.[11] At some point in the future I hope to be able to send to you, *gratis* and *franco*, an analysis of this remarkable character. With Max Strauss you shouldn't forget that he has one invaluable virtue: his very natural indolence allows other people to speak, and people like this. If I'm not mistaken, already in 1917 I was won over by this characteristic of his. It's not only, as you wrote, that he doesn't have much interest in the few things Schocken could actually do. The truth is even worse: he's not interested in anything, and this is what gives him his power. His is the repressed yawn of a handsome old gentleman who is full of suggestions and in the end doesn't lift a finger.

Only very rarely do I read *Aufbau*. The speech you mentioned given by Jaspers during the opening of the university, I'm hoping to get soon from our friend Jonas. With a little hullaballoo, he has returned from the Jewish Brigade back to civilian life. In case you're interested, he married a young woman, a woman who is, in Fanja's and my opinion, a perfect match for him, and is someone with some excellent character traits.[12] Jonas brought back with him from Göttingen a university course catalogue from winter semester 1945, which isn't half-bad. I've discovered in it that that pig of a theologian Gogarten is still around. The only one given his walking papers was Emanuel Hirsch, who admittedly was completely useless. Jonas tells us a variety of interesting things about the development of the universities. Apparently, he himself wants to come up with his own philosophical system here.[13]

You were of course entirely right in what you wrote concerning the question of language. But still, if we just paid decent salaries we would definitely get many good people. Lerner, whom I was surprised to hear you don't know—he's not a journalist, he's an economist whose first name is Abba—turned us down, and he didn't do so because of language. He already speaks Hebrew. The difficulties we are going to have in finding suitable young talent are going to grow exponentially. We know this.

That'll have to be all for today. I just ask of you not to wait in answering this letter until the two manuscripts mentioned above arrive. It's better to write two letters than one. Kurt Blumenfeld (on another occasion I'll write about him) told me that together with your husband you are coming here. You mentioned nothing about this in your letter. Where did Blumenfeld get this information? Is something cooking? And what about Youth Aliyah in Paris? People really need you there. Are you not at all interested?[14]

Give my greetings to everyone over there, and to yourself as well.

Your Gerhard Scholem

Greetings,

Your Hans J.[15]

LETTER 19 From Scholem

January 28, 1946

My dear friend,

I received your package with the articles along with the issue of the *Menorah Journal* that was sent to me directly. Many thanks.[1] I find myself in the extraordinarily disagreeable position of having to give you my opinion on the essay "Zionist Reconsidered," though I really don't want to get into a life-or-death squabble with you. It's impossible for me to offer a detailed discussion of all the many issues I could raise concerning an article which disappointed me so profoundly and which, to tell you the truth, somewhat embittered me. Please don't be offended by my sharp tone.

While basically agreeing with your starting position in the first paragraph, as your argument unfolded I found myself vigorously shaking my head.[2] In vain I asked myself what sort of credo you had in mind when you wrote it. Your article has nothing to do with Zionism but is instead a patently anti-Zionist, warmed-over version of hardline Communist criticism, spiced with a vague Diaspora nationalism. You can sit comfortably in the Galut and denounce Jews in Palestine for building castles on the moon,[3] but when these same Jews make efforts to fend for themselves, in a world whose evil you yourself never cease to emphasize, you react with a sneer that itself stems from some celestial source. Your mishmash of arguments is extremely odd, and the whole displays such inconsistency of scale and perspective that I can make sense of it only by viewing it as an assemblage pieced together by someone who wishes to separate herself from the "reactionary" concerns of Zionism. Herzl's reactionary personality; the shameless exploitation of anti-Semitism for the purposes of Zionist propaganda; the infernal theory of eternal anti-Semitism; the otherworldly sectarianism of aristocratic kibbutzim which don't give a damn about the fate of the Jewish people; the arrogance of this entire Palestinian project vis-à-vis the question of the Jewish people as a whole; the anachronistic opinion that organizing a community into a state still makes sense in an age of international federations;[4] the flirtation with Hitler through the transfer agreement and the scandalous undermining of the boycott; and finally the utter mindlessness of Zionists toward Jewish history, a subject they should know more about—all this, my dear friend, is a lovely potpourri of anti-Zionist positions. In order to prove my claim that your essay is—*sit venia verbo*[5]—an act of political tomfoolery, I would really have to go into specifics. Instead I can only register spirited protest against your "better insights" and "self-criticism." Of course, there are many points on which Zionist politics are completely wrong, and you zero in quite rightly on these weak points. You do this, however, not from a Zionist perspective but from one propped up by patently Trotskyite, anti-Zionist arguments. If none of this has yet been brought home to you, it will be with the publication of your article. I'm not certain if it is necessarily advisable to be a Zionist after Zionism failed in such an important matter as convincing the Jews to come to Palestine before it was too late. I can understand if someone feels this way. What I don't understand, from the viewpoint of your critique, is how Zionism—that is to say, the opinion that what is happening in Palestine is the most decisive event in Jewish history of this generation, even if the Jews here are a sect of fifty or five hundred thousand people—how this Zionism is still possible. With great repose I declare myself guilty of most of the crimes you attribute to Zionism. I am a nationalist and am entirely unfazed by ostensibly "progressive" denunciations of a position that people repeatedly, even in my earliest youth, wrote off as obsolete. I believe in that which can be called, in human scales, the "eternity" of anti-Semitism. Nor can any of the clever inquiries into the roots of anti-Semitism ever prevent it from generating new crusades in perpetual fresh constellations. I am a "sectarian" and have never been ashamed of expressing in print my conviction that sectarianism can offer us something decisive and positive. I couldn't care less about the problem of the state, because I do not believe that the renewal of the Jewish people depends on the question of their political or even social structure. If anything, my own political credo is anarchistic. But I cannot blame the Jews if they ignore so-called progressive theories which no one else in the world has ever practiced. Even though I have a clear notion of the vast differences between partition and a binational state, I would vote with the same heavy heart for either of these two solutions. You make fun of both with truly breathtaking ignorance.[6] The Arabs have never accepted a single solution that includes Jewish immigration, whether it be federal, national, or binational. I am convinced that the conflict with the Arabs would be far easier to deal with after a *fait accompli* such as partition than it would be without it. In any event, I have no idea how the Zionists could go about obtaining an agreement with the Arabs, even though each and every one of us came to this country without any agreement—and if we were still on the outside waiting to enter the country, we would still be prepared to come. I regret to say so, but Zionist politicians are not being complete idiots when they declare that, given the sabotage efforts made by the British administration, there is no chance of reaching any kind of understanding, however formulated. Certainly, as an old Brit Shalom[7] follower, I myself have once belonged to the opposite camp. But I am not presumptuous enough to think that the politics of Brit Shalom wouldn't have found precisely the same Arab enemies, enemies who are mainly interested not in our morality or political convictions, but in whether or not we are here in Palestine at all.

I was frequently surprised by the way your arguments relate to the facts. I'd like to meet the person who told you that people in Palestine, or even in the kibbutzim, aren't interested in the Jewish people outside Palestine.[8] That person must be a complete fool, and I'm offended that you put such pure nonsense into print. I've been living here for twenty-two years and believe I have a fair grasp on the inner life and psychology of my fellow citizens. As a self-declared sectarian, I also know what we could be accused of, but I've never sensed for a second that people here aren't interested in the Jewish people. With the sweat of the brow I have studied Jewish history my entire life, and I'm able to come up with an instructive treatment on the true weak points of our lives here. But for myself and other Zionists, I can't draw one lesson out of your harmless Galut nationalism, which you combine with a spirited American something or other, I just don't know what.

I was just as speechless when I read your arguments about the anti-Hitler boycott, the Jewish army, and even Rommel. People will *really* resent you, in my opinion justifiably, for writing that the appearance of Rommel on the borders of Palestine exposed the absurdity of the Zionist claims regarding the building up of the country.[9] No Zionist has ever said that, before the coming of the Messiah, Palestine cannot be destroyed, be it through an earthquake, a deluge, a moral catastrophe, and so on. More than anything thing else in the essay, I flew into a rage when I read your paragraph on page 181, for it showed me that the two of us are no longer arguing at the same level. I wish the only thing I had against Weizmann was his comment that building Palestine is our answer to anti-Semitism, for rarely has he ever come out with such a simple truth. You must have developed a monumental anti-Palestine complex for you to argue the way you do against this sentence of his.

Anyone who has given it any thought, I believe, realizes that the transfer agreement presented us with a moral dilemma.[10] You should really know that the Revisionists responded to this dilemma with rhetorical denunciations—because they carried none of the responsibility for it![11] I believe that subsequent experience has proven that each and every one of us, if placed in the same position, would have made the same decision as the Zionist organization. The only thing to regret is that in this damned world of ours we didn't make more and better use of this possibility in freeing Jews from the grip of fascism. You should know—and if you don't, I'll say it in the strongest possible terms—that we were already at war. The people behind this precarious operation that bought Jews their freedom from the Gestapo—and yes, sent a pile of hard cash from the Joint[12] and the Zionists back to Germany—were not traitors to the Jewish people, as your reasoning would lead one to assume, but were people doing their duty. I'd like to know if you would have permitted us to undertake such a transfer to save the life of Walter Benjamin! I have to say that I thought you had a better grasp on such dialectical situations. To me your naïve indignation seems as entirely out of place here as it is in a discussion of the merits of Zionism.

Your outrage at the Jewish army is just as baseless and even more annoying because it doesn't even have the excuse of a dialectical moral situation as in the question of transfer.[13] I'm afraid I'm going to provoke your anger against me for saying so, but I have to tell you that your treatment on this point strikes me as pure rubbish. Anyone who read the Hebrew newspapers in Palestine for six years knows how much the facts and the discussions of our position vis-à-vis the army and the formation of Jewish units completely contradict what you allege. For anyone who lived here at the time, the notion that the Agency[14] sabotaged the Jewish army, ostensibly due to a sectarianism more interested in cutting deals with Hitler than in fighting against him, is so grotesque and fictitious that one can only be stunned by your sources or your interpretation of them.

Allow me to conclude with a comment on the verbiage of "reaction," which plays a role in your thinking. The moral debacle of socialism, which is unparalleled in the history of the past generation (since fascism, as is implied in the fact that it wanted to eliminate morality altogether, had no moral idea to defend), has created such confusion over what is reactionary and what is progressive that I can no longer make heads or tails out of these notions. Everyone today is a reactionary, quite often for a completely defensible reason. Moreover, the willingness to go to any length to avoid falling into this category, a willingness written all over every page of your essay, is one of the most depressing phenomena to be seen among clever Jews. It hits me each time I read *Partisan Review*, which you yourself have sent me. I feel free enough in my thinking not to be rankled when I'm accused of holding reactionary opinions—opinions amply demonstrated by pointing not only to my professed religious sympathies but also to my conviction that the social revolution, however desirable it may be, has less to do with the Messiah than commonly thought. I consider it abundantly obvious (and I hardly need emphasize this to you) that the political career of Zionism within the exclusively reactionary world of ours has created a situation full of despair, doubt, and compromise—precisely because it takes place on earth and not on the moon. About this I haven't the slightest illusion. The Zionist movement shares this dialectical experience of the Real (and all its catastrophic possibilities) with all other movements that have taken it upon themselves to change something in the real world. As things have stood for the last twenty years, if we've managed to escape from the Charybdis of imperialism, no form of socialist politics would have been able to save us from striking the Scylla of real-world

Stalinism. Yes, we've certainly compromised to the bone. This I can say with a lot more certainty than I would have fifteen years ago, when with a harmless dialectic reasoning I still believed it was somehow avoidable. (I've written an article about this in Hebrew, as well as a letter. I'll read the letter to you one of these days, in case we see each other.)[15] I really have to pity you if today the only thing you see in Herzl's writings is its reactionary character—already in 1920 I brushed off this aspect of the man. I have to tell you that I still can't read Herzl without quivering. What shocks me about him more than anything is how one person can embody both foolishness and greatness. It's so mind-bogglingly easy to ridicule Herzl that I've trained myself not to do it. If I were to believe you, reactionary Herzl hadn't the foggiest idea about what Jews should do. My only suggestion for you is to spend an hour in dialectical reflection, which shouldn't be hard for someone like you. Anyone who tries today to question Herzl's insights by reference to his most naïve writings, this person knows nothing about us. I'm not such a highfalutin gentleman that, at all cost, I need to hold up the purity of my sect. And if I may duly and respectfully mention this as well, your cynical use of lofty, progressive arguments against something that is for the Jewish people of life-or-death importance is unlikely to persuade me to abandon the sect. Never in my dreams had I thought it would be easier for me to agree with Ben-Gurion than with you! After reading your essay, I now have no doubts about this. I consider Ben-Gurion's political line disastrous, but at the same time it's much more noble—or a lesser evil—than the one we would have if we followed your advice. You don't seem to be aware how close your position is to that of the American Jewish Committee, though no reader of your essay will miss this.[16] I'm counting on hearing from the more noble abysses in your heart. But we'll never be able to connect through the arguments evidenced in your essay.

Being a longtime religious reactionary, I hope for your repentance—or, as old Buber has rendered it in his marvelous style—your "return."

With warmest greetings, but also, so to speak, with determination (I'm determined not be made a fool of).

Your Gerhard Scholem

> P.S. Just as I was about to send this letter to you, I received a telegram from Stephen Wise inviting me to New York this coming July. For various pressing reasons, I can't accept the offer. If I manage to push off the invitation until January, then I'll be heading in your direction!![17]

LETTER 20 From Arendt

New York
April 21, 1946

Dear friend,
I would have replied to your scathing letter long ago but, operating according to the rule First Things First, I decided to wait until I had settled a variety of matters related to Benji's literary estate. *Voilà!* After a lot of effort, it became clear to me that there is no chance to publish Benjamin's "Historical-Philosophical Theses" here, however dearly I want to see it in print. It is too "philosophical." People really can't wrap their minds around it—they brush it off as utter nonsense. What they want is exclusively literary criticism. Eric Bentley, a young English writer who teaches here at the university and who has exquisite German, agreed to publish Benjamin's "Discussions with Brecht" in the *Kenyon Review*. He'll then try to get Reynald & Hitchcock, where he works as an editorial advisor, to publish a volume of essays (with the "Theses" among them). I then engaged in long negotiations with Brecht: he seriously believes that "Benjamin's death is the only major blow Hitler dealt to German literature." Brecht has already "borrowed" the manuscript from the Horkheimer clique and plans to add some necessary marginal notes.[1] Brecht is hoping to get his hands on the other manuscripts as soon as there are serious possibilities for publishing them. Anyway, Bentley is his translator, at least for some of his writings, and Reynald & Hitchcock is his publisher. German or Swiss publishers are the only ones who could bring out the collected works, and Brecht will do his best to make this happen. Schocken's the only other possible publisher, but he's more hopeless than ever. I'm furious that there is no Jewish publisher or journal that will publish the "Theses." Regrettably, that's just how it is. We're caught between the American philistinism on the one hand, and the European half-educated philistinism on the other.

Since nothing is going to happen before the fall, we'll presumably have the chance to discuss these things while you are here. Please, you should bring a list of everything in your possession. You should also give some thought about which essays and articles one could include in such a volume. I've heard here that you'll probably be in Europe in the summer. Could you take a side trip to Switzerland and meet with publishers? You could also ask

Dora Benjamin, who might know who really possesses the copyright. I discussed this with Strauss and asked him to phone the Institute. It seems that the Institute doesn't hold the copyright; accordingly, the son probably owns the rights. We're really going to have to clarify this. American publishers are very cautious, and with anything going beyond publishing in a magazine, Strauss was very apprehensive about the rights situation. What's crucial, I think, is that Brecht be the one to spearhead negotiations with the Institute. He's probably the only one who can lean on them—the only one they might fear. Besides, he knows that gang. I know that you don't like Brecht, but believe me that compared to Wiesengrund and Horkheimer he's not only a gentleman, he's also a friend capable of devotion.

It seems that, sadly, I've said everything for today that the two of us can agree on. Let me begin with a couple general remarks, or rather a list of things I find completely perplexing. The first and most important thing I don't understand about your credo (if there is anything beyond a credo, you didn't think it was important enough to share it with me) is this: how is it possible that someone can spend his life in the serious study of philosophy and theology and, ignoring all possible insights that can arise from these fields, can present himself as a believer in an "ism"? I don't want to squabble with you over nuances, over whether nationalism is better than socialism, Zionism better than communism, Stalinism better than Trotskyism, or Marxism better than whatever. I don't really care. What matters to me is that they all share a common fanaticism, a shared screen against reality. Let me put it this way. I have always considered your position as a Jew to be a political one, and I've always had the greatest respect for your decision to take the political reality of Palestine seriously. To be honest, not even in my darkest dreams did it ever occur to me that you had a Zionist "worldview," perhaps because deep down I was hoping you didn't. The second general remark I feel compelled to make is this. I think it's obvious that I wrote my article out of panic-stricken fear for Palestine, and not because of an "anti-Palestine complex." If I have any complex at all, it is this "complex" of panic and fear I've had for nearly ten years. For me, more important than this is the fact that you apparently have no such fear whatsoever. You may say that fear is a poor counselor. Far more dangerous, however, is the inability to properly assess power relations, and especially one's own power. (This political idiocy began with your dear Herzl's insane notion that anti-Semitism can be a positive force for us.)

Let's get down to details. If you had any knowledge of the relevant literature, you would find the idea rather shocking that my article is "warmed-over

Communist critique." Obviously, you reached such a conclusion not because of my essay but because of my work with *Partisan Review*, which today is one of the best-known literary journals here, and has nothing whatsoever to do with Trotskyism. You are really basing your opinions on obsolete information. As for me, I have never been a Marxist (nor have I ever been "dialectical"). People here generally consider me to be an anti-Marxist, which is far closer to the truth. The fundamental difference between us is this, that in contrast to you I'm of the opinion that the renewal of the Jewish people depends above all on the question of its political and even social organization, though I consider the political to be the more important of the two. I am the furthest thing from being an anarchist, and the fact that you are one seems to me to be the real reason for your "Zionism." Moving on to the attitude among the kibbutzim and Yishuv[2] toward Diaspora Judaism before 1939, pardon me for saying so but what I wrote is so well known, and so confirmed by the innumerable conversations I had had with kibbutzniks both inside and outside Palestine, that there is really no point in going into the matter. The only relevant question is how to interpret this attitude. In writing about the Jewish army, I wasn't describing positions taken by the Hebrew press, or even the Yishuv, but solely the behavior of the leadership, above all Weizmann with his talk of the "so-called Jewish army."[3] The entire Jewish people stood behind the demand for such an army. You've clearly misunderstood Weizmann's remark about the building up of Palestine and about Rommel's forces. I didn't write that Rommel's army was an argument against Palestine: this would have been palpable nonsense. I said that Rommel was an argument against the Zionist ideology according to which building up Palestine can be an antidote to anti-Semitism. In Palestine Rommel wouldn't have become a friend to the Jews. I can't prevent you from being a nationalist, though I find it hard to understand why you are so proud of the fact. I am also not of the opinion that nationalism is dead. Quite the contrary. What is dead is the nation, or better put, the nation-state as an organization of peoples. This principle should be clear to any historian who knows that the nation depends on its sovereignty and on the identity between state, people, and territory. That the nation isn't eternal should come to no surprise to anyone who realizes that the only real argument is whether the nation has existed in Europe since the sixteenth or the eighteenth century. I lean toward the latter. Since this is the case, there is a very real danger that a consistent nationalist has no other choice but to become a racist. My dear friend, this danger won't become any less acute when on top of everything else one is an anarchist. The metamorphosis of a people into a racial horde is an ever-present danger in our times. And you'll surely agree with me that a racial horde has precious little to do with renewal, but it has a lot to do with ruin and destruction. The real question, which doesn't just confront the Jewish people in Palestine because of the Arabs, is quite simply what is the most rational political organization. I strongly believe that a Jewish nation-state would be a stupid and dangerous game, and I'm just as opposed to your anarchist attempt to defend this very proposal. As for the partition, I can only hope that we can dodge this bullet. It would only exacerbate all the existing problems and render impossible the JVA project—and this would be a catastrophe for immigration and for the country.[4] I think it very likely that the British proposed partition in order to scuttle the JVA project. My comments on the transfer agreement had nothing whatsoever to do with the issue of ransoming Jews during the war, or extermination. During the war there was just one possible political position for us, and that was raising a Jewish army. Once this effort failed, for whatever reason, all means were obviously legitimate. Which means that politics, as I define it, no longer existed.

You have no choice but to look at me with consternation, for in my case repentance can hardly be expected. And if I may say so, the Buber citation won't work very well either. The more pertinent question seems to me how we will get along after this orgy of truth-telling. While I really wasn't offended in the least by your letter, I have no idea how you will respond to mine. When all is said and done, you are of a *masculini generis*, and for this reason perhaps you are naturally vulnerable. For God's sake, despite this letter, you shouldn't take me for a "fanatic for truth"! For me, human relationships are far more important than "heart-to-heart talks." In this particular case you have demanded more provocation from me than is reasonable and fair. Maybe you can bring yourself to follow my example here: know that a human being is far more valuable than his opinions, for the simple reason that humans are *de facto* much more than what they think or do.

So you should make your way here as soon as you can (fall is around the corner), and let's do our best to remain friends.

The warmest greetings to you and Fanja.
Hannah

LETTER 21 From Scholem

c/o AJDC, 019 Rue de Téhéran, Paris VIII
[undated]
Mes chers amis—what a melancholic sight to be again in Paris and be reminded of the past days.[1] I will have to proceed to Frankfurt during the next week.[2] You will always reach me through the above address. I hope to write to you in a quieter hour.

Yours,
Gerhard Scholem

LETTER 22 From Arendt

New York
May 20, 1946

Dear friend,
I just got your postcard from Paris, and my apologies for writing this on official stationary.[1] I'm sitting in the office and I'd like to get a few words out to you right away.[2]

You are probably already in Frankfurt.[3] The sadness of Paris must have been nightmarish. I wish I could have been there with you. Even if it wouldn't have helped at all, sometimes a witness from earlier times can at least help a person snap out of the unreality of melancholy.

In case you're still in Paris, or if you plan on returning there and you're feeling lonely, you should ring up my friends Anne and Erich Weil and Käte Mendelssohn[4] (1 Avenue Rene Samuel, Clamart/Seine, a suburb of Paris). The two women are the only friends I still have from childhood: Annie and I have been "best" friends since I was fourteen. You'll no doubt see Jaspers in Heidelberg. I'd do anything just to pay him a visit, but until now I haven't succeeded. If you'd like you can tell him (or his wife) that I sent you. Unfortunately, a lot of people have already made unauthorized use of my name, which has the advantage that I can send packages. I'm afraid that Jaspers is even sicker than usual. Write and tell me how he looks. I'm always worried about him; it just doesn't show up very much when I write. In Heidelberg you should meet an old friend of mine from university, Dolf Sternberger.[5]

He's an excellent fellow and is now editor of the *Wandlung*. *À propos Wandlung*, try to nudge Sternberger into sending me regular issues. As soon as it is possible again, I'm prepared to pay. Jaspers sent me the first edition, and I managed to track down the second edition somewhere. Since then, I have nothing. If you manage to make it to Berlin, go see Ernst Grumach, Schlueterstrasse 53. He lives in the garden house. He knows more than anyone about what happened to Jewish libraries in Berlin because the Gestapo assigned him to the libraries. I haven't had any contact with Grumach, an old, old friend of mine, since 1930.[6] He's a good philologist of classical languages and knows a thing or two about Judaica.

I'm writing on official stationary, and to let you know what's going on I'm enclosing a memo we gave to Philip Bernstein[7] (he is the new Jewish administrator in the American Zone). Of course, this is confidential. There are negotiations taking place here between Senator, Ben-Gurion, and others. Magnes is expected any day.[8] Pinson can give you a better report than I can from here.[9]

All the best, from my whole heart,
Your Hannah

[Enclosure]

Memorandum Submitted by the Commission on European Jewish Cultural Reconstruction to Rabbi Philip S. Bernstein

May 17, 1946
The Commission on European Jewish Cultural Reconstruction was started a year ago as a fact-finding agency whose ultimate goal was to combine with similar bodies in England (British-Jewish Historical Society) and in Palestine (Hebrew University) to form an international advisory board to the Allied governments for the salvage, restitution, and ultimate redistribution of Jewish cultural and religious treasures in Europe.

In order to help with the identification, location, and the ultimate establishment of losses, the Commission published an extensive catalogue—"Tentative List of Jewish Cultural Treasures in Axis-Occupied Countries"—of all Jewish libraries, museums, and archives as they existed before Nazi confiscation, with an appendix listing more important collections of non-Jewish libraries, archives, and museums.

In October 1945, Professor Koppel S. Pinson, the Secretary of the Commission, went over to Germany as Educational Director of the American-Jewish Joint Distribution Committee. Shortly thereafter, he was appointed by Judge Rifkind to head a three-man committee assigned to the huge depots of Judaica and Hebraica in the American Zone, especially in Offenbach.

The following Jewish organizations during the last year tried to win some kind of recognition for the looted Jewish book and art collections—a memorandum signed by the Board of Jewish Deputies in England, the American Jewish Conference, the World Jewish Congress, and the Jewish Agency of Palestine proposed to establish the Hebrew University in Palestine as the sole trustee of the Jewish Cultural treasures in Europe. The Hebrew University itself contacted different agencies such as the American section of SHAEF[10] and the American Consul General in Jerusalem. No answer to the general claim of the Hebrew University has been given, but two experts have been granted transport facilities and are expected in Germany shortly.

In March 1946, the Commission received various letters from Captain Pomrenze and Professor Pinson, stressing the following points:

1. It would be advisable to transfer all unidentifiable objects of the Offenbach Depot (probably the bulk of the material there) to America because there is a very immediate and great danger that the Soviet Union may claim everything that comes from Russia, Poland, Lithuania, the Baltic States, Czechoslovakia, and Russian-occupied Germany—regardless of legal ownership.
2. Official claims at this time from Palestine, a country from which no part of this collection has come and which, unfortunately, is not recognized as possessing any legal claims in restitution proceedings, would not only be not recognized, but may serve to stimulate Russian claims.
3. The Library of Congress Mission, which had secured official representation, will have facilities to have all unidentifiable books sent to the United States, where the Commission on European Jewish Cultural Reconstruction can take over and ultimately help in the redistribution. This would solve the main problem, which is to get the books out of Germany as quickly as possible.

The Commission thereupon contacted the State and War Departments and the Library of Congress. During an extensive talk with Dr. Luther Evans of the Library of Congress, he took the following stand:

1. He was convinced that we will never get any international Jewish trusteeship, simply for the reason that no private group would have any chance with military authorities.
2. He suggested that the War Occupational Authorities should appoint their respective national libraries as trustees of all cultural Jewish property found in the respective zones of occupation. These trustees again should appoint Jewish bodies to act in an advisory capacity.
3. The Congress Library, at any rate, would be willing to accept the trusteeship. Packing, transport, and cataloguing would be its responsibility. Jewish experts appointed by the Commission would be taken on their own staff. They are prepared to add Jewish experts to their own missions in Germany.
4. Redistribution of heirless and unidentifiable property would be made upon the advice of the Jewish bodies.
5. In the case of Russian claims for identifiable Eastern Jewish collections, Evans suggested that the Russians may accept military libraries now in the American Zone in exchange for Jewish cultural property originating from Russian or Russian-dominated territory.
6. Evans concluded by emphasizing that the occupying powers had decided to seize all military or party collections. The latter would apply anyhow to the Offenbach Depot since most of the property there comes from the Rosenberg Party Institute, and can be confiscated if it is not identifiable Allied property.

The Commission then contacted the following national Jewish organizations with which it has been in close cooperation throughout its existence: The American Jewish Committee, The American Jewish Conference, and the World Jewish Congress. During a full meeting of the Commission on May 12, it was decided to submit to the State Department a memorandum which fundamentally accepts the proposals of the Library of Congress. This would mean that the American Government would appoint the Library of Congress as trustee over all existing depots of Jewish art, archival, and book collections in the American Zone—*this trusteeship to be exercised in the interest of the Jewish people and for the purpose of reestablishing Jewish cultural and religious values*. The Commission should be recognized in an advisory capacity in all phases of the work, especially when pertaining to questions of restitution and redistribution. In this respect, the Commission adopted the following principles:

1. Identifiable objects belonging to *private owners* shall be restored to the owners or to their successors in title.
2. Identifiable objects formerly property of German or Austrian Jewish *communities* should be dealt with in the following manner: In View of the fact that these communities have dwindled down to a negligible size, that the majority of their former members now live in other countries, and that a majority of the present members is likely to emigrate in the near future, these objects should not simply be restored to them, but be held in trust for a certain period until it is determined that the community will be able to use the objects for religious and cultural purposes and will not sell or dissipate them.
3. As to objects which belonged to institutions of higher learning, theological seminaries, and other corporate owners, it was decided to take into consideration the fact that all these institutions did not serve only the needs of local Jewry, but those of European Jewry as a whole and even those of world Jewry. In other words, a majority of the students and teachers in theological institutions in Vienna, Berlin, Breslau, etc. were foreigners. Rabbis trained in these institutions served in all eastern and central European communities and even in America, regardless of nationality. If the money for the establishment and support of these institutions came from European countries up to the outbreak of the First World War, their support depended mainly on American Jewry after the inflation of the early twenties. Moreover, since none of these foundations have been reestablished, it was decided to put these objects into the common pool destined for ultimate redistribution.
4. This common pool will also comprise all unidentifiable objects, all heirless and unclaimed objects, and all communal properties not subject to restitution.

Redistribution shall be determined by the cultural and religious needs of the Jewish people all over the world as well as of those Jews who have suffered at the hands of the Nazis. The erection of a Memorial Library at the Hebrew University to commemorate the millions of slaughtered European Jews should be seriously considered.

LETTER 23 From Arendt

New York
September 2, 1946

Dear friend,
I sent you a *meschuggene* telegram, and I'm sitting down now to write you a letter presumably every bit as *meschuggene*.[1] Schocken surprised me with the news that you're probably not coming here, and all because of a crazy misunderstanding.[2] I was so panicked by the news that I sent the telegram.[3]

I'm naturally not going to persuade you. I'd be very disappointed, but that's of course beside the point. When I saw Marie Syrkin she told me that you were not only enraged by my article (something you made abundantly clear), you were also dismayed.[4] Hearing this likewise deeply dismayed me because I honestly didn't know you felt this way. Somehow I hadn't anticipated this reaction, even in my response to you.

I haven't written you since, and not because you've just been sending postcards. It was because I had been anticipating your imminent arrival here, and I hate writing letters. You obviously are aware that I am now working for Schocken Books.[5] For now I can't say what I'll be doing here, or at least I can't say so in writing. You see that I haven't in the least given up the hope for a face-to-face conversation.

Putting these things to one side, there are some other things to report. Last year I worked so hard that I was barely able to collect my wits. For the last months I've felt somewhat better, and I managed to cobble together a few insights. I'm not about to erect a monument out of them; they can, however, be of some use as tools, and without such tools intellectual labor can seem like Sisyphus pushing his stone up and down the hill. With this I'm slowly, slowly getting over the unavoidable, predictable, and very real postwar and post-Hitler hangover.

I'd start having a bit of fun too if the situation in Palestine didn't appear so catastrophic, and if the situation of the Jewish survivors weren't so unimaginably scandalous.

Greetings to Fanja; and don't forget that we're still waiting for you here.

Your Hannah

LETTER 24 From Arendt

317 West 95th Street, New York, NY
September 9, 1946

Dear friend,
I can't say if I am filled more with fury or with sadness, and I am not in the mood to find out. There is no point in crying over spilled milk, or rather unspilled milk. I am sad and disappointed and somehow I can't understand you.

I wrote to you in Paris; one of these days the letter should get to you. So what are your plans during your free months? When will the book on Sabbatai Zvi be finished?[1] Completing it will be the only thing that will comfort us here, and at the same time it'll be your only chance to make amends. You are certainly mistaken in case you feel innocent and morally pure. What's going to happen, for instance, with Benji's estate? Who holds the rights now that Dora is dead? (How uncanny everything is. It seems like yesterday that we sat together, all of us.) Do you have the address of Georg's wife and their child?[2] Dora was very attached to the brother. His wife is supposed to be a marvelous person. I don't know her, though we have some common friends from the university and I know who she is. In case she and the child are still alive, one should at the very least see to it that they get some care packages. Don't you agree?

Things are going well at the publishing house, that is to say, I'm having a great deal of fun. I've fallen a little in love with the old man, who is very clever and lively. I find him charming, and at least for now he's giving me enough freedom. Regarding my writing, once I'm finished with "Human Rights" and the "Philosophy of Power," I'm going to take a break for a few months.[3] (I'll send you both, against the resolve I made at one point never to send you anything again for the sake of our friendship.) Which means that I'm looking forward to a couple months without panic. I already feel refreshed.

In the Schocken Series here at the publishing house I absolutely want to publish Berl Katznelson.[4] My God, this man deserves to be honored. Excerpts from his conversations with Youth Aliyah Midrachim, which came out in *Jewish Frontier*, are the best things about fascism I've ever read in print.[5] It would make a really lovely small book to include such pieces together with excerpts from his superb lecture, which was of great importance for the Second Aliyah,[6] "The Way to Palestine." S[alman] S[chocken] told me that you were a close friend of his. What do you think about taking charge of making the selection and writing a few pages of introduction? What do you think?

How is Kurt?[7] His health, I mean.

That in writing I have to ask you how you are doing makes me so furious, so I'll leave it. Modern desks, which anyway are not equipped for people, no longer have ink pots. It would be wonderful to smash one against the wall.

On this note,
Your Hannah

LETTER 25 From Arendt

September 25, 1946

Dear friend,
I wish you all the best.[1] I hope you complete the book on Sabbatai Zvi, and above all I hope that by the end of next year there will no longer be any Jews left in concentration camps. Do you agree that momentarily this should be our only political program? I really don't want to discuss, that is to write, about politics because I don't want to distract from the things we actually agree on. With that said, if you agree with me about this, could you try to do something, for heaven's sake, to win over a newspaper or something? Concentration camps are the beginning of death camps. This lies in their very nature.[2]

I didn't sit down to write about this; the topic just crept into my typewriter. But for weeks I really haven't been able to think about anything else. What I wanted to do was to write to you something very beautiful for the New Year: that Schocken has decided to publish a volume of Benjamin's writings. This will happen over the coming year. I'm pushing to do it as soon as possible.

Please, write me soon your thoughts about the following selection:[3]

1. Elective Affinities.
2. Baudelaire.
3. Kafka, in an expanded edition, possibly with an excerpt from the last pages of his extraordinary letter to you.[4]
4. The Art of Storytelling (that was published in Lieb's[5] journal).

5. Karl Kraus (from the Frankfurter *Zeitung*).
6. Maybe "The Work of Art in the Age of Mechanical Reproduction" (I don't like the essay, though it was very important to Benjamin).
7. From the literary estate, the "Historical-Philosophical Theses"; and
8. Conversations with Brecht (which, thank God, B[recht] managed to rip from the teeth of those sharks in the Institute).

One last thing. Would you be willing to write an introductory essay?

Now on to the matter of Katznelson. Wilhelm wrote to me about a memorial book by Agnon that appeared in Schocken Books.[6] If you think this essay is sufficient, and if you don't want to write anything, this essay might work. Please, just tell me what you think.

So, that's all for the time being. At the moment we're looking for your photo for *Mysticism* (that is to say, the man in production just asked me if I had the original).[7] Apart from that, we're thinking about you, even though, as you know perfectly well, in truth you should go to hell.

Sincerely yours,
Hannah

LETTER 26 From Scholem

Abarbanel Rd. 28, Jerusalem
November 6, 1946

Dear Hannah,
I was so worn out when I returned from Europe that I immediately collapsed into a heap, and I'm only now slowly recovering. I couldn't drum up the concentration needed for writing letters, and for days on end I lay instead on the chaise lounge and slept. In the coming three weeks I hope to have recovered enough to decide whether to take my vacation in order to sit and work on my Hebrew book on Sabbatianism, and to thumb my nose at the idea of a trip to America. Anyway, the idea was spoiled for me by S[alman] S[chocken]'s manner of negotiations. (Just between the two of us, he behaved shamelessly.) Or do I push off the vacation for a year and travel to America now. If I felt *well* enough, I'd choose the former so I could finally do something productive. For over six months or more what I've been doing or experiencing has pushed scholarship into a *very* distant corner. That I wrote neither to you

nor to anyone else during my time in Europe just goes to show how incapable I was of lifting my pen. What I saw didn't exactly stir up my desire to write but instead ended up adding considerably to my melancholy.

I relayed your greetings to Jaspers. From Paris I also sent you, with J[aspers]'s personal dedication, his book on the question of guilt.[1] Inferring from your silence, I sadly have to conclude that you haven't received my two letters from September 2 and 9. For the time being, there is no possibility to send things directly from Germany—mail gets returned to the sender. For this reason I brought the book for you myself. Jaspers is very proud of you and quotes you often. In the aforementioned book, he cites you a lot. Some of the Germans I spoke to told me that if the Americans were to leave Heidelberg, Jaspers would be dead within three days. I say this to throw light on the situation in Germany at the moment. Everywhere I turned, people assured me that in Germany the theme of German guilt *as such*, however the issue is approached, is taboo.

However valuable the libraries in Offenbach are for cultural purposes in Palestine, the most important libraries are not there, as the press would have people believe, but are hidden away in Czechoslovakia.[2] I'm hoping people can get to these libraries and procure them for Palestine.

My experiences in Europe were very gloomy and depressing, and I was extremely despondent by the time I returned home. In my opinion, there is a catastrophic chasm opening up between various Jewish communities in Europe, America, and Palestine. There is no overcoming this through any conceivable theory. Everything is falling apart, and people don't understand one another. We have no idea what is going on among the Jews in Europe, and they are clueless about what is happening with us here. If they could, the European Jews would run off to every other country on earth, just not here. For we can't give them what they expect from us, insofar as they expect anything: namely, rest, more rest, and no goyim. And who can blame them? In parallel, in France and elsewhere there is the process of radical assimilation. I noticed a lot of this.

While I accomplished everything I was sent to do in Europe (I hope that when all is said and done the books will end up in Palestine, through a detour via the USA or in some other way), I'm afraid that this trip broke my heart, if I have such a thing (as I presume). In any event, I left behind in Europe all my hopes. I'd really like to know where I could recover this hope.

Now to your letters. I understand perfectly well why you don't want to send me any more of your work. I got a fresh dose of dismay of just how far apart the two of us are when, a week ago, I read your essay on the jubilee of

Herzl's Jewish State, and then I moved on to your reply to my letter regarding your piece in *Menorah*.[3] I saw the letter only after my return because Fanja wanted to spare me the agitation. It's really a shame for both of us. I had thought that we could at least agree on something, and that you could sympathize with certain of my basic anarchistic convictions, but you seem to pity me that I have them. But what hurts me more than the contents of your anti-Zionist performances, which at least one could debate, is the tone you use, a tone that shuts off discussion. So let's drop the matter.

—Three weeks later.

I've been resting and I'm now a bit more relaxed. Meanwhile, I received new letters from you. Mysteriously, the Jaspers book I sent to you from Paris was returned to me here. From here I dispatched it to you forthwith. At the same time, Schocken turned up. He's a real delight to have around as long as you don't have to do business with him, which is what I mostly want to do with him. Now that he has totally wrecked my America trip, he's full of regrets and he's offering me the sky. I'm on my guard now and don't really buy what he says. He's a wretched man.

I saw Grumach often in Berlin. He's very intelligent. The same goes for Sternberger, whose essays in *Wandlung* I don't much care for. By the way, someone sent you a copy of *W[andlung]* but the censor sent it back. It is *verboten* to send German literature abroad due to the crazy way the Americans interpret the Potsdam Agreement.[4] Perhaps this will change now, or already has, for the senselessness of this ham-fisted policy with books is appalling. I've brought all the back issues with me. The *Wandlung* is an awful metaphor for the state of Germany: weak and *passé*, something like *Frankfurter Zeitung* circa 1932. It is spiced up with very little that is impressive; especially among the poetry there are some poignant things. I came across some very dramatic poetry in Germany.

Walter Benjamin's estate: in my opinion, his heirs own the rights. I visited his son Stefan in London (63 Leinster Square W. 2 London), as well as W[alter]'s wife Dora. If she were still alive, his sister Dora wouldn't have any claim. Unfortunately, I didn't have the address of Georg's wife—I had neglected to take it with me to Zurich. She is in Germany with her child. As she is a member of the KPD, it must be possible to track her down there.

I have the same problem in writing about Berl as I have with Walter: I'm not able to do it, and therefore I have nothing to send you.[5] I've tried a number of times to put down on paper something about WB. The selection you are planning sounds good. Perhaps you could add his short but highly important review on Keller and Julien Green.[6] Now that Schocken wants to publish an English edition of Brod's scandalous biography of Kafka, I'd like to make public (in the *Jewish Frontier*, perhaps) the devastating attack Benjamin made on the book in a letter to me. Do you have a copy of the letter?[7]

Agnon's essay in memory of Berl, while perhaps beautifully written, is completely inadequate. Berl was no great writer, but he compensated by being an uncommonly good and clear speaker. The stenographs of his speeches are much better than anything he wrote. Above all, he was a pivotal person, a rare and modernized "Rebbe," and these qualities are hard to put into words.

In the spring I packed up and secured Walter's things together with my own, as I thought we would be traveling to the USA. I didn't want to leave anything for some marauding Soldateska to break into my house and destroy. The things are still packed up, and at the moment I can't get at them to tell you what I would recommend of Walter's writings. Is there anything new to report about what the Institute is doing with WB's estate? Is the Institute's journal really back up and running? For me, all lines of communication have been cut. I would almost bet that they found among the estate one of my letters in which I honestly expressed what I was thinking about Horkheimer.[8] Apart from that, I heard from Benjamin's sister that the suitcase from the Bibliothèque Nationale in Paris hasn't even been sent off yet but is with someone on Quai Voltaire.[9] Three days before I flew out of Paris I called on the man, but of course like *tout le monde* he was in the countryside.

In light of everything that is happening, it's completely up in the air when we will finally make it over to you. I assume sometime over the coming two years, but even then not for as long as I had planned, unless of course someone comes up with the idea to invite me for a year as an exchange professor, which has already come up.

This letter must finally be sent, and it should prove to you that I am really still here.

So until the next letter, my greetings to you and your husband. From your

Gerhard Scholem

November 6, 1946

> P.S. Blumenfeld isn't doing so well: he's 3/4 a wreck. It's heartbreaking to see. Berl's essays on Lawi and Eliezer Joffe are really worth reading.[10] (This relates to your question on September 9.)

LETTER 27 From Arendt

317 West 95th Street, New York, NY
November 8, 1946

Dear Scholem
Apparently you're angry with me again. I can't do anything about this. But why, for heaven's sake, don't you reply to my letter about Benjamin? There was a time when the two of us agreed that Schocken was the right publisher for Benjamin; he just didn't know it yet. And now Schocken has finally seen the light, and we're letting the opportunity slip through our fingers. Without you I can't do a thing, not least of all because I don't have my hands on the material. I am dependent on your famous archive. I also don't want to do anything without you. Practically speaking I can't, but more generally I don't want to. I get physically ill at the very idea of having to get involved with the people at the Institute ("people" here is a euphemism). In case we have to do so because of the copyright, Strauss can take care of it. To do the book you'll have to come up with the material. This takes care of the "practical speaking" part. As for the "more generally" part, I hope I don't have to jabber on about this.

How are things? What does it mean that you have an eye problem?[1] What's wrong?

Warmest greetings from both of us.

LETTER 28 From Arendt

November 27, 1946

Dear Gerhard,
For the last couple weeks your letter has been so much on my mind as if it has been sitting around for years. The only reason I'm answering—though in truth you've nearly cut off the possibility for a reply—is that I don't want to wait until it no longer bothers me.

In a certain sense I am naturally relieved that you, too, realize that this is the deluge that has swallowed up the world. Now here we sit, the two of us survivors (and we can't really help it that we are still alive, we don't need to be happy about it, just accept the fact), and like Noah on his ark, we haven't been able to salvage even the most necessary things. Even worse is that the two of us Noahs also seem to be dogged by the additional problem of being so bad at steering our arks that we pass by one another without meeting. And even if I'm against the idea of bringing all the Noahs onto the same ark—which unfortunately would be a simple matter given the small number of those who know what's going on—I would like it if we could hitch a couple of the ships together, or at least steer them in such a way to allow us to say Hello and How are things?

O Gerhard! Put your heart back together. Try to be like Odysseus. The only reason the gods could give him a heart that couldn't be broken was because he was sly enough to renew his heart over and over. You must know that this isn't yet the end; it can always get worse. And one should even be able to withstand the end (which doesn't necessarily mean to survive it).

I was duly cheered up and relieved to read about your plans to publish Walter's letter about Brod's concoction. That would be a divine coup. For now, though, we shouldn't do it. I'm afraid that either Brod could stir up trouble with the literary estate, which he's working on, or Schocken could scuttle my Benjamin plan. As soon as my plan is secure and Mr. Brod no longer has his hands on the estate, we should proceed. With Benjamin's things, I'll have untold difficulties in bringing them together if you don't make your archives available.

Above all, I need "Elective Affinities"; "Karl Kraus" (if at all possible); "The Art of Telling Stories" (absolutely); and the smaller pieces you mentioned on Keller, Julien Green, etc. With regard to these last essays, I don't even know any longer where they first appeared. The journal *View* will soon be coming out with Walter's essay on epic theater in Brecht.[1] It's poorly translated, and I don't even think the article is very good. He allowed himself to be too influenced by Brecht. Perhaps I'm mistaken about this. If the suitcase wasn't sent out from Paris, then the Institute has been lying through its teeth, which sounds likely. And if so, this would clarify all their inconsistencies. The fact you haven't received a reply from them can be explained through a mixture of these gentlemen's arrogance, angst, and secretiveness. With regard to your prologue, *for the time being* I'm going to stop pestering you.

You are no doubt right about Germany. If Jaspers could only decide to get out of there for the time being! The blabber just like in 1932—the ridiculous talk of forging forward amid the ruins—is bad; even worse is the lack of vitality, the absence of rage, of fury that is most apparent in Sternberger's essays. And Sternberger is a nice, upright fellow.

I haven't heard a word from Kurt in ages. I'm always afraid he'll suddenly die on us. Is Jenny at least leaving him alone?[2] I've heard there is a chance that Lilli will be going to Jerusalem.[3] That would be the best solution for Blumenfeld. Rosenblueth has turned up here. I saw him recently; and while I really like him, nothing can penetrate his philistine tranquility.

My heart goes out to you—and for this no passport is required, no money, and no "vacation time." My heart got a ticket and is sailing peacefully, in tourist class, to Palestine. You will then be at the port in Haifa to make sure that my heart isn't allowed to land. (Being an exchange professor would be much better. Can't Spiegel arrange this? I'm angry with you for not holding your end of the bargain and meeting with me in a cafe at five o'clock, right after the end of the World War. But I'll have to admit, somehow, that the cafe no longer exists.)

All the best to both of you. Monsieur sends his greetings.
Your Hannah

LETTER 29 From Arendt

December 16, 1946

Dear Scholem,
I am sending you enclosed a copy of a letter which I received today from Alfred Cohn. I would like to know what you think of Schoen's idea.[1]

Please answer me by return mail, since I am going to wait with my letter to Schoen until I get your reaction to his plan.

Will you please also let me know whether you have the German original of Walter Benjamin's "L'oeuvre d'art à l'époque de sa reproduction mécanisée," and if so, I would greatly appreciate if you could let us have it for a while, since we would rather have the English translation made from the original text than from the French translation.[2]

With regards,
Yours, Hannah

Pardon me for this "business" letter. A lot to do. The *Question of Guilt* has arrived. *Merci!*

[Enclosure]

Dear Hannah,
I'll get right to the point, as in general there isn't anything new to report. Ernst Schoen, a common friend of Walter Benjamin's and mine, asked me what is happening with Walter's literary estate. I replied to him—which I'd also heard from Walter himself—that all of his manuscripts, as photocopies, are either with the Institute for Social Research, or they are with Gershom Scholem at the Hebrew University.

I know nothing about the precise distribution of the manuscripts. Now Ernst Schoen, who better than anyone else perhaps is familiar with, and has mastered, Walter's manner of thinking, has offered to collaborate on the publication of his literary estate. In case the question of the publication of the estate ever comes up, I'm of the opinion that one should accept this offer. It is not necessary for me to spell out for you my friend's qualifications.

Perhaps it would be simplest for you to be in direct contact with him, and then the two of you can discuss all the details. He wrote: "Perhaps you can tell Mme. Blücher-Arendt exactly what I wrote Gershom Scholem, and I'm fully convinced of it: that neither Palestine nor the US would be the right place for such a publication, but rather first of all it should be in German, that is, it could be in Switzerland. And then perhaps there could be a French translation because still today France is the one country where one could expect his manner of thinking to be best understood. Finally, maybe at the very least there could be an edition for a very narrow circle of readers in England and the US. All of this, and precisely in this order, is what I could attempt to undertake."

Hence, my dear Hannah, I am merely a middleman, though a middleman who out of self-interest is highly motivated to see the plan carried out, and quickly. I am convinced that Walter told you about Ernst Schoen. He's basically a musician, though is passionately engaged in all things related to culture, and for years he's been a program director for London radio. His address is:

43, Kingfisher Court
East Molesey
Surrey, England

I have done my duty, that is to say, I've carried out what I set out to do. I very much hope that the immediate consequence of this will be a positive result. One last thing. Since his days at Frankfurt radio, Ernst Schoen has had serious quarrels with Wiesengrund. He specifically asked that his plan not be shared with Wiesengrund. I have no idea if and how you get along with

Wiesengrund-Adorno, nor do I know if he is interested in Walter's literary estate. Be that as it may, I urge you to respect my friend's wishes.

Drop a line to keep me up-to-date on what happens, and my very best to you,

Alfred Cohn

LETTER 30 From Scholem

Abarbanel Rd. 28, Jerusalem
December 25, 1946

Dear Hannah,
In front of me are your letters from November 27 and December 16, with Alfred Cohn's supplement. The second letter arrived yesterday, exactly three days after I wrote Ernst Schoen that we are hoping to publish, under your guidance, a volume with Schocken. I wrote him how, in my opinion, so long as there is a serious chance for this to happen, I don't want to do anything that could derail it. If it turns out that Schocken can't be budged, the two of us can gladly return to his friendly offer. It seems that Schoen no longer has any of Walter's letters, which is a great disappointment for me. By contrast, Wiesengrund wrote me in 1941 that Alfred Cohn supposedly has a pile of things (I barely know Cohn: isn't he married to Walter's first fiancée?).[1] This information, however, seems to be very vague. This is something you can see in Cohn's erroneous comment about the photos I am supposed to have (if I haven't misconstrued his statement).[2] I advise you to write Schoen about *what* Schocken's volume might include. You should treat the man well. (While he can also be abrupt, he's very good-natured.)

Schoen wrote to me that Wiesengrund is angry with him because it had come to his attention that he, Schoen, called him a "little snob." I'm wondering if something similar doesn't lurk behind the manifest break in correspondence with me. Say, my letters to Benjamin about the Institute?

Moving on. Very, very sadly I do not have the German text to "The Work of Art in the Age of Mechanical Reproduction." I saw it at Walter's in Paris and I immediately tried to confiscate it for my archive. But Walter didn't want to part with it because he said it was his only copy. Perhaps by chance the translator Pierre Klossowski, who is still alive in Paris, still has the original. It won't be easy to translate this text, especially, from French back into German.

With Dr. Wilhelm[3] I'd like to make the photos you need of Walter's things. (We'll do this on our own so as not to give the Old Man the opportunity again of interfering.) "Elective Affinities," however, can surely be transcribed, without any difficulty, from the Neuen Deutschen Beiträgen, which no doubt can be found in one of the three German collections at Yale, Columbia, or Harvard. I have a better edition of "Karl Kraus" than the published one: it is a corrected typed copy. I'll also photograph Leskow and Kafka. With Kafka, Gustav Schocken[4] already had it transcribed, so I'll have you sent the collated copy.

I've heard it from some people here, who got it straight from Brod, that our Dear Ole Schocken dangled Walter's letter about Kafka in front of his nose but didn't allow him to read it. Schocken was delighted when I told him I would publish the letter if he brought out an English edition of Brod's biography. "That'll be quite some fun," he said. "Do it." But you're probably right that, if pressed to the wall, he might react differently, especially if I wasn't standing right in front of him.

For now, I'm writing Sabbatai Zvi, in Hebrew.

Indirectly I received from you, by way of the September edition of *Commentary*, your *very* interesting critique on the *Black Book* and on Weinreich.[5] I read the latter book and find it hard to stomach.[6] I read the book in Berlin, the perfect place to get a good sense for his somewhat arrogant stupidity. Please send me more fodder—I *love* to collect.

When I'll be traveling to New York? *Between the two of us*, before your letter arrived I had already put out feelers through the right channels to be an exchange professor. I don't think anything is going to come of this very quickly. On top of everything else, I might not be kosher enough. Maybe one of these days it will happen anyway. It might illuminate things by referring back to my nature as an Odysseus (though you did so in a context I didn't quite understand).

Warmest greetings to you and Blücher,
Your Gerhard Scholem

LETTER 31 From Arendt

January 7, 1947

Thanks so much for your letter from December 25. Now I'm only missing from you the essays on Karl Kraus and Leskow. You've already sent me the Kafka, and everything else is easy enough to find here.

I especially relished the anecdote on Brod. I once had an exchange of letters with him that rather turned my stomach, and for no other reason than he's a creep, a stuffed shirt, a nothing. The fellow makes me want to puke.[1]

Returning to Benjamin, we're busy at work. We have a contract with the son, and I think it's unlikely that any problems will crop up on that end. I'll write Schoen at once.

I'd like to send you the Broch, but only if you want it. Kurt got a copy from Schocken and is thrilled by it.[2] (Tell Kurt that I love him but have no time to tell him so in writing.) Take a peek at the book, and if you want I'll get you a copy. It's already sitting on my desk, waiting to be sent to you.

Sincerely,
Your Hannah

LETTER 32 From Arendt

February 20, 1947
You are now an honorary member of I don't know what kind of society. An honor or not, you are supposed to pay $5. I wonder how you like this kind of promotion?

We received here the Karl Kraus and the Leskov.[1] Thanks. Thanks also for the old article you sent me.[2] Excellent. I begin to wonder what we are quarreling about. But quarreling or no quarreling, I think it would be nice to publish that piece right now in this country. Anything against it?

Yours,
Hannah

LETTER 33 From Arendt

February 25, 1947
I received your letter and the Benjamin material.[1] Thanks. Language question: I never wrote you of a German edition.[2] This we couldn't do for so many reasons that I don't care to enumerate them. So it is in an English edition, or rather, it will be, because S. S. decided in the meantime to "postpone" the project. That is not very serious, but I still feel that a letter from you may have a very desirable effect.

On the other side, I am glad about the postponement for the following reason: I remember that apart from the Baudelaire, published by the Institute, there are more chapters ready from the Passage and I'd love to have them. The Brecht piece I don't get, and I won't get, because Brecht obviously doesn't want to spoil his relationship with the Horkheimer people.[3] The real difficulty is of course that I very much doubt whether we have any right to non-published posthumous writings which Benjamin apparently left to the Institute. The price which we would have to pay to get this material or permission to publish part of it would probably be an introduction from Adorno. What do you think about that? I received the Hölderlin.[4] Thanks. I enclose another honorary membership.[5]

As ever,
Yours,
Hannah Arendt

LETTER 34 From Scholem

Jerusalem
March 16, 1947

Dear Dr. Arendt:
I am writing to you in connection with Dr. Adorno's letter concerning his possible part in the Schocken edition of Benjamin's Essays.[1]

It seems to me that Adorno supposes that Schocken Books are planning a complete edition of Benjamin's writings in several volumes. While a comprehensive essay on Adorno's part on Benjamin's philosophical ideas would be in its place and possibly not out of proportion, yet I doubt very much if anything would be gained by a too voluminous essay on his part. I think I wrote you last week[2] that at any rate I would favor an introduction by him only in case you need him sorely for handing over some parts of the manuscripts in his possession, or if you yourself are not willing to write the introductory essay. In that case, it might be advisable to limit his introduction to a fair proportion of the whole volume.

The curious wording of Adorno's letter makes me think that he is "afraid" I might write the introduction, though he does not say so *expressis verbis*. I suppose you have given him some information as to the real purpose of this volume, and if you want to make him cooperate, by all means do so. Anyhow, it could do no harm.

I understand from his letter that I was correct in my assumption that the manuscripts were only this winter still in Paris, and not at all in the possession of the Institute. Thus they cannot have hidden it away, and I hope they will make a study of it in the future.

With kindest regards,
Yours,
G. Scholem

LETTER 35 From Arendt

Schocken Books, 342 Madison Avenue, New York, NY
March 19, 1947

Dear friend,
Go ahead and write as unclearly as you want, I can read your writing—alas, I have a lot of practice because sometimes I have to read my own damned handwriting, and also Jaspers's. And you should continue writing your lovely, long letters.[1]

Getting down to business, copies have gone out to Grumach (do you know that he was my first love, from the glorious age of thirteen to seventeen?). In a letter, Jaspers confirmed to me that he got his copy, though he added that the book would be difficult for him to read because of the language.[2] Bultmann and Schaeder also received copies. It just took a while because the postal service to Germany for printed materials still wasn't in service at the time, and I didn't have an address for them in America.

You really can't expect there to be any reviews yet. I spoke to an editor at the *New York Times* and asked him to give the book to Niebuhr, and he promised he would. I assume that *The Nation*, whose literary editor I get along with quite well, will review the book.[3] But the reviews will take about four to six months.

Tillich encouraged me to send copies to certain professors here (you'll get the list), and I got back two truly enthusiastic letters in response. I've included copies. (By the way, one of these days you should drop Tillich a line or two. He considers you a friend and, after all is said and done, he's a nice fellow.) I sent them a boilerplate reply, not the worst thing in the world. It might be good if you could also make up your mind to answer them. From now on you'll be getting a constant stream of such opportunities.

I sent the invitation for your honorary membership more out of curiosity than anything; I would suggest not replying at all. In case you want, I'll send the routine answer that you are in Palestine, etc., in which case you need to send once more the names and addresses because I sent you the invitation without giving it much thought.

What is your opinion of Herr Schoeps?[4] Please, please, don't say you have a better opinion than I do. It's a pure loss for us when these literati turn into dandy schmucks. I would rather not honor the man by giving him the German literary rights. Moreover, I recently spoke with Schocken, and he told me that for an entire year he hasn't been able to give away the German rights because he doesn't know if one of these days he might want to return to the publishing business in Germany.

As I now work for a publisher, I can't really publish my own review.[5] *Menorah* would very much like to print the thing, and eventually we'll be able to add a footnote somewhere so we can weasel our way out of this pickle. While unfortunately I no longer have a copy of my remarks, Hurwitz will surely be able to send me the copy that he has.

Benjamin. With Adorno there's no way you can put me in a sourer mood than I already am. Still, as I've written to you the gang have gotten their hands on the Arcades papers from Paris. I'd dearly like to publish some of the materials, together with Baudelaire; but of course I won't be able to unless Adorno gets to schmooze about it. After he already officially made it clear that's what he wants, I wrote him very cautiously that first of all I'd very much like to see the manuscripts from the estate. After that, no answer from him.

As for my qualifications, there are a number of reasons why I shouldn't do the job, above all the objective fact that I knew Benjamin only in the final years of his life, that I know but little about his biography, and which disqualifies me even more, I didn't know the circle of people, or better the circles, he belonged to during the various phases of his life. You see, unfortunately there is a grain of truth—but only a grain—to the rather nasty remark my friend Jonas made years ago: that I knew only philosophy professors, or those who would go on to become professors. My personal objection is much more plausible: I still haven't been able to come to terms with Benjamin's death, and therefore over the subsequent years I've never managed to have the necessary distance one needs to write "about" him. When it comes to the duty of friendship, you know perfectly well that you were the closest to him. In passing, Günther Stern gave me a marvelous photograph of Benjamin as a thirteen-year-old. If you don't have it, I'll gladly make you a copy.[6]

Even if both the Gottfried Keller and Leskow articles are wonderful, I'd like to suggest we just include the Leskow because in America Keller is completely unknown, nor is there anything equivalent to him in the English literature. The article would simply be too bizarre. The same thing applies, if in a somewhat less extreme manner, with the "Elective Affinities" essay, but in this case it really must be a part of the volume, perhaps in a somewhat shortened version. I'd like to take another look through *Die Gesellschaft*.[7] Incidentally, I got my hands on a bibliography of everything Benjamin wrote up to the year 1930, which we're trying to complete. (Where I got it, I'd rather not say—I stole it.) I assume you, too, have the bibliography, but in case you don't, I'll make you a copy under the condition you use your archive to add to it. (I'm not serious when I say "under the condition." My God, you are turning me into a pedant, and only because you say that I'm stepping on your toes. I haven't the foggiest idea what I wrote, but whatever it was, I certainly didn't mean what you think I did. Phooey! Feel free to send me what you want: believe me, I'm not stepping on your toes.)

At this very moment a heap of copies of *Major Trends* are on their way to France, according to a list Koyré was kind enough to put together for me. Koyré also received a copy. Feel free to send me any additional requests.

Best wishes to both of you,
Your Hannah

[Enclosure]

Oberlin College
Oberlin, Ohio
The Graduate School of Theology
Walter M. Horton
Schocken Books, Inc.
342 Madison Avenue
New York

My dear Miss Arendt:
I appreciate very much your sending me Gershom Scholem's "Major Trends in Jewish Mysticism," at Professor Tillich's suggestion. It seems to me to fill a great gap in the history of religious thought. I was aware of the importance of the modern Hasidic movement associated with the name of Israel Ben Eliezer (Ba'al Shem-Tov) and aware that he was influenced by the Kabbala; but I was quite unaware of the continuity of the Hasidic movement throughout the Middle Ages, as indicated by Scholem's richly documented study. I

am by no means an authority in this field, but think I can recognize an authoritative work when I see one. I must henceforth refer my students to this book whenever the subject of Jewish mysticism comes up.

Sincerely yours,
Walter M. Horton (signed)

[Enclosure]

Union Theological Seminary
Broadway at 120th Street
New York 27, N.Y.
March 31, 1947

Miss Hannah Arendt, Editor
Schocken Books Inc.
342 Madison Avenue
New York 17, N.Y.

My dear Miss Arendt:
I wish to express my very warm appreciation of Professor Gershom Scholem's book on *Major Trends in Jewish Mysticism.* While I am not an expert in the field which is covered by this book, it impresses me as a first rate performance. It is without question an important contribution to the understanding of the Kabbala, and its religious and philosophical bearings. The documentation is superb, and the employment of sources, so far as I can tell, judicious and fair. The discussion is throughout discriminating and penetrating. Above all, what has always been for me a difficult and complicated, and sometimes very distasteful area of Jewish religion, has acquired profundity and fascination. I am deeply indebted to you for sending me this substantial work.

Very truly yours,
(signed) James Muilenburg

LETTER 36 From Scholem

[No date]

Dear Hannah,
I just wrote a long letter to Schocken and hope I'll now be able to come up with one for you too, in spite of my bad handwriting (and what should I do about this? In the evenings around ten PM my secretary isn't around for dictation and, besides, in my personal correspondence I have this desire, which I don't want to suppress, of producing original manuscripts). Added to this is the political situation, which at the moment means a curfew and, for me, days freed from giving lectures.[1]

Today I already wrote to Schocken about W. B., and I don't want to repeat what I told him. I am *against* shortening texts, and I stand by the *Keller essay*.[2] It makes no difference *whatsoever* whether people over there know who Keller is or not. *C'est le ton, que fait la musique*. Do you really think that Benjamin's other essays will strike people as any less *strange*? There is no convincing me on this point. In case he travels to Switzerland I've encouraged *Ernst Schoen*, with you and with your blessing, to at least try putting together a Swiss edition, in German.

I *don't* have the *picture* of *Walter* as a thirteen-year-old; I only have the magnificent photo taken in Paris by Germaine Krull.[3]

Do you think that Adorno will give you what *you* want from the estate? And do you really need the estate? Please keep me abreast of how things develop with this friendship. Did you tell Adorno that you're talking about a selection of essays and not a collected edition?

I don't have the partly mentioned, partly stolen (which in logic is called an incomplete disjunction) *bibliography until 1930*, and I'm not in the least averse to getting a copy of it at some point. So please!

Now on to *my* book. Until now, the only people on the list I had requested to send books and who have confirmed receiving them are Margarete Susman, Jung, and Benjamin in London. From the others, in France, England, and Germany, either I haven't heard a word or (like Jaspers) they've just mentioned something to you. Jaspers told me how interested he was in having the book—but had I known he doesn't know English, I wouldn't have sent it to him. He didn't reply to my letter from November 1946. I won't even consider personally responding to perfunctory acknowledgments sent to the publishing house, no matter how nice they are. This is asking too much, it seems to me. For crying out loud, *why* should I be writing to Professor So and So? Only because he considers, and quite rightly, that my book is a splendid contribution to the field, a book given to him free of charge and about which he hasn't yet even published a review? I assume that's the way things are done in the USA, and I don't have anything against it. But do I therefore have to start writing all kinds of letters? Tillich of course is a different story. Send my greetings to him and his wife. If I had a good reason to do so, I'd write him myself. Neither one behaved badly toward me. I'm not going to respond to this "honorary membership," whose character I'm not certain about.

I've always had a *very low* opinion of Mr. *Schoeps*: I was being ironic when I spoke about giving him the German rights because *he* asked for them. In my opinion, by the way, he's not a schmuck; he's something else, but not any better. He came calling here to offer his greeting, not knowing (as happens so often in Judaicis and Palestienicis, which just goes to show) that one of my most famous polemical pieces of writing was an open letter to Mr. Schoeps. It came out in 1932 and adorned my eightieth-anniversary volume of the *Studies of Jewish Stupidity and Critique of Jewish Rancor*.[4] (If you ask for it from the publishing house or from Schocken, Wilhelm will get you a photocopy.) Suddenly, over the past year this failed Nazi-Jewish youngster[5] (and apparently, *horribile dictum*, he had seriously meant what he said) has been pursuing me with his veneration. With Schoeps you don't have to do anything more than send him a *review copy*. Why Bultmann called the man to Marburg is a mystery to me. Maybe it's Schoeps's exceptional hustle and bustle, which seems to spring from natural diligence but which doesn't impress people like us.

I suggest that review copies be sent to Professor Karl Ludwig Schmidt in Basel, for his (very serious) theological-historical journal. Also, copies should go to the English journals of philosophy and history of religion, journals that were more or less passed over the last time around.

Could you send me the review of the first edition that appeared in the *Jewish Frontier*?[6] I understand perfectly well that there can't be any new reviews yet. I can wait patiently. What's more important is that people buy the book! The reviews, whether read or (mostly) unread, aren't what will get people to buy. Reviews are in my opinion an archaic rite that must be endured but whose utility lies at the level of the irrational. (As unlikely as it sounds, I've noticed the way Schocken is extremely influenced by reviews.)

I'm giving you a copy of a letter from a "reader of my books" from Michigan who wrote that if Schocken doesn't finance a translation of Tischbi's book on Lurianic Kabbalah, he will.[7] How should one reply to him? This gentleman is a well-to-do Yiddishist who doesn't know Hebrew and who understandably therefore has such a burning desire to see the book translated.

Now finally I have to thank you for the letter that arrived last week. I had to put off reading such an extensive missive, but I'm excited to dig into it now. In any event, it looks quite formidable.

I'm afraid this year I'll be deluged with Festschriften and anniversaries, and I won't even be able to think about doing any productive work beyond doing my duty to the incalculable row of seventy-year-olds who want to be honored. I shudder at the very thought of this. Suddenly, everyone I'd ever had anything to do with is celebrating an anniversary between July 1947 and July 1948. All this makes me want to pass out. I ask you, as one says in Yiddish, "Who's allowed to do such a thing?" The upshot is that I'm going to be busy with these honors and won't be able to concentrate sensibly on anything.

Since you don't read Hebrew it is of no use to send you any of my work, however much I would like to. Your exhortation, "You could also go ahead and send me something, too," is more than appropriate. But I've never written anything in English. The first attempt—of course in one of these Festschriften mentioned above!!!—I sent off in manuscript form to Salman Schocken, and I did so out of fun, just to show Schocken how well I can mangle the English language. With English I can write about light, *historical* themes only, not about anything difficult. German doesn't exist for me anymore.[8] Why don't you be so kind and learn Hebrew one of these days? Then I could send you this and that or the other, and besides, you could then enter heaven. My essay on the bankruptcy of the Science of Judaism, for instance, is an exceptional piece of writing, which makes it universally unpopular.[9] The essay is also composed in the best literary style. Impressive! If you had some Hebrew, you could translate it into English, and by doing so, you would offend a lot of people. Or, as I would put it, it would truly be a voice from better days.[10] So enough of singing my own praises! Right now, on my desk, is the first proof of my latest book, *Development of the Kabbalah* (this is the new chapter left out of the second edition as a result of not having a translator). It's difficult material, and no easy slog for the "well educated." I'll be happy if I can get it published this year, along with my book on the Sabbatian hymns and songs.[11] This tome has been preoccupying me the *most*, during the entire Shabbat. With all these things on my plate, the revolution isn't going to happen anytime soon, and I suffer *a lot* from this. (What do I need? A year of complete rest and a break from all this business, then at least I'd be able to wrap up the work on Sabbatianism.) I have to stop here. You at least have proof of my good intentions with writing. Warmest greetings to all (to Ha-Adon Blücher[12]), from Fanja and I.

Your Gershom Scholem

LETTER 37 From Arendt

May 14, 1947

Dear Scholem,
This is not a reply to your long letter, just a quick Hello together with a letter from Bultmann.[1] I wrote to Bultmann and gave him your address.

Otherwise, nothing new on my end—which is the reason I'm not answering your letter. The Benjamin volume will hopefully happen, after all, even if I still have a lot of doubts. You've been familiar with the situation longer and better than I, and you know how one never gets a straight answer. Even if Gideon is a really nice fellow, the sons don't understand very much and are therefore not sure of themselves.[2] Beyond this, everything depends on imponderables that you simply cannot oversee or control. Can you tell how furious I am?

I'm working a lot. God willing, in July I'll have a vacation. On top of everything, today I have the sniffles, which makes me particular angry at the world in general and at certain aspects of it in particular.

Soon I'll send you more and better.

To both of you, sincerely yours,
Your Hannah

LETTER 38 From Arendt

July 6, 1947

Dear Scholem,
Over the coming days Dr. Glatzer will be sending you the book reviews we've received thus far. The *New York Times* promised me a review from de Sola Pool. (I'm not overly thrilled by the choice.) I had tried to suggest someone better, but Pool's not too bad. With your book I did what we otherwise never

do: I wrote directly to the editor of the Book Section and, miraculously, he helped. The review appeared on June 1. Over the coming days I'll send you a copy.[1]

I'm quite friendly with the book editor at the *Nation*, and he sent the book to Van Dusen at Union Theological Seminary, who agreed to review it.

Please, have some patience! And please don't be impatient with people to whom you've sent your books, people like Jaspers and others, who haven't responded yet. What do you think? In order to give your book a judicious reading a person needs at least one or two weeks of free time. Take me, for instance. I'm not completely dense and I needed even more time than that.

I have a vacation in July, and I'm now playing around with a vague plan to write you a properly long letter. This one here I'm writing within the typical rat race of office work.

Why the devil don't you come here?

Sincerely yours,
Hannah

P.S. you'll be receiving Benjamin's photo and bibliography soon.

LETTER 39 From Scholem

Jerusalem
June 15, 1947

My dear Hannah,
Yesterday I received your letter of June 6 and thank you very much for it. I can wait for the reviews you are announcing, and I hope that they will be to our general benefit. Are you satisfied with the sale of the book? I hope to receive a longer letter from you during your vacation, and wish you godspeed.

In order to help you to quicken your mind, I think it will be best to return to you the enclosed letters, which by somebody's flight of fancy in your office, I found together with your letter to me. I think that you will be glad to have them back, especially the long letter without a date which I wrote to you about everything and nothing, some time ago. If you returned these letters to me on purpose, please send them back to me a second time. I read it through and found it a very charming document....

A while ago you asked me for names of people to whom I would like to have copies of my book sent. May I ask you to be so kind and mail copies to the following people:

1. Professor A. D. Nock
   Harvard University
   (He is professor of comparative religion)
2. Mr. Menachem Ribalow
   Editor, *Hadoar Hebrew Weekly*
3. Professor Dietrich Gerhard
   Erlangen, Henestrasse 8
   German-American Zone

The latter is the son of one of the most decent Gentiles I have ever met, and has kept up a very good record during the Nazi Regime in Halle.[1] He is very interested in Jewish things, and I would like my book to reach him. Since we cannot send it directly to him to the Russian Zone, I have arranged to try to send it through his son in Erlangen.

There is another small matter I would like to ask of you, if you possibly could attend to it. My uncle in Rio de Janeiro wants to send me some money, but there are difficulties in transferring monies from there to Palestine. I would like to send this money, the sum of sixty dollars, directly to you and then ask you to forward it to Dr. Siegmund Hurwitz, Rigistrasse 54, Zurich, to whom I owe some money. Would it be too much to ask you to act as an intermediary in this matter?

The next time I hope to be more spiritual! Kindest regards to Blücher and yourself,

Yours

LETTER 40 From Arendt

Hanover, New Hampshire
July 29, 1947

Dear Gerhard,
The legendary holidays have nearly come to an end, and the prospect of having to return to New York draws nigh. The vacation was wonderful, and

I was once again able to do really focused work. I went on walks, took in the smells, swam, and even managed to get in some reading.

I no longer hear a word from you, which I find natural enough given the necessity of carrying on what has almost become a commercial correspondence. What are the prospects of your coming here? From time to time I hear rumors. I can't help but think it would probably do both of you some good to get out of there for a spell. The last time you did, it was really lovely. While I can't imagine who would be all that interesting for you here, that's not the point. In this country everything is interesting, and there are plenty of very amusing things not connected to the university. With the university, admittedly, the picture is pitch-black.

I'm not getting along with the old man Schocken because of this business with Benjamin. Since you know him better than I, I can't tell you very much you don't already know. Wealth is more than an indecency; it's a curse, especially for Schocken. At the moment he's becoming so "Jewish" once again that he doesn't even want to hear about Benjamin. This can of course change. With his two sons there's not much new to report. See the above.

I received a marvelous letter from Bultmann.[1] Why he has to make Schoeps his postgrad is also a mystery to me—or, to speak the truth, it is clear as a bell. It's the old refrain: there are those who will never accept a Jew because he's a Jew, which then forces other people to accept all Jews because they are Jews. By the way, Bultmann wrote to me about Hans Jonas (Jonas and I studied together in Marbach several eternities ago, which out of habit we call the past), and he told me his letters aren't getting through to Palestine. What sort of nonsense is this? It that true? In any event, please kindly tell Hans (whose address I don't have) that Bultmann sends his greetings and that "he expects something important from his philosophical studies, but he also wishes urgently that he successfully wraps up his work on Gnosticism." And thanks.

Do you have any contact with Hans Schrader?[2] Could you ask him what has become of Richard Harder?[3] I fear that he behaved like a pig, I'm just not certain. He was once a friend of mine.

I'm a little afraid of New York. I'm always fearful of being pulled under in the hustle and bustle, and there is this constant struggle to find time to do my work. There is a permanent lack of time to develop any kind of friendship. One could barely design a system that goes more against my nature (to the degree that there is such a thing).

It has been really lovely up here. It is an old story with me that people so easily disgust me. It might help if I was still arrogant, but I don't think I'll be able to conjure up my old arrogance any longer.

Cordially to both of you,
Your Hannah

LETTER 41 From Arendt

New York
September 30, 1947

Dear Scholem,
I just had a long talk with Koyré, who just arrived to give lectures at Chicago University.[1]—(By the way, I like him very much.) About reviews of your book in France: Koyré himself is writing one for the *Revue Philosophique*. Vasta (I'm not sure that the name is spelled right) is writing one for the *Revue d'Histoire de Religion*, and a third review is going to appear in the *Revue d'Histoire et de Philosophie Religieuse*.[2]

Did you see the long review of your book in *Critique*? If you haven't, I'll send it to you.

Yours,
Hannah

LETTER 42 From Scholem

Jerusalem
October 15, 1947

My dear Hannah,
Returning from Nahariya, I found your letter of September 30. I am very glad to hear about the reviews which have been promised by French journals. Please be good enough and send me the review from *Critique* which you mention in your letter. I have not seen it.

Moreover, some time ago I received information that Jean Wahl had expressed his willingness or eagerness to write an article about the book. Since then I have not heard any more about the matter.

I met Koyré in France. He is a very intelligent man, but a dreadful assimilationist, which I hope will not prevent his keen intellect from seeing the finer points in the book. We had a long discussion one evening at Edmond Fleg's house.[1]

I am enclosing copies of two letters I received from the *Revue Thomiste* and the *Vigiliae Christianae*, both important scholarly journals, who would like to have copies of my book for detailed reviews. Please arrange that shipment to them be affected immediately. I think that we should be very interested in their reviews, through which the European public may be made aware of the existence of the book. I have written to them, informing them that I transmitted their letters to you.

With all good wishes and kindest regards,
Sincerely,
G. Scholem

LETTER 43 From Arendt

November 10, 1947

Dear Scholem,
In the meantime you will have received the review from *Critique*. I saw Jean Wahl in New York and we talked about your book, which he admires of course, but he didn't say anything about his writing an article about it. On the contrary, he asked me if I had anything. I promised (but forgot to send to him) the old odd remarks which you know. These, by the way, are not going to be printed up in *Menorah*; they have a new editor there who thinks they are absurd.

We have mailed a review copy to the *Revue Thomiste*, but we have not done the same for the *Vigilae Christianae*. The feeling here is that we have been very generous with review and free copies in your case, and that the *Vigilae Christianae* is a brand-new magazine (Vol. 1, No. 1). There was nothing I could do about it—at least not at this moment (for heaven's sake, don't get angry. Believe me every other publishing house would have done much less).

I saw Ernst Simon, who somehow gave me a little idea of how you are and how you live.[1] Tell Fanja to give my love (and I mean love) to Kurt,[2] and to demonstrate it with as many kisses as he wants. I somehow miss him very badly right now. No special reason.

Yours,
Hannah

LETTER 44 From Scholem

December 5/6 1947

Dear Hannah,
We barely hear from each another these days. The last time we did, you asked Fanja to deliver kisses to Kurt Blumenfeld, a task she faithfully carried out though the kisses barely connected because, as she says, he's become too spoiled with all the declarations of love he's getting. Anyway, lately he's had some good weeks and made a real contribution to history with his truly marvelous birthday letter to Schocken. The letter can honorably counted among his few contributions to literature.[1] You should read the letter if it has made its way over there to you. Try to get your hands on it, if need be from the author himself.

I'm sorry to hear that you're not going to have your essay published. Unfortunately, in the end I'm only getting garbage to read, and because you've already done so much for my book—and on this point we agree, even if you wrongly seem to attribute to me the opposite opinion—I should just relax and let things take their natural course.

When you read about the unrest over here, don't take the reports so seriously, at least not yet.[2] Everything is very different than what it seems.

I'd like to go to America, but I don't think anyone will be inviting me again anytime soon. Fanja is emphatically against accepting offers from Schocken. So you, too, will have to practice a bit of patience if you want to amuse yourself with our presence or otherwise communicate face to face. I have no idea if, as a surrogate, you'll be able to strike up something sensible with Ernst Simon. Assuming he's not your cup of tea, I didn't ask him directly to drop by and pass on my greetings, though I'll be delighted if the two of you get along. In the last couple days I received a long and *quite* bizarre letter about my work and me. It is from a young man from Zurich who is now in New York at the Jewish Theological Seminary. The man doesn't seem to be half bad. His name is Doctor Jakob Taubes.[3] I don't know the man personally, but if you happen to meet him sometime I'd be grateful if you could pass on your impression. It seems that he has really plunged into the study of my work.

Be well and all the best,
Gerhard Scholem

LETTER 45 From Arendt

January 8, 1948

Dear Gerhard,
Quickly, first to the issue of reviews: you're not just getting "garbage." Don't be so unfair! Right now I can't go into details; to do so I'd have to pull your review folder out from the files, and I don't want to do this now.

However, your request prompted me to send my notes to the *Jewish Frontier* because the people there don't intend on having the book reviewed again.[1] (They reviewed the first edition.) With the helping hand of God and Haim Greenberg, the notes will be published. In this matter I feel really quite awkward because editors aren't exactly supposed to be writing reviews of books they publish. The justification I'm giving them is that my notes are not a review.

I don't know Jakob Taubes, but if I happen to meet him I'll look him over. Ernst Simon and his wife were at our place one evening. He's very nice and quite intelligent. It'll be difficult for me to see much of him, however. I don't want to complain, but you can't really imagine what my days look like. Given my basic laziness, I still can't get over how I'm being coerced into being industrious by a strange series of circumstances coupled with living in this work-obsessed country.

I'll write more soon, with affection,
Hannah

LETTER 46 From Arendt

January 26, 1948
Just a quick note to tell you that Schocken has decided in the end *not* to publish Benjamin. The official reason is that Benjamin, it seems, is too highbrow, and not "Jewish" enough. (I should point out in passing that he was every bit as Jewish as the Jewish Bismarck.) The real reason is naturally a mixture of motives. There's an element of rancor against me and perhaps, though I'm not sure, against you, too. Even more important is that the old man naturally can't make heads or tails out of Benjamin. Benjamin is simply too hard, and Schocken has a powerful grudge against anyone who writes in a way he

doesn't understand. He suspects people who write like this, even if it's Kant himself, of wanting to pull a fast one on him. *Voilà*. What to do, says Zeus? I'll write Schoen that, for the love of God, he should try to do something in Switzerland. Here I'll talk to Broch, who has good contacts in Switzerland. Moreover, I've found a place to publish two essays, the one on Brecht and on Baudelaire. I'll be overseeing the translation on the latter, which has stirred a great deal of interest here. It is of course ridiculous that Benjamin can't be sold here. The opposite is true: especially now, the kinds of things people are interested in could be of great use for Benjamin. Of course, he's never going to be a bestseller. Here I come back to your old suggestion to publish Benjamin's letter to you on Brod, as a kind of literary review. Now I'm no longer opposed to the idea. Back then I didn't want to ruin our chances with the old man out of hope that he would publish Benjamin.

There is one matter I didn't want to write to you about from the office. I don't quite understand why you don't take money from Schocken, at least this one time, and come here. I understand Fanja's sense of nobility—I understand but I don't agree. For your article in *Haaretz* alone he should have easily paid you 2,000 dollars.[1] What good is all this money of his if there aren't people like you doing their level best to burn through it? And anyhow the minute the old man is dead the days of generosity will be over.

That's all for today. I only hope that you don't do with this letter what you did with the one on Zionism, and show it to the old man.[2] Between the two of us, that wasn't very clever of you for a variety of reasons, including Benjamin.

With affection to you both,
Hannah

LETTER 47 From Scholem

February 1, 1948

Dear Hannah,
Apparently many letters these days haven't arrived (I'm receiving next to nothing: 250 bags of postage have been stolen), but yours from Jan. 26 came today. I'm replying by return post.

However bad it is, given the entire course of things and your reports over the past year, your news was to be expected. I don't think I've heard a peep out of Schocken since last April. I'm going to hold off before responding (assuming you are expecting a response out of me) until I have the chance to react in an effective and dignified manner. One of these days I will respond, that you can bank on. By the way, who is this "Jewish Bismarck" supposed to be? You wrongly overestimate my bibliographical knowledge. With the exception of a small anthology of the Zohar I'm putting together, I have no idea about Schocken's other books.[1] I think he is soon going to drive his publishing house into the ground (unless he has a *large enough* income from some other sources that can cover the losses for a long time. I don't know anything for certain about this).

You can go ahead and *publish the letter to me on Brod*, along with an indication from where you got it. Just do me a favor and let me know when you do. In case there are any queries, and if you want to stay in the background, you can make it look as if I was the one directly presenting the letter. I'm independent enough to be able to speak my mind, and Schocken will think twice before trying to "retaliate."[2] I have no problem accepting from Schocken an *honorarium* for my work or $2,000 dollars for an article (which article do you mean?). My misgivings are about accepting any kind of advance from him. Over F[anja]'s objections, in the past I was ready to do so; now, given the present situation, I have serious doubts whether I would do the same. I'd rather not go to New York at all if it means I would be dependent on Schocken's money. That's the way things look for the time being. (I don't like the accustomed style of having to pull strings to get invitations. That's not my way of doing things.)

When you get a chance, could you send me the old review of my book from *Jewish Frontier*?[3] I haven't seen it yet, and I want it for my archives.

Regarding B[enjamin], I would be equally grateful if you could send me anything in *writing* you might have between you and the old man. If the subject comes up for discussion, I want to be well armed. By the way, your break from Zionism is much too much in the same line of development as Schocken's (when it suits him) for my statement to have done any damage. Quite the opposite: the fellow was completely on your side. Of course, your Gerhard took you a lot *more seriously* by (futilely) admonishing you to be more cautious.

Your Gerhard (appealing for caution)

LETTER 48 From Arendt

April 4, 1948

Dear Gerhard,
This time the reason I haven't been writing is that the newspapers have been forcing me to think so much about the two of you over there that I was simply incapable of it. I don't want to write today, either. I just don't want you to get the impression that people aren't thinking about you when, in reality, I can't get my mind off anything else.[1]

Meanwhile, I'm so enraged that it's robbing me of all my joy. I've done nothing about the permission you gave me regarding Benjamin. At the moment I can't do a thing, it's as if I'm paralyzed. (By the way, you misunderstood one thing. My comment "Jewish Bismarck" referred to the old man. That's what I call him sometimes.)

I'm often seeing and talking to Ernst Simon. He's able to maintain a certain high-spiritedness that I sometimes envy. I like him a lot.

If you weren't so completely in the center of the storm, and if I had a bit more confidence that the two of us could come to some kind of political agreement (I mostly still believe this is possible), I'd write to you about the unbelievable and sudden shift among American Jewry in its attitude toward America, and America's toward it.[2] Out of caution, I won't do it. But it is one of the most shocking, worrying, and absolutely sudden mood shifts I've ever witnessed.

Despite everything, I'm trying my best to work. My publisher sent me a very positive assessment of the first two-thirds of my book.[3] What I've been writing about concentration camps will also probably come out in the *Wandlung*, and I'll send it to you.[4]

If only you were here![5] In general, it would make a lot of sense. At the moment, no one is more useful than our good friend Ernst Simon.[6]

Thank God I've had some lower back pain and couldn't go to the office. This has allowed me to rest a bit, and to work.

Don't you want, at some point, to write about what you really think?

I knew I would write an utterly awful letter, and therefore I haven't written anything at all. Please, make do with this for today. Don't be angry and be well.

Sincerely,
Your Hannah

LETTER 49 From Scholem

Abarbanel Rd. 28, Jerusalem
April 18, 1948

My dear Hannah,
Before the Iron Curtain comes down on the postal service, I'm taking this opportunity to thank you for your letter from April 4 and the clippings from the *Jewish Frontier* containing two reviews of my book, which reached me only a moment ago through the large convoy which broke through the famous first siege of Jerusalem. (Let's hope that it may be the last one!)

During the past few days I have been busy with spiritual matters and have given myself wholly to studies of magic which is a most actual issue, and to Sabbatianism which may serve as a fitting epitaph to what has been going on in our time.

But now I am afraid we will have to turn to more temporal matters, as the Church would put it, and I am busy filling my tanks with water, getting fish to eat, and jam to put on my bread. (Bread seems for the time being the one thing you get without a queue.) Rumors have it that enormous stores have been brought to sustain your friends and admirers in Jerusalem. Besides, I have been called up by my Jewish Civil Guard to take up some duties which are as yet unidentified.[1] During the last slaughter on the way to the Hebrew University, one of my best friends was killed, and the consequence seems to be that, for the time being, there will be no more sending up of professors to the University although I am not altogether sure if our turn will not come too.[2] There are not very many people to guard the place, as we are very short in manpower here. So everybody has to go where he is needed.

I thank you very much for your good thoughts about us and hope to hear from you with the last mail that may come through to us or, after the renewal of the postal services with, I hope, another authority.[3] Please give Fanja's and my greetings to anyone who may be in need of them, both inside Schocken Books and beyond the pale, especially to Ernst Simon to whom I have written some days ago but you never know which letters reach their destinations now.

I have a kind of invitation to America which I want to put through for the next year, but I am unable to do it without settling the previous difficulties with Schocken who I hope will make no difficulties this time as he has committed himself back in '46 to agree to a certain settlement. If everything goes well, it may be that we will still meet sometime in '49, but keep this to yourself as it is not public knowledge. Many hearty greetings to Blücher and you.

Yours,
Gerhard Scholem

LETTER 50 From Scholem

November 23, 1948
Yesterday Ernst Simon gave me your "Six Essays," together with your dedication. I'm writing quickly to thank you. The only essays I'm familiar with are the ones you've already sent me, and I am delighted to have the others.[1] Perhaps we'll be able to discuss them in person if our travel plans for March are realized and my wife and I are able to go to New York for three or four months. I've received the invitation and have accepted, but a lot can happen between now and then given the prevailing conditions here. In any event, this time around it won't be my fault if something intervenes.[2]

As I haven't heard from you in months, I've just recently heard that you have left Schocken Books.[3] (Is it about to shut its doors?) For me this was upsetting news.

I'm not opposed to your doing some public relations on my behalf so I can get some offers to deliver well-paid lectures in April or May. Otherwise, Fanja and I will be on a tight budget.

Affectionately yours,
Gerhard Scholem

LETTER 51 From Arendt

New York
September 8, 1949[1]
Dr. G. Scholem
c/o Dr. S. Hurwitz
Rigistr. 54
Zurich, Switzerland[2]

Dear Scholem,
Your letter of September 5:[3] Dr. Heller will return to America around September 15, and you will find in Wiesebaden Dr. Lowenthal, who actually is in charge.[4]

Hermann Cohen Library:[5] The next meeting of the Advisory Committee is on September 19. I don't see how there could be any difficulties with regard to the claim of the Hebrew University.[6] After all, you have top priority. When you are in Wiesbaden, please let me know if I am right to assume that the Hebrew University also claims the 1,100 rare books which are still there and of which we received a catalogue. However, please bear in mind that JCR has not yet received official title to these units.[7] As far as I know, Lowenthal is now busy with 12,000 volumes of the Breslauer Theological Seminary.[8]

There is one more issue which I would like you to discuss with Lowenthal. You probably heard that we plan an investigation into the whereabouts of Jewish collections which possibly may still turn up in university and other public German libraries or be in the hands of booksellers. Lowenthal is supposed to devote much of his time to this task in the three Western zones, and I asked him for a program of what he intends to do. There are, of course, all kinds of legal complications, the most serious of which is that German institutions were supposed to report all confiscated Jewish property which they might have received during the Nazi regime, but not a single such report was ever made.[9] What is needed in this matter is a kind of detective gift, and I must confess that I have great confidence in you as far as that is concerned.

I am glad to hear that you had such a good time in Europe. Brecht is in Berlin. You may be interested to know that a special edition on Bertolt Brecht appeared in Berlin, published by the magazine *Sinn und Form* which carries a long essay of Brecht on poetry. I have not seen it. If by any chance you get hold of two copies, I should be glad to receive one.

Give my best to Fanny.

Yours,
Hannah

P.S. Included here is the first piece of writing we have from Walter. It is from the year 1899 and was written for the wedding of William and Clara Stern.[10] I thought the collector's instinct in you would be thrilled. Warmest, Hannah

[Enclosure]

Polterabend-Scherz, as told by Walter Benjamin

Endlich bin ich angelangt
Und an wohlbekanntem Ort,
Bräutchen, gieb mir schnell die Hand!
Sag', erkennst Du mich sofort?

Bin ja doch der Schelm, der lose,
der dir oftmals saß im Nacken,
Wenn mit Witzen ganz famose
Wußtest alle Welt zu packen!

Seit du Braut nun bist geworden
Sag', wo blieb dein Scherzen, Lachen?
Wo hielst du den Schalk verborgen?
Clärchen, was machst du für Sachen!

Glaubst du dass Dein Schelm verschwunden?
Nein, in deinem neuen Heim
Hab ein Plätzchen ich gefunden,
Stets mit euch vereint zu sein.

Wenn ihr dann als junges Paar
Tretet über Eure Schwelle,
Bei Euch bin ich immerdar
Weiche nicht mehr von der Stelle

LETTER 52 From Scholem

Wiesbaden
September 29, 1949

My dear Hannah,
I am writing on my last day before leaving Germany, and I use the opportunity to answer some points in your kind letter of Sept. 8, 1949 which reached me in Prague where I tried to find out about the next shipment of books still due from there. (This will take some time since we are up against an extortionist maneuver of the Czech government to which we are not going to submit.)[1]

As to Berlin, Shunami[2] has given you yesterday a picture of my findings there. For your information, I am enclosing a copy of my letter to Rabbi Schwarzschild, dated Sept. 26. I do not see any difficulty in handling the Berlin situation, with a little patience and initiative.[3]

Many thanks for your decision regarding the Cohen Library.

As to the 1100 rare books, I want to tell you that they were ready for shipment to Jerusalem just as other Hebrew rare books went there. But M. G. Authorities,[4] for reasons of their own, intervened and did not allow the shipment. We hope that they will be free for shipment in the near future, and I think it is clear that according to the Board's decision, Jerusalem has priority on items not yet in their possession. On the other hand, there can be no doubt, that quite a number of these books are not required by us and will go to the US. Anyway, there is no case for any special provisions regarding the disposal of this "collection" which, in my modest opinion, should not have come at all into existence.

As to your question concerning detective work in the Western zones, I think

A) that there is quite a lot of work to be done

B) that Mr. Bernstein[5] is unfit for this type of work

C) that it would require a man of more scholarly education to do this work, but that it will be exceedingly difficult to find one (I rather doubt whether my university would give me leave for such a mission.)

D) That there can be no doubt as to the unwillingness of German libraries to report anything. They all keep to the good old rule of "My name is Hase, I don't know a thing about anything." I was in Berlin and spoke to some very suspect libraries about which we have heard rumors—and all are innocent like children.

I regret Lowenthal is on leave and I could not talk the matter over with him. But L is a man of a very "correct" type and the kind of work which is required for detecting things hidden is of a rather different kind, as I need not tell you.

Give my kindest regards to Baron and to yourself.

P.S. My address till October 15 will be the Zurich one. Tomorrow I will be in Paris for about one week. Every mail after October 15 should go to Jerusalem.

LETTER 53 From Arendt

Dear Scholem:

This is *not* an official reply to your letter of September 29. I am writing you mainly because of the rare books and want you to know the following: Both Marx and Kiev are pretty convinced that their needs should be considered in the allocation.[1] Kiev said that if you will consult your own catalogue, you will find that no more than 19% of these so-called rare books are not in the library of the Hebrew University. He, therefore, suggested that the whole unit be shipped here, and those items which the Hebrew University should receive could be shipped to them from here together with the periodicals.

Kiev also insisted that the books which he chose (German Judaica) should be given him for the German Jewish Memorial Library, which, as you remember, was decided to be established in the Jewish Institute of Religion.[2]

Let me make a proposal. I trust that you have a list of these rare books in Wiesbaden, and you will find it easy to find out in Jerusalem which books are actually needed by the Hebrew University. As soon as I have this information, I am sure we can come to an agreement on this matter.

I shall write you about detective work at some other moment. I noted with great satisfaction that in principle you would be interested to help. I hope the Gesamtarchiv business will soon be straightened out.[3]

As ever,
Yours,
Hannah

LETTER 54 From Scholem

October 23, 1949
JCR 1841 Broadway, New York
ON RETURN FOUND JERUSALEM RECEIVED NO COPY WIESBADE RARE BOOKLIST PLEASE DESPATCH IMMEDIATELY COPY OR PHOTOSTAT STOP UNIVERSITY MUST INSIST ON EXERCISING PRIORITY RIGHT FOR BOOKS NOT IN JERUSALEM STOP SEE NO REASON FOR DIFFERENT PROCEDURE HANDLING THIS INTEGRAL PART GREETINGS

SCHOLEM

LETTER 55 From Arendt

October 24, 1949

Dear Scholem,
I received your cable. No change in the priority rights of the Hebrew University Library have ever been contemplated. As I wrote you in my letter of October 11, it was felt here that only a small portion of these "rare" books are not yet in the possession of the Hebrew University.

However, I am disappointed that Dr. Shunami did not send copy of this letter to the Hebrew University. As you see from the enclosed copy of my letter to Dr. Wormann,[1] I requested Dr. Lowenthal to send you copies immediately. I also asked them to cable us in case they have no copies left.

Many, many thanks for the gift.

Many regards to both of you,
Yours,
Hannah

LETTER 56 From Arendt

November 7, 1949

Dear Scholem,
Enclosed is copy of my letter to Shunami in re Breslau collection.[1] I just learned of your letter to Baron, which was read to me over the phone. I did not yet talk to Baron, and give you my first reaction.

Shunami misunderstood the decision with regard to the German Jewish institutional collections.[2] I hope you have received the Minutes of the meeting of the Board of Directors in the meantime. It was only decided that "the destination of each collection should be considered separately, after pertinent information has been received from Wiesbaden."[3] If, for instance, we follow now Shunami's proposition, roughly 25% of the Breslau collection would go to Israel including the Hebrew University, and not 40% which would have been the old key. In other words, the destination or the destinations of each collection will be considered separately.

It is somewhat unfortunate that Shunami failed to inform me that the Hebrew University was interested in books from the Breslau collection. I was under the impression that the Hebrew University would not claim any of these books. In case of all these requests, moreover, I shall need a breakdown between the Hebrew University on one side and of other Israeli institutions on the other.

As to the decision to keep the Breslau unit intact and send it to Switzerland, I should like to tell you that I think you are 100 percent right. Our difficulty here is that the representatives of the Council for the Protection of Rights and Interests of Jews from Germany have some difficulties to reconcile themselves to the fact that we deal only with remnants and that these remnants are not representative of the former collections and do not constitute organic units. The case of the Kirchheim and Hermann Cohen collections are, of course, different.[4]

However, I want you to be aware of still another factor in this connection: The German Jewish institutional collections, in distinction from the other Offenbach material, have been claimed by JRSO under Law 59,[5] and JRSO is likely to take a much stronger interest in the allocation of these books than it did with respect to the other books which were given over to JCR directly. I do not yet know how this new influence will make itself felt, but I do know that JRSO also has the problem of the German Jewish communities, past and present.[6]

I hope this clears the matter up. I shall circulate a vote on the Bresau collection among the Board of Directors in the next few days, and I do not expect to have difficulties, except from the Council for the Protection of Rights and Interests of Jews from Germany.

Yours,
Hannah

LETTER 57 From Scholem

November 10, 1949

Dear Dr. Arendt,
I am in receipt of the Minutes of the Board of Directors' meeting of October 17, and am very much concerned about Paragraph 3 "Problems of Allocation," particularly the first and third paragraphs of the section.[1]

Permit me to point out that the Hebrew University is not represented on the Advisory Committee and we obviously represent public interests which could not and should not be decided upon without consultation with us. We cannot accept decisions of the Advisory Committee in direct contradiction to the decision and priorities made in January 1949.

The University must exercise the limited priority rights conceded to it by that decision. I can certainly see that we might agree to the allocation of one or two of the institutional collections to other places—that would be only fair—but I do not think this should be done without consulting Mr. Shunami on the spot.

Referring to the Breslau collection, which I myself have examined, there is undoubtedly a collection in which we are interested, as is the case too with the Kirchheim and Berlin community books.[2] I would therefore ask the Board of Directors to reconsider the matter and to concede to the University the right of priority previously granted.

It would be most unfortunate if precisely those items of special value for the scholarly work of the University should be disposed of without previous consultation with us. These libraries contain many volumes which could not be expected in the kind of stuff which was distributed until now as unidentifiable books. The Hermann Cohen library, containing principally non-Jewish material, was an exceptional case. When it was under discussion, it was expressly stated that other libraries would be allocated according to accepted rules of priority.

I hope you will bring this matter to the attention of all concerned.

With kind regards, I am sincerely yours,
G. Scholem, V.P.
JEWISH CULTURAL RECONSTRUCTION, INC.

LETTER 58 From Scholem

[Undated]
MANY THANKS YOUR NOVEMBER SEVENTH INFORMATION AND STEPS PROPOSED SATISFACTORY TO US LETTER FOLLOWS
GERHARD SCHOLEM

LETTER 59 From Scholem

November 16, 1949

Dear Hannah,
Your letter of November 7th reached me two days ago and I wish to tell you that I was very happy to have your information and private opinion which sets my mind at peace as far as that is possible given my mental constitution. I send you today a cable saying:

"MANY THANKS YOURS NOVEMBER SEVENTH INFORMATION AND STEPS PROPOSED SATISFACTORY TO US LETTER FOLLOWS"

This means of course also that if the line which you take in your letter is followed there is no further reason for other steps such as envisaged by my official letter to you ten days ago. I understand that none of the more important collections will go to other places without our being consulted. This applies specially to Berlin, Breslau and Kirchheim which contain a certain amount of highly desirable and sometimes absolutely necessary material. Shunami will certainly make this concrete proposals to you and I am very glad to hear that you are ready to back them. You will have seen from our last letters that we are not unreasonable in our demands and especially the rare book collection holds attraction for us as our desiderata list shows only in a rather limited measure. Shunami thinks that the idea is to distribute, if not collections as a whole at least all material on a special subject to one place.

This makes him very uneasy as in the several sections there is scattered some amount of material which should go to Israel. I hope this will be taken into consideration.

As to your remark that you shall need a breakdown between the Hebrew University and other Israeli institutions as far as Breslau and other collections are concerned I can only say that we certainly agree with your demands but we cannot give such a list before we have the full lists of the books chosen by Shunami or if no such lists exist the books themselves. The case of the periodicals was an exceptional and easy one because we got a list which enabled us to act.

I hope that the queer idea about the Breslau unit being sent to Switzerland will be given a decent burial as it should.

I do not share your fears in connection with JRSO's interest in the allocation of books. I think there should be no difficulties with them. As far as the memorial to the German Jewish community is envisaged you know that it was decided to put up some thing of that kind under Rabbi Kiev's responsibility at the Jewish Institute of Religion, and as for the books for the present German Jewish communities there will certainly be no real problem since the books which they require do not come under the category which interests scientific institutes elsewhere.

Between you and me I would say that I was not a little astonished to find the Hebrew University representative absent at the meeting of the Board of Directors on October 17. Do you think it would be feasible to give them a polite hint that they should take care of our interests—I have done so from our end, but it may be worthwhile to remind them that things might be decided par default if the Hebrew University's representative does not show up. Perhaps you know a gentle way to handle that from your end, may be a telephone call to Mr. Salpeter before the next meeting.[1]

What about the trip to Germany which you planned for November or December? Are you postponing it? I am afraid it will be extremely difficult to set up a machinery in Germany which will not prove much too expensive and on the other hand effective for digging up hidden treasures as there certainly are. Perhaps you tell me your ideas if you have any on that subject.

I hope you have enjoyed the Brecht volume.[2] I have not yet found leisure to look into mine. There are 250 volumes clamoring for my attention and between the Devil and the deep sea I am doing exactly nothing.

As ever
Yours
G. Scholem

LETTER 60 From Scholem

Jerusalem
November 20, 1949
Along with this letter, I am sending you a copy of a handwritten letter I wrote to Mr. Sternberger regarding Benjamin.[1] I understand that *you* referred him to me. But you must have been fully aware of what I told you in our conversation about the matter, based on my recollection. In the meantime, I've located Benjamin's critique on S[ternberger]'s book as well as the letters in which he characterized Sternberger's book as a "shameless attempt at plagiarism."[2] Was Benjamin mistaken about this, or not? Without question, you must have known that I would have no choice but to respond to Sternberger's request—for advice and help on selecting Benjamin's writings for the *Neue Rundschau,* and even for a literary portrait of Benjamin he wants me to write—by sending him the accompanying letter. I hope you'll bear witness to just how polite I've managed to be in such a delicate matter. I *didn't* tell him that I was sending you a copy of the letter, I'm doing so because I want you to know how things stand. Have you in the meantime read the book *Panorama*?

One last thing. I reread Ms. Gurland's description of W[alter] B[enjamin]'s death (on October 11, 1940), and what strikes me very clearly is that, at least before his suicide, he did not write *any sort* of last will and testimony benefiting Wiesengrund. Rather, he left behind just five lines.[3] The lines only request that Adorno and his son be informed.[4] If W. had given Wiesengrund anything that was halfway legally binding, it had to have been long before this.[5] Can you remember any such thing?

That's all for today.

With warmest greetings,
Your Gerhard Scholem

LETTER 61 From Arendt

Wiesbaden Bahnhof
December 10, 1949

Dear Scholem,
Hopefully you can read my scrawl. Naturally I was fully aware of Benjamin's accusation of plagiarism when I told Sternberger that he should speak to you. That was the reason I did it. Seeing that Sternberger, as editor of the *Neue Rundschau*, wants to publish materials of Benjamin, it didn't seem to be a good idea simply to prevent him from doing so. Besides, as I told you in New York, I had already given him some essays to take a look at before I knew anything about this entire story.

As for the matter itself, St[ernberger] will send you his book *Panorama* so you can judge for yourself. I've taken another look myself, and the impression I have is that the influence is just as obvious as the impossibility to prove plagiarism. Under *normal* circumstances St[ernberger] would be seen as a pupil of Benjamin's without him having to say so explicitly. Perhaps—or rather almost certainly—Benjamin wouldn't have been very happy with the piece because of its tendency toward conformity.

I've spoken to St[ernberger]. Your letter was not in the least insulting; rather, it was a masterpiece of restraint *and* clarity. St[ernberger], who didn't know I had read your letter, said of it that it was exceedingly friendly and not in the least offensive. He says: a) given the chaos of the time, accusations of plagiarism would have been (nearly) a daily affair, and that b) his best defense is his no doubt strong desire to publish Benjamin again in Germany, and as soon as possible. *Voilà!*

The other issues will have to wait. Germany is terrible. I'm haunted by this place; I'm filled with inner revulsion. Disgust. Every conversation I have leaves a bad taste in my mouth.

My address in Germany is: Jewish Cultural Reconstruction, Landesmuseum Wiesbaden

Affectionately always,
Your Hannah

LETTER 62 From Scholem

January 20, 1950
Frau Dr. Hannah Arendt,
Wiesbaden

Dear Hannah,
After receiving your letter about Sternberger in which you hinted at more letters to come, I haven't heard a word from you, though today I received your Field Report No. 12 in the *New Yorker*.[1] In the meantime, I've noticed that the issue we raised concerning Breslau has been decided in favorable terms for us, for which I'd like to congratulate us all.[2] Today I'll be sending you my vote regarding Berlin.[3] I'm hoping that Wiesbaden can soon send to Israel the entire shipments Shunami has requested. The importance for us of these books has risen exponentially because of the ongoing blockade of Mount Scopus and the collections in the university library. I probably can't emphasize this too strongly. This has grown into a calamity of the first order for scholarship and for students.[4] We'll be able to make use of any books we can get our hands on. Unfortunately, I don't share the optimism of certain gentlemen who believe in a quick resolution of the political issues surrounding Mount Scopus.

Your Field Report is exceptionally interesting.[5] I hope you'll be able to push through your plan for a decree from the German educational ministers of the various German states; nonetheless, I'd like to point out (which for you is probably superfluous) that my impression is that such decrees will have no practical effect. You may know that while I was in Germany I spoke to many of the people you list, and they didn't leave me with the impression that we can expect much from them. I had extensive negotiations with Eppelsheimer, and without question he is the most well intentioned of the entire lot. But he's also terribly weak. You can almost bet that the minute you turn your back, he won't do a thing.[6] On p. 5 of the Field Report you characterize contact with Dr. Hänisch from the Near Eastern section of the Prussian State Library as something to be welcomed.[7] I should mention that in Berlin I established contact with him long ago. I had a lengthy discussion with both him and the general director of the library over the issues you are pursuing. They were quite emphatic that they had never received Jewish books from either the Gestapo or any other similar source. They responded with moral outrage when I countered that "persistent rumors" say otherwise. Both are former Social Democrats and were fired or persecuted by the Nazis, and they are both absolutely sincere and decent. That said, I don't think you can trust any of these people an inch. According to them, the former general director of the State Library under the Nazis was a civil servant, a conservative, and a man with no love lost for the Nazis. He adamantly refused to have anything to do with collections that the Gestapo or similar institutions had picked up.[8] It is possible, they said, that shortly before the end of the war the Gestapo stored a certain number of books in the cellar of the State Library. Those books, though, were whisked away by the Russians; and anyway, as far as they knew, the books weren't of a Jewish nature. They cautiously implied that in Berlin the Russians made off with a lot of books, whereby, as you know quite well, the Russians were just following in the tracks of the Americans. On this latter point, you say something on p. 3 about the Munich Institute for the Study of the Jewish Question.[9] I'd like to remind you that during my time in Munich, in 1946, people's memories were fresher and the American officers admitted to me that a substantial part of the collection they had found in Munich was shipped off to America. My interest in documenting evidence of these shipments met with understandable resistance. But you can be sure that the Library of Congress Mission as well as other American authorities took more than they admit to us.[10]

In any event, it would be very welcome indeed if you see to it that all verified collections from the various libraries you mentioned get transferred to Wiesbaden, or if not Wiesbaden then to the JRSO. Of course, what will bring about more success than a short visit is an extended stay in Germany where constant pressure can be applied on numerous places. Your description of Held and the library in Munich demonstrates to me just how much caution is needed here. I know Held personally very well.[11] He received me with great ecstasy and Kabbalistic effusion, but in 1946 and '47 he didn't think it was necessary—he was perfectly aware of the purpose of my visit—to inform me about the existence of Jewish collections, acquired wrongfully, inside his own library. I mention this just so you know how little we are standing on firm ground here.

I want you to know that I suggested to Dr. Kreuzberger from the JRSO that, should the organization's extensive negotiations with the Bavarian state on the restitution of Jewish property come to a resolution, the JRSO should demand from the Bavarians, as a symbolic gesture, that they hand over some historically important Jewish manuscripts in the possession of the Bavarian state and with a financial value of approximately half a million marks.[12] The manuscripts should, first and foremost, include the only complete manuscript of the Talmud, which is of great value to the Jewish people. It is in the Codex 95 in the Hebrew collection of the Munich Municipal Library. I wanted to negotiate directly over this manuscript while I was in Germany but couldn't due to political considerations involving the relations between the State of Israel and Germany. It probably would have been possible to raise the issue, though only in the wider context of Israel's official response to such a gesture, a response our officials have until now been unwilling to give.[13] That said, one shouldn't be deterred from working to get the Munich Talmud through the JRSO. Kreuzberger was enthusiastic about the possibility, and perhaps you can raise the issue again with him and Ferencz. In any event, it's good that you know about my efforts. There is of course no way for this to happen officially by way of JCR, as the German libraries' legal ownership right of the manuscripts is clear.

Regarding the main archive in Berlin, both Dr. Bein and I have been promised the sky. Unfortunately, we'll just have to wait and see what practically comes out of this.[14]

That's enough for today. Dear Hannah, if you think it is possible and technically feasible, I'd appreciate it if you could send me a copy of your next Field Report direct from Wiesbaden. That way I can stay better abreast of developments.

Steinberger's book that you mentioned still hasn't arrived, and as such I can't reply to his letter.[15] How long are you planning to stay in Germany?

Warmest regards,
Your Prof. G. Scholem

LETTER 63 From Arendt

February 5, 1950

Dear Scholem,
I'm making use of a few free minutes and a weekend in Basel in order to write you quickly and thank you for your letter from January 20 (Jaspers is literally my "immobile pole in the occurrence of flight."[1] By the way, did the coffee and chocolate arrive which I sent at the end of December?)

Shipments to Israel: Everything is set. The sections Shunami requested from the Berlin library have already been approved in New York. The only difficulties are some German-Jewish journals that Kiev has also requested, along with the rare books that Kiev would also like to have. It seems to me that we can agree on some sort of 50-50 split. At the end of the day, you shouldn't be disappointed: you've really gotten everything you wanted. What we're talking about now aren't really large collections and, as far as I can tell, nothing all that valuable. Shunami also wants the remainder of the Wünsche collection, and New York has already been informed of this.[2] The decision seems to be a pure formality, as the collection is composed of exclusively non-Jewish books. One other question. In Wiesbaden we have a heap of non-Jewish light fiction. Nothing special, and plenty of garbage. Does Israel have any interest in any of it? I wonder ...

Now on to my various undertakings. I'm doing everything I feel is necessary and possible, and without entertaining any grand hopes. God knows mistrust is certainly in order, but there is also a kind of mistrust that can be just as blind as blind trust. Or, to put it differently, you can take the position that everyone is lying, everyone is hiding something, that no one has any goodwill. But if you do this, you're not only closing off discussion, you're also preventing any possible action. As a matter of fact, in this context I can say that many of the people at the top of public institutions in Germany are first-rate. (And Gerhard, don't hit the roof: this is a brute fact!) But in these very same offices I see the people—and I have names—trying their best to sabotage everything. Without question, the power of those who are trustworthy has never been very great, and at the moment it is constantly dwindling as the de-Nazified people stream back. This said, I had to act as I did because we need some basis for our search operations. Senator's idea of sending a bunch of "detectives" over to Germany, so to speak, might work at some point in the future, but at the present there is no point.[3] None of these detectives will be able to crawl into the closed and stacked boxes and take a look at what they contain. This is purely a technical issue, and in this technical sphere no one can really know anything for certain because of what's going on in Germany (the alternative storehouses, collections placed in cellars, the big turnover in personnel, and the fact that so many employees died in the war).

With the Berlin Municipal Library, it seems in fact that the Oriental Department didn't buy any of the collections that were constantly being offered to it. By contrast, after the war hundreds of thousands of books flooded into Berlin, and among them one can most likely find Jewish collections. It is no doubt true that the Russians confiscated a large number of collections and simply drove off with them. And your suspicions against the Library of Congress seem more than justified. Above all, Munich and the administration of the Collecting Points there are very dubious, and at the moment I'm trying to get the Collecting Points searched through once again.[4] It may be that ceremonial artifacts will turn up.

You'll find in my next official report a list of the things, based on our instigation, the JRSO is now claiming.[5] The most important artifacts are eighteen chests and two golden goblets from the Jewish Museum of Frankfurt, all of which are safely stowed away and guarded at the Historical Museum of Frankfurt.[6] The behavior of the present director at the museum is an example of how damaging blind mistrust can be. The local management had paid the Gestapo six thousand prewar marks alone for the two goblets, and did so to preserve them from being melted down. The director told me right away that the museum would naturally not be getting the goblets back, and that he was happy they had been able to save as much as possible and could now return everything.

Munich. I don't like Held but nevertheless I managed on the spot to get a list of all German Judaica (of around 2,500 books). Nothing special about them at all.

Thanks for your news regarding your negotiations with Kreuzberger. While this is very useful, I also think it best to separate completely these operations, operations that are fundamentally distinct.

The most pressing problem at the moment is that of the Jewish communities, that is to say, those people who, as individuals, claim to be the Jewish communities.[7] The danger here is that things will be given back to them, and they'll just end up selling them. There is scarcely any material necessity here, for they already have enough community property they can sell. This is a very ugly matter.

From Shunami you've heard about Mainz and the library there.[8] The collections from the local museum were also rescued and, temporarily, handed over to the museum of the city of Mainz. The local gentlemen have already tried to gain ownership over property in Worms, which unfortunately according to French law they are entitled to. The community in Mannheim sold the Laemmle Klaus Library for three thousand dollars—and they are very proud of themselves, despite the fact that the library had never belonged to them.[9] It had belonged to a special foundation that is now extinct. There is no doubt that the JRSO is its rightful successor.

I'll be in Berlin in about ten days. From there I'll travel to the British Zone, and then home. I am rather tired. It often seems that I'm gagging on the disgust at the general conditions in Germany, among both Jews and non-Jews.

To sum up, perhaps you know that I suggested that all major collections in Germany, above all manuscripts and archival material in German hands, be microfilmed. I've already done some preliminary negotiations with the Germans. This doesn't have to be too costly, and it could be of great importance. I'd similarly like to microfilm the archival materials (related to JRSO claims in Bavaria and Württenberg) that we're now expecting back, and before they get distributed. It seems to me that the Gesamtarchiv should also be sent to Wiesbaden to be microfilmed.

I believe that this project of microfilming will gain us unrestricted access to German warehouses and therefore permit us to combine detective work with microfilming. I'm writing about this in my next report, but I just want you to know about it and perhaps get your opinion on the matter. The technical side of this in Germany could be done, and with good terms, by a newly established central office for microfilming.

Sternberger. I swear that the book was sent. You'll get a copy of the Field Report that I'll get around to writing only at the end of next week because I'd like to wait for the results in the French Zone. On March 15 I'm taking the *Queen Mary* back to New York.

This has been a long letter. How are things with you and Fanja? What's going on with the supply of food?

With all my heart,
Your Hannah

LETTER 64 From Scholem

February 16, 1950

Dear Hannah,
Yesterday I received your letter from February 5, and I'm replying right away. I believe I've already confirmed receiving your friendly parcel from Basel. I got it at the beginning of February. Everything arrived and we were really delighted.

With regard to "Shipments to Israel," we at the university will offer Rabbi Kiev a reasonable compromise: he has always responded in a very friendly manner to our concerns. Of course, we don't wish to create any problems. But whatever the eventual compromise we work out with him, I suggest that the books be sent here as soon as possible. I'm stating to you officially that the university will not make any kind of fuss about sending periodicals or rare books from here to Kiev, per agreement. My suggestion (and I've run this past Dr. Wormann, and he fully supports me) would be to make two lists of periodicals and rare books that both Kiev and we want. Until now we have received no such detailed list. With it we can gladly go about searching for the books we can give up most prudently in a compromise solution. I can't imagine any difficulties standing in the way of an amicable agreement.

The Wünsche collection is an easy one. I don't suggest that you send over the non-Jewish light fiction you mentioned. These books would just be an unnecessary burden on our apparatus here. We'd rather be loaded down with processing the more sensible items we're getting from Wiesbaden.

I wish you all the best in your activities, and I'll be pleased at whatever you manage to achieve. The items from the Frankfurt Jewish Museum are excellent examples of what's possible. It would be magnificent if you could manage to snatch the things from Worms from the greedy people in Mainz and to give the items over to the wider Jewish community. Could we threaten to take the Mannheim people to court for illegally selling the Laemmle-Klaus collection? At the very least one could perhaps go on record with an official letter.

It would be very welcome indeed to have the manuscripts and archivalia in Germany on microfilm. Who would bear the cost of this? We are stretched so thin by the expenses of this entire operation that I frankly can't say how much more money I can come up with. Don't forget that we have already poured thousands and thousands of pounds into the operation, which doesn't just include Germany but also Poland, Italy, Czechoslovakia, and now there's a special mission to Morocco.

I hope to hear from you again before you leave Germany. Sternberger's book arrived three days ago. It seems that you were rather on the mark with your assessment. I'll be taking a closer look at the book.

Please give Dr. Lowenthal my warmest greetings. And be so kind as to send me copies of all your reports so there won't be any delays from New York.

Yours,
Gerhard

LETTER 65 From Scholem

March 6, 1950

Dear Hannah,
I am very grateful for your two reports from February; the special report from Berlin was of particular interest to me.[1] I hope these few lines reach you before you leave Germany. I'm also hoping to hear something soon about the conclusion of your mission and your impressions from the British Zone.

With regard to Berlin, it is interesting to compare the information two different people get from the same source. I've even discovered how the same person, namely Dr. Grumach, within three years told me entirely different stories; and not everything he uttered with the utmost certainty turned out to be true. Completely contradictory are the reports about the removal of the library of the Reich Office of Genealogy, and the behavior of the Jewish community in this matter. In 1946 I took a look at these books. I went through them for two days, and among the collections I didn't find anything Jewish (maybe there's something in the archives I didn't manage to get my hands on). What I found were general books on German history and especially on genealogy, things that mostly were of no interest to us. As for your remarks on the Eisenacher Strasse and the presence there, still in 1946, of large portions of the Jewish Central Collection, I can just say that there, too, people gave you half the facts.[2] The truth is that during my stay in Offenbach a number of wagonloads of books, I estimate there were about 150,000 books, arrived from Eisenacher Strasse. I saw them as they arrived in Offenbach. The vast majority of the books, I would say, weren't Jewish and, I'm afraid, were substantially more valuable than the Jewish books. In Berlin, people including Capt. Benkowitz, the director of Offenbach, were saying back then that there was nothing left there. What part the National Library and the Bergungsstelle had in the plundering of what was left at the Eisenacher Strasse I can't say for certain.[3] Maybe they got the things, or took them, rather, before July 1946, when everything was transferred to Offenbach.

With regard to the Gesamtarchiv, I unfortunately share your skepticism. I would be very pleasantly surprised if any of us manages to achieve anything here.[4] Mr. Schwarzschild promised us the non-Jewish items you saw in the collections of the Berlin community, but of course he hasn't come through.[5] I was more interested in the complete series of *Zukunft* and the Akademie edition of Aristotle than in the Jewish periodicals you mentioned.[6] Schwarzschild—who with all his doubtless intelligence, with regret I have no choice but to consider him awfully flighty and unreliable—claims that the superb collection of bibliophilic non-Jewish literature belongs to a particular owner and therefore can't be given away. It seems he said nothing about this to you.

The archives in Berlin are exceedingly valuable and should have been sent for us to Wiesbaden or, depending on the decision by the community, directly to Jerusalem. As you can tell, nothing of the sort has happened. The leadership of the community consists of the chief hyenas of the black market and the leading sharks; the less one has to do with them, the better. Due to their obvious dollar value it's uncertain if we'll get our hands on the truly historically valuable Pinkassim[7] of the old German communities, in particular from Berlin, Breslau, and Posen—which no one in Berlin is even capable of reading. I tried to take them out of Berlin and to add them to our collection of manuscripts in Wiesbaden, but Schwarzschild prevented me from doing so, and this despite the fact that clearly no one would have noticed the existence or non-existence of these things if Schwarzschild had given them over to us at JCR. I don't need to tell you that these things are more valuable to us than the Torah scrolls.[8] In Wiesbaden, because of Schwarzschild's promises to compel the communities to surrender items that are of interest to JCR, I insisted on separating out a couple boxes of things useful for the needs of the present community; and as far as I can tell, it was done even though, as you write in your report, the community has done nothing for us.

I hope you received my previous letter and you've seen to it, as I suggested, that the entire collection of rare books be sent here, with the understanding that in the spirit of friendship we will come to an amicable compromise with Kiev over the volumes he has set his eyes on. I would be very grateful if you could work out something along these lines.

For your information, I'd also like to let you know that the Czech government has in fact sold, on the international market, the sizable collections of Hebraica and Judaica that were found in various castles and then confiscated using the infamous Law No. 2 from 1946.[9] (This doesn't include the collections promised us from Theresienstadt and the Nimeser and which we transferred to the Jewish community in Prague. Some of these books are still there because we refused to pay the shameless ransom of one million krones.) Some of these books ended up in Switzerland in manifest mockery of legitimate private ownership claims based on the ex-libris of their owners and living heirs. (Seeligmann in Amsterdam, for instance, who now lives in Jerusalem.[10]) With my own eyes I've seen some of these books in antiquarian bookstores in Zurich, and I've brought two back with me to Jerusalem.[11] The Czech government sold a large number of these books to Wahrmann. Unfortunately, taking into account all the circumstances of the case, I can't even say that Wahrmann was acting against Jewish interests when he bought the books and then introduced them into the general antiquarian market. The only consequence of his having refused to buy them would have been that they would have ended up with other bidders, or they would have been parceled out to Czech libraries by the Czech government or, if they had no dollar value, pulped. It is patently obvious that the government in Prague is determined to turn Jewish collections from Germany into much-needed hard currency. Together with the collections from Germany, the government has sold a very large number of Jewish and Hebraic materials from private Judaic libraries in Prague. As far as I've been able to tell, the collections from Breslau do not seem to be among the books sold.

I wish you a pleasant return journey and hope to hear from you again soon.

Your Gershom Scholem

LETTER 66 From Arendt

March 31, 1950

Dear Scholem,
Thanks for your letter, which at this moment I cannot find. Somehow it got lost, but will turn up again. I just came back, or about just, and only the tip of my nose is outside of the mountains of papers and so-called urgent matters which awaited me here and which by now have buried me.

Therefore, quick.

1. Did you see the enclosed item?[1] Can you please explain or find out? I am, of course, interested, because of our own microfilm program in Germany, and wondering whether we are about to duplicate efforts. And please let me know as soon as you possibly can.

2. Did you or the library ever get a list of incunabula and old prints contained in the Cosman Werner collection Munich?[2] Is the Hebrew University interested? If you didn't get the list, 13 items altogether, please let me know immediately.

Please tell Senator that I found his letter only upon my return, and will answer him shortly. And give him my very best regards.

Shalom, Shalom!
Hannah
Hannah Arendt
Executive Secretary

LETTER 67

Jerusalem
April 6, 1950

Dear Dr. Arendt,
I trust by this time you are back in New York and ready to report to the Board of Directors meeting which I am unfortunately unable to attend. But I hope that the matter which I feel obliged to raise in this letter will be brought to the attention of that meeting by you and Prof. Baron.[1]

I am concerned about a fact which I learn indirectly from the last reports of Dr. Lowenthal in Wiesbaden with regard to the operations in Germany. It follows from these reports that the archival material which is collected in Germany is shipped to New York without further ado. From some of the reports I understand that somebody is planning to have this material included in the Memorial Library to be built up as a part of the Jewish institute of Religion Library. The position, however, is this that we all were agreed that a decent collection of books on German-Jewish history and Judaica should be concentrated at the JIR. But no suggestion has ever come before the Hebrew University that we should give up our priority right to things which exist only in one copy (which certainly applies to manuscripts and archival material) in favor of this collection. I am sorry to say I have never been asked about this matter and I consider it of great importance that the position of the Hebrew University is made clear to everybody concerned. Archival material shipped to America is not a matter for the American institutions alone to be decided upon and we expect no decision to be taken without consultation with us. I fail to understand why the material has not in the first place been shipped to Israel, but conceded the technical necessity for shipping it to the USA. This does not change the claim in principle of the Hebrew University to have these materials assigned to it. If we are asked to give up certain things there will be surely good will on our part to come to a friendly agreement with other parties concerned. There are certain materials which could be assigned to one place or the other. The Darmstadt Archives for instance are considered by us as forming an integral part of our claim.[2] It contains important documents from the beginning of the 18th century onwards and should not be divided. If there are archives from other sources we should like to have some kind of description enabling us to form an opinion as to their character. The Hebrew University will be agreeable to any sensible suggestion as to the assignment of such collections. But we do not agree that these things are decided upon in a committee on which we are not represented such as the Committee for Allocations.[3] I propose therefore that the Board of Directors shall resolve to confirm the priority rights of the Hebrew University as to manuscript material it considers essential. This of course is not meant to exclude the making of microfilm copies of all such material to be kept in both Israel and America if this will be decided upon and financed by JCR. We certainly have objection to such a procedure, quite the contrary.

I have not received a further indication as to the fate of the rare books for the shipment of which I have asked. I would appreciate it very much if you will let me know what has been done and whether you have taken the matter up with Rabbi Kiev in the spirit of a friendly compromise which I suggested in my last letters to you.[4]

There is a last point I should like to discuss. You mention correspondence with Berlin about the archives in Merseburg.[5] I am sure you understand that this Merseburg affair is a very delicate matter. There can be little doubt that no headway can be made by JRC in that matter because the authorities of the Deutsche Volksrepublik will not allow such material to be given to JCR owing to its formally American character. They have made that quite clear. If there is any hope to get the material it will be only for Israel. The Central Zionist Archives in Jerusalem are in charge of these negotiations and I am afraid that the only thing that could be achieved by competition is that nothing would be obtained at all. It is the same case that we had in Prague only that the political situation has since become much more precarious as the anti-American line of policy has become more outspoken. I would therefore suggest that JCR takes no independent steps in this matter which might make the Russian or pseudo-Russian authorities suspicious. I understand from your report from Berlin that you have not talked to the Keyman, namely, Mr. Julius Meyer. But it is precisely through him that we are trying to achieve the transfer and I think there is good reason to hope for a good outcome of that enterprise with his help. I am sorry to say that Rabbi Schwarzschild has proved very uncooperative in the whole affair, but it may be that he as an American is practically without influence in such matters.

It would be a pleasure to hear from you in the near future.

With kindest regards to Professor Baron and you.

Yours sincerely,

Prof. G. Scholem

LETTER 68 From Scholem

April 9, 1950

Dear Hannah,

I just got your letter from March 31, and then I noticed a letter lying around I had written to accompany the official missive I sent by express mail three days ago. I'm including that letter with this one.

To the inquiry about the announcement by the JTA[1] regarding photographing the manuscripts, I am a member of the commission that will negotiate this matter with the government: together with Assaf and Dr. Wormann, I will be representing the university.[2] While till now no meeting has been set, we expect to meet over the coming days. From the university's perspective, we've already discussed the general outlines of the position we will present and will stick to. It's too early to tell you if anything will come out of this. Everything depends on two rather murky factors, namely the budget and the minister of finance, and the extremely headstrong Rabbi Maimon, whom we have to deal with. Of course we'll make sure that what the government is planning won't end up duplicating the work of JCR.

We don't have a list of the Cosman Werner collection of incunabula and are of course interested in getting one as soon as possible. I thank you in advance for this.

Just a final word on my official letter. I'm hoping for your support in figuring out this business with the archives that has been raised over there. I haven't the foggiest idea what's going on, I have to admit. Can it be that some sort of commission for allocations, of which I am not a member, has made decisions of which we have not been informed, decisions moreover that are all the more incomprehensible given the basic decision about such matters that was made in January 1949 and which cannot be unilaterally revoked?

For me it's a mystery what is happening, mostly because steps have been taken that are apt to prejudice the entire affair. I am certain you know just how concerned we are with this.

I would also be grateful if you could attend to the legal questions I raised with JCR when you weren't around. These questions were made necessary because of the outrageous claims made by the former owner of the Jüdischer Verlag in Berlin.[3] The only information I received was from Mr. Ben-Horin, who told me that they would ask a legal advisor. Since then I haven't heard anything. We'd really like to know how people there assess the situation based on the submitted documents. Perhaps you can take a look at the materials I sent.

I hope that I can soon read some kind of a concluding report on your final weeks in Europe.[4] Are you perhaps planning to return in the summer? It might be that we will meet there, as I might be traveling to Paris for a congress of historians.

In any event, I hope you can give me your personal opinion regarding the questions raised in the official letter. The protocols of the board meetings are not very informative, and it's impossible to glean anything from them about the actual situation. I would be very indebted to you if you could give me a picture of the actual discussions, in case they've taken place. I sent the letter by express mail because it is important to me that these matters be formally raised before the meeting of the board takes place.

Meanwhile, kindest regards,
Your G.S.

LETTER 69 From Arendt

April 13, 1950

Dear Scholem:
I received your letter of April 6. All your assumptions as to archival material are wrong. No decision has been taken up to now. So that now as a few months ago it was perfectly unnecessary that a letter of Professor G. Scholem was written to Dr. Hannah Arendt.

1. Archival Material.—Up to now, JCR has received only the Darmstadt archives. Other archival material, mainly from Bavaria, has been claimed through JRSO. We do not know as yet how much of such archives will even-

tually fall into our hands. No shipment is being planned for the time being. Lowenthal has orders to receive archival material as it comes in and to do nothing with it for the time being.

The eventual disposition of archival material will depend upon two factors:

1. *Archival Material.*—Up to now, JCR has received only the Darmstadt archives. Other archival material, mainly from Bavaria, has been claimed through JRSO. We do not know as yet how much of such archives will eventually fall into our hands. No shipment is being planned for the time being. Lowenthal has orders to receive archival material as it comes in and to do nothing with it for the time being.

The eventual disposition of archival material will depend upon two factors: (a) If the Israeli succeed in getting the Gesamtarchiv, there may be a feeling among the members of our Board that communal archives should go to the United States. During a meeting of the Advisory Committee a few weeks ago, I explained that the outcome of these efforts is very dubious. (b) The second factor is that, in view of the special nature of archival material, many members of our Board feel that its allocation should not be handled like that of books and art objects. The value of these documents may depend upon their being centralized in one institution. This, of course, does not mean that the Gesamtarchiv *and* the communal archives should go to one institution. Every discussion of allocation, however, seems to be premature as long as we do not know how many archives and what kind of documents we shall eventually receive.

There was also agreement among the members of the Advisory Committee that it might be advisable to microfilm archival material in Wiesbaden before it is shipped out of the country. In that case, one institution in one country should receive the originals and another institution in another country a complete microfilm set. The countries mentioned were, of course, Israel and the United States.

2. *Rare books.*—Very few conflicting claims between Rabbi Kiev and the Hebrew University exist. Therefore, it will not be important to decide right now if the few items in question are to be shipped first to New York or to Jerusalem. This is a technical matter, and I do not yet know if it can be handled in Wiesbaden the way you proposed. The point is simply that we do not want to unpack and repack cases for one or two items.

3. *Merseburg affair.*—Here you are right. Lowenthal wrote during my absence. I am also quite opposed that eastern zone officials be contacted by JCR. I wish you the best of luck for your negotiation with Julius Meyer.

I shall show your letter to Professor Baron, but, for reasons mentioned above, I do not think it necessary to put this matter before the Board of Directors at the present meeting. I do not know of a single instance in which the Hebrew University was not consulted and has not been in a key position as to allocation decisions. It is not very likely that this will change in the future.

Yours sincerely,
Hannah Arendt

LETTER 70 From Arendt

April 18, 1950
Dr. G. Scholem
Hebrew University
Jerusalem, Palestine

Dear Scholem
Thanks for your letter of April 9, and please find enclosed copy of my letter to the Executive of the Jewish Agency.[1] Dr. Gerling had written to JRSO Nuremberg with reference to a report of Narkiss which I did not see.[2] However, I would like to tell you that Narkiss' evaluation of the paintings which had been found in Germany (50,000 pounds) has been proved entirely wrong. The collection as far as I know is now estimated at between $5–$10,000, but I may be wrong about these figures. I may assure you that, selling or not selling, nobody is particularly happy about this business.

Please keep me informed about the microfilm business.

Enclosed please find list of incunables. I have not yet shown it to the New York librarians. I hope that we shall soon get a selection from HUL.

Archival material I think is finished for the time being.

Judische Verlag.—Have not yet been able to get the legal advice, but have reminded people of it.

I hope you received in the meantime my last field report and the report to the Board of Directors.[3] Please let me have, as in the past, your detailed reactions.

For heaven's sake, don't worry about the archives. First we have not them yet; second, difficulties will arise only if Jerusalem gets the Gesamtarchiv.

One more question about archives: A certain Mr. Benjamin Orenstein, a former DP in Bamberg, received in 1946 from the Director of the Bamberg

Staatsarchiv books, ceremonial objects, Torah scrolls and, *sage und schreibe*,[4] 310 folders of documents covering the period of 1658–1938, 29 volumes of community archives from 1814–1876, and a number of birth, death, and marriage registers. In Germany I was told by the gentlemen of the Bavarian Landesverband that Mr. Orenstein had left Germany with this collection. We finally, and with considerable effort, established contact with Mr. Orenstein, who now lives in Canada. He wrote us that all archives were sent to Israel through the Historische Kommissie in Munich.[5] He speaks of tens of thousands of documents from 24 communities plus municipal archives. Have you any idea what could have happened to this material? Or where I could at least try to find out?

With kind regards,
Hannah

[Enclosure]

April 18, 1950
Dr. H. Gerling
The Executive of the Jewish Agency
P.O. Box 92
Jerusalem, Palestine

Dear Dr. Gerling:
Dr. Katzenstein sent me copy of your letter to him of March 26 referring to your plan to send a team of ten persons into Germany in order to search for Jewish cultural objects.

I just spent almost four months in Germany for exactly the same purpose. I visited the three Western zones and Berlin and wrote detailed reports about my findings in each of the three zones.

My reaction to the three points of Dr. Narkiss is the following: (1) Although Jewish Cultural Reconstruction asked only for Jewish-owned objects of Jewish content, following the advice of Dr. Shunami, I made one exception: The American military authorities have at one time transferred to the Hessen government more than 100,000 books of non-Jewish content and not marked with Jewish names, from the Offenbach depot. These books, consisting of general German literature and of no special value, are now under the custodianship of Professor Eppelsheimer in Frankfurt. The majority of the books is unidentifiable as to ownership. After restitution to proper claimants has been made, it was intended to give the unclaimed books to German libraries. I came to a *tentative* agreement with Professor Eppelsheimer that 50% of these books should be returned to JCR, since they are doubtlessly former Jewish private property.

2. Because of material conditions in Germany (destruction of buildings, return of large material from war-time caches, and great turn-over of personnel) it is impossible as yet to assess how much material will eventually turn up. The unpacking of cases will in many instances be a matter of years. However, it seems as though more archives and more ceremonial objects were saved than books, largely because the German-Jewish book collections were more strictly centralized in Berlin while synagogue silver and archival material more frequently found their way into local institutions.

Unfortunately, I cannot share Dr. Narkiss' optimism about the amount of material which can still be expected from German institutions. The situation briefly seems to be the following: German Jewish collections, as distinguished from the Jewish collections from abroad, were strictly centralized in different depots of the Gestapo in Berlin. We can expect only material which by some miracle escaped this centralization (such miracles happened in Hamburg). The Berlin material was partly put into caches in eastern Germany and Czechoslovakia and partly disappeared into German libraries in Berlin which are located in the eastern sector of Berlin.

3. Largely because of material conditions but also for other technical and psychological reasons, I am now even more convinced than I was before that we depend upon the good will of German personnel to a very large extent and that all other methods of investigation are impractical. To quote but two examples: (a) it took our library investigator more than four weeks of hard work to discover a few archives in Bavaria where Jewish confiscated material had been deposited during the Nazi regime. One single letter to the general director of Bavarian archives resulted in a reply which gave a probably complete list of such localities without omitting a single "discovery" of the investigator. (b) I discovered the valuable Frankfurt art-collection through contacting the respective museum-directors and without using any detective methods.

As to the paintings which JRSO recovered, I hope that Dr. Narkiss has been informed in the meantime of the decision of JRSO New York which was taken in full agreement with the representatives of the Jewish Agency. Unfortunately, the pictures had been largely overestimated. A number of paintings requested by Israel will be shipped to Israel.

In conclusion I would like to say that it is a debatable question if a mission of a ten-men team will result in any discoveries to justify the costs involved. There is, of course, always a possibility that a systematic search could discover caches, probably still in existence and hidden by former SS men, which the Allied authorities have not been able to find. I was specifically told of the existence of such caches in the British zone.

Hoping that you will find this information usefull for your purpose, I am,

Very sincerely yours,
Hannah Arendt
Executive Secretary
cc to Messrs. Katzenstein
Scholem

LETTER 71 From Scholem

April 30, 1950
Dr. Hannah Arendt
Executive Secretary,
Jewish Cultural Reconstruction, Inc.
1841 Broadway,
New York 23, N.Y.

Dear Hannah,
Many thanks for your letters of April 13th and 18th. I am very glad to hear that in the matter of the archival material our misgivings were based on a misunderstanding and I note with much satisfaction that we will take up every question of incoming material according to the merits of the case. So far there are no reliable news about the "Gesamtarchiv" except a letter from the Israeli Consul in Munich[1] saying that he has already heard from Berlin that the files would be shipped to Munich. That may mean very much if they are actually under way, or nothing if it is only an announcement of a pious intention. But since the responsible official on the German side seems to be very much in favour of giving the material to the Berlin Community with a view to having it shipped to Israel there might be really a chance of things moving in the right direction.

In that connection I wish to answer your question about the Bamberg Staatsarchiv material. I have taken the matter up and it appears that the material has been brought over by the Historical Commission in Munich to Israel and handed over to Yad wa-Shem.[2] Now as you may know, Yad wa-

Shem is a stillborn child. It was planned as a central organization which was to establish a memorial to the Jewish dead of the Hitler War. It was to erect also a memorial library and a collection of documents pertaining to the history of the Jews under Hitler. We have been always very sceptical about the whole business and have opposed the extravagant dreams of the initiators. The only thing that has been done was a lot of harm as for instance in the present case. Material which should not have gone to them under no circumstances has been rather irresponsibly given to an institution that has ceased to function. Practically there is now nobody to whom to speak and with whom we could settle the matter of finding where exactly the files are to be found. We will try to clear that mess up with a view to having the files transferred to the Historical Archives of the Hebrew University and the Historical Society. I learn that to this very day there are still 12 cases of documents from the Historical Commissie in Haifa Port that have not yet been taken out. The whole thing is preposterous and I am glad that you have drawn my attention to it as we may be able to do something about it. But as far as I learn here the material from Munich contains chiefly protocols and eye-witness reports collected by the Munich Commission during the last four years and I doubt very much whether they are really tens of thousands of documents from twenty-four communities as you were told.

Many thanks for your interesting reports.[3] It will be a wonderful thing if you can bring the negotiation with Eppelsheimer concerning 50% of the so-called non-Jewish stuff to the favourable conclusion.[4] Do you think that there is anything I could help by going to Frankfurt in September? By that time there should be a decision as to the principle involved. Is there somebody in Germany who can make a choice of the books in case they decide to give them to us? I have a strong suspicion that quite a number of books among this material may contain Orientalist literature which I saw in Offenbach and which was not included or classified as Jewish, my protests to that purpose notwithstanding. Of course we are not interested in shipping a single volume of German fiction and all that, but there should be quite a lot of other valuable stuff.

We have been notified by Dr. Lowenthal that the rare books for which we asked and also the Breslau and Berlin material assigned to us is being shipped to Israel. We are very glad to hear that.

I wish to draw your and Baron's attention to the extremely unfortunate interview Dr. Bernard Heller has found appropriate to give to *The Yiddish Vorwärts* (12. II. 50) regarding his activities in Germany.[5] It seems that this man is quite something of a fool. We are very unhappy over his remarks about the Baltic books that have been shipped to Israel.[6] It was understood and the gentleman should have known about it that this matter of the Baltic collections was a very delicate one and not to be given any kind of publicity. We were to keep the books here until the end of the stipulated period without opening them and without making any fuss about them. Now Dr. Heller has put the Russians who may screen Yiddish newspapers in New York for material interesting to them, on the scent. They may come and put us in a very awkward position by claiming books from Russian territory which we are said to hold. The diplomatic position of the United States and of Israel with regard to these territories is not the same. Of course we will deny everything if it comes to that. A newspaper can tell a lot of lies. But I think JCR should register its protest at least on behalf of the Hebrew University regarding the indiscretion which Dr. Heller has committed by giving away facts of this kind.

I will take up the matter of the microfilms as proposed in your memorandum and put it before the Government Commission if it assembles.[7] So far, I do not see that anything is done in spite of our repeated requests for fixing a date for that meeting. But I am very glad to have your detailed proposals and we will certainly make up our minds about it. In general we are more inclined to have photostats in normal size, but of course there is much to be said for the procedure which you suggest.

As to your letter to Mr. H. Gerling I have spoken to him. The idea of sending a team of ten people to Germany for detection work seems utterly out of place to me and I have made it clear to him that I share more or less your opinion about locating hidden material in Germany. I said, and he agreed to it, that the most that would be justified under the present conditions might be a mission of one or two men for tentatively 6 to nine months on the understanding that these could not be people of the type of Mr. Bernstein,[8] but people of academic standing with a full command of German who would be able to talk to German authorities in a responsible way and to establish conditions if not of friendship at least of mutual trust without which nothing could be gained. Of course the question would be to find the right people if the Agency would be willing to foot the bill.[9] Gerling has promised they would do nothing without consulting me before.

This is enough for today. Finally let me say that I have read your last article on Bert Brecht with very much pleasure.[10] Have you met him in Berlin? I did. A very queer fish. I spoke to him about Walter Benjamin's papers, but it was obvious that he has no use for the dead ones which are not longer there to extoll his greatness.

It sets me thinking that both the "Neue Rundschau" and "Der Monat" are written at least 50% by Jews.

Cordially yours,
Gerhard

P.S. I forgot to tell you that Shunami has already written to Lowenthal about the incunabula from the Cosman Werner Library. I think from the whole list we have claimed only four or five volumes which are not in the Library.

G. S.

LETTER 72 From Arendt

May 5, 1950
Dr. G. Scholem
Hebrew University
Jerusalem, Palestine

Dear Scholem,
You may remember my report on the Mombert library.[1] Unfortunately, this collection was claimed, and returned to a niece of Mombert a few weeks before JCR got ready. The library at this moment is in Karlsruhe and belongs to Mrs. Klara Vogel (Green Lea, Hendre Gardens, Llandaff-Cardiff, Wales, G.B.). The library is for sale. According to Dr. Richard Benz, a friend of Mombert, who prevented the Gestapo in 1940 from selling the collection at public auction, the library consists of 4–5,000 volumes in the following chief categories:

German poetry and literature, with an almost complete collection of periodicals
German philosophy
Modern literature, mostly dedicated copies
Indian religion in English translation
A beautiful collection of traveler reports, many of them rare
Mystical literature, such as original edition of Bachofen, etc.

A small collection on Greek music

I took these details down just in case the University should be interested. If so, the best way would be to contact Mrs. Vogel directly.

Yours,
Hannah

> Just received your letter of April 30. Thanks. Baron took already the Heller-business up with Mr. Heller; we were also taken—by surprise.

LETTER 73 From Arendt

June 2, 1950
Dr. G. Scholem
Hebrew University
Jerusalem, Palestine

Dear Scholem,

Many thanks for your letter of April 30 and the information about Gesamtarchiv and the Bamberg material.

As to the material which is now under Eppelsheimer's trustee-ship, I am wondering why you believe that it contains Orientalia and other valuable stuff. Eppelsheimer told me that an overwhelming majority of these books are modern German fiction plus such "scholarly" items as Gundolf, etc.[1]

Heller:—The interview in question was given without our knowledge and came to my attention by accident, that is, no copy of the newspaper was sent to the office. I telephoned Baron immediately and he protested to Heller. Some days later I received a protest from JRSO, Nuremberg, which I forwarded to Heller. I called him up and wrote him myself—I think that will do for the moment.

We shall have another discussion of the microfilm project next Monday at a Board of Directors meeting, but the chances are slim. I shall propose a 35,000 mark budget for the negatives of 200,000 manuscript pages. The positives can be done in this country at a cheaper rate than the one quoted to me by the central German microfilm association. It is very doubtful whether JRSO will grant us a mark budget and it is almost certain that the additional dollar budget will have to come from other sources. I still think that this microfilm business may eventually prove to be the most lasting contribution of JCR to Jewish cultural life, especially if we could take Germany as a starting point only and through some kind of revolving fund (recipient libraries all over the world refunding at least part of the expenses) proceed to microfilm manuscript material in Austria, Italy and possibly France.

Dr. Wormann wrote me that you in Jerusalem are anxious not to have cultural property included in any bulk arrangement between JRSO and the German authorities. As a matter of fact, Mr. Ferencz, when he was in New York, mentioned the possibility of including cultural property, but we did not discuss the matter at this point. I can understand your misgivings, but I should like to point out to you the following:

1. If a bulk arrangement between JRSO and the German government materializes, it will mean the very rapid liquidation of JRSO offices in Germany. This in turn will mean that cultural property in the hands of German institutions can no longer be claimed by a successor organization.

2. JRSO is extremely anxious to terminate the activities of JCR for budgetary reasons. We are having great difficulties with our budget up to the end of the year, and the chances are that this will be the last budget for operation in Germany even though a few finish-up jobs may be left for next year.

In other words, what is the alternative to a bulk arrangement—which admitedly is not a good idea for cultural property? Moreover, I am afraid that you overestimate the quantity as well as the quality of Jewish owned material in German public institutions.

In order to give you an idea of how things stand, let me tell you that during a recent executive Committee meeting of JRSO, it was reported that JRSO will probably get recognition as successor organization in the French zone. There was strong opposition to spending any dollars for initial operations, that is, it seemed doubtful if JRSO would be willing to become the successor in the French zone. The reason behind all these recent developments is very simple. There is very little "heirless" Jewish property in Germany; almost everything has been claimed through proper channels.

Did you see Benjamin's Baudelaire-Essay as it was printed in "Sinn und Form"?[2] I didn't meet Brecht, I never liked him. Moreover, he certainly resents my article in the "Rundschau" for obvious political reasons.

Yours,
Hannah

LETTER 74 From Scholem

June 7, 1950
Dr. Hannah Arendt, Exec. Secretary,
Jewish Cultural Reconstruction, Inc.
New York

Dear Hannah,
I understand that several pending matters are being settled between you, Dr. Wormann and Mr. Shunami and I need not go into these, but want to report to you on other matters.

Thanks for your information with regard to Mombert's library. We cannot take any interest in it if we have to buy it. German literature is not high up on our priority list. God may give that we have in any other literature what we have in German.

As to the microfilming project I suppose that the meeting of JCR has made its decision to proceed according to the proposals. In this case I am authorized to declare that the State of Israel will take one copy of the whole set which is planned. We have now had a meeting with the Prime Minister and the Minister of Education and it was resolved to take steps to establish a collection of photographs of every available Hebrew manuscript text. "The Committee for the Photographs of Hebrew Manuscripts" consisting of representatives of the Government and the Hebrew University will be the responsible body to handle these matters and also will be in charge of the administration of the budget to be allocated by the Government. The photographs themselves—photographs, photostats and microfilms—will be preserved as a trust for the Government by the University. We will appoint a special expert who, in his capacity as a government official, will attend to all these matters. Apart from that we intend to apoint a second expert whose function it will be to travel to places where manuscripts should be photographed.

If JCR proceeds to put into effect its German microfilming program we will join it and not take separate steps of our own. I should like to hear in detail what are the plans and have information whether the personnel and equipment for the execution will be ready by August or September. I shall be in Europe in August and may be free to go for a certain time to Germany after the 10th September. If the work proceeds by that time it may be desirable for myself to go and see how the program is carried out. In the meantime we would proceed with our preparations for the same kind of work in other countries, especially those of the popular democracies.

I am leaving Jerusalem about August 15th for Switzerland and I hope that you will let me have full details as to the execution of the program in order to enable me to make a decision whether to go to Germany or leave it alone.

In the "Gesamtarchiv" affair we are without information. I will let you know as soon as any news comes in.

Cordially yours,
G. Scholem

LETTER 75 From Arendt

June 15, 1950
Dr. G. Scholem
Hebrew University
Jerusalem, Palestine

Dear Scholem,
Thanks for your letter of June 7th. You will receive the minutes of our last board of directors meeting in a week or so and will see that the budget for our microfilm project has been approved, but that the JDC and the Jewish Agency has turned us down as far as the money is concerned. You will also see that we are now trying to get a grant from one of the American foundations. We shall apply for $25,000 and then try to do the microfilming not only in Germany, but at least in Austria, Italy and France as well.

In spite of our financial difficulties we are going to take all the necessary steps to put into effect at least our German microfilming project. In July we shall send to Germany Meir Ben-Horin who knows Hebrew (former student of the Hebrew University) and he will be more or less in charge of all of our activities in Germany.[1] We are planning to have the negatives made by the German documentation services in Frankfurt, whereas the positives will be printed by the central microfilming firm in this country. This seems to be the cheapest way to arrange things.

Mr. Ben-Horin will travel in Germany and find out if the Hebrew manuscripts are available (already unpacked, etc.). It would be just wonderful if you could be in Germany in September because by that time we shall know the material conditions in each place.

We are thinking first of all, of course, of the manuscript collections in Munich, Hamburg, Frankfurt and Berlin. If my information is correct, the Berlin manuscript should now be in Marburg and Göttingen.[2] Part of the Frankfurt manuscripts were sold in a restitution deal to a private person in New York. We may be able to microfilm them here. The Hamburg manuscript I saw myself, including the Levy collection.[3] They *seemed* to be complete. In Munich I was told that all manuscripts—nearly 400—were saved.

As to manuscripts in other university libraries, I would be very grateful to you if you would draw up a list of those institutions which we overlooked in our Tentative List, which, I trust is in your hands.

There is another question which has come up: Marx questioned the wisdom of microfilming bible manuscripts and he proposed to omit the following numbers of Steinschneider's catalogue for Hamburg:[4]

1–13, 15–30, 36, 39, 43, 44, 47, 49, 50, 54, 58, 59, 61, 62, 63–66, 70–82, 100, 157, 159, 161–65, 167–68, 172, 174, 200, 221, 223–24, 226–28, 235–45, 252 (?), 254, 259–62, 268–81, 298, 311, 315, 317, 322B, 331, 337, 338–51;

Spanish and Portuguese (?), 352, 354, 355.

H. B. Levy—4, 7, 9, 17, 26, 28–34, 40, 64–67, 80–92, 99, 103, 107, 108, 110, 111, 116, 117, 119, 125, 139, 140, 141, 142, 143, 164–67.

We are figuring here a total of 200,000 manuscript pages, which also includes photostating of the catalogues of the Jewish divisions in German archives.

If the Israeli government could do the same kind of work in the countries of the popular democracies, that would be very valuable. Please don't forget that there may be a possibility to "sell" sets of microfilms to Jewish and general libraries in the United States. I found out that Cincinnati, the Jewish Theological Seminary and the New York Public Library are almost certain to be "customers."

The possibility of covering part of the cost through refunds by subscribing libraries has not yet been sufficiently explored by us, but in planning our budget we have been thinking in terms of a revolving fund. Needless to say, that I am glad to hear that the State of Israel will take and (presumably) pay for one copy of the whole set.

With kindest regards and cordially yours,
Hannah

I just received the following information from Germany:

(1) The Hebrew Berlin manuscripts: These were not put into one cache as a unit but the various numbers were put into different places together with other manuscripts so that the definite whereabouts of each manuscript have to be established.

(2) You may be interested to know that the Varnhagen Archiv, which, as you probably know, contained a considerable amount of Jewish correspondence of the early emancipation period, was shipped to Silesia and nobody knows what happened to it.[5]

Hannah

LETTER 76 From Scholem

26th June, 1950
Dr. Hannah Arendt
Executive Secretary,
Jewish Cultural Reconstruction, Inc.
1841 Broadway,
New York 23, N.Y.

Dear Hannah,
I received your letter of June 15th and hasten to answer. First of all I want to remind you of the legal problem submitted to JCR nearly five months ago. It concerned copyright claims of Dr. Katznelson formerly of the "Jüdische Verlag," Berlin, now Jewish Publication, Jerusalem, and we should by now have indeed a detailed opinion on all the legal aspects of this matter. Please do not forget this problem which involves a number of books which are very much needed by other institutions in Israel.

I am awaiting the minutes of the last meeting of the Board of Directors.

As to the microfilm project I think I must observe that there seems to be a misunderstanding which is apt to result in serious overlapping. You write that JCR intends to include France, Italy and Austria. As far as France and Italy are concerned I do not see what business JCR has to go into these fields. I told you that the Government of Israel intends to undertake a microfilm project which will include the Hebrew manuscripts everywhere and it will certainly not limitate its activities to the Eastern countries where, as a matter of fact, very little is likely to be achieved. Russian manuscripts are unavailable for the time being, Czechoslovakia and Poland have left very little, Rumania never had anything of great value. This activity may thus boil down more or less to do the work in Hungary which by the way may be done anyway by the people of the Budapest Rabbinical Seminary who have already told us that they will take microfilms of everything with them if they cannot remove the original manuscripts together with the whole library from Hungary when they will establish themselves in Israel.

The department to be established by the Government will be under the responsibility of an expert in these matters which of course cannot be said of Mr. Ben-Horin whatever his other merits are. I think therefore that if JCR proceeds with the German and possibly with the Austrian project; this should be all of it and the other parts should be left to the activities and financial responsibility of the Government of Israel which seems to be willing to foot the bill and to look at the whole thing as a governmental and diplomatic action on its part.

We are much concerned about, and interested in, your information that part of the Frankfurt manuscripts were sold to a private person in New York. Please let me have precise details as far as you have got them. Who is the gentlemen in New York and which manuscripts has he got? When I was in Frankfurt I was informed that all the Hebrew Manuscripts except those in the showcases were burnt. If this is true the restitution deal could comprise a very small number of manuscripts only, though possibly valuable ones.

The Hebrew manuscripts from Berlin are mostly in Tübingen and Marburg and only a small part if any has been sent to Silesia and is of course considered as lost for the time being unless we can uncover them in one of the collections of the University of Cracow.

Now as to my movement: I am leaving Israel probably on August 17th for Switzerland. As I shall have to be at the Eranos meeting[1] in Ascona I shall have no time to go to Berne to the Inter-Allied Permit Office and see whether I get a German visa. I shall then have to leave directly for Paris where I shall also be for a couple of days only. If it should be found advisable for me to go to Germany and to meet with Mr. Ben-Horin about the tenth of September arrangement for my visa should be made with the Inter-Allied Permit Office or the American Consulate in Amsterdam where I shall be likely to stay on September 3th–10th. Last year's experience proves that there was no point whatsoever in IRSO's refugee to handle my entrance permit using the pretext that I was a "hot case" for the American authorities. This was just as much idle talk. I therefore think that JCR should insist on my receiving the German permit as Vice-President of JCR for a short visit and on their behalf. I am giving you hereunder the necessary data from my passport in case you want to arrange for a permit from your end. I see no reason why it should not be prepared with your assistance in a way to be available for me the moment I come to Amsterdam. It is of course better to meet Mr. Ben-Horin in Germany, preferably in Frankfurt or Hamburg, than to arrange for a meeting in Amsterdam or Paris. At any rate I would be glad if practical steps for cooperation between us and a personal meeting could take place.

I also suggest that JCR contribute $ 100,– towards my travel expenses to Germany in case I go there. The money should be forwarded to me to Amsterdam.

With kind regards
Yours cordially,
Prof. G. Scholem.

> P.S. Amsterdam seems to involve exchange difficulties for me, I am advised. Therefore I would prefer or the money to sent to me to Switzerland (Ascona, c/o Mrs. Olga Froebe, Casa Gabriella) to be available there on the 20th August; or to have Mr. Ben-Horin authorized to pay the amount when we meet.

LETTER 77 From Arendt

July 7, 1950
Dr. G. Scholem
Hebrew University
Jerusalem, Palestine

Dear Scholem,
I am replying to your letter of June 26th in an hurry because I am going on a vacation for four weeks. If you want to reach me, my address is: c/o Mrs. S. Franc, Menomet, Mass.

I discussed your letter with Dr. Baron and he feels that if the government of Israel really has the intention to carry out the microfilming project, then JCR might do better to withdraw from it completely. After all, this is only a tangential development of our own work and we shall have great difficulties in financing it. Mr. Ben-Horin will however carry out a pilot study while he is in Germany, possibly beginning with the Hamburg manuscripts, and we shall be glad to let you have the benefit of our experiences.

As to the sale of Frankfurt manuscripts in New York, I advise you to get in contact with Prof. Alexander Marx of the Jewish Theological Seminary, 3080 Broadway, New York, N.Y. I know the following: 88 manuscripts were sold by Frankfurt to a certain Mr. Levy of New York, formerly of Frankfurt, in a restitution deal between the municipality of Frankfurt and Mr. Levy. I don't know which manuscripts he received. Eppelsheimer told me in Frankfurt that he sold all the manuscripts of the Frankfurt library. This, however, does not seem to be true. Mr. Ben-Horin will talk with Eppelsheimer about this in the near future.

Your information—that the Hebrew manuscripts from Berlin are partly in Tübingen. Are you sure? I heard that they were in Göttingen.

As to your trip to Germany: If we drop the microfilm program, it may still be advisable for you to go, provided we receive in the meantime more material from the American Zone. We shall try once more to get a share of the books under Eppelsheimer's trusteeship. If however that is not the case, I wonder if there will be anything of interest for you.

You will find it very easy to receive a permit for Germany wherever you are. I don't believe that you will need our help, but I shall be glad to ask JRSO to facilitate matters for you. As matters stand today, it has become well high impossible for JRSO to get military facilities for our people before they get to Germany. The tourist visa is now really open to everybody.

If you should decide that your presence in Germany is necessary as a result of developments within the next few months, we shall of course be glad to contribute $100.00 toward your travelling expenses.

Yours,
Hannah Arendt

LETTER 78 From Scholem

July 25, 1950
Dr. Hannah Arendt, Exec. Secretary,
Jewish Cultural Reconstruction, Inc.
New York

Dear Hannah,
I'm glad you're getting the chance to recuperate a bit. I wish for you a pleasant vacation; I can only begin mine when I leave here.

Very quickly, in response to your last letter from July 27[1] you should know that I got a visa to Germany for 2–3 weeks, so technically I'm set to travel. I'm waiting for final word from Berlin in matters related to the Gesamtarchiv to see whether it makes sense to travel there for a few days. Should the archive from Merseburg in fact be transferred (Julius Meyer wanted to go there around now), it would seem right for me to travel to Berlin in order to make sure "on the spot" that the transfer to the Israeli consulate in Munich really takes place. The consulate will then take charge of the transport from there. In which case I would also head to Berlin. Naturally, I'll only believe anything will come of this when I see the documents. For now, I prefer to regard the entire story as a pipe dream.

I would in any case propose that I meet Ben-Horin in Germany, either in Hamburg directly after Rosh Hashana (so I can fly directly from Hamburg to Berlin), or in Frankfurt before I leave Germany. Could you be so kind and share with me the addresses where Ben-Horin can be reached? Is Wiesbaden still open? Is it still the center? As soon as your vacation is over, please put me in contact with Ben-Horin so we can make all the necessary arrangements. My addresses are:

August 17–27: Ascona, Tessino, c/o Mrs. Fröbe, Casa Gabriella

August 28–Sept. 2: Paris, Hotel Louis-le-Grad, 3 rue Rouget de L'Isle, Paris 1

Sept. 1–10: Amsterdam, c/o Congress for the History of Religion, Indian Institute, Mauritskade 63

Please share these addresses with Ben-Horin.

Has Dr. Lowenthal left his position at JCR?

Before I leave you'll be hearing from us about the microfilm project. We have someone here who will do the traveling, but we still don't have anyone for the processing. I'm hoping that over the coming days decisions will be made in all these matters. Without question, we would prefer for JCR to undertake the *German* side of the project, which would naturally be cheaper. Should JCR withdraw from the project altogether, especially because of lack of money, we of course would have to move in and do it.

Thanks so much for your information on the Frankfurt manuscripts. It seems that Eppelsheimer said very different things to different people.

As for the manuscripts in Berlin, you must be suffering from a loss of hearing. As far as I know, nothing has been sent to Göttingen, though a large portion of the Near Eastern manuscripts are in Tübingen, another part is in Marburg, and the rest must have been lost in Schlesien. Not only did I get this information directly from Professor Hänisch, and I wrote it down, but I've also ordered a Syrian photograph from Tübingen. I would be very surprised if there is anything in Göttingen. Perhaps someone should go there and take a look.

Once you get back, please don't forget to reply to me—or if I'm already gone, to Dr. Wormann—about the still unresolved legal issue with Dr. Katznelson. Because everyone is off in the countryside, the expert report by your nameless legal advisor will probably be delayed until October.

In the meanwhile, be well and warmest greetings,
Your G. Scholem

LETTER 79 From Arendt

August 8, 1950
Dr. G. Scholem
Hebrew University
Jerusalem, Israel

Dear Dr. Scholem,
Thanks for your letter of July 25th. I hope this letter still finds you in Jerusalem.

1. *Microfilming*—The Munich State Library raised difficulties and put conditions which, in our opinion, are inacceptable. They are the only ones. The same does not hold true for Hamburg and the Berlin manuscripts. However, since the Israeli government wants to do microfilming in Europe anyhow and is certainly better qualified for all diplomatic negotiations than we are, it may be better that they undertake the German job as well. We still may

decide to do a pilot study, either in Hamburg or on the Berlin manuscripts. Ben-Horin is supposed to discuss this matter with you in detail.

Another question is the microfilming of archives. This too Ben-Horin will discuss with you.

2. Ben-Horin must leave Paris for New York on September 7th. I therefore think the best thing would be for you to meet in Amsterdam prior to his departure. I think you will find it necessary to go to Germany and we shall then of course send you the $100.00 check. Please let me know when and where you want to have the money.

3. One reason why it would be good for you to go to Germany is that the Kultusministerium of Hessen has notified me that it is ready to abide by the tentative agreement between Eppelsheimer and myself, according to which we would get 50% of the books under Eppelsheimer's trusteeship. However, they warned me of the bad quality of these books (70% pamphlets or unbound). Up to now it has not been possible to inspect the books, which are in a bunker. You may want to look into the matter.

4. You were right with Berlin manuscripts in Tübingen.

5. For your planned trip to Berlin, please find enclosed a lovely note from the community gentlemen. For your information, the books are now in the Oranienburger Strasse in the attic, and when and if you are there don't forget the climb a little stairway which leads from one attic to the one above.[1]

6. For your general information: The British Trust Fund has seen the light.[2] Ben-Horin goes to London in order to decide if JCR or the Committee on Restoration of Continental Jewish Museums, Libraries and Archives, i.e. the Cecil Roth–Rabinowicz group will take over the job.[3] We are not over-anxious, but would do it if we are asked to. JCR work in the American zone will definitely be liquidated by December and possibly earlier. There are occasional in-shipments, but the big claims, the Frankfurt art collection and the Bavarian archives, have not yet come through.[4] The latter are also claimed by the Bavarian Landesverband. Auerbach is very busy and also successful in preventing anything which we want to do. My opinion on the activities of this gentleman are no longer fit even for typewritten print. (By the way, his hold on the German government officials is politically the most interesting aspect of the story.)

7. Katznelson—I finally got the opinion of our legal advisors and am sending them on to Wormann. According to American and British law, Katznelson's claim is non-existent.[5]

Yours,
Hannah

LETTER 80 From Scholem

16th August, 1950
Dr. Hannah Arendt, Exec. Secretary,
Jewish Cultural Reconstruction, Inc.
New York

Dear Hannah,
I am glad to hear that you are back from your vacation and I just read your letters to Dr. Wormann from August 8th and 9th.[1] Many thanks for the legal opinion on the Katznelson case of which we will make use in due course.

The microfilming project of the Government is under way so far as we are now waiting for the final allocation of the budget to begin our operations. Meanwhile we have appointed two people, namely, Dr. Paul Klein from Paris, formerly the Librarian of the Alliance Israelite—who changed his name now to Moshe Katan. He is a trained archivist. Secondly Dr. Nehemya Aloni who in the fall will go abroad in order to arrange for the operation there. It is very important for us to know whether JCR is going to proceed with the German microfilm project or not. In the latter case Dr. Aloni will be sent to Germany this fall. In case you write me about this to one of my addresses in Europe which I gave you in my letter of July 25th please send a copy of it to Dr. Wormann who is a member of the Government Committee responsible for the action in order to keep him informed. At any rate we are starting on the presumption that JCR is unlikely to undertake the enterprise because of its financial difficulties and we have given Dr. Aloni instructions to prepare also for Germany.

I hope to hear from you in Switzerland or Paris, or at the latest in Amsterdam about a possibility of meeting Ben-Horin who I assume is to continue at the old address in Wiesbaden. Meanwhile, the matter of the Gesamtarchiv seems to proceed and although there has not yet been a formal transfer of the Merseburg material to our people, we hope that no obstacles will arise in the last hour. It is well possible that in connection with this matter I shall proceed to Berlin. In case I go to Berlin and possibly also to Hamburg I shall pass through Frankfurt and Wiesbaden only on my way out of Germany.

You have promised that JCR will contribute $100.– to the expenses of this trip and I would like you to send it in a cheque in my name to my address in Zürich (Kurhaus Rigiblick, Krattenturmstrasse). It should be there by the end of September. In the meanwhile I will pay the expenses from my own funds.

I hope to hear from you and am with cordial regards

Yours,

Prof. G. Scholem

P. S. I wrote to Dr. Sternberger about the *Panorama*-business a carefully worded letter, but I have not heard anything from him. Do you think I should call on him when passing through Germany? Is he at present in Frankfurt, Berlin or Heidelberg?

LETTER 81 From Arendt

August 24, 1950
Dr. G. Scholem
Hotel Louis-le-Grand
3 rue Rouget de l'Isle
Paris 1, France

Dear Scholem:
Thanks for your letter of August 16. I am happy to see that the Israeli microfilming project is so well on its way.

Ben-Horin will tell you that we made a pilot study in microfilming manuscripts in Germany. (I do not yet know whether he decided to microfilm Hamburg, for which Prof. Marx had made a selection, or Marburg-Tübingen, where we would ask you to select the manuscripts.) Anyhow, the experiences of this study will be available to you, but we would then withdraw from this project altogether and keep in mind only the possibility or rather the desirability of a microfilming project for archives.

Ben-Horin will meet you in Paris the first week in September. I enclose copy of a letter to him in order to give you an idea of what is going on and what we expect from you. But please keep this letter as an internal office affair because of the unfinished stage of our negotiations with London.

Since you are going to Berlin: We received angry applications for books from Rabbi Freier for the Berlin Jewish community.[1] He wants 1,500 to 2,000 books and on principle we are willing to let him have them. However, we want in exchange, the books and documents in Oranienburger Strasse. We shall let him have 500 books now—elementary stuff, Hebraica and Judaica—as a show of good will. Do you think you will be able to negotiate on this basis?

You will receive a check, as you requested. Since we issue checks at the beginning of each month, you will get your check earlier than you indicated.

Sternberger: The best way to reach him is still at the old Heidelberg address. Eppelsheimer surely knows where he is. I think he plans to come to the United States this fall.

With kind regards,
Sincerely yours,
Hannah

[Enclosure]

To:
Mr. Ben Horin
M. G. Club
Alexandrastr. 6-8
Wiesbaden, Amer. Zone

Dear Mr. Ben-Horin,
Enclosed please find copy of my letter to Dr. Rabinowicz, which, I trust, is self-explanatory.

1. In view of the scarcity of available material in the British zone, the British zone job can only be a side job. Their budget seems to me exaggerated. However, if they want to and succeed in establishing a whole new administration, let them do it. I don't think that we should take responsibility without having any administrative power. And we would take responsibility if we were to follow Dr. Rabinowicz' propositions.

To make this point even clearer, let me summarize to *you* what we can expect in the British zone.

(a) Sephardic archives in Hamburg. These were community archives; we probably won't get them.

(b) 2,000 kilos of silver in Hamburg. This is (1) non-Jewish, though of Jewish ownership. That is not strictly in our line; and (2) former individual property, the majority of which in all probability will be claimed precisely because it is very valuable.

(c) The microfilms in Düsseldorf, which were made from Jewish owned archives. There is very, very, small hope that the British authorities will decide to confiscate this material in favor of the Jews because the microfilms themselves were made by the Reich. But even if such confiscation were possible, there are again the Jewish communities, who will almost certainly claim them.

(d) The Jewish community in Hamburg has valuable ceremonial silver which was given into their custody by the British authorities and which never belonged to the Hamburg Jewish community. I think it very unlikely that they will part with these objects.

(e) There are a few odds and ends: some ceremonial objects in the museum in Altona, the Königsberg archives in Golslar, etc. You see?

However, I think that some kind of cooperation or at least basis for mutual information will develop between JCR and OR in JCT. Frankly, neither Prof. Baron nor I, after many unhappy experiences to which you will find allusions in my letter to Dr. Rabinowicz, think that it would be very wise to elect this organization as a successor to JCR, i.e. as a successor address after January 1, 1951. The best solution would be to have outstanding claims shipped via JRSO. At a later date, in case anything new materializes, and after JRSO has left Germany, we may ask the Jewish Agency to handle pending claims, incoming information, etc.

2. Lowenthal. Let's postpone this until you come back. Since the breakdown of the individually owned books is not possible now and may not be necessary at all, I really do not see what he is supposed to do full time. The main thing is to clear the Wiesbaden depot.

If the Frankfurt collection should be entrusted to us, we are going to ship it directly to New York in unopened cases. Distribution can be made only with expert advice and Schoenberger of the Jewish Museum is the best man in the field.

A real headache would be the Bavarian archives and I do not know any solution to this problem except that registers are available for everything. Some registers were sent in by Bernstein. It may be worth while to ask Lowenthal to draw up, together with Bernstein, a list of these archives for which registers are available.

3. I suppose you will be in Nurenberg before you leave Germany. Will you kindly take up the following with Kagan:

Since JCR is very eager to terminate activities in Germany as soon as possible and is bound to do so by the end of the year, we hope that JRSO will be able and willing to help us with the few matters which may still be pending. What we would require would be of course only a shipping job. As far as we can see now, the following shipments may be necessary:

(a) The Frankfurt collection to be shipped directly to New York (see above).

(b) The Eppelsheimer books, if they are not sorted, to be picked up and packed in cases, to indicate to us the number of cases and then probably to be shipped to Israel and to New York.

(c) Odds and ends, the allocation of which should be decided in each individual case.

I meant to write to Kagan, but I think it much wiser for you to discuss this problem with him. This procedure may start even before January 1st, since we hope to have the depot cleared well before that time. This would mean, of course, not only part time work für Lowenthal, but the termination of his appointment.

4. I am awaiting Scholem's opinion on the Eppelsheimer books. The main question is: Will this material be sufficiently valuable to warrant the expenditure of the necessary time for sorting and processing according to categories? If the material is not good enough, we should ship as I indicated before. If however Scholem is of another opinion, this may mean once more full fledged operations in Wiesbaden. But here is the real problem. After my experiences with Lowenthal's general education and attention to cultural matters (as distinguished from administrative matters), I do not think that he is the right person for the job. (I guess I told you the story of the "Dilthey ms." which turned out to be a notebook of excerpts from one of Dilthey's published writings—and it said so at the head of the first page.) Since this is only German material, I could easily do it and I might go to Germany to do the job. I am wondering, however, if it would be worth the expense. I must confess that I do not quite see any other reasons for my coming to Germany in the near future, even though you insist on it time and again. Don't think that I shall be able to fight Mr. Auerbach tooth and nail. I won't. And whatever turn the British zone job may take, the material which is there does not justify any great expense.

With kind regards
Sincerely yours
Hannah Arendt
Executive Secretary

LETTER 82 From Scholem

September 14, 1950
Frau Dr. Hannah Arendt, Exec. Secretary,
Jewish Cultural Reconstruction, Inc.
1841 Broadway, New York 23, N. Y.

My dear Hannah,
I'm writing to you, in German, from the Frankfurt office of the JRSO, and from the midst of the well-known office conditions. I'm writing to give you my opinion about the books in the State of Hesse under the charge of Prof. Eppelsheimer.[1]

1. The findings: For two days I've looked through the collections in the bunker at the Wittelsbacher Allee. A worker helped me take some samples from the books from every possible place, including from deep inside the bunker. I think this search enables us to make a rather fair assessment of the collections and what could be done with them.

There are two cement rooms completely stacked to the ceiling with books. Another room is nearly filled with brochures. There are about six rooms in which the book collections are on shelves. Someone has already pulled some of the books from the shelves to check them out. I estimate the total space taken up by the books to be between 50 and 60 cubic meters.

The content of the collections includes Judaica, socialism, economics, history, philosophy, psychology, psychoanalysis, art—in German, English, and a bit of French. There are works of literature and newspapers. Added to all this is a heap of catalogues, military literature, and what looks like a large number of dissertations from German universities. My search turned up very few technical publications, and I came up with a lot of pure rubbish, such as address books and the like.

My search convinced me of two things above all:

1. There is more Judaica than we had expected. In some places I came across entire shelves of Jewish books and brochures. Somehow, and for reasons that can scarcely be explained, entire boxes of Judaica ended up among so-called non-Jewish material. In my opinion, the Property Division of the military government in Offenbach should never have sent them here in the first place. I estimate that Judaica makes up five, possibly as much as ten per-

cent of the whole. More importantly, I am fully convinced that the Judaica is important for us, especially for Israel and the Hebrew University Library. I found some truly valuable things: really fine volumes of old Judaica from the seventeenth and eighteenth centuries; literature on emancipation from around 1800; and works on Jewish history. I think the collection of brochures is also very valuable. I am ready to take all the brochures, along with the other Judaica, to Jerusalem. Immediately, I had everything Jewish set aside along with the other Jewish materials that had already been separated out. Among the newspapers, while we can't expect to find complete series, there are a large number of bound individual volumes.

Quite valuable among the non-Jewish literature, I think, are the books on socialism, economics, philosophy-psychology, and art. Many of these books belong to multivolume collections of which there are only parts. Still, the value, for instance, of the materials in philosophy, socialism, and history is nothing to scoff at. The fiction leaves me cold. The art books are partly quite good, some even valuable.

I can't say that the JRC should renounce the legal rights to these collections. The problem arises, then, of how we should proceed.

2. Suggestions:

I've had two long discussions over this subject with Prof. Eppelsheimer and Dr. Wehmer, who manages the collections at the bunker, and we've weighed the various technical options. We have to be clear that we can only move forward on the basis of an amicable agreement. We shouldn't expect any difficulties coming from Eppelsheimer. The question remains, what should we do? There are two possibilities:

1. To go inside the bunker in Frankfurt to make a selection or division of the books, and to do so according to the general line I will describe below. From there the books could be shipped directly to Israel or, for instance with the newspapers, to the common pool in New York.

2. To send everything back to Wiesbaden. What should be taken into consideration here is not only the need to get permission, once again, from the military officials but also the very substantial transport costs.

This option admittedly involves legal and administrative issues I can't decide on. Apparently, Eppelsheimer is under the impression that he, that is, the state of Hesse, has the authority over the collections. At most he has to get approval from Wiesbaden, where there is no opposition to handing the books over to us.

When, say, the question of divvying up the books comes up for review, I can't say if Wiesbaden will insist that this take place at the Collecting Point. It'll also be a problem for JCR because of the substantial costs involved.

With the division of the books, I would shy away from coming up with an entirely new procedure with subdivisions according to subjects and so on, as was the case in Wiesbaden. I would suggest a much simpler procedure that would look more or less like this:

JCR commissions Dr. Lowenthal to devote half of his free time to this matter. Dr. Lowenthal will take two assistants and go through the volumes that are in the bunker in Frankfurt. According to row, the books will be brought to him in the empty rooms, where there is plenty of shelf space. All Judaica will be set aside for us. Books we have no interest in will also be separated out, and the people in Frankfurt can do what they please with them, that is to say, send them to be pulped. (Don't forget that the main problem for the people in Frankfurt is to get rid of the books because they have to clear out the bunker.) The non-Jewish books that are of interest to us will be divided up according to an amicable arrangement between Dr. Lowenthal and the person authorized by Eppelsheimer. The proportion could be 1:1 or, in case we end up pulling out a large amount of Judaica, 1:2, or some other equation that takes into account the value of the individual works. I see no difficulty in coming up with a generous agreement.

If questions arise, we will always have Dr. Eppelsheimer on our side. If JCR were prepared to act according to my suggestion and to ship these collections to Israel (with the exception of the newspapers that would go to New York), then the books could be packed up immediately, and there would be no further problems with sorting through the books. I think, given the nature of the collections that come into question for us here, that we are the most natural and best choice among those interested in them. We can make full use of the non-Jewish scientific literature, especially.

The other option would require a complicated division of the books between Israel and other countries. I see no reason to do this.

If this operation were to take place in Frankfurt, Eppelsheimer would go along with my suggestions. As for the costs involved, the idea is this:

JCR will pay Dr. Lowenthal and his assistant 220–230 DM per month. The time in which his assistant is not working for us (Dr. Lowenthal will be available at most three days a week), he'll be used in the library, and we'll be compensated for the costs. The second assistant will be paid by the library in Frankfurt.

We think that with such assistance, and if a simplified procedure such as I have proposed is adopted, the organization and shipment of the books could be carried out quickly and systematically. Even if the books first need to be transported to Wiesbaden, a fast-track procedure would still be the way to go. I would argue against an extensive sorting procedure.

The decision has to be yours. My only advice is to come to a quick resolution and to negotiate directly with Eppelsheimer or the Property Division, and with Mr. Heinrich in Wiesbaden. Time is of the essence because the bunker isn't heated and it can be bitterly cold to work there in the winter. A small room in which Dr. Lowenthal can work could be heated with a small oven. Another reason to hurry is that we only have Dr. Lowenthal for another three months. I therefore push for beginning negotiations along the lines as I have set forth, and for settling this affair as soon as possible.

Enough said on this topic. Tomorrow I am flying to Berlin. I'll be there for about a week, and I'll try to find out more details on the issue of the Gesamtarchiv.

I write all this to keep you happily in the loop, with warmest greetings,

from your old friend,

G. Scholem

LETTER 83 From Scholem

Fischerhüttenstrasse 24
Berlin-Zehlendorf
September 20, 1950
Dr. Hannah Arendt,
Jewish Cultural Reconstruction, Inc.
1841 Broadway,
New York 23, N.Y.

Dear Hannah,
I'm rushing before my departure from Berlin to send you a report on the negotiations and on the status of the two questions of interest to us.

1. *The Gesamtarchiv*

I've spoken to all parties involved. Three-fourths of the archive arrived here in Berlin ten days ago, and I've looked it over in the Oranienburgerstrasse. Once the remainder of the archive comes next week, the technicalities of the handover will have to be discussed between the Jewish and German offices. As you can appreciate, this will involve certain psychological difficulties. Nevertheless, it is expected that these formal issues will be resolved over the coming two to four weeks. From Switzerland I'll write you more about the situation as it develops. The older community files that are here have been added to the Gesamtarchiv. As you yourself know, under the prevailing conditions the only possibility is to transfer the archives to Israel, and the gentlemen involved here have in principle agreed to give everything over to the Central Archive in Jerusalem—this without doubt—or perhaps to the Hebrew University.[1] We've undertaken some preliminary sorting of the books that you saw during your time here. In sum, we can count on sending to Jerusalem all the important documentary material here. Nevertheless, before believing anything I still strongly advise waiting until you receive news of the successful transferral, at least to Munich. This is important for the question of the other archives that JCR controls.

2. *The Community Library*

I've heard a lot of loud complaints from Dr. Freyer, the local rabbi, and from the gentlemen from the community council that, until now, nothing has been sent from Wiesbaden to the community here. I strongly suggest that if Dr. Lowenthal hasn't yet received the necessary authority from JCR, you give instruction that the collection that was set aside for Berlin be transported here right away. If I've understood Dr. Lowenthal properly, there are around five hundred books from the various categories that until now have been separated out and which the community needs. I believe that at least twice this amount should be sent to them. The people here also want a number of rabbinical foundational works. Dr. Freyer stated that in Berlin he doesn't even have a single complete copy of the Talmud so he can write sermons or look things up. Likewise he is missing copies of the third or fourth most important codifications (Poskim). Nor is there even a single copy of Goldschmidt's German translation of the Talmud, while for instance in London there are five, and no one knows what to do with them.[2] For the community Freyer also urgently needs the Pentateuch with commentary from Samson Raphael Hirsch. In Wiesbaden there were also plenty of exemplars of Theodor Herzl's writings and other fundamental Zionist works. Dr. Freyer said to me that there are about thirty or forty people studying either with him or independently who would have keen interest in such books. While I'm not entirely certain that these numbers and comments by Feyer are one hundred percent accurate, I believe we wouldn't be losing anything if JCR took these needs and requests into account. I told these gentlemen that I would immediately do everything in my power to come to a friendly settlement.

As soon as the community receives at least a first shipment from Wiesbaden (and perhaps one could get Dr. Rabinowicz to agree to make available a couple of the relevant books that are in London), JCR will have no trouble in obtaining the transferral of the scholarly Judaica, the modern Hebraica, and above all the periodicals. Objectively, in the interest of JCR, I place the most weight on the journals. From here I'll also be writing a letter to the community in which I'll request the corresponding transferral of these collections to JCR.[3]

Sadly, I have to say that we should expect only trouble from Dr. Freyer with this matter, but not from the community leaders. In contrast to the latter, Dr. Freyer declared that if JCR comes up with the books he wants, he will see to it that at least one hundred Torah scrolls, which Dr. Lowenthal had wanted, are made available. In a word, we won't get anywhere without a positive step on our side that shows goodwill.

We encountered some substantial psychological difficulty at the news of the transfer of the Breslau collections to the Swiss community federation.[4] Some people here are quite embittered by this. They bring it up over and over. I have my doubts whether we acted prudently because, as far as I can tell, the books in Switzerland will without question end up rotting. (I had a sad conversation about this with a member of the Swiss distribution committee.) Do you think something still can be done here? Couldn't one give the rabbinic literature to Israel?

That's enough for today.

Meanwhile, warmest greetings from Ernst Grumach, and from yours truly,

G. Sch.

LETTER 84 From Scholem

[Undated]

[page 8][1]

I just finished reading Walter Benjamin, which he presented me. Moreover, he pulled out the manuscript of the Arcades fragments, which in fact can at most yield aphorisms, say, for a posthumous publication; nowhere do they offer, however, a continuous text one could use.

Of course, I offered him my help in preparing manuscripts and materials for the publication of the writings.[2] He presented himself as the picture of innocence, if not exactly as a fool. I did nothing to hide my opinion of Porkheimer.[3]

I write all this to keep you happily in the loop.

My warmest greetings, your old friend,
Gerhard Scholem

P.S.

1. Best greetings from Baron and Ben-Horin. With Ben-Horin in Paris I had two very thought-provoking conversations. It turns out that he's an old student of mine.

2. For the next edition of the *Neue Rundschau*, Adorno is contributing an article commemorating the tenth anniversary of Walter Benjamin's death. I'm now reading it in manuscript form, and it's in part truly outstanding. It will interest you.

I took a look at the remains of the Judaica collection of the Frankfurt municipal library. The collection is supposedly completely preserved. It turns out that only the catalogue pieces 1–6,000 were there, and even among these there are gaps that of all things include the valuable pamphlets and other similar material.[4] The rest of the very large collection of Judaica listed in Freimann's catalogue—in other words, an even larger number of items than what I saw—was burned, and this includes nearly all of the most valuable pieces. This was very unpleasant news to me. We're talking about all dissertations written on Judaica before the eighteenth century. A very small number of works in Yiddish are also in the library, though most of them were burned. Of all the manuscripts, two boxes from the Merzbacher collection have been preserved. I had one of the boxes opened and I counted inside fifty-six Hebrew manuscripts.[5] That is to say, of the approximately 800 Hebrew manuscripts, around a hundred have survived and are still in the municipal library. This proportion is worse than we had expected.

LETTER 85 From Arendt

September 27, 1950
Dr. G. Scholem
Kurhaus Rigiblick
Zurich, Switzerland

Dear Gerhard,

Thank you very much for your two letters of September 14th and 20th. Upon receipt of your report on Frankfurt, I immediately wrote to Dr. Lowenthal, following your suggestions in every detail. I shall write to Prof. Eppelsheimer and hope that work may start in Frankfurt on October 1st.

As to the allocation problem: We are having a Board of Directors meeting on October 9th, at which we shall submit your proposition. I am pretty convinced that the bulk of the non-Jewish material will go to Jerusalem. The Judaica are another question. Please believe me that I shall try to do my best for you. However, this whole allocation question is really never decided by me, either formally or informally. My argument in your favor will be that JCR as a rule does not claim books of non-Jewish content and that I started my negotiations only because of the Hebrew University's (Shunami) special interest in this material.

It would be wonderful if you really succeeded in your Berlin negotiations. Please find enclosed my letter to Dr. Lowenthal, from which you will see that we will do everything in our power to carry this through.

As to Switzerland, this decision was taken because it was felt that one substantial part of our recovered material should remain in Europe. When I was in Zurich, I saw the Zurich community library which seemed to me in good shape. I was told then that this material would be incorporated into the Zurich Library, and that through a special system which they have there these books would be available to scholars in all Western European countries. Unfortunately, I was not in a position to make this promise a condition *sine qua non* for the allocation of the Breslau books because, as you know, according to our rules, we have no right to interfere with local national distribution. Since you are in Zurich now, maybe you can do something about it. I talked at the time with Rabbi Taubes and some other gentlemen from the community. Unfortunately I could not see Brunswig.

Mr. Ben-Horin reported delightedly about his meeting with you in Paris.

He already told me of your objections to the Switzerland business (you were the only one to vote against this allocation, don't forget this).

We have now decided not to microfilm any manuscripts in Germany and to let you have a complete report about our preliminary negotiations. You will find this report upon your return to Jerusalem. On the other hand, Prof. Baron still thinks about the microfilming of archives. I don't know if anything will ever come of this, but we shall make a pilot study of the Worms archives.[1]

Last but by no means least, please read once more Dr. Lowenthal's report on Austria. Does the Hebrew University intend to do anything about this? As far as I can see, there are two chief collections:

(1) The remainder of the Tanzenberg collection, which originally probably had the same character as the Rosenberg collection in Offenbach. The remainder consists of (a) 400 cases in Klagenfurt "likely to be handed over to Carinthia" (whatever that may mean); and (b) 200 cases still in Klagenfurt, but probably on their way to Vienna. It seems that the 400 cases are unidentifiable as to ownership, whereas the 200 cases contain books marked with the names of individual owners. Among the Tanzenberg material there seems to be Judaica from the communities of Berlin, Königsberg and Karlsruhe.[2]

(2) 250,000 heirless books in Vienna, part of them identifiable, and probably comparable to the Eppelsheimer books in Frankfurt.

We have communicated with Mr. Harold Trobe, Director General of JDC in Vienna, and asked him to ascertain in whose custody the Tanzenberg books are at this moment, the British occupation authorities or the Austrian government. If these books are still under British authority, we shall try to get the JTC in London to do something in London itself. We have taken no steps with regard to the 250,000 non-Jewish books because, strictly speaking, they are not in our domain.

Please let me have any ideas or suggestions you may care to make. I think that it may be wise for Dr. Wormann to go to Vienna and possibly to Klagenfurt to see if there is anything that can be done.

I forgot Mainz. Did you come to an arrangement with the community? If not, JCR may be ready to accept a deal.[3] In this case too, we should need a detailed expert opinion from Dr. Wormann.

That's all for the moment. Have a good time.

Yours
Hannah

[Enclosure]

September 25, 1950
Dear Dr. Lowenthal:
I just received Prof. Scholem's report about his negotiations in Berlin, which were quite successful. The following information is confidential:

1. It seems that the Gesamt-Archiv will be transferred within the next two to four weeks (unberufen). The other archival material which I saw in Oranienburgsestrasse will probably also be shipped to Jerusalem.

2. Prof. Scholem has come to an oral agreement, which he confirmed in writing, that the following categories of the present Berlin Jewish community's holdings should be exchanged for books from JCR: Judaica, scholarly; Hebraica, including Rabbinics, if these are not needed; Hebrew and German periodicals; non-Jewish scientific literature. In exchange, the Berlin community needs, in addition to the 500 volumes which we have set aside, books in the following categories:

(a) If possible, one or two complete sets of the Talmud;
(b) Poskim;
(c) Pentateuch with commentary;
(d) Zionistica;
(e) Goldschmidt-Talmud.

Dr. Freyer told him that five sets (?) of the Goldschmidt-Talmud were shipped to London, where nobody needs them. Is this correct? If so, I would suggest that we ask Dr. Rabinowicz to return at least one set. Please let me know from you about this.

The community also seems willing to let us have 100 Torah Scrolls.

If the 500 Berlin books have not yet left Wiesbaden, please ship as soon as you can overcome the technical difficulties and advise Dr. Freyer as well as Mr. Galinski (Joachimsthaler Strasse 13) that the books are en route.

Also try as much as possible, even if you have to take books from the South American allotments, to fill the above enumerated needs of the community. They should get a minimum of 1000 and a maximum of 1500 books.

At this moment I do not see any need for your going to Berlin. Let's see what is going to happen. As soon as I hear from you that the books are being shipped, I will write to Mr. Galinski, who, according to Prof. Scholem, is more sympathetic to our requests than Freier.

With kindest regards
Sincerely yours
Hannah Arendt
Executive Secretary

LETTER 86 From Scholem

October 4, 1950
COPY

Dear Hannah,
I hope you get these lines before the meeting of JCR. Yesterday I had the visit of Dr. Lowenthal and we discussed in detail the whole question of the Eppelsheimer books. He will take the matter up with E. and decide whether he can undertake the job. He thinks that a much larger budget will be required for technical help, crating, etc. than I anticipated; *more* workers, etc. but he will see for himself. If there is any hope to finish the job in the remaining 10 weeks,[1] it can be done only by an extremely simplified procedure which forgoes all bureaucratical niceties. We have no time to loose, so we better forget about sorting out duplicates and other good things which are likely to make the work more difficult—which under the circumstances of the work in the Bunker, will be difficult enough anyway.

I earnestly urge the Board of JCR *not* to *divide* the Judaica but to allocate the whole lot to Jerusalem. They contain material of exceptional value for us, especially the old Judaica and the pamphlets. After the shipment to Switzerland of thousands of books which nobody needs and which will be lost to any serious purpose, JCR should not repeat the error of allocating books which are very much needed in Israel to other places. Please speak in my name if that can help you.

Do not make any *final* decisions on the allocation of archives before we actually have got possession of the Gesamtarchiv material for Israel. And please, if you have to mention our negotiations in Berlin, for heaven's sake ask the gentlemen present to keep quiet and not to give the matter any premature publicity. You will understand the obvious reasons for this warning. As yet, no instruction of a final decision of the East German gouvernment has reached us and if it comes through, somebody will have to go to Berlin to receive the stuff (and to pack it and ship it)—either myself or Dr. Bein. As I plan to return this sunday (Oct. 8th) to Jerusalem, it will probably be Bein. The Israel government has consented to either of us going.

About Tanzenberg, etc. I can only talk the matter over with Wormann; ditto re Mainz, where I had no time to go. As to Mainz, I am sure we are ready to pay for the collection, if it comes to that (a moderate sum).

Kindest regards
Yours
Gerhard

LETTER 87 From Arendt

October 11, 1950
Dr. G. Scholem
Hebrew University
Jerusalem, Israel

Dear Scholem,
Thanks for your letter of October 4th, which came just in time for the Board of Directors' meeting.

Eppelsheimer Books: I quite agree with you that we should forget all bureaucratic niceties. I am worried, however, because I have not as yet heard from Dr. Lowenthal, who is a good administrator, but overfond of bureaucratic procedures.

You will probably receive the minutes of the meeting of the Board of Directors some time next week. It was decided not to divide the Judaica, but to allocate the whole lot to Jerusalem. As to the non-Jewish books, 2/3 will go to Jerusalem und 1/3 to New York. That is the best we could do. On the archives, no final decision has been reached.[1]

May I add that neither Mr. Salpeter nor Ben Halpern, who after all are supposed to speak up for your interests, were present.[2] And this, even though they indicated on the response card that they would attend.

Mainz: I am afraid you misunderstood. The gentlemen do not want 1,000 Marks; they want 1,000 dollars. Quite a difference![3]

As ever, yours,
Hannah

LETTER 88 From Scholem

7th December, 1950
Dr. Hannah Arendt, Ex. Secretary,
Jewish Cultural Reconstruction, Inc.
New York

Dear Hannah,
Thanks for the Notice of Annual Meeting of November 28th with enclosures.[1] I have talked the matters over with Dr. Wormann and in the following wish to explain my views and make my suggestions as representative of the Hebrew University.

ad 1) § 1b[2] Since matters with regard to the "Gesamtarchiv" are not yet finally settled and we are expecting this final settlement, I would ask you kindly not to make any decisions on this point. We are willing to take all archives over, also the Bavarian Jewish community archives. If the transfer of the "Gesamtarchiv" should meet with difficulties in the last minute—I will not hope that it actually does—I feel that the Bavarian archives should be allocated to the Hebrew University. Incidentally the Berlin authorities have asked for a document in which the State of Israel asks formally for the transfer of the "Gesamtarchiv." This document has only recently been handed over to the German authorities in Berlin. If necessary Dr. Bein will once more go to Berlin.

ad 2) § 2[3] As to the decree which you hope the German Länder governments might issue I have no objections to it although I feel compelled to give vent to my scepticism. I do not believe that we will actually receive book collections or similar material which will be found at some future time through a decree of this kind. As I stressed, such a decree would indeed be of use if Hebrew manuscripts of institutions and individuals which we are all looking for should turn up in whole or partly. It would make possible legal steps regarding the enforcement of the transfer. This is an object of such importance to Jewry as a whole that it appears worth while to secure the legal claims. As in this case property of dissolved institutions or individually owned items are involved the matter comes under the jurisdiction of JRSO. I do not wish however to give the impression as if I would think that there is much chance of finding such material in Germany herself or that it would turn up there within the next two years. I rather think it will be found <nat.ly> and can be identified, in Poland. The man who will be charged to make microfilms there in behalf of the Israeli Government—and we hope he will start at the beginning of 1951 (the main difficulty of the budget seem to have been removed by and by!)—has been specially requested to take care of this matter.

ad 4)[4] § 4 I do not think that legal steps would produce any results in Berlin. The Jewish Community may be prevailed upon to give us things in accordance with amicable agreements. In any event it should be taken into account that much was actually destroyed by fire, etc. and that there may not exist caches in Berlin. For this reason I do not recommend that JCR should make a new effort next year.

ad 6) § 6 If it should prove possible to liquidate the stock of 12,000–14,000 Judaica and Hebraica of the privately owned books by distributing them among American institutions we have nothing to say on this point. But if only a part could be placed I suggest that the remainder be sent direct from Wiesbaden to Israel. We can use the items for distribution here. I request you to consider this alternative. We are ready to take closed cases from this holdings without further sorting.

ad 7) § 7a[5] If there will remain duplicates of periodicals which do not find a claimant we want for Israel Hebrew and Yiddish periodicals (the latter without American dailies) only. Duplicates in other languages are not required, but we hope that the Hebrew and Yiddish duplicates can be shipped to Israel.

ad 7d § 8 The same principle as above may be applied for remaining books. We are willing to take over all Hebrew and Yiddish books. I propose to let us have this material and in no circumstance to offer it to American libraries or to sell it on the market.

ad 8)[6] I herewith file the claim of the Hebrew University of Jerusalem with regard to the material in France. We are prepared to take *all* of it. I most sincerely urge you to take this decision and not to start sorting and various allocations. As it has become clear, rabbinical literature—and the Paris holdings consist of such material in its *major* part—is anyway needed in Israel only. The Ministry of Religion as well as the Ministry of Education and Cultural have frequently applied to us and inquired whether we are not ready to supply more material of this kind to new settlements. I request you to state this point in our behalf. The precedent of the Breslau Rabbinica must deter us. During my stay in Switzerland I followed up the fate of the Breslau rabbinica which were allocated to this country. As a result of my investigation I may say that not more than five or six people will use these 7000 volumes. I suggest to stress the public interest which exists in Israel for this material and not to allocate this material in accordance with the accepted percentage key. This would mean that no material that nobody wants there will be sent round Europe and that it can be prevented that the books finally find their way into the bookshops. We also claim the Baltic material the contents of which we know very well. There is no doubt that all of it can be used here. As to the individually owned books in Paris we feel that not more than 10% of them will be claimed by their owners. The majority of them will be Hebrew books which are of vital importance to Israel and we would suggest that all the material that cannot be returned to its owners should be sent to Israel. The acceptance of our suggestion would facilitate the handling. The Baltic books need not be processed at all and could be forwarded at the beginning of Sept. 51, next year, as we have a specification of the cases.

If special problems in connection with the individually owned books should arise there might be a possibility that the Hebrew University places some one at the disposal of JRC. This person would then come to Paris if necessary. But I think that a summary disposal as I suggest would make such a mission unnecessary. Dr. Shapiro can handle the matter by himself.[7]

As stated above we do not expect more than 10% of the books to be claimed. As far as we can we are prepared to do our best to facilitate the additional work you anticipate. Details may be settled later on.

ad 9)[8] We propose that the material you mention will be given to the Hebrew University in Jerusalem after conclusion of JCR activities. It should be added to the national archives. I believe that JCR archives are of general Jewish national significance and it is fitting that such documents covering an interesting period and important activities should be deposited in Jerusalem.

I trust, dear Hannah, that my suggestions which you will be kind enough to submit to the meeting in my behalf will facilitate your work. I wish JCR all the best for what I suppose to be the last year of its activities.

With kind personal regards and best wishes,
Sincerely yours,
Prof. G. Scholem

P.S. I read your article on Germany in the *Commentary* in nearly full agreement. Many thanks.[9]

LETTER 89 From Arendt

December 27, 1950
Dr. G. Scholem
Hebrew University
Jerusalem, Israel

Dear Gerhard,
Thanks for your letter of December 7th, which was duly read at the meeting of the Board of Directors on December 21st. You will receive the minutes shortly, so let me summarize first.

All the archives will go to Jerusalem, but you will be *strongly* requested to make microfilms available to other institutions, especially to Cincinnati (the Täublers, etc.).[1]

I quite agree with you with respect to the decree. However, the feeling here is that this is a matter of principle, so I am supposed to continue. I am also wondering if under the radically changed political circumstances we can expect anything from the German Ländergovernments. Frankfurt, and Hessen in general, are exceptions to the rule.[2]

I just cabled to Wiesbaden to ship all remaining Hebraica to Israel. You are wrong in assuming that a high percentage of the privately owned books are Hebraica. Our estimate is not higher than 25%. As for periodicals, duplicates in Hebrew are not available. We have duplicates of German Jewish periodicals only.

We have quite a few demands for "Left-Overs," including Latin American countries. No sale will be considered.

No decision has been reached as to the material in France, but the chances for you are good. However, you will probably be interested only in the Baltic collection. There are very few Hebraica among the individually owned books. We do not expect to ship anything to the United States, but the European offices of the JDC, who were quite helpful in handling this material, will have a certain claim for their distribution among European communities.

You did not send me your Kabbalah & Mythus.[3] Please do. I shall try to get the "Berliner Kindheit" here.[4] Sternberger did not inform me.

How is everything? How is your chocolate and coffee supply?

Yours,
Hannah

LETTER 90 From Scholem

29th January, 1950
Dr. Hannah Arendt, Ex. Secretary,
Jewish Cultural Reconstruction, Inc.
New York

Dear Hannah,
I am in possession of the Minutes of JCR, December 21st, 1950 and the attached statements.[1] As I was ill during the last weeks I could not answer you at once, but having recovered now from my 'flu I am taking the first opportunity to thank you. I have read the Minutes with much attention and I wish to thank you and Baron for your help. I hope that everything will go smoothly. As far as the archives are concerned I wish to state that we certainly will do our best to make a list of this material after it will be received here and to forward a copy of such a list to Cincinnati (or perhaps should we send it to you for transmission to Cincinnati?) which should enable them to state which of this material they wish to have microfilmed. I assume that only a part of it will be of real value to them. At any rate I should like to know who is going to foot the bill. We assume the receiving institution is supposed to pay for expenses. Up to now we have had no information about the archives being shipped to us, but I assume that this is only a matter of some weeks. You will be informed by us as soon as the cases containing the material will be in our hands. Please notify the gentlemen in Cincinnati about this. We very much appreciate the sympathetic attitude taken by practically all concerned towards the general policy the Hebrew University has advocated.

As to the Frankfurt Museum I understand that Dr. Rabinovicz has asked for a reconsideration of the resolution about it. In case such a discussion should be resumed I wish to state that I certainly would vote in favour of the proposals made by the British Committee.[2]

As to the Paris books, especially the Baltic collection, I understand that there will be further negotiations before a final decision will be reached. I hope very much that by then all parts will agree that these books should go to Israel where they are so urgently needed. I can tell you that we are under constant pressure from the Ministry for Religious Affairs to give them more and more books of this kind for the libraries they are setting up in new and old settlements and this is indeed one of the vital functions we should fulfil here and in which JCR will have every interest to take a share. This books cannot be bought today and those offered are to be had only at prohibitive prices. It is this situation which prompts us to insist on a maximal allocation to Israel.

With kindest regards to you, as always,
Yours sincerely,
Prof. G. Scholem

LETTER 91 From Arendt

March 6, 1951
Professor G. Scholem
The Jewish National & University Library
POB 503
Jerusalem, Israel

Dear Scholem,
This is in reply to your letter of January 29th. I agree with you that it would be best to send a list of the archival material to Cincinnati to enable them to decide which part of the material they wish to have microfilmed. I am also inclined to think that the expenses for microfilming should be borne by the recipient institutions. However, the Board of Directors did not decide anything about this and I am afraid I will have to bring it up once more.

Baltic Collection: We are now preparing the procedure for claimants of individually owned books of six or more per owner. In the roster which shows the names of the people found in the books, we included the names of the owners of the Baltic collection on the same principle: We shall publicize only private owners of six or more books and we shall not publicize, *at least for the time beeing*, the names of the institutions in the Baltic countries, to which the majority of the Baltic books belonged. I don't believe that you will have any trouble in getting the bulk of the unclaimed Baltic collection allocated to Israel, even though the demand for books of this kind is also quite considerable strong not only in the United States but in all of the Western hemisphere (Latin American countries).

On February 12th, I wrote to Dr. Wormann about a discussion with Rabbi Maimon, Minister of Religious Affairs.[1] I do not want to repeat myself and I am sorry that I omitted to send you a copy of the letter. You will see from it that we too are by now "under constant pressure."[2]

With kindest regards
Yours
Hannah

LETTER 92 From Arendt

March 26, 1951
Dr. G. Scholem
Hebrew University
Jerusalem, Israel

Dear Scholem,
Please find enclosed copy of letter to Dr. Wormann, which I trust is self-explanatory.[1]

I am bothering you because I think that a telephone call from you to Gustav Schocken might persuade the *Haaretz* to publish the list.[2]

I just received a letter from the American Jewish Archives in Cincinnati in which Dr. Marcus tells me that he presumes that they will be willing to pay for microfilms of material which they request. On the other hand, it seems obvious that they should not be charged for the *listing* of this archival material.

With kindest regards,
Yours
Hannah

LETTER 93 From Scholem

July 19, 1951

Dear Hannah,
I'm in the very awkward position of having to explain to you my inexplicable and entirely baseless silence, and now of all times when I own you a direct reply as well as my gratitude for so many things. But my low spirits have caused me more and more to procrastinate in my writing. The only thing I can claim is that I've been battling the lung infection I got at the beginning

of spring, and this has caused a rare drag on my life that is otherwise very busy, as you are certainly well aware of. I've had no desire whatsoever to do any kind of writing. And of all times, I got your wonderful package, which resonated with all my desires and vices, and then came your important book which I read with great interest and should otherwise have inspired me to engage you in every aspect of the book. I can only say that this stubborn paralysis affecting my work for months has nothing whatsoever to do with the lively feelings that your packages inspired in me. What has become clear is that I am quite simply worn out, and in the near future I'll be doing a cure and undergoing an operation. Afterwards, you'll see me again full of spirit sitting at my writing desk.

So I really beg your forgiveness by responding to your testimonies of friendship with nothing more than this dark cloak over my helpless silence. Because of necessary medical treatment I'm going to stay in the country over the summer. This coming fall, with all of my powers restored, I'm hoping to return to my manuscripts, which are all lying around half-written.

Allow me, with inexcusable tardiness, to congratulate you on your magnum opus.[1] It reads so marvelously well and inspires all kinds of unexpected reflections. This book of yours, which sets out to engage in fundamental categories, must come across as exotic indeed in the USA, with all the reigning intellectual wishy-washiness. Aren't a lot of people shaking their heads?

In principle I have to say, even after reading your book, that you haven't convinced me that there is an inner, essential connection between totalitarianism and anti-Semitism. While I consider your presentation in part 1[2] to be really quite useful, I don't think the recent phenomenon of totalitarianism, which after all entered into history with Lenin and not with imperialism, sheds a lot of light on the subject itself (*sub specie*, looking at Jewish history, for instance). Moreover, I would also suspect (if my memory doesn't fail me) that the anti-socialist thinkers of the nineteenth century, and in particular the "reactionaries" which you take so little account of, saw the totalitarian aspects of unrealized socialism with much greater clarity than did the thinkers on the left. In this context perhaps it would be of great value if you could also explore in its depths the ideological specter of the Communists' liquidation of "cosmopolitanism." One could really do an exemplary dialectical analysis here. It's a pity you didn't closely engage this subject, say in your conclusion, after having done such an excellent job of studying related phenomena.

Are you satisfied with the reception of the book? The only offer of thanks I can give you from my end, in a language you can understand, is my lecture at the Eranos conference I gave last year in Ascona. I'll send it to you right away with this letter.[3]

With JCR, you'll be interested to hear that after long, indescribable torment the microfilm initiative with the government is at last getting under way (though *much* too slowly—there is no hard currency!!).[4] This week Dr. Aloni should be heading out on his first trip to Central Europe and, if possible, mainly Eastern Europe. I've noticed in the most recent protocol that JCR is taking up the project again, after all—provided the Ford Foundation gives the money. Please write and let me know how things stand. For in the best-case scenario you'll have more dollars for the project than us, and it would be good to know what we could do together. (For now our grant totals 15,000 dollars.)

The boxes from Frankfurt and Wiesbaden have finally arrived. In accordance with your agreement and obligation to JCR, for the time being we've given over *six* boxes with the Darmstadt archive material to the archive for an inventory. This information is also for the gentlemen in Cincinnati.

Who will do the distribution of the Baltic books? Shapiro all by himself? I don't want to be the one to complain after the feast, but I don't really believe the books will be used fruitfully in the European countries. The minute we process the books (from Offenbach), people are grabbing the Polish rabbinic literature from our hands. We could use a lot more of the books here. But because we've lost the dice roll, there is no point in complaining.

For the fall agenda, now that Salpeter has left the service of the university, do you think there is any point in nominating a representative to the board of JCR? Or are we going to disband already?

Dear Hannah, don't play tit for tat with me but write back soon, and cut me some slack for mitigating circumstances.

My sincerest thanks and greetings
Your old friend,
Gerhard Scholem

LETTER 94 From Arendt

130 Morningside Drive
July 26, 1951

Dear Gerhard,
I'm writing at once because I'm worried, and because I also know how easy it is, even with the best efforts, not to write. Drop me a line or two after the operation, and don't be annoyed about losing time for work. This sort of thing always pays off in unexpected ways. Tell me honestly if you need anything, and what. Thank-you cards are never necessary. Really, they're not!

I was really delighted by what you wrote about my book, mostly because you came up with a similar critique that I have of the book, just not in relation to anti-Semitism. Anti-Semitism seems to me more important than you think: perhaps not as "origin" (in this respect the book's title is a misnomer, and should have been called "The Elements of Totalitarianism") but as an element injected into its crystallization process.[1] More than anything, it seems to me that with the Jewish Question I can demonstrate the disintegration of the nation-state in Europe better than using anything else. I agree with your criticism of leaving out socialism. I had my reasons for this—first of all, not to end up blowing through the horn of these disgusting ex-communists; second, I wanted to hide my true opinion somewhat behind the curtain.[2] Also, what you write about cosmopolitanism is entirely correct, though the topic can really be illuminated, on the one hand, by a truly fundamental ideological critique of Marxism, and on the other by tracing the factual development of Marxism from Lenin to Stalin. At the moment I'm mulling these things over a little, or rather I'm examining them for the *n*th time. But I don't regret that I'm taking so long even if my hesitation has taken away from the book.[3]

I'm happy to hear about the Eranos lecture because I'm pleased every time you send me something of yours.

JCR: With the Ford Foundation, it is very uncertain. I've gotten to know some fellow with connections, etc. All at once it seemed to me that I couldn't simply let things slide, and so I made the application. It was an awful task, and I worked like a dog on it. Over here, this sort of thing has to be "written beautifully," whatever that means; and it should be as long as possible. Besides this, we are in fact closing up shop. And by the way, all of a sudden around eight hundred books arrived in Nuremberg[4] from the Municipal Library (of Marburg), probably as a result of the decree that we're not even getting any longer in Wuerttemberg-Baden.[5] Meanwhile, while looking through the claims to the individually owned books (there are more than 300 such claims, whereas we always have to find out if a cousin or a nephew is the most closely related), all at once it struck me what sort of extraordinarily valuable things had been privately owned and then more or less simply vanished.

I wrote to Wormann about the Baltic collection. HUL has without any question the old claim of priority. Shapiro can only do something about it once you tell him what you want. Naturally, you won't get all of the rabbinical literature, but in proportion to what we have, you'll get the first choice.

In passing, Baron isn't thinking about completely closing our doors. The organization will continue existing, just without the office. The situation will change, of course, if the Ford Foundation comes through.

All the very, very best. Your old friend,
Hannah

LETTER 95 From Scholem

Ababanel Road 28
October 7, 1951

Dear Hannah,
A lot of time passed before being able to respond to your most delightful letter from July 26. In the meantime, thank God, I'm healthy again; and, as you can see, I can put pen to paper. I have the operation behind me, it's done and over with, and there is no longer cause for worry. For several weeks I lay in a Tel Aviv hospital (because—my rotten luck—the best surgeon in the country isn't on our medicine faculty), and I got the best treatment. Rested and refreshed, now I have every intention of taking up my work again. With all my illnesses, I just have to write off last year as a loss. I feel tip top, and I'm beginning honestly to pay off my debt I owe in letters. It's a good sign. You wrote that I should tell you if I need anything. The truth is that this coming winter we will have some real difficulties, and I would be thrilled if you could send one or two packages like the one in the spring—and don't make it kosher, in fact quite the contrary. I counsel against using the newly introduced quasi-monopolistic service. You'll get a lot more for your money

by just putting things together yourself, like you did in the spring. Along with meat, you could include jam and condensed milk. Tongue and ham is always the best. Sugar and butter wouldn't be bad, either. I think that in the spring we might have an improvement in supplies. But for the moment the situation is wretched. Despite your ban on showing gratitude, I thank you from the bottom of my heart!

I sent you the second lecture at Eranos; please confirm when it arrives. As the sequel to the first lecture, you might have some fun with it. They've invited me to speak again next year. I have half a mind to do so, which I'll combine with a few other exploits. Do you have any plans to travel back to your beloved Paris or to some other Mecca? Then we could do a proper rendezvous. There are some things related to our work for JCR in Germany, and especially in Berlin, which I'd like to share with you confidentially. You shouldn't conclude from my, or our, official silence about the archives that we at the university are sitting on our hands.[1] For the time being I'd like you to be satisfied with this quite positive hint. Officially (and this you should say if asked about it somewhere), the only thing we know is that, for now, we've encountered insurmountable political difficulties in Berlin. I prefer not to mention what we're doing in any official letter to JCR.

We've unpacked the books from the bunker, and among them are some absolutely superb things. The two of us, in particular, can congratulate ourselves on this operation. It is completely unfathomable to me how carelessly such valuable Judaica from Offenbach had been hastily given over to the Germans!

This week Dr. Aloni sets out on his first journey to do the photos for the government.[2] We're afraid that in Eastern Europe the window of opportunity has already closed and that, initially, we'll only be able to take photographs in Western Europe. All because of the accursed budget! How do things look with the Ford Foundation? If something comes of it, I suggest coordinating our efforts.

A few months ago I dug up a brochure from Bruno Bauer[3] from 1862 titled "Jews Abroad." In the scholarship about the development from Hegel to whoever, this article has escaped attention. The brochure from ninety years ago shocked me as a document of undiluted Nazism. A former pupil of mine, who specializes in the Hegelians, wants to write an article about this.[4] Being someone interested in this entire bundle of issues, you should take a look at this fantastic piece of writing, if you can find it in New York.

Have you read Adorno's *Minima Moralia*?[5] What do you say about it? Faced with this production, I find myself in a moral dilemma. If you've seen the book, you'll know what I mean. Should I *thank* him for dedicating it to "Max" and not to Walter B.? Should I be astounded by it? Truly, a strange pack, these people.

Sincerely yours,
Your Gerhard

LETTER 96 From Scholem

Jerusalem, 27th November, 1951
Dr. Hannah Arendt, Exec. Secretary,
Jewish Cultural Reconstruction, Inc.
New York

Dear Hannah,
I did not reply to your last letter regarding the meeting of the Board of Directors which I presume will be the last during its activity.[1] The reason was that I wished to make a sensible suggestion to the agenda. But nothing occurred to me and I think that there is nothing new to be added and the old business must be wound up. Apart from that our friend Dr. Wormann will be in New York and probably attend the meeting and you will thus be able to talk everything over with him.

I regret that the Ford Foundation did not accept your application for a grant to make microfilms of manuscripts, but we had to take this refusal into consideration. I, on my part, can report that the photographing of manuscripts was started from our end. Dr. Aloni is at present in Germany and already started to photograph. Professor Baron will be interested in this. Let us hope that enough foreign currency will be available to continue the work in the next few years so that the more important texts will be available here. Naturally everything depends on the foreign currency question.

There is nothing more for today. I trust to hear from you personally and remain with very best wishes

Yours sincerely,

LETTER 97 From Arendt

January 1, 1952

Dear Gerhard,
I don't even know why I've waited until today before replying to you, so I won't even try to explain. I was immensely relieved to hear that you're feeling well once again. Above all, I want first to thank you for your Eranos lecture. The essay is quite interesting, even if reading it was a little spine tingling. Speculation is one thing, and as long as it remains speculation, one can understand it; but as soon as speculation takes on the actual form of ritual, one experiences a proper shock of just how foreign and strange that world is.[1]

I'm thinking of traveling to Europe at the end of March, and if so then I'll make a quick foray to Palestine. I still don't know when I'd show up, most likely in April or May. When are you planning your trip to Europe? Aren't the Eranos meetings always in August? That would be too late for me. No doubt we'll see one another if I travel to Israel.

As you know, I'm liquidating JCR, and it's costing me more headaches and troubles—maybe because I'm starved for vacation and I'm simply worn out—than the entire story did during my two-and-a-half-year stint. The truth is I'm nearly dying to get back to the peace and tranquility of scholarship. I've got a lot of tomfoolery in my mind, and probably nothing sensible will come out of it. I'm as plagued with ideas as your Kabbalists were with demons. Anyhow, I'll end up with the same things they did.

Dear friend, the letter you wrote about me for the so-called dinner was enthralling and embarrassing. (Had I known the dinner was for me, I would have prevented it from taking place.) I can't reply to it; I don't have the words.[2] With JCR, it was Baron's baby from start to finish, and I didn't do much more than create an organization to carry out what he wanted.

Jonas was here.[3] It was so nice and cheerful to have him around. It did me a lot of good, too, and made me so happy. He's become such a mensch and has plenty of new ideas in his head.

I saw Worman here, and the impression he left me with was one of a good, solid, sensible man. Moreover, he saw to it that we got from you per agreement the lists of books that the university received. All of us here considered that to be a kind of miracle, and we're sincerely grateful.

Baron wants me, once again, to try to get decrees sent out to the other

German states (I had success only in Hesse). Following the decree in Hesse we've already received 3,000 books from the West German library in Marburg, along with a couple ceremonial artifacts. Not yet anything of great importance, but you never can tell what will turn up. I'm not traveling to Germany on behalf of JCR, but I'll nevertheless try to get something done there, especially in Bavaria. I'd also like to see what I could do for you about the archives.

Many congratulations on the Gesamtarchiv. Will the Berlin community cough up its book collections? As you know, it was only by the skin of our teeth we were able to get three hundred Torah scrolls out of them. It cheers me up to think that Auerbach is now sitting behind bars.[4]

So, perhaps we'll see one another soon. Have a good and happy New Year.

Your old friend,
Hannah Arendt

LETTER 98 From Arendt

January 8, 1952
Dr. G. Scholem
Hebrew University Library
Jerusalem, Israel

Dear Scholem,
This is to inform you even before you get the official minutes of the Board of Directors meeting that the microfilm negatives which we made of the Worms Jewish Community Archives and of parts of the Jewish Division of the Worms Municipal Archives have been deposited with the American Jewish Archives, at Hebrew Union College, Cincinnati, on condition that they make available at cost the positives of these archives to all interested libraries.

The costs are very low in this country and I assume that the National Archives in Jerusalem will be interested in procuring positives. Could you kindly inform them and ask them to communicate directly with the American Jewish Archives in Cincinnati, since our organization is more or less "out of business."

Yours,
Hannah

LETTER 99 From Scholem

February 17, 1952

Dear Hannah,
Last week your marvelous package arrived (sent last November), and by the way it was in good condition. Thanks from the bottom of my heart. I can't deny that it came just in the nick of time given the situation here! And it contained all the right items. Admittedly, in the wake of the recent economic and monetary measures, customs duties have been significantly raised. I don't know whether I can and should encourage you to send off another such package.

I was electrified by the news of your trip here, and let us say that with open arms we want you to stay with us. You'll be perfectly at home in a beautiful room. It would be awful for you to have to stay in a hotel. In any event, this is very good news indeed, and I'm counting on some wonderful days with you. I had planned my trip for August and September (I'm supposed to give a talk at Ascona on August 25 on the concept of the Shekhina[1]), but with the current changes in foreign exchange I can only travel if I can count on getting a substantial subsidy from abroad. Originally I had planned to spend a few weeks in Germany and Prague because of books and archives. Do you think JCR could pitch in with some other organization on a grant of between $250 and $500? Given the situation here, I can only squeeze something from my superiors if someone else can pay the lion's share of the costs. I would be very grateful to you if you could be of help.

What are your other plans in Europe? It would of course be lovely if the two of us could meet again.

Would you be interested one of these days in inviting my niece over (the daughter of my dead brother Werner, the ex-communist)? She's written me that she's in the USA doing a guest performance with Laurence Olivier's troupe. She doesn't know a soul and is a very pretty and melancholy twenty-eight-year-old. She goes by the name of Mrs. Renee Goddard (she's already divorced) and can be reached c/o Ziegfeld Theatre 54 Street (or thereabouts) in New York. Perhaps it's worthwhile for you to make her acquaintance. Among all my relatives, she's the one I care most about and find the most likable.

What do you say about Buber's performance over there?[2] Has he managed to make himself incomprehensible? To quote one of our American students writing from there: "Since Pepsi-Cola hit America there was nothing like Buber!"

Apart from this, keep yourself healthy. In my experience, Europe makes one sick. Let me know soon about your plans, and write to me your addresses.

Sincerely,
Your Gerhard

Dear Hannah, I'm so deeply touched by how much you've done to keep us fed that even I am putting pen to paper to give you my warmest thanks. Because according to all signs we are probably on the edge of eschatological times, we are hoping for a corresponding miracle in order to get back on our feet. You'll see everything for yourself when you come.

It would make us so happy if you could be our guest during your time in Jerusalem. The bed in the dining room is awaiting you.

Be well, and send all our greetings to H. Blücher.
Your Fanja

LETTER 100 From Arendt

Basel, April 5, 1952

Dear Gerhard,
I'm not coming. It was impossible to get a seat on the airplane at the right time and for the dates I needed. I can't afford waiting an extra week because all kinds of things require I return to Paris at the end of April. In New York no one warned me, because of Passover, it would be so hard to get a reservation from Rome to Tel Aviv; and I wanted to book the ticket in Paris because the difference in the value of the franc could save me 25–30%, no small sum. So we are not going to see one another, and I'm quite sad about it. When will you be in Europe? Perhaps we can figure something out after all. I'll probably be back here at the end of July. I'll be heading to St. Moritz with Jaspers. Plans are still very uncertain—but there might be a chance.

At the moment, we also can't discuss a JCR subsidy for your trip to Germany. Could you write Baron or me a couple lines detailing what you'd like to do? Wormann made a few hints but then we dropped the whole matter because, anyway, I was going to see you.

I'm floating around happily in the world, and I'm reading as few newspapers as possible. Being in Basel, here with Jaspers, is like an oasis in the desert of time. I haven't been in such high spirits for ages because of the conversations without end, conversations in which you can talk about everything and, in the spirit of freedom, be certain to get a response. There's a lot of back and forth without either one of us trying to force a point, not even with the famous "conclusive evidence."

Yesterday I was in Zurich, at Taubes's and the library there.[1] What do you think about Bredo, the librarian in Zurich?[2] The three communities of Geneva, Basel, and Zurich are somewhat up in arms because of the JCR books. Bredo says he's the only one in Zurich able to make a decent catalogue of the books. *Please*, this is all *entre nous*. It's really none of our business, and we're hardly in the position to do anything anyway. But just for the record, I'd like to hear your opinion. Taubes believes that Basel and Geneva will be very proper in terms of management.

Taubes also told me that Jerusalem has meanwhile received, via Poland, the manuscripts from the Fraenkel Foundation. Is this true? This would be fantastic![3]

Wormann is in Europe already but I haven't heard from him yet. Baron wrote to the presidents of the Hague Conference[4]—Goldmann etc.—about the manuscripts in German possession. Next week I'll meet with Leavitt[5] from JDC either in Paris or the Hague (he phoned here a couple days ago). In case I get the chance, I'll keep you abreast of what's happening.

Be well. Think about how and when we can see one another. Life is short and World History, so-called, is full of unpleasant surprises.

You can reach me until the beginning of May at the American Express in Paris, 11 rue Scribe.

Sincerely, and as always yours,
Hannah

LETTER 101 From Arendt

Hotel d'Angleterre 44 rue Jacob, Paris 6e
April 10, 1952

Dear Scholem,
Sausage, chocolate, and coffee are off, but I wasn't able to get the medicine without a prescription. Moreover, it seems that you've mixed up the name a bit.

I received your lovely letter in Basel.[1] Even though I'm really not at fault for this confusion, or just a little, I have a really bad conscience. Added to this is the natural sadness that for now nothing will come of our reunion. What's happening with your European plans?

All the best to you both, and warmest greetings,
Your Hannah

I can't yet write about anything in detail yet. I just got here and I've yet to see anyone.

LETTER 102 From Arendt

Munich, May 16, 1952

Dear Gerhard,
Between August 7–10 sounds good. Till that point I'll be in St. Moritz and can ramble down from there. I'm so delighted—how wonderful that it'll work out after all.

I'm writing in a rush. This JCR business plus lectures and writing obligations would be too much for a horse. But it's also really lovely to be once again tramping around in the world.[1]

I can't give you an exact address, but so long as I am in Germany, until June 20, you can always reach me in Nuremberg through JRSO, Fuertherstr. 112. After June 20 I'll be in London, where I'll meet up with Baron. Around the first of July I'll be back in Paris for a couple days, and from Paris—to the extent that it's still possible—I'll fly to Berlin. From the middle of July I'll be back in Germany.

In terms of the JCR grant, the best thing to do, it seems to me, is to write Baron directly, and do it quickly.[2] Or then again, perhaps you should wait for Wormann. By the way, working with him was a real joy, and we've struck up a bit of a friendship. I'll probably be seeing him once more before his return. Next week I have to go to Lugano because of the Broch estate,[3] and I'd like to try meeting Wormann in Zurich or Basel.

I have nothing important to report from here. I'm trying to pry loose the archive for you. It's happening, just slowly and with all kinds of entirely unimaginable difficulties.[4] In Munich even candidates for prison hold a lot of power.[5] Munich is pretty much the most unpleasant city I know in Germany.

I wish you all the best and warmest greetings,

Hannah

LETTER 103 From Arendt

Paris, July 3, 1952

Dear Gerhard,

It's so wonderful that things are working out after all. From July 30 you can reach me best in St. Moritz/Engadin, at Prof. Jaspers's Villa Nimet. I'll be there until around August 8. I suggest we meet somewhere over the weekend of the 9–10.[1] When I'm with Jaspers, I don't have a lot of time and it wouldn't be right to meet then. But if you happen to be coming to Engadin anyway, we could perhaps meet in Sils Maria. Write me about your plans and where I can get in touch with you in Switzerland.[2]

In July I'll be hard to reach. Between July 20 and 26 you can probably reach me in Berlin c/o JRSO Fontanestr. 16, Berlin-Dahlem. I'll hardly be doing anything for JCR, and I certainly won't be having any contact with the community. Instead, I'll be delivering lectures and roving around. What I do anyway.

I'm so happy we can see one another again, just don't be irascible! Let's have a couple wonderful days together. We both know we're capable of this.

Greetings to Fanja, and see you soon!

Your old friend,

Hannah

By the way, I got to know George Lichtheim in London.[3] I like the man. Don't forget to pass my greetings on to Wormann!

LETTER 104 From Scholem

Frankfurt
October 1, 1952
Dr. Hannah Arendt
Dr. Hannah Arendt c/o Jewish Reconstruction, Inc.
1841 Broadway,
New York 23, N.Y.

Dear Hannah,
I'm at the end of my Germany trip, and today I'm off to London. Until the 16th you can reach me at Walter Benjamin wife's, c/o Mrs. Dora Morser, Pembridge Crescent, London W. 11. In London I have two main things to accomplish:

1) The business with the German Book Association. Everything has been settled, and there will be a direct contribution to the Hebrew University, with approval from our government.[1] With this there is no need for the other plan that Baron and I cooked up.[2] How much we'll end up getting I can't predict. Anyhow, Lambert calculates it will be 10,000 DM per year, which considering the stinginess of booksellers this is at least something. I have to confess that I had counted on a lot more.

2) In Berlin I had a number of discussions and negotiations, which over time I hope will enable us to get various things out of East Berlin, Schwerin, Magdeburg, and possibly Dresden, as well. It was probably a good thing that I was able to be there myself (I spent 14 days), so I could have direct contact with the relevant people. I'm very grateful to JCR for its help in enabling the trip.

I suggest that, if needed, Baron and you get the Board to vote on a change in the shipping address in Israel. There are technical problems with the address that have caused major spats and months-long delays. Until now, everything has been sent to Dobkin at the Jewish Agency. There is enormous chaos there, and since millions of things are going to that address, no one can find a thing. You know the story of the shipment of Narkiss's pictures.[3] I suggest that future shipments of scholarly materials be sent directly to the Hebrew University library, and all art objects should go to the Bezalel Museum. I would be most appreciative to you if this could be done.

In Berlin I spoke with Fraulein Dr. Von Schwartzkoppen.[4] Her boss was still ill and only showed his face only after I left. She promised to write you directly and tell you what she could find out.

Dr. Moser[5] in Berlin said that the legal advisor of the Berlin Senate had raised juristic doubts on the possibility of the sort of decree we are asking for, both in terms of the JCR's authority and in terms of the formulation of the decree. You can just imagine how I replied to this. First of all, I told Dr. Tuch and Ferencz,[6] who was in Berlin at the time and we had a very pleasant meeting, about this so they could pursue the matter. Dr. Moser said that these doubts had been expressed by their man in the American office in Berlin. If this is true, it is based on a misunderstanding by some minor official and has to be dealt with.

I'm now fresh and fit. Before the trip back to Israel I'm hoping to spend a few days in Paris and then again in Zurich, where I'll be staying with Katzenstein, Mühlebachstr. 140.[7] In Vienna things are moving slowly forward. Shunami is now in Vienna and will let me know if there is any sense in me traveling there before the end of October. If not, I'll be returning to Israel on November 3.

I was awfully happy to spend time with you and hope we'll soon see one another again in Europe or in America, where for me there are some concrete prospects.

Warmest greetings to you and our friend Baron, from your old friend

---

LETTER 105 From Arendt

October 20, 1952
Dr. Gerhard Scholem
28 Abarbanel Road
Jerusalem, Israel

Dear Gerhard,
This is a belated acknowledgement of your letter from Frankfurt, which I showed to Salo and which we both found quite interesting.

I am writing you today in this impersonal manner only to tell you that we already decided that all art objects will again go to Narkiss from now on. Scientific material, by the way, always went directly to the Hebrew University Library.

I almost forgot to tell you about a very unfortunate incident of which I learned in London. The remnants of the Königsberg Jewish Community Archives were found in the state archives in Goslar, which is in the British zone. Dr. Kapralik of the Jewish Trust Corporation informed me that this material will have to be returned to Russia because it originated in Russian territory (sic.). After a few futile arguments on my part, I suggested that at least the material be microfilmed before we part with it for ever. Now Kapralik writes that he expects us to pay for the microfilming, which of course we cannot do. In my opinion, the Jewish Trust Corporation is obligated to have this job done, but if they really refuse to pay for it, maybe the National Archives in Jerusalem could undertake this job. Do you think you can communicate with Dr. Kapralik on this? I am writing him that I would inform you of the state of affairs.

Best regards
Yours
Hannah

LETTER 106 From Arendt

April 9, 1953

Dear Gerhard,
Samburski was here, and I liked the man so much that I'm sending you a quick thank-you for having sent him my way. All at once it seemed like I was back in Zurich and we were sitting together in the circus. How was it at the Eranos conference? Your lecture hasn't yet arrived. For all that, I've sent you a short offprint from Jaspers's Festschrift.[1]

I'm doing well, but that's about all I can say. Here things are rather revolting; and what Samburski rightly liked here (I was happy to see that he had an open mind and noticed things that are good), while not exactly holdouts from the past, are sadly highly endangered achievements.[2] In the process, externally everything will become so quickly normalized that not even the vague inkling people have that "not everything is OK" will remain. This will be especially true if the Russian peace offensive is serious (which this time seems to me possible), that is, if it keeps going for a couple years. Meanwhile, with each passing day this country changes visibly and tactilely, and the power of Mr. McCarthy grows. In short, it isn't fun at all to have to watch this happen.

But, as I said, I'm doing well. I work in peace, I live in peace, and sometimes I even believe I'm coming up with some nice things and am getting a little bit of solid earth under my feet. Such are my pleasures in life, and already quite immodest pleasures at that.

How are things with you? I'm curious to see what will become of the old Mapam.[3] Those people are such idiots that you couldn't put it past them to return, filled with a sense of relief, to old familiar stalls and the familiar pile of manure. Perhaps you're of a different opinion. From the very beginning it seemed to me that the entire story was nothing more than an anti-Zionist—that is to say, anti-Israeli—maneuver with anti-Semitic overtones. I'll change my opinion on this only if the Jews get deported from Moscow.

What are you up to? What are you working on? Of course, Taubes has turned up here, as always duplicitous and shameless and bluffing people with his Levantine cleverness.[4] I've only seen Finkelstein once, and very briefly.[5] What's become of your sort-of-plans? Are you coming here for a year, after all? The Jewish Theological Seminary is exactly one block from our apartment. I've put off all my travel plans until 1955, and so far nothing has changed. I want to make use of a couple years of rest and normality, but any longer than that I won't be able to handle. But for the time being, after the incredible ramble through Europe, this suits me just fine.

Drop me a few lines. I have no clue what you're really up to these days. In the event you have someone such as Samburski on hand, send him my way. Much better would be for you to come in person!

Sincerely, and in friendship,
Your Hannah

LETTER 107 From Scholem

May 24, 1953
Jerusalem

Dear Hannah,
Your letter from April 9 made me very happy, and if I failed to reply right away it was because I thought I might be able to mention the prospect of a rendezvous in the USA. There was this possibility of an exchange professorship for a year in which someone from the university was supposed to head to America, and I was one of two candidates. But now we are in the end of May and no decision has come from Wellington. I'm assuming that nothing will come out of it. I mentioned, among other places, Columbia as a place where there might be interest in having me (for free! Our State Department pays

for everything). But I don't have the impression that anything is moving; otherwise, Baron would surely have written about it in March. Upshot is that we'll probably have to postpone our next rendezvous. JTS is hardly the right place for me. All they want is for me to go to California on their behalf; this they really want.[1] But for New York, I'm too radical for them. And I have no desire to head off to California. This year we'll have to make do with around six weeks in Switzerland, and for the one Eranos lecture (in August) they've invited us for the entire time. *Just now* I've received the offprint of my first lecture there.[2] I'm sending it to you today through the post as printed matter. It might be of interest to you as, say, an in-depth introduction into the history of a symbol. I've packed a lot into it. Now I'm working on the next lecture, on the history of the Golem. ("Do you know how Scholem goes? God! What the Golem knows!" With this limerick, I'll conclude!)

This year I've been up to my ears in apocalyptic literature. If, as I wrote, nothing comes of the trip to the USA, I'll take an 8–9-month sabbatical beginning in the summer of '54 or winter of '54–55. I'll then try to wrap up my large tome on Sabbatianism. If I get some money, I'll sit myself down in some small European town with a library, where I can write without any interruptions for six months.

I'm so pleased you liked Samburski. Last week his daughter (she's around 25 years old) left for New York for one or two years. She's a very shy but nice example of a Sabra,[3] a woman with a Mapam education who is still very indecisive. She also has no clue about the world. Shall we suggest she make contact with you? (If yes, call up Saul Liebermann, whose wife is her cousin. He'll give you her address.)

I see that a memorial book has come out on Starr.[4] Have you already sent me a copy? May I ask for one? Send my warmest greetings to Baron.

Sincerely,
Your Gerhard

LETTER 108 From Arendt

August 15, 1953

Dear Gerhard,
Just a quick and warm hello as a reply to your letter, and above all thanks for the "Shechinah," which I just finished reading. It is a wonderful essay, clear and deep and very thought provoking. I'm completely enraptured by it, and

I wish we could have some of you here. Maybe one of these days you'll decide to write something more general, from this field of experience, about the "Revolt of the Images."

What astounded me the most, and which becomes so evident here, is what has remained unnoticed within our tradition and as such has only been expressed through the "Revolt of the Images." And therefore it really doesn't matter if we're talking about the Jewish or the Christian tradition. When your attention is turned to what gets left out, the orthodoxies are more similar than people realize. I mean by this, in essence, the "Life" of God, the *processus dei*, which is the inversion of the Aristotelian conception according to which everything dynamic (in the original double meaning of power and possibility) has no reality, only *potentia*. Through Hegel this then flowed into conceptual philosophy.

One last question: "God's dwelling place" surely can't mean the "Omnipresence of God." Doesn't it mean that God cannot be everywhere and all-present to the extent that he dwells and lives in the world? Or?

Has anything changed in your USA plans? I haven't seen Finkelstein[1] for ages. In September he's planning on moral renewal of the world (moral awakening!) and what's stupid is that somehow he roped me into discussions on the subject. I'm furious but I can't do anything about it now.

I'm absorbed in work, and I'm writing what seems to me to be a sort of book on the modern challenge to tradition. First I'm doing a lecture series on the subject at Princeton.[2] I'm doing well, even if I'm losing more and more contact with most people here—partly because of politics (this McCarthy business is serious and the differences run very deep), and partly because people don't have any sense for philosophical questions, while in my old age I'm naturally returning to my beginnings, which is only fitting.[3]

There's a chance I'll be heading off to India in the winter of 54–55, and on the return journey I'll stop off in Israel.[4] For now it's all rather vague, but at least there's a real possibility. Besides this, Heinrich and I have plans for an extensive trip to Italy and Greece, a trip that would culminate in a visit to you, or at least if I have anything to say about it (I dare not even raise my hopes too high). But this is all too far away: you should come here first.

By now you must have gotten a copy of Starr's memorial volume; it was already sent out. Baron has plans again to raise money for the microfilming of archives. If something comes of it, I'll let you know. Otherwise, the office is dead, dead just not buried. Incidentally, we've gotten "decrees" throughout the entire American zone.[5]

Greetings to your wife, and to Samburski
and Wormann. Be well, and much love,
In friendship,
Your Hannah

LETTER 109 From Scholem

December 18, 1953

Dear Hannah,
I only received your letter from August upon our return from Switzerland, where this time I was alone with my wife, and I want to thank you so much for it. Hopefully you'll enjoy my latest European concoction. Next spring "The Golem" will come out as an Eranos lecture; another essay, on the Christian kabbalist Pico (you can read it in German!) will appear in the Baeck Festschrift; and a third major work of mine was just included in the *Revue de l'histoire des religions*.[1] This one I'm sending you together with this letter as printed material. The translation into French (it is a detailed look at Sabbatianism in Poland), which enables you to read it, was a truly selfless act of friendship by Georges Vajda in Paris. The original I wrote in Hebrew.

The news from my end is that *nothing* is going to come out of the America trip, whereas I've been given the opportunity to spend my sabbatical half-year in Europe, and there I'd like to sit undisturbed for six or seven months and work on my opus. It's still unclear, and still under discussion, if we'll go to England or Switzerland (say, Oxford, London, or Bern, a city I have a real soft spot for). Copenhagen would also be not bad at all (and cheap!). So those are the options from around April 1 to the beginning of November. You could meet us again, this time in Israel, in the spring of 1955. Leo Strauss will be here at the time, for ten months.

In order not to be diverted from my work (not to mention being the director of the Judaic Institute) I have to leave Jerusalem, otherwise I'll get nothing out of the vacation, and what I'll have least of all is concentration. My papers are already stacked up far too high.

What you say about the seriousness of the McCarthy business is cause for reflection. Are there major differences even in your circle of friends? How so?

I've received the Starr memorial book, and many thanks.

As for your question: "God's" dwelling, as such, does *not* need to mean omnipresence. There is an *additional* thesis according to which this dwelling everywhere A) *occurs* or b) *can* occur.

My warmest greetings,
Your old friend Gerhard

LETTER 110 From Arendt

July 8, 1954

Dearest Gerhard,
The office just forwarded me your letter, and yesterday morning I got your Golem essay.[1] Oh, what is wrong with me! I've been meaning to write to you for so long, and every time nothing has come of it. One reason is that I'm irritated at you for not coming here, despite all the hopes you raised in Zurich. Another reason is that I've sometimes thought that I'll soon be traveling to Europe. As you know, there's no chance of that now. The Claims Conference, based no doubt on some kind of intrigue, has rejected our application; in September we'll definitely be resubmitting. I have no idea what will happen if, God forbid, the application gets approved after all.[2] By that point I won't be in the position to worry about it. Early next year I'm heading off to a university in California for a semester, in which case I'll scarcely be able to manage an additional absence from home. This was the reason I turned down the idea of spending an entire year in California.

I read "The Golem" with the greatest pleasure. It is so enormously enjoyable to get both history *and* essence without the modernistic nonsense and the superficial fantasies of the Master Interpreters.[3] I'll send you something that might amuse you—I hope I haven't already sent it. It's the first part of a lecture series I held last fall at Princeton.[4]

À propos lectures, at one such lecture at Harvard I met Mr. Taubes. He introduced himself as my intimate friend. In the most recent edition of the *Partisan Review*, which just came out and where he presented his thoughts on mythology (I haven't read it), he described himself like this: "Teaches social philosophy (sic!) at the HU, Jerusalem, and is now in the Un. States on a Rockefeller fellowship."[5] Do you want to put an end to his game, or are you not interested? He hasn't changed his methods. In his mind there isn't a person on earth who can't be won over through the most vulgar flattery. And he's right about a very high percentage of people.

Everything here is becoming less and less pleasant. (Which has been, of course, one of the chief reasons behind my long silence.) You must be following almost everything in the newspapers, but you probably can't imagine how the atmosphere is changing nearly by the day. But we're doing well. During the winter I really worked hard, and now I'm inclined to lounge around for a spell. For this reason we're heading to Chestnut Lawnhouse in Palenville, NY, till about September 1. Afterwards Heinrich has to go back to the College and the New School. *À propos,* you must know that Jonas is coming to New York, to the New School's graduate faculty of philosophy.

Now something serious: What's happening with your Sabbatai Zvi book that is already finished in Hebrew but has never come out in a European language? By chance, a couple days ago I discussed the book with Kurt Wolff, and he's of the opinion that Bollinger would consider it both an honor and a pleasure to pay for the translation costs and to get the book out.[6] (These two things, translation and publication, should be kept separate. The first would be taken care of through a grant, and the grant has nothing to do with the publishing the book. This separation is advantageous because of royalties!!) What do you think? Years ago, when you were in New York, you said that you needed nothing more than a secretary for you to dictate your entire bag of tricks—into English or German. My dear friend, don't let this matter simply slide. Pull yourself together and think hard about this. Let me know if I can help.

Once again to the question of the Golem study: at the beginning, you mention the relationship to Adam, and you distance yourself somewhat from the telluric implications of *Adam-adamah.* Above all, you say that the "servant" idea in the Golem is quite late. I have a question. It states explicitly in Genesis that Adam was created in order to look after the earth. Here, then, the telluric element already seems connected to "service," if not, of course, in the sense of the Golem story.[7] I've always been interested in this passage, for a different reason. People normally think that work is somehow connected to the expulsion from paradise; but it seems to me that work, in the sense of tillage, is implied in the creation story from the very beginning. According to the text, the only difference after the expulsion is that work became arduous and difficult.[8]

Write a few lines about how things were for the two of you in London. Please, no revenge! Are you traveling again to the Eranos conference?

Warmest greetings to you and Fanja,
Your Hannah

LETTER 111 From Scholem

August 3, 1954

Dear Hannah,
In the evening, when I'm tired, I lose all desire for writing, especially when I've already been scribbling all day. This might be the one chance for movie houses to convert me back into being a fan and lure me over to the movies for some relaxation. (But there's no longer anything happening with this art form, and so for many years in Jerusalem I'm staying home!)

I'm using the bank holiday to thank you for your lovely letter. I can only hope to succeed, as you praise me for doing, at carrying out the scope of work for my book. You're mistaken here: the Hebrew is far from finished. Sabbatai Zvi is, at this very moment, emerging out of the fog of London, just in Hebrew.[1]

It's turning out to be a long book, and I'm not at all sure I can wrap it up during this holiday, as I had hoped.

After fifteen years of unbelievable mining and nosing around, I've amassed so much fantastical material that I can scarcely use any of my earlier manuscripts and drafts, and nearly everything has to be completely rethought. Seeing that the Bollinger made possible the completion of *this* part of the book, I really doubt if I can go back to them for the translation into English (which is probably going to be endlessly complicated). They gave me a grant that I then (as planned) used for this work. The awful fact is that the only European language I could dictate the book into would be German. Even the Hebrew text takes me forever because I'm always seized by major inhibitions whenever I begin formulating something for the so-called minor immortality. At any rate, whatever happens I'm not going to take a break until I put the manuscript into shape, however long it takes, into the coming year if need be. This is my primary concern. Naturally, you'll say that in works of scholarship of such scope, history overshadows what is essential (which can be expressed in far fewer words than history can). That is in my book, in fact, the nub of the matter!

I'm going to Eranos, even if I won't be speaking because, like an idiot, it occurred to me too late that I have a finished essay on the topic Man and Transformation, just under a different title!!!! It's one of my lectures from 1949.[2] Next year I'll certainly give a talk.

With Taubes, the only thing to be said is that I will not have anything to do with him. It is easy to be a genius at other people's (spiritual) expense, and I can't congratulate him on this sort of career after I've already told him what I think about him.[3] I think he's better suited for America than he is here with us. He'll introduced himself to Jonas as my friend—please, *WARN* Jonas on my behalf. But he'll probably end up winning Jonas over anyway.

As far as I can recall, since the Middle Ages some interpretations of Genesis regarded agricultural work as part of the original task in paradise. You are completely correct that telluric service is a part of this story. I was just being overly cautious—I had been reading too much philology of the Near East.

I can't say much of anything about London. I see nothing outside the four walls of my workspace here among the Warburg people.

Next year I'll decide whether in two years I'll be going to the US after all, for the entire academic year (9 months). (The idea is to be in a quiet place to write something again without constant diversions.) I'm certain everything will work out. This is the only *conceivable*, practical plan I have for a trip to the USA.

From the 15–28 of August we will be in Ascona, and afterwards we'll be back in London until October 28, c/o Warburg Institute.[4]

Warmest greetings
Your old friend,
Gerhard

LETTER 112 From Scholem

Jerusalem[1]

My dear Hannah,
Since my plans for the summer seem to be getting clearer, I want to write a few lines in order to make sure that we see each other in case this summer you'll be in Europe (as you wrote last year), or even in Israel. For me, it would mean a lot. Until August 15 I'll be in Jerusalem; Zurich until around August 22; and then I'll be in Ascona at the Eranos conference until September 1. Afterward, I'll be on vacation for around ten days in Sils Maria. From there I'll mostly be in Germany until the end of September, especially, as is expected, if the edition of Benjamin's writings (which is finally coming out with Suhrkamp) will be out around the end of September. I had planned on

returning earlier to Israel to finish up my book, but then I received from the University of London a highly prestigious invitation to deliver two or three lectures, and I want to accept.[2] If I end up delivering these lectures, I would be in London until around October 16, and from there I'd fly back to Jerusalem directly. In the unlikely case the lectures are not until early next year, I'd be finished up here in Europe at the *beginning* of October. The question is, Where are you? Could you make your trip to Israel when I am back there? And if not, in which train station in Europe could we meet? As you can see, I've given you my details so we won't miss one another. Please, give this some thought and write me what you're thinking. I'm most likely traveling alone this year. I only hope you don't end up coming to Israel during one of our heat waves!

All in all, things are going quite well here. But there's no way the world will be standing much longer (standing still, at least).

I wish you all the best,
Your old friend,
Gerhard

LETTER 113 From Arendt

Berkeley
May 28, 1955

Dear Gerhard,
I'm writing immediately upon receiving your letter, which followed me here. I've been working here during the spring semester as a professor of political science, and I'll be back in New York at the middle of next month.[1] I've been meaning to write you for a long time, but I keep putting it off. Here at the end of the semester I'm swept up into this fantastic whirlwind. It's hard for me to fend off the students. I don't know how one does it—and I don't want to learn. It's been devilishly fun. With no attention to curriculum, I've been able to do precisely what I wanted, at least in political theory. What I've noticed, even given my tendency of coming out with rubbish, is that I can still count on my ability to reach out for direct contact.

In the middle of the hustle and bustle—and that's what it is—I received an invitation to Milan to attend the International Congress for Freedom, which is from September 12–17.[2] Of course, I accepted at once. Now things are starting to move. It's possible that I'll travel to Italy a couple days early and check out Venice. After the seventeenth I'll head to Rome for a week, and then for the highlight of the trip it'll be on to Athens and Greece for about 2 1/2 weeks—and from there, to Israel. If everything works out the way I think, hope, and plan, I'll be in Israel for 2–3 weeks in October. Afterward, I'll fly to Basel, Germany, possibly London, and then back home, where I'm thinking of arriving around the first half of December. *Voilà!!!*

According to the plans you described, we should best meet in Jerusalem. And so in the second half of October I'll presumably, or certainly, be there. Yes?

Until June 15 you can reach me at the Women's Faculty Club, 2200 College Avenue, Berkeley 4, California. And then I'll be at my New York address: 130 Morningside Drive, New York 27, N.Y.

It was lovely to see your handwriting again, dear Gerhard. It's wonderful that I'll see you again soon. But for now, I can't write—the above I've written just to give you my dates.

As always,
Your Hannah

My greetings to Fanja

LETTER 114 From Scholem

June 5, 1955

Dear Hannah,
I'm answering you by return post. Chances are that during the second half of October I'll be back in Jerusalem. If the University of London pushes back my lectures to October 10–17 (I haven't yet received a reply to my request), then I won't be back until around the twentieth, but we'll still have a couple days to meet. To counter any unexpected developments, I'd therefore like you to give some serious thought to accepting my proposal: at the beginning of September fly to Zurich and come to Sils Maria for at least 2–3 days. I've already made reservations September 3–15 at the Hotel Alpenrose. It would be easy for you to go directly from there either to Milan or Venice. This way we'd be sure to have a comfortable environment. I'd be *immensely* delighted if you could make this change in your travel plans.

Auf, Torrera!!!

No one invited me to Milan[1] this year (last year I got an invitation to

Hamburg but declined). This year I'd go if I had the chance. From Sils I'll head to Germany and from there to Paris. I'll stay in Israel until August 16 or 17.

Warmest greetings and auf Wiedersehen,
Your Gerhard

Fanja has traveled down to Tel Aviv for a couple days.

LETTER 115 From Arendt

New York,
July 1

Dear Gerhard,
I'm now starting to make my arrangements. Though it would be very, very lovely to meet in Sils Maria, I just can't make it. You know how complicated it is to get there via Zurich, and I'm flying directly from here to Milan. I have to use the trip to get to know Italy a bit. You see, this will most likely be my last big trip for years, not because of money but because of time. I'll probably have to buckle down at my writing desk for a couple years if I want to accomplish what's swimming around in my head, and what I began presenting in outline form at Berkeley. And because I want to write about the world, that is to say, about the public-political world, I especially want to take a good look at an aspect of the world—its beauty—which afterward I won't have very much to do with.[1]

I can fly out of here around the first of September, and by the following day, via Milan, I can be in Venice. And since you are of the opinion that it is so easy to go up to Sils Maria, why don't you come down to Venice? How's that for an idea? But please, write at once so I can make arrangements. I don't know yet where I'll be staying, but by that point I certainly will. I know of a lot of good, small hotels. Think about Venice—but you've probably been there already. But what difference does that make? *Dis kai tris to kalon* was a famous Greek saying.[2]

One way or another, auf Wiedersehen. If everything goes the way I want, I'll be in Israel on October 7 and will stay until the twenty-eighth, a full three weeks.

I've been back here for a week, and I'm slowly beginning to unwind. We'll be once again in Palenville in August, as it's already starting to get really hot here, which doesn't really bother me too much but is grueling for Heinrich.

Gerhard, just think how beautiful Zurich was—and come down to Venice!

Your Hannah

Greetings to Fanja

LETTER 116 From Scholem

July 11, 1955

Dear Hannah,

I'm afraid that this business of seeing one another again in Europe is not going to happen. During the month of September, Venice (or, for that matter, Milan) isn't the place for someone looking to cool down. After Eranos I want to have some rest and relaxation up in the mountains. Yes, I admit that the road from Zurich to Venice via Engadin isn't the easiest, and I can't blame you for not wanting to take it. What a shame! But I'm even more worried about October!! I'll be coming to Israel only on October 18/19 or on the 22nd, which means that if you arrange to spend your *final* days in *Jerusalem*, we'll *just barely* manage to work things out.[1] Fanja (who's at the moment in bed with a foot ailment) has asked me to say that in case you're in Jerusalem you could also stay with us *earlier*, and you're warmly invited. You'll have the library all to yourself without being bothered by a librarian.

Be *very* quick with the reservation for the flights: around that time of year everything gets filled up, and I really don't want you to find out too late (like last time) that you can't get a seat. So reserve a spot, it's *not* too early. (The same goes for the return flight.)

Sincerely,
Your Gerhard

LETTER 117 From Scholem

Jerusalem
January 21, 1956

Dear Hannah,
By now you must be back from the Old World, and you're getting down to do some new work. I hope you enjoyed your trip. Right in front of me sit two heavy memories of you: the German version of *Origins of Totalitarianism* and your edition of Broch's essays.[1] The formulations in your magnum opus are much more splendid in German, I think (which isn't surprising given my linguistic affinities). Everything is so precise, and I sense I wouldn't lose a thing by taking up the book again and reading through.

I'm very eager to read the Broch essays; until now I haven't had the time.[2] I'm busy preparing the first volume of my opus on Sabbatai Zvi for publication. It'll come out in the spring, and it's absorbing all of my free time. I'm afraid I'll have a lot of inhibitions with the Broch book. For me, he has some particularly annoying idiosyncrasies of style that don't make the reading any easier. (For instance, the inversion of the genitive, which for my taste is a really awful habit among philosophers.) From your very loving and penetrating introductory essay I can tell I have a lot to look forward to. For all this, I am most grateful to you.

In Germany did you hear anything about the reception of the two volumes of Walter Benjamin's works?

It'll be decided soon if I'll be going to America next fall or if the entire project will be buried. I'll let you know.

For now, all the best
Your old friend,
Gerhard

LETTER 118 From Scholem

April 1, 1956
(This is no April Fool's Day prank!)

Dear Hannah,
Alea jacta est,[1] that is to say, I've accepted the invitation from Brown University for the academic year 1956/7. Fanja and I will settle down in Providence in September. On the flight there, and maybe at some other point, there will possibly be a stopover in New York. There shouldn't be any lack of opportunity. We hope that you won't be in India, Tibet, or California at the time. We'll be going to New York, say, between September 5 and 10. Will you still be up in the mountains on summer vacation?

I'd like (or need) to earn some money but will have very little time to do so. If by chance you hear of someone needed to deliver highly paid, short lectures, think about me.

My opus Sabbatai Zvi vol. 1 goes to print this month.[2] If I can, I'll work on vol. 2 (continuation until Frank) in the USA.[3] Perhaps I'll also find an English translator. It is a very extensive book.

I was delighted to hear that the Leo Baeck Institute has picked up the rights to your Rahel manuscript.[4]

We're having here a harsh cold snap to prepare us for the winter in America.

With no takers I'm looking for someone in Israel (after all the hubbub) who'll make a bet with me on war.[5] What this shows is how, in the end, everyone believes that nothing is going to happen. And so I remain "betless."

How are things with you? I suggest you honor me with your New York telephone number so I can give you a call.[6]

With love, from Fanja too.
Your Gerhard

LETTER 119 From Scholem

Tuesday, October 7, '58

Dear Hannah,
By sheer coincidence I stumbled across the *Börsenblatt*, and I read your and Jaspers's excellent, or should I say magnificent, speeches in Frankfurt.[1] I had no idea you were in the region. I'm writing out of the blue to give you my greetings and thanks, but also, in case you're still around, to try to see if we could perhaps meet here or in Basel. I'm now at the Hotel Urban on Stadelhoferstrasse in Zurich. Tomorrow I'm delivering a lecture, and I'll be heading back to Israel in eight days, on October 15 at night.[2] (My telephone number is 32-70-52.) Perhaps we're due for a miracle and might see one another!

If these lines reach you in Basel, give my regards to Jaspers.

Best wishes,
Your Gerhard

LETTER 120 From Scholem

Jerusalem
December 26[1]

Dear Hannah,
I was so delighted to receive within a *single* week: 1) both of your books from Piper Verlag, 2) your opus magnum *The Human Condition*, and 3) news from a newspaper report of your appointment as professor at Princeton.[2] No one can digest so much good news in such a short period of time. I'm going to have to set aside a free evening for the reading of the *Philosophicum*. (It seems to read very well.) My warmest thanks and congratulations for your accomplishment and distinction! What exactly will you be teaching to the youngsters at Princeton? I assume it'll be political philosophy, where you'll be able to say whatever you consider important. Are you moving away from New York? (I can hardly imagine it!)

Let me at least know if you have any trips planned for Europe, where and when and how. Maybe we'll manage to have a couple days together.

Meanwhile, I'm writing away on the continuation of my gigantic novel on Sabbatai Zvi and whatever goes along with it. In the course of this study, maybe I'll succeed in making my way to Poland, but who knows what this summer will bring.

Warmest greetings to you and Blücher
Your old friend, Gerhard

LETTER 121 From Arendt

June 27, 1959

Dear Gerhard,
Your "Ten Unhistorical Sentences" are in my opinion among the loveliest things you've ever written.[1] The essay on the "Righteous" also just arrived and I've begun reading it. It's really beautiful to see the way you transform things back into ideas after you've already turned ideas entirely into things. So thanks!

But today I'm writing mostly because of the business with Benjamin. Cohen wrote that you don't want to write the introduction.[2] I really don't understand this because this is really something you should do—which in no way means I couldn't. But, without question, you have the priority, and from every angle, not just due to chronology. Cohen seems to think that you will do the selection only if I write the introduction. I replied to him, of course, that I would write it if you don't. And if you think you don't want to do it now, you'll naturally change your mind after you begin making the selection. I didn't say this to Cohen—he doesn't care who writes the introduction, you or me. When he mentioned it to me the first time, my immediate response was that this was something Scholem should do. I didn't say this because I was trying to pressure you.

I think this letter will reach you while you're still in Israel. How long will you be in Europe this time? I hear from Moses that there will be a meeting of the Leo Baeck Institute.[3] Regrettably, I won't be able to attend, for I'll be traveling to Europe at a later point. I have to be in Hamburg during the last week of September, and I'll most likely tramp around Europe for most of October.[4] Maybe, or even probably, I'll also be in London. Maybe we can meet up. It would be lovely!

Warmest greetings and in old friendship,
Your Hannah

LETTER 122 From Arendt

July 2, 1959

Dear Gerhard,

This is just a "p.s." to my letter from a couple days ago. Alan Stroock[1] from the American Jewish Committee called me up today. An Israeli by the name of Itzhak Norman approached the Committee with plans to create a sort of Israeli *Partisan Review*. He similarly dropped in to see me in order to stir up my interest in the project. The Committee is interested and is, in principle, prepared to help. I think the plan is a good one. The question—the main question—is of course what sort of fellow he is. What we know here is that he was the secretary of the cultural foundation, or something along those lines. (I don't know this for sure, but the others do.) The information I got from a close acquaintance of mine wasn't at all flattering, and my own impression of the man isn't very positive. I said none of this to Stroock but instead acted as if I knew next to nothing in order not to sabotage the project through flippancy. I told him we would have to make some inquiries. He has no idea who to ask. I promised I would write you and so, *voilà*! Decisive, of course, is what Israeli intellectuals think about him. Whether the country's most important writers would trust him, etc. Naturally, people here will treat whatever you say with the greatest discretion.

I thank you in advance,
Sincerely yours,
Hannah

LETTER 123 From Scholem

July 10, 1959

Dear Hannah,

I was so pleased to get your letter. I hope we'll see each other, if around October you're able to steer your movements to be in the same place and the same time as me. From September 30 to October 5 Fanja and I are in Stockholm; from October 5–13 in Uppsala; in Copenhagen from about 18–25; and then probably before November 1 we are in Zurich for a few days. Maybe you'll be in Switzerland, or in Basel, around the same time.

I'll be here in Jerusalem until August 13. We then head off for Ascona and, after the meeting in London, it's on to Poland, where we'll be tracking down some Frankist manuscripts.[1] From Poland we travel to Sweden. After we leave Jerusalem, until August 31 our address is Hotel Tamaro, Ascona.

I'll reply straight off to your discreet inquiry regarding Y. Norman. I can give you both my own unambiguous opinion and that of every other serious *homme de lettres* I know in Israel: Y[itzchak] N[orman] is a bag of hot air, and the hot air streams out of him in an endless gush of words. I've never experienced anything from him beyond catchphrases and towering heaps of verbiage. His gravitas as an author is zero. His reputation rests exclusively on the fact he is related closely to the very rich founder of the Norman foundation (I think it's now called the American Foundation for Israeli Cultural Institutions). He's the Israeli representative. The deceased Norman (he was the husband of Dorothy N, whom you must know) depended on him as his Hebrew cousin. But people neither trust nor respect him. The reputation he has here is one of an uncommonly efficient gramophone. Personally, I barely know him; a few years ago I saw him once or twice in passing. As a "doer" and a Hebrew author, he's well known as someone who instead of writing one sentence will write three pages. After receiving your letter, I buttonholed three very well-regarded and responsible writers—I met them yesterday at the twenty-fifth anniversary of Bialik's[2] death—pulled them to one side and asked each one separately about the man. All were of the same opinion: he's full of ideas, he's just incapable of accomplishing a thing.

I've decided to agree to Cohen's suggestion that I do the selection for the W. B. volume; the introduction, however, I cannot do. I said explicitly that I consider you to be an excellent choice to write a proper introduction for American readers. So don't worry about me. The two of us will work together quite well. In case we end up meeting, we could discuss the matter.

All the very best,
Your old friend Gerhard

LETTER 124 From Scholem

July 21, 1959

Dear Hannah,

Piper Verlag sent me the book on Rahel, as your personal gift.[1] With my gratitude for the book, I recall the first time I read the manuscript and how it survived your flight through safekeeping with me in Jerusalem. These are pleasant memories, though mixed with bitter memories of Schocken. I have to repeat once again what a pity it is that your magnificent book, which is really about the darker traits among us German Jews, wasn't published twenty years ago when it should have been. But even today the book will invoke all kinds of mental associations, even though the curtain has already been drawn in the middle of the final act of this tragic play. Yesterday, just like today, I read again much of your book—since it's in English, *a priori* I couldn't take it in—and I am very impressed with the direction you take the story. Isn't it curious that in these weeks, of all times, I've been spending my free time reading, and continue to read, Varnhagen's memoirs?[2] These memoirs for me are an exceedingly important document for understanding the group of Jews Rahel was raised among. (Almost half of the volumes deal with these families, mostly by concealing their Jewish heritage, which makes the books even more instructive.)

Just in passing, I don't want to discount the possibility that Varnhagen's literary estate, like so many other collections, was transferred to Schlesien and is now in Warsaw (or was deposited in Wroclaw).[3] As I've told you, we're traveling to Poland on September 12. While I'm there, perhaps I can make inquiries about its whereabouts.

In case you will be heading north from Hamburg, we would see one another in Stockholm on September 1. In any event, I'm giving you my addresses:

Sept. 1–5 Stockholm, Hotel Gillet

Sept 5–13 Uppsala, also the Hotel Gillet

Otherwise, we always have Switzerland. We'll be in Zurich between October 25–30. It would be a real pity if we don't manage to cross paths.

Warmest greetings,

Your Gerhard

LETTER 125 From Arendt

July 29, 1959

Dear Gerhard
Thanks for your letter. Yes, with Rahel you are no doubt right. Twenty years too late. I only doubt whether I would have found a publisher for this book twenty years ago. Jews are all secretly of the opinion that I'm an anti-Semite. They don't see how much I liked Rahel when I was writing the book, they don't understand how one can both be friendly and tell the truth, to oneself for instance. For this reason these gangs never understood Heine. What undoubtedly made Heine even harder for them, on top of everything else, was his ability to laugh at everyone. I have the secret suspicion that in Germany nothing was so sacred among Jews and non-Jews as the so-called Life Lie.[1] One of these days someone should illustrate how in Germany the petty bourgeois Life Lie fused with the Jews' unique political and social position. If at all possible, this should be done with a bit of humor directed at the facts themselves as well as at the people affected.

I have a question regarding the meeting in London:[2] I don't know what you think, but I'm of the opinion that one should leave Rudolf Borchardt alone.[3] The follow is simply too pathological to be representative of anything. He is of course unbelievably talented, with nearly half a dozen *very* beautiful poems to his name. But if one wanted to tell the truth here, one would really have to start lying. And I am very much against not telling the truth and fudging things.

Meeting up. I have to go from Berlin to Hamburg, and from there most likely I'll head via Frankfurt to Switzerland or perhaps (for a week) to Italy. It seems to me very likely that I'll be in Switzerland at the end of October. In which case I'll probably be in Basel and can drop by. Write me your address in Zurich. It's always best to reach me via Jaspers in Basel (Austrasse 126).

Warmest greetings to you and Fanja,
Hannah

LETTER 126 From Arendt

370 Riverside Drive, New York 25, NY
November 3, 1960

Dear Gerhard,
I hadn't yet thanked you for your wonderful essay on Jewish messianism—and then the Kabbalah gets washed ashore.[1] I had been so hoping we could meet in New York so I could tell you what marvelous work you've done in the messiah essay. Siegfried Moses told me about Fanja's illness. I hope everything has turned out well. Give her my warmest greetings. Your work is becoming ever better, and there are few things I read with such relish.

Nanda Anshen asked me for your "Messiah" essay;[2] she apparently intends on publishing it in her series. I'll hand it over to her as a loan: I assume you have no problem with this. For myself, I'm going to take a dive into the Kabbalah.

I've also taken the liberty of sending you the German edition of my *Vita Activa*, although I believe you've already received the English version, *Human Condition*. I would have gladly written a friendly dedication but the publisher mailed it to you directly from Germany.

It is not out of the question that next year I'll be heading to Israel, as I'd like to "amuse" myself with the Eichmann trial.[3] A local magazine will make this possible. If you happen to hear from a reliable source about when the trial begins, and how long it'll last, it would be nice of you to share the information with me. This state of "not knowing anything precisely" is really exasperating because I have all sorts of commitments that, if worst comes to worst, I'm prepared to cancel—but, of course, I don't want to cancel things for no reason.

Warmest greetings,
Your Hannah

Pardon me for this disgusting letter: dictated—I just wrote it finally to give you a sign of life. It would be lovely to see you again. H.

LETTER 127 Jerusalem

November 28, 1960

Dear Hannah,
Your letter from the third of November, which you described as "disgusting," nevertheless provided me with a great deal of amusement. I flatter myself that my work on the messianic idea would hit the bull's-eye with you and a number of others. I hope you will have the opportunity to cite me. I sent a copy of the essay to Nanda so that she can ascertain whether it is of interest to her and to her Christian and Jewish readers and their "universal" concerns. Once more I am "too Jewish," which of course does not bother me in the least. Meanwhile I hope that you have lovingly read your way through the Kabbalah volume, in particular the chapter on the meaning of the Torah. Its philosophical implications will not have escaped you. These thoughts were in fact the source of Walter Benjamin's attraction to the Kabbalah, insofar as I was in a position to explain them to him during my youth (when I was guided intuitively, rather than through learning).

Yesterday a friend of mine received a copy of your *Vita Activa*; my own should be on its way. You'll have the opportunity to write me a personal dedication here in Jerusalem, as you in fact planned. This brings me to your travel plans. According to an official statement, the trial should begin on the sixth of March, if no new events cause yet another delay. This was announced here a week ago, so plan accordingly! It's also important for you to come in March if you want to see me. At the beginning of April, at the latest, I'll be in London for about six months. There I will finish writing a more or less immortal book on the development of the Kabbalah, something I owe the world of scholarship and which will appear in both German and English.

The volume of Walter Benjamin's correspondence is coming together. Please check to see if you have any letters. If anything turns up, please send me the original or two copies. I would be most grateful if I could include his letters to you. Naturally, most letters have disappeared. Ernst Bloch finally explained that he had destroyed all letters from Walter Benjamin immediately after receiving them, and had done so "out of principle." This is what I call utopian principles.

If you want to do me a favor, send me the issue of *Life* magazine containing Eichmann's confession. Strangely, they left it out of the international edition.

Warmest greetings,
Your Gerhard

LETTER 128 From Arendt

Hannah Arendt, 370 Riverside Drive, New York 25, N.Y.
December 26, 1960

Dear Gerhard,
Thanks so much for your letter. Nanda will print whatever you write: famous people are allowed to be Jews, too. Moreover, I really doubt if she knows enough German to understand anything.

But I'm now writing about Benjamin: it's wonderful that you will edit a volume of his letters. I have just one letter, from July 8, 1940, sent from Lourdes! It is a reply to a card I had sent him. We had just spent fourteen days together and, determined to find Monsieur, I had just left, which Benji considered complete madness, and he was right. He stayed in Lourdes and I wrote to him at once—because crazily I was really able to track down Monsieur. The letter is in French. I would send it to you but I'm afraid to. I'd rather have it photocopied here first.

Besides the letter, I have the original of his historical-philosophical theses, written entirely on small, colored, ripped-up pieces of paper. It's fabulous stuff for a facsimile. Perhaps the best would be for me to bring everything with me when I come. For in case the March 6 date remains, I'll be in Jerusalem around the 15th. I'll stay at the Hotel Morijah. Then we'll meet.

I was very upset by Erich Neumann's death.[1] I knew him well when we were young.

Many thanks for your Kabbalah volume. It arrived in one piece, but because of momentary overwork I haven't yet had the chance to take a look at it.

Dear Gerhard, I wish all the best to you and Fanja.
From your Hannah

I just noticed that I have a copy of a fantastic letter from Benjamin to you, the one on Kafka and Brod.[2] You'll surely include it in the book.

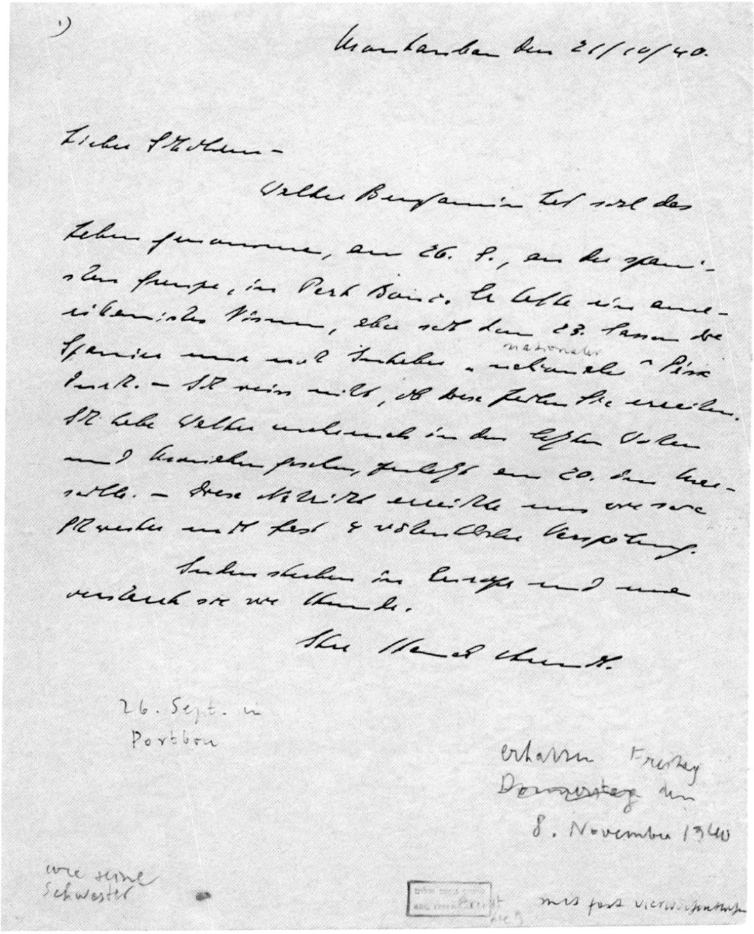

Montauban den 21/10/40.

Lieber Scholem –

Walter Benjamin hat sich das Leben genommen, am 26. 9., an der spanischen Grenze, in Port Bou. Er hatte ein amerikanisches Visum, aber seit dem 23. lassen die Spanier nur noch Inhaber „nationaler" Pässe durch. – Ich weiss nicht, ob diese Zeilen Sie erreichen. Ich habe Walter mehrmals in den letzten Wochen und Monaten gesehen, zuletzt am 20. in Marseille. – Diese Nachricht erreichte uns wie seine Schwester mit fast 4 wöchentlicher Verspätung.

Juden sterben in Europa und man verscharrt sie wie Hunde.

Ihre Hannah Arendt.

26. Sept. in Portbou

erhalten Freitag ~~Donnerstag~~ den 8. November 1940

wie seine Schwester

mit fast vierwöchentlicher

Figure 1. Letter from Hannah Arendt to Gerhard Scholem, 21 October 1940. Courtesy of the Hannah Arendt Blücher Literary Trust.

Figure 2. Walter Benjamin (left) with his brother Georg; see Letter 35.

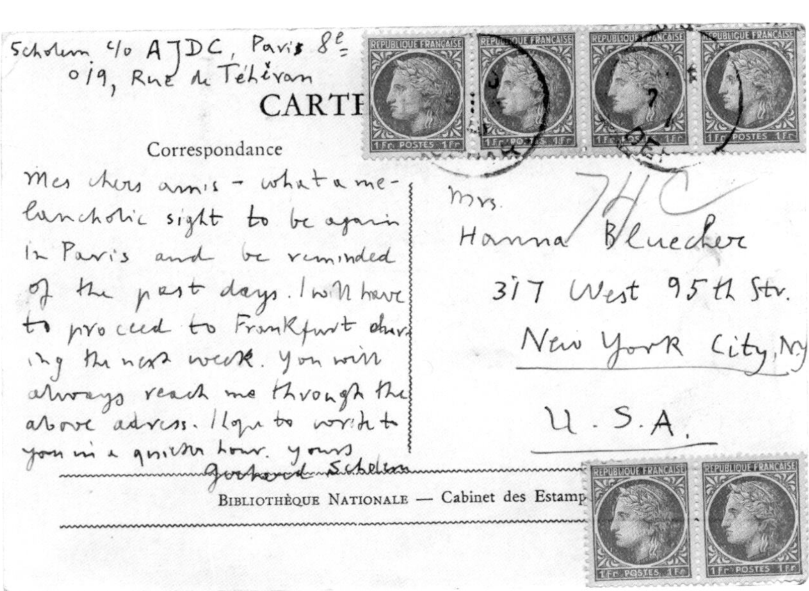

Scholem c/o AJDC, Paris 8e
19, Rue de Téhéran

CARTE

Correspondance

Mes chers amis – what a melancholic sight to be again in Paris and be reminded of the past days. I will have to proceed to Frankfurt during the next week. You will always reach me through the above adress. I hope to write to you in a quieter hour. Yours
Gerhard Scholem

Mrs.
Hanna Bluecher
317 West 95th Str.
New York City, N.Y.
U. S. A.

Bibliothèque Nationale — Cabinet des Estamp

Figures 3a and 3b. Postcard from Gerhard Scholem to Hannah and Heinrich Blücher, Paris 1946.

Figure 4. Gershom Scholem with an unknown woman, Paris 1946. Courtesy of the Gershom Scholem Collection at the National Library of Israel.

Figure 5. Dr. Hannah Arendt and her colleagues from JCR, Inc. (Jewish Cultural Reconstruction), 27 December 1951, in Schreiber's Restaurant, New York. Courtesy of the YIVO Institute for Jewish Research.

Outside row (from left to right): Irvin Weintraub, Dr. Aaron Margalit, Dr. Lawrence Harwick, Prof. Alexander Marx, Prof. Salo W. Baron, Dr. Hannah Arendt (hidden), Rabbi I. Edward Kiev, Miss M. Gruber, Isaac Goldberg, Rabbi Hermann Neuberger, Jacob Dienstag, J. Kagan.

Inside row: Dr. Joseph Reider, Dr. Popper, J. Novak-Schwimmer, Abraham G. Duker, Miss Dina Abramovic, David Rosenstein.

Figure 6a. Storage space immediately after the arrival of the books. Courtesy of the Yad Vashem Photo Archives.

Figure 6b. Sorting of the books according to their (possible) origin. Courtesy of the Yad Vashem Photo Archives.

Figure 7. Torah scrolls found in the American zone.
Courtesy of the Yad Vashem Photo Archives.

Figure 8. Hannah Arendt in her library, 1972.
Courtesy of the Hannah Arendt Blücher Literary Trust.

Figure 9. Gerhard Scholem in his library. Courtesy of the Gershom Scholem Collection at the National Library of Israel.

Telephone: Circle 5-7826

Jewish Cultural Reconstruction, Inc.

1841 Broadway, New York 23, N. Y.

September 8, 1949

Dr. G. Scholem
c/o Dr. S. Hurwitz
Rigistr. 54
Zurich, Switzerland

Dear Scholem:

Your letter of September 5: Dr. Heller will return to America around September 15, and you will find in Wiesbaden Dr. Lowenthal, who actually is in charge.

Hermann Cohen Library: The next meeting of the Advisory Committee is on September 19. I don't see how there could be any difficulties with regard to the claim of the Hebrew University. After all, you have top priority. When you are in Wiesbaden, please let me know if I am right to assume that the Hebrew University also claims the 1100 rare books which are still there and of which we received a catalogue.

However, please bear in mind that JCR has not yet received official title to these units. As far as I know, Lowenthal is now busy with 12,000 volumes of the Breslauer Theological Seminary.

There is one more issue which I should like you to discuss with Lowenthal. You probably heard that we plan an investigation into the whereabouts of Jewish collections which possibly may still turn up in university and other public German libraries or be in the hands of booksellers. Lowenthal is supposed to devote much of his time to this task in the three Western zones, and I asked him for a program of what he intends to do. There are, of course, all kinds of legal complications, the most serious of which is that German institutions were supposed to report all confiscated Jewish property which they might have received during the Nazi regime, but not a single such report was ever made. What is needed in this matter is a kind of detective gift, and I must confess that I have great confidence in you as far as that is concerned.

I am glad to hear that you had such a good time in Europe. Brecht is in Berlin. You may be interested to know that a
Sonderheft

Figure 10. First letter from Hannah Arendt to Gershom Scholem on JCR stationery, 8 September 1949. Courtesy of the National Library of Israel.

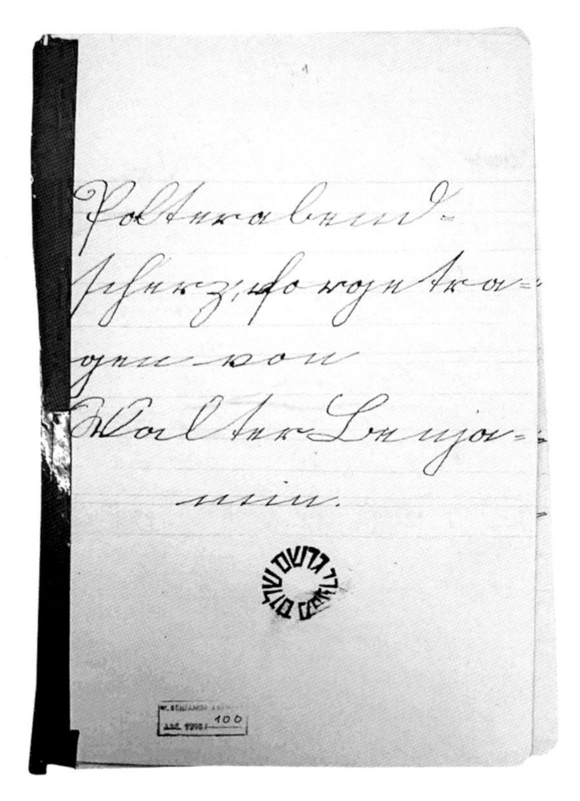

Figure 11. Cover sheet of Walter Benjamin's *Polterabend-Scherz* for the wedding of Clara and William Stern; see Letter 51.

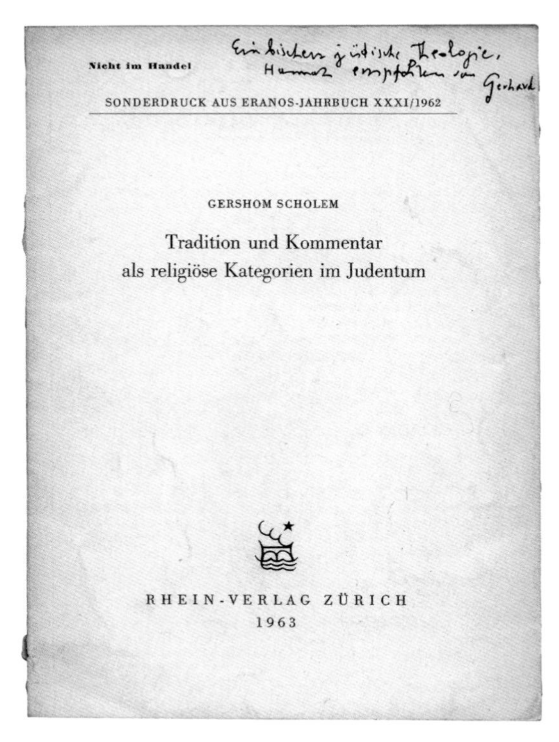

Nicht im Handel

SONDERDRUCK AUS ERANOS-JAHRBUCH XXXI/1962

GERSHOM SCHOLEM

Tradition und Kommentar
als religiöse Kategorien im Judentum

RHEIN-VERLAG ZÜRICH
1963

Figure 12. Dedication (1963). "A bit of Jewish theology, recommended to Hannah from Gerhard." Courtesy of the Hannah Arendt Collection, Stevenson Library, Bard College.

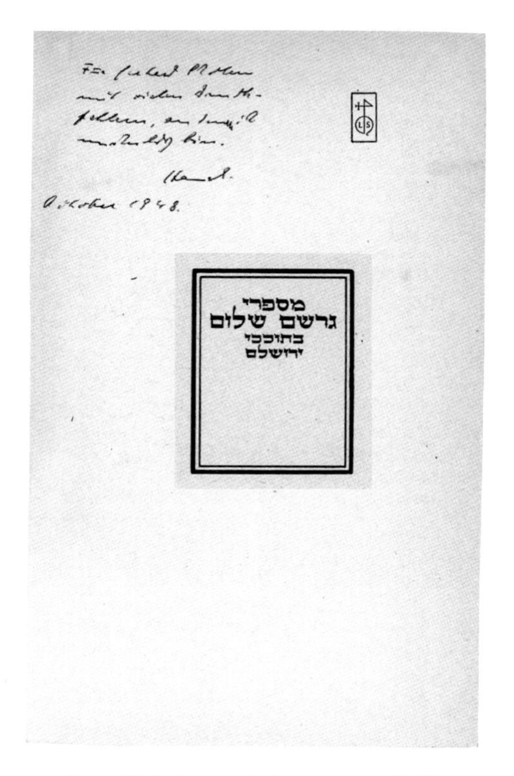

Figure 13. Dedication in *Sechs Essays* (1948).

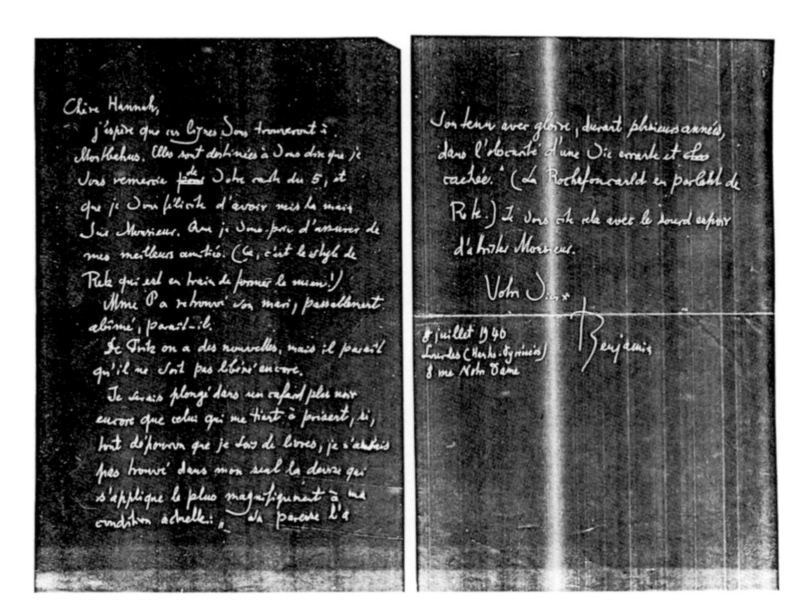

Chère Hannah,

j'espère que ces lignes vous trouveront à Montauban. Elles sont destinées à vous dire que je vous remercie de votre carte du 5, et que je vous félicite d'avoir mis la main sur Monsieur. Quant je vous prie d'assurer de mes meilleurs amitiés. (Ça, c'est le style de Retz qui est en train de former le mien!)

Mme P a retrouvé son mari, passablement abîmé, paraît-il.

De Fritz on a des nouvelles, mais il paraît qu'il ne soit pas libéré encore.

Je serais plongé dans un cafard plus noir encore que celui qui me tient à présent, si, tout dépourvu que je sois de livres, je n'avais pas trouvé dans mon seul la devise qui s'applique le plus magnifiquement à ma condition actuelle: „La paresse l'a soutenu avec gloire, durant plusieurs années, dans l'obscurité d'une vie errante et cachée." (La Rochefoucauld en parlant de Retz.) Je vous cite cela avec le sourd espoir d'attrister Monsieur.

Votre vieux

Benjamin

8 juillet 1940
Lourdes (Hautes-Pyrénées)
8 rue Notre Dame

Figure 14. Negatives of the original letters (8 July 1940) from Walter Benjamin to Hannah Arendt.

Jewish
Cultural Reconstruction

gabe, besorgt von Oscar Schmidt, Professor an der naturwissenschaftl. Facultät der Universität Straßburg. Mit Abbildungen, gebunden . . . . 80 Pfg.

Geologie von A. Geikie, Professor der Geologie an der Universität Edinburg. Deutsche Ausgabe besorgt von Oscar Schmidt, Professor an der naturwissenschaftl. Facultät der Universität Straßburg. Mit Abbildungen, gebunden . . . . 80 Pfg.

Weitere Bände sind in Vorbereitung.

Naturwissenschaftliche Elementarbücher.

Physik

von

Balfour Stewart,

Professor der Physik in Manchester.

Deutsche Ausgabe

besorgt von

E. Warburg,

Professor der Physik an der Universität Freiburg i/B.

Mit Abbildungen.

Zweite Auflage.

Straßburg,

Verlag von Karl J. Trübner.

1877.

Figure 15. From the private library of Hermann Cohen, first edition from 1877.

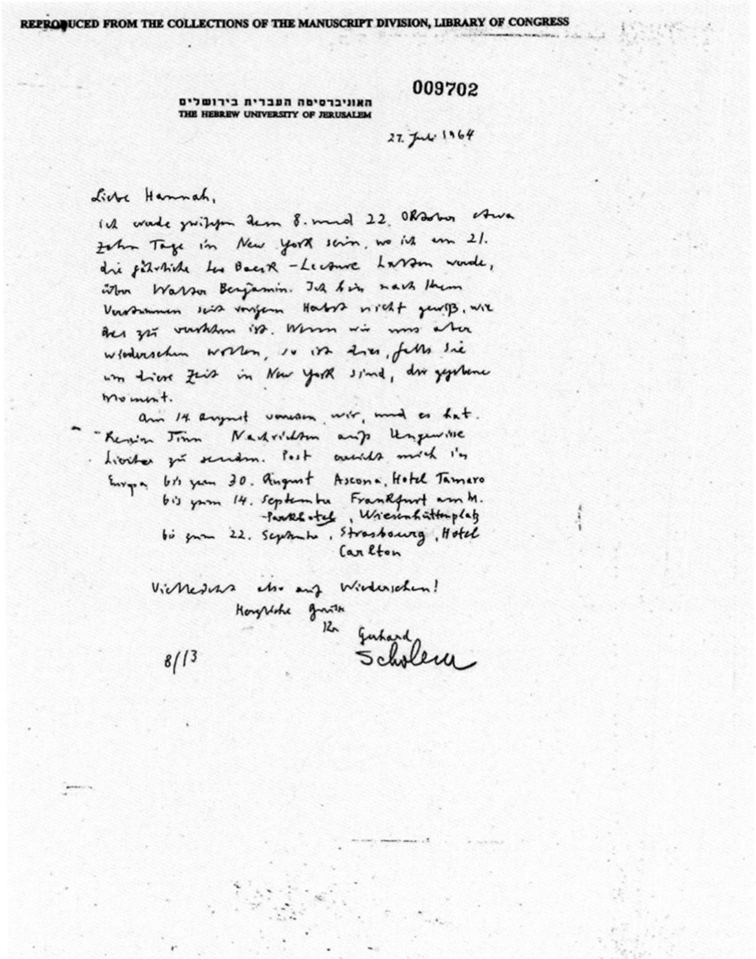

האוניברסיטה העברית בירושלים
THE HEBREW UNIVERSITY OF JERUSALEM

27. Juli 1964

Liebe Hannah,

ich werde zwischen dem 8. und 22. Oktober etwa zehn Tage in New York sein, wo ich am 21. die jährliche Leo Baeck-Lecture halten werde, über Walter Benjamin. Ich bin nach Ihrem Verstummen seit vorigem Herbst nicht gewiß, wie das zu verstehen ist. Wenn wir uns aber wiedersehen wollen, so ist dies, falls Sie um diese Zeit in New York sind, der gegebene Moment.

Am 14. August verreisen wir, und es hat keinen Sinn Nachrichten aufs Ungewisse hierher zu senden. Post erreicht mich in Europa bis zum 30. August Ascona, Hotel Tamaro
bis zum 14. September Frankfurt am M. Parkhotel, Wiesenhüttenplatz
bis zum 22. September, Strasbourg, Hotel Carlton

Vielleicht also auf Wiedersehen!

Herzliche Grüße

Ihr Gerhard Scholem

8/13

Figure 16. Letter from Gerhard Scholem to Hannah Arendt, 21 July 1964.

LETTER 129 From Scholem

Jerusalem
January 29, 1961

Dear Hannah,
In the event the trial isn't delayed, I hope we will see one another in Jerusalem. I'm not traveling before the end of March or April 3. The papers of Walter Benjamin you mentioned won't have any place in the planned book. Only the one letter. Don't weigh yourself down with them, and bring just the photocopy of the letter, or send it to me. Of course, the letter to me on Kafka will be a highlight in the book of letters.

For now, auf Wiedersehen and warmest greetings,
Your Gerhard

LETTER 130 FROM ARENDT

[Undated]

Dear Gerhard,
I fear we won't see one another again. I'm arriving in Israel on the ninth, most likely for around three weeks. Thus I'm including here the photocopy and the transcription in case your typist has difficulties with the French (handwriting, photocopy, etc.).

Clarification: Montbahus. During the collapse of France I was with Benjamin in Lourdes. Montbahus was a place where friends of ours were living at the time. Monsieur is Blücher. I don't remember Mm P. and her husband. Fritz is Fritz Fraenkel, the psychiatrist who was also living at 19 rue Dombasle in Paris. A close friend of Benjamin's and Blücher's.

Any chance of seeing you in Europe? I'll probably travel from Israel to Zurich. Let me know where you will be, and when. In Jerusalem you can leave a message for me at Hotel Moriyah or otherwise at my family's in Tel Aviv: Dr. Ernst Fürst, 16 Bar Illan Street.

What a pity!

Warmest greetings to you both,
Your Hannah

LETTER 131 From Scholem

Jerusalem
April 13, 1962

My dear Hannah,
You made me so happy by sending me your *Between Past and Future*.[1] When the book first appeared I read some of your spiritual exercises in political thinking, but now I am taking them in as a whole, relishing the way you fit them together. I'm hoping to be able to match your gift of six exercises with six of my own, as soon as the Rhein-Verlag publishes my book on some, to wit six, central concepts of the Kabbalah.[2] They won't be forgotten. The book is now being sent into production. I haven't heard from you in a while, and I don't even know if you have embarked on one of your European forays. Speaking of which, let me tell you that I'll be in Paris for the last week of May. Believe it or not, I'll be at a colloquium on "heresy and society" at the École des Hautes Études. I'll speak on Frankism and the phenomenon of religious nihilism. This will be my French debut and I'm eager to see how it goes.

I'll stay in Paris until June 3 and will then make my way back to Jerusalem, where we will still be in the middle of the semester. Is the Agathodaimon[3] arranging matters so that you'll be in the region around this time? For this year I won't be turning up in America.

With warmest greetings
As always,
Your Gerhard

I didn't send you my article on Buber in the October edition of *Commentary* because I didn't have copies, and I had hoped that on your own you would come across this serious piece of creative writing.[4]

LETTER 132 From Scholem

June 23, 1963[1]

Dear Hannah,
It's been six weeks since I received your book on the Eichmann trial. I am just now writing because at first I couldn't concentrate on the book.[2] I have only recently gotten to it. I won't concern myself here with whether you got all the empirical or historical facts right. So far as I can assess some of the details, the book is not lacking in misunderstandings and errors. A number of your critics—and there will be many—will take up the issue of factual accuracy. But this isn't central to what I want to say.

Your book orbits around two centers: Jews and their behavior during the Catastrophe on the one hand, and Eichmann and his responsibility on the other. For many years I have given thought to the subject of the Jews and have studied no small amount of literature on the subject. It's utterly clear to me—and this probably goes for every reflective observer of these events—how bitterly serious, how complicated, how far from transparent and reducible this matter is. There are aspects of Jewish history (and this is what I have occupied myself with for the past fifty years) which are hardly free of abysses: a demonic decay in the midst of life; insecurity in the face of this world (in contrast to the security of the pious, whom your book, bafflingly, does not mention); and a weakness that is perpetually confounded and mingled with trickery and lust for power. These have always existed, and it would be odd indeed if they didn't come to the fore in some form at times of catastrophe. This happened in 1391[3] and in the generation of disaster that followed, just as it has happened in our own day. The debate on this topic is for the most part legitimate and unavoidable, even if I don't think our generation can pass anything resembling a historical judgment. We lack, as we must, the true distance that could also inspire prudence. Still, the questions continue to press themselves on us. The query that young people in Israel are asking has real merit: "Why did they allow themselves to be killed?" The answer that one always starts to give cannot be reduced to a formula. In every important respect, particularly when it comes to your choice of focus, your book addresses only the *weakness* of Jewish existence. And to the degree that there really was weakness, your emphasis is, so far as I can tell, completely one-sided and leaves the reader with a feeling of rage and fury.

Nevertheless, the problem you pose is genuine. Why, then, does your book evoke such emotions of bitterness and shame for those who recognize this—indeed, not for the author's subject matter but for the author herself? Why does your account so dominate the events it records, which you rightly want people to reflect on? To the degree that I have an answer, I cannot hide it—if only because of my high regard for you. It will clarify what stands between us. It is the heartless, the downright malicious tone you employ in dealing with the topic that so profoundly concerns the center of our life. There is something in the Jewish language that is completely indefinable, yet fully concrete—what the Jews call *ahavath Israel*, or love for the Jewish people. With you, my dear Hannah, as with so many intellectuals coming from the German left, there is no trace of it. An exposition such as yours demands, if I may say so, the old-fashioned kind of objective and thorough treatment—especially where, as in the case of the murder of a third of our people, such deep emotions are necessarily at work and are so greatly aroused. And I see you as nothing other than a member of this people. I haven't the slightest sympathy for the lighthearted style, by which I mean the English word "flippancy," that you employ all too often in your book. It's inappropriate for your topic, and in the most unimaginable way. In treating such a theme, isn't there a place for the humble German expression "tact of the heart"? You may laugh; I hope not, for I say this in earnest. Among the many passages in your book which have gnawed at me, I can point to no clearer example of what I mean than your description of the way in which residents of the Warsaw Ghetto[4] bought and sold armbands bearing the Jewish symbol; also your comment on Leo Baeck, "who in the eyes of both Jews and Germans was the 'Jewish Führer.'"[5] In *this* context your use in German of a Nazi term says a lot. For instance, you don't call him simply the Jewish leader, without quotation marks, which would have been sensible and free of any malicious aftertaste. You say the very thing that is most offensive and farthest from the truth. No one I have ever heard or read considered Leo Baeck, whom you and I both knew, a leader in the sense that your readers will be induced to adopt. Like you, I have read Adler's book on Theresienstadt.[6] A lot can be said about the work. But I have not found that the author, who speaks resentfully about people I have likewise read something about, has ever characterized or indirectly portrayed Baeck in such a way. What our people have gone through may be clouded on account of dark figures who earned or would have earned their bullets—and how could it be otherwise with a tragedy of this magnitude? But to discuss this in such a wholly inappropriate tone (to the benefit of those Germans whom your book mentions with stronger tones of disgust than those it uses to discuss the misfortune of the Jews) is not the way to lay out the true dimensions of this tragedy.

I don't find any balanced judgment in your discussion of Jewish behavior under extreme conditions—conditions that neither of us experienced; instead, it's more like a demagogically twisted overstatement. Who of us today can say which decision the "Elders," or whatever one wants to call them, should have made under those conditions? I don't know, and I have read no less on this issue than you have; nor do I get the impression from your analysis that your knowledge is any better grounded than my ignorance. Jewish councils existed. Some of the members were scoundrels, others saints. I've read a great deal about both. There were also many average people, like most of us, forced to make decisions under conditions that will never recur and that are impossible to reconstruct. I have no idea if they did the right thing or wrong thing. I don't presume to judge. I wasn't there.

Certainly, Rabbi Murmelstein[7] from Vienna, who was in Theresienstadt, deserves to be hanged by the Jews—all the people I spoke to and who were in the camp confirmed this. Murmelstein's career in particular has been one of my special interests. But there is no unanimity at all when it comes to judging many others. Why did the Nazis shoot Paul Eppstein,[8] for example, who was one of these controversial figures? You say nothing about this. The reason they shot him was that he did precisely what you said he could more or less do without any danger: he told people in Theresienstadt what was going to happen to them at Auschwitz. Twenty-four hours later he was shot. I heard this from the lips of Baeck, Utitz, and Muneles.[9]

Your thesis that through well-known maneuvers the Nazis blurred the clear line separating torturers from their victims, a thesis you used to the disadvantage of the prosecution against Eichmann—this thesis I consider wrongheaded and tendentious. As you write, people were humiliated in the camps, and they were made to collaborate on their own destruction, to assist in the execution of their fellow prisoners, and the like. And this supposedly blurred the line between tormentors and victims? What perversity! And we should then come along and say that the Jews played their "part" in the murder of the Jews? This is a typical *quaternio terminorum*.[10]

Over the past few days I read an essay on the book by the rabbi from Pjotrkow, Moses Chaim Lau.[11] During the time of destruction, and aware of what was about to happen, he wrote the book *The Sanctification of the Name*. It was recently published. Given the circumstances in which he found himself, Lau tried to determine precisely what obligations Jews have who are living under extreme situations. Not everything in this searing text (and there are other books like his) contradicts the substance (not the tone) of your observations. In your book there is absolutely no mention of how many Jews, in full awareness of the situation, faced their fate with their heads up high. Rabbi Lau went with his community to Treblinka, though he urged the members of the community to run away, and they urged him to run away. The heroism of the Jews hasn't always involved shooting, nor have we always been ashamed of our heroes. I can't disprove someone who says that the Jews had earned their fate because from the beginning they didn't defend themselves differently, that they were cowards, and so on. In the last few days I first came across such an argument in a book by a dyed-in-the-wool Jewish anti-Semite named Kurt Tucholsky.[12] I'm not as subtle as this Tucholsky. Of course he was right: if all Jews had run away, especially to Palestine, more would be alive. It's another question altogether whether this was possible given the circumstances of Jewish history and Jewish life, or whether in a historical sense not doing so counts as guilt and participation in the crime.

I won't say anything about the other central issue of your book, which is Eichmann's guilt, or the extent of guilt that should be allotted to him. I have read the judge's verdict against Eichmann, along with your substitute text. The judge's account strikes me as far more convincing than yours. Your verdict is a curious example of a massive non sequitur. Your justification holds true for hundreds of thousands, perhaps millions of people, and your last sentence could just as easily be applied to them.[13] And only your last sentence provides justification for Eichmann's hanging, because in the earlier parts of the essay you explain in detail why, in your opinion (which I by no means share), the prosecution failed to prove what it should have proved, and on all essential points. I would like to mention that, in addition to signing a letter to the president urging him not to carry out the execution, I wrote an essay in Hebrew explaining why I consider it historically misguided to carry out the death sentence (the primary reason being our position with regard to the Germans)—even if Eichmann has it coming to him in every way and in accord with the arguments of the prosecution.[14] I don't want to burden this letter with a discussion of his sentence. I wish to say merely that your depiction of Eichmann as a convert to Zionism is conceivable only when it comes from someone like you, filled with ressentiment for everything connected to Zionism.[15] I can't take these pages of your book seriously; they do nothing but mock Zionism—which is, I fear, the main point for you. I don't want to get into this.

After reading your book, I am not in the least convinced by the notion of the "banality of evil." If the book's subtitle can be believed, you strove to develop the theme. This banality seems rather more of a slogan than the result of the kind of in-depth analysis you presented far more convincingly under very different circumstances in your book on totalitarianism. Apparently, back then you had not yet discovered that evil is banal. The radical evil which your previous analysis testified to so elegantly and knowledgeably has disappeared without a trace into a slogan. If this is to be more than a slogan, it must be taken to a deeper plane of political morality and moral philosophy. I regret that, given my sincere and friendly feelings toward you, I have nothing positive to say about your theses in this work. I expected something else, especially after your first book.

All the best to you, from your old friend Gerhard

June 24, 1963
Dear Hannah, I wrote the above yesterday evening, and I hope it reaches you somewhere. Do you have anything against my publishing this letter, perhaps by removing its epistlatory character and printing it in the third person? These questions relating to your book are of interest to far more people than just the two of us.

Your Gerhard

LETTER 133 From Arendt

370 Riverside Drive
New York, 25, New York
July 20, 1963

Dear Gerhard,
I found your letter waiting for me when I arrived back home eight days ago. You can easily imagine how things look after a five-month absence. I am truly writing at the first possible opportunity, though perhaps not with the detail I should.

Your letter contains a number of uncontroversial claims—uncontroversial because they are quite simply wrong. I'll begin with them so we can move on to the issues worth discussing.

I do not belong to the "intellectuals coming from the German left." This you couldn't have known, because we weren't acquainted in our youth. It's hardly a fact to boast of. In fact, I say so unwillingly, particular since the

McCarthy era descended upon this country. Only later did I learn something about Marx's importance. In my youth I was interested neither in history nor in politics. If I hailed from anywhere at all, it was from German philosophy.

Unfortunately, I can't say you couldn't have known a second point. I thought it peculiarly touching when you wrote, "I see you as nothing other than a member of this [namely, the Jewish] people." Not only have I never acted as if I was something else, but I have never even felt the temptation to do so. It's as if I were to say I am a man and not a woman. In other words, it would be sheer lunacy. Naturally I know this can be a Jewish problem, but it's never been mine. Not even in my youth. That I am a Jew is one of the unquestioned facts of my life, and I've never wanted to alter such brute facts. Such an attitude of fundamental gratitude for something that is as it is, given and not made, *physei* and not *nomoi*, is pre-political. But under extraordinary circumstances, such as the circumstances of Jewish politics, this attitude has negative consequences: it makes certain manners of behavior impossible, and these kinds of behavior, it seems to me, are precisely what you are reading into my exposition. (To give you another example, in his obituary for Blumenfeld Ben-Gurion spoke about his regret that in Israel Blumenfeld had never changed his name. That Blumenfeld didn't do so was naturally the result of the same impulse that led him to become a Zionist as a youth.) It seems to me that you were well acquainted with my style of thinking in these matters, and it is baffling to me why you would want to shove me into a pigeonhole in which I don't fit and never have.

Let's get to the real issue. Tying in with what I just said, I'll begin with *ahavath Israel* (by the way, I would be extraordinarily grateful to you if you could tell me when this expression began to play a role in the Hebrew language and literature, when it appeared for the first time, and so on). How right you are that I have no such love, and for two reasons: first, I have never in my life "loved" some nation or collective—not the German, French, or American nation, or the working class, or whatever else there might be in this price range of loyalties. The fact is that I love only my friends and am quite incapable of any other sort of love. Second, this kind of love for the Jews would seem suspect to me, since I am Jewish myself. I don't love myself or anything I know that belongs to the substance of my being. To illustrate what I mean, let me tell you about a conversation I had with Golda Meir, who by the way is a person I quite liked, so I ask you not to read into what I'm about to write any personal animosity. We were talking about what I consider a disastrous lack of separation between religion and state in Israel, which she defended. She said more or less the following (I don't recall her exact words): "You understand, of course, that as a socialist I do not believe in God. I believe in the Jewish people." This is a horrible comment, in my view, and I was too shocked to offer a response. But I could have replied that the magnificence of this people once lay in its belief in God—that is, in the way its trust and love of God far outweighed its fear of God. And now this people believes only in itself! What's going to become of this?[1] In this sense I don't love the Jews, nor do I "believe" in them. I belong to this people, in nature and in fact.

We could speak politically about this issue, and then we would discuss the question of patriotism. We would both agree that patriotism is impossible without constant opposition and critique. In this entire affair I can confess to you one thing: that injustice committed by my own people naturally provokes me more than injustice done by others.

It's a shame that you first read the book after the Israelis and the American Jews kicked off a distortion campaign against it. I'm sorry to say, but there are very few people who can remain uninfluenced by such campaigns. If you had read the book without prejudice and not under the influence of so-called public opinion—which in my case has been manipulated—I can hardly believe that you would have so misunderstood me. I never turned Eichmann into a "Zionist." It's really not my fault if you didn't understand the irony of my language, which through indirect speech I made crystal clear, namely, in the way Eichmann described himself. I can assure you that dozens of people over here, who read it before the book was published, never had any doubt about this. Moreover, I never asked the question of why the Jews "let themselves be murdered"; rather, I accused Hausner of asking the question.[2] There was no nation or group in Europe that, under the direct compulsion of terror, behaved any differently than the Jews did. The question I raised concerned the cooperation of the Jewish functionaries during the phase of the Final Solution. These people one cannot simply accuse of being traitors. (The fact that among them there really were traitors isn't interesting.) In other words, until 1939 or 1941, depending on when one dates the beginning of the Final Solution, everything is still understandable and forgivable. The problem begins after this point. This issue was brought up during the trial, and I couldn't avoid it. And herein lies the "un-mastered past" that concerns us. And if you are perhaps correct, though I doubt it, that a "balanced judgment" cannot yet be made, I believe we will only get this past behind us if we begin to make judgments, forceful judgments in fact. I've spoken out my opinion in this business loud and clear, an opinion you've obviously not understood. There was no possibility of resistance, but there was the possibility to *do nothing*. And in order to do nothing, one didn't need to be a saint. One only had to say I am a *poscheter*[3] Jew and don't want to be anything else. Whether all of these people in each and every case deserve to be hanged is a very different question. The issue at hand revolves around the arguments they've used to justify their actions to themselves and to each other. Faced with such arguments we are obliged to make a judgment. These people were also not subject to the direct pressure of terror; the terror was indirect. In these questions I am well acquainted with the different degrees of terror. There always remained a certain space for free decisions and free actions. Precisely the way it was with the SS murderers, who as we know now had a limited amount of freedom: they could have refused to go along without anything happening to them. Since in politics we are not dealing with heroes or saints but with human beings, this possibility of *non-participation* is manifestly decisive for judging the individual, but not the system.

And in the Eichmann trial, we were concerned with an individual. In my report I only discussed issues that came up during the trial. As a result, I couldn't bring up the saints you spoke about. Instead, I had to limit myself to the resistance fighters, fighters whose resistance, I explained, has to be held in such high regard because it took place under conditions in which, in fact, there could be no real resistance. Among the witnesses that Mr. Hausner presented there were no saints. There was just one fully pure human being, and that was the old Grynspan,[4] about whom I gave an extensive report. From the German side, there were actually more of these pure humans than I mention. I had to limit myself to Sergeant Schmidt[5] because during the trial no other names were mentioned and no other cases named.

In *Origins of Totalitarianism* I demonstrated with great detail how, in the concentration camps, the line separating victims from persecutors was blurred, and in a calculated and intentional way. To repeat: my point is not to shift part of the guilt over to the Jews. The system was guilty and in this the Jews had no part in the guilt whatsoever.

That you could form the opinion that my book is a "mockery of Zionism" would have struck me as completely incomprehensible if I didn't know the extent to which Zionist circles have forgotten that they should avoid listening to opinions set in stone and embraced by everyone from the start. A Zionist friend of mine told me quite naïvely that the last chapter (on the jurisdiction of the court and on the justification for the kidnapping) is especially pro-Israel, which is of course true. But it threw you off because you didn't expect my arguments or my way of thinking—in other words, my independence. I mean on the one hand that I do not belong to any organization and speak only in my own name, and on the other that a person must think for himself and, whatever you may have against my results, you won't understand them unless you know that they are my results and no one else's.

It's a pity you didn't want to "weigh down" your letter with your argument against carrying out the death sentence because I think that in our discussion of this question we could have clarified our real, not apparent, differences. You say it was "historically wrong," while I think that the execution wasn't just *politically* proper (I'm not interested in the historical angle here), it in fact would have been utterly impossible not to carry it out. One could not have carried out the death sentence only if one had accepted Jaspers's suggestion and "extradited" him to the United Nations. No one wanted to do this, and it was perhaps not even possible; therefore, he had to hang. Clemency wasn't an option, and not for juristic reasons—clemency lies outside the legal system. Clemency is applied to the *person* and not to the act: it doesn't forgive the murder but pardons the *murderer* who is more than his action.

In conclusion, I come to the only point of agreement between us. I am happy you discovered it, and I wish to say a few words about it. You are completely right that I have changed my mind and now no longer speak of radical evil. We haven't seen each other for a long time; otherwise we would perhaps have gotten around to discussing this. It's unclear to me why you characterize the phrase "banality of evil" as a slogan. So far as I know, no one has ever used it before. But this isn't important. The fact is that today I think that evil in every instance is only extreme, never radical: it has no depth, and therefore has nothing demonic about it. Evil can lay to waste the entire world, like a fungus growing rampant on the surface. Only the good is always deep and radical. As I said, however, I don't want to go into this here, since I intend to deal with these issues in a different context and in greater depth. If you were to look up the concept of "radical evil" in Kant, you'd find that he doesn't mean much more than ordinary baseness, which is a psychological rather than a metaphysical concept. But, like I said, I don't want to say much more about these things, for in a different context I'm intending to return to the topic and elaborate on it. But Herr Eichmann will certainly remain as the concrete model for what I have in mind.

You suggest publishing your letter and you ask if I have anything against it. I would advise against transforming it using the third-person voice. The value of our debate is that it takes place as an exchange of letters and is carried out on the foundation of friendship. Naturally, I am not at all opposed to this if you are prepared to publish your letter together with mine. But let's keep this in the form of letters.

I'll write some other time about your extraordinary book on the philosophy of the Kabbalah, which I still haven't read to the end.

In old friendship,
Your Hannah

LETTER 134 From Scholem

28 Abarbanel St.
Jerusalem
August 6, 1963

Dear Hannah,
Thank you for your letter, and I am in agreement with the suggestion that we publish our two letters. In this country I've approached the *Mitteilungsblatt* of the Irgun Olei Merkasz Europa to see if they would print up both letters together.

But first of all I've had someone ask Mrs. Golda Meir if she'll agree to have in print the comment from a personal conversation, which you cite on page 2 of your letter. Just like you, she doesn't remember the exact wording of the conversation and therefore has suggested either not to mention the conversation or, instead of using her name, to mention an anonymous source. The relevant passage in our letter would therefore more or less go like this:

To illustrate what I mean, let me tell you about a conversation I had with a leading political figure who defended what I consider a disastrous lack of separation between religion and state in Israel. She said more or less the following (I don't recall her exact words): "You understand that, as a socialist, I, of course, do not believe in God. I believe in the Jewish people." This is a horrible comment in my view, and I was too shocked to offer a reply.

Since I'm traveling in a few days I would be very grateful to you if you could send me a telegram and let me know if you agree to the alteration to your original letter.

In Europe I will show the letters to the editor of the *Neue Zürcher Zeitung* (he is the one who wrote a review of your book).[1] I think the paper might be the right place for the letters.

I'm leaving on August 18, and I can be reached in Ascona (Hotel Tamaro) until September 9, and then I'll be in Copenhagen (Hotel Codan) until October 1. I'll be writing you a few more things about your letter before I leave. I'm now in a rush.

Sincerely,
Gerhard

LETTER 135 From Scholem

Jerusalem
August 12, 1963

Dear Hannah,
I'm assuming that by the end of this week our exchange of letters will appear in Tel Aviv as a supplement in the (widely distributed) *Mitteilungsblatt* of the so-called "olej Germania."[1] You'll get a copy sent to you by airmail. In the spirit of your telegram, I've changed the comment you made about Golda Meir in your letter to accord with the text I suggested. I didn't include the final sentence of your letter that refers to my book on the Kabbalah. If the chance arises, I'd like to see our correspondence also printed up in a European paper, be it the newspaper in Zurich where I know the editor Dr. Streiff (he wrote the review to your book, and I'll show him our letters), or in some other appropriate place. I'd still like to make a few comments to your letter. In one respect, your letter confirms what I say, and in another respect your letter is simply strange.

I have to admit that I find the idea completely new and incomprehensible that you don't belong among the intellectuals who have grown up out of the German left. I recall the lively discussions we had in Paris years before 1933 about you and your first husband. Whatever you say! I must have dreamed it all up. My comment and strong emphasis on your belonging to the Jewish people meant precisely the opposite of the sense you gave it. It was a riposte to all those who consider themselves (and, as you must have noticed, there are many) members of what has lately been characterized as a "post-Zionist assimilation"—that is, those who think they have cut themselves free from the Jewish people, or who would very much like to do so if it's at all possible, etc. By writing this, I showed that I don't count myself among the critics who accuse you of such a thing, but that on the contrary I am in full agreement with you here. You are so irritable and tense when it comes to anything related to this topic (which of course is understandable) that you want to write off your critics, myself included, as victims of an organized campaign, manipulated from above. You seem to take me for a more or less harmless victim of this campaign. I doubt very much whether such a campaign has been "set in motion" from the Israeli side (something I'm in a position to know about). The bitterness aroused by your book among so many readers hardly needed an organizational hand in order to find literary expression. Since I believe you've brought up a problem of absolutely critical importance, but you've blocked yourself from any access to the heart of the problem, I've had a number of conversations with people here about this; and I've made my thoughts clear to you in my letter. It seems evident to me that the misunderstanding of your presentation, in particular those statements you now tell me were meant to be ironic, are possible without needing any "manipulation" from above. Your irony is so subtle that not just me but also others were incapable of picking up on it. I would say that it is hard to imagine irony being more out of place than here, in this context. Someone like yourself who writes about Zionism the way you have, and who continues to do so in the same vein in so many pages of your book, should hardly be surprised when your readers fail to pick up on your irony about Eichmann's conversion to Zionism. Today, after rereading your statements, I still scarcely notice it. The fact that you fail to take up a clear position against Eichmann's scandalous nonsense hardly makes one predisposed to catch your fine-spun irony—your absence of any reproach against Eichmann's remarks, while you muster a robust and direct assault against others without the slightest hint of irony.

I don't believe I've forgotten the art of listening to opinions that haven't been pre-manufactured or haven't already been formulated by someone, even by myself, for instance. What arouses my opposition to your presentation isn't what can't be pigeonholed; it is the heartlessness and the certainty of your judgments, a certainty that at decisive points to me seem to be entirely ungrounded. By "decisive points" I mean above all what you say about "non-participation," which, by presenting as a feasible humane and political strategy, and not for individual Jews but for millions of them, you end up elevating into a kind of *postfestum* measuring stick of judgment. More than anywhere else, as I have written, this is the point where I can least go along with you. You haven't offered up even the slenderest scrap of evidence that, to any serious extent, this political strategy—that *nolens volens* the Jews would have had to come up with because of pressure from the outside—could have been a realistic option, both given the reaction of the Nazis against the first sign of such a strategy, and the social and psychological realities of the Jewish community. What you recommend one can only sketch out and argue on a piece of paper, but it couldn't have been actualized in any realistic way given the conditions in Germany, Poland, Lithuania, Latvia, and Rumania. Millions of Jews would have had to become autonomous individuals, and in the midst of nations whose anti-Semitic predispositions and their willingness to collaborate with the Nazis were so evident as to leave no room for illusions. I'd really like to know how you think the Poles or Latvians or our dear Germans would have been willing to take up and save the lives of masses of Jews wandering around, each one trying to find a place to stay. All of this talk of yours, it seems to me, is entirely unrealistic. I would say the opposite as you. If Jews had done as you say they should have, people would use it against them today by saying, Why did you run into the arms of your oppressors instead of organizing yourselves where at least you might have had a chance to save tens of thousands of lives? I don't even know where to begin with the claims you make. Jews in Poland could have known the Germans only through their memories of the way they behaved during the First World War, when they were infinitely friendlier than anything the Jews had been used to, day in and day out, during the twenty-year history of the Polish republic. What's the purpose of bringing up such naïve fairytales as you do in your book? I have no idea which political strategy would have been "correct." My argument against you is that you also don't know, but you claim to.

My opinion on the execution of Eichmann is different from yours, though I know that under present circumstances someone (or even you) could accuse me of unrealistic thinking in this case. My point was that we should not make it easier for the Germans to confront their own past, as we did in fact with Eichmann's execution. A great sigh of relief spread through the forest of German newspapers (and not only there) when the Israelis hanged Eichmann. He now stands as a representative for everyone, and will remain so. This notion filled me with the deepest unease. No one who signed the letter thought about clemency; instead, they all thought about non-execution.

One of these days the two of us will no doubt discuss evil and its banality through bureaucratization (or evil's banalization within bureaucracy). Though you think you have proven it, I have not seen the proof. Maybe this kind of evil exists; but if so, philosophically it would have to be considered differently. I don't picture Eichmann, as he marched around in his SS uniform and relished how everyone shivered in fear before him, as the banal gentleman you want to persuade us he was, ironically or not. I refuse to go along. I've read enough descriptions and interviews of Nazi functionaries and their conduct in front of Jews—while the going was good—to mistrust this innocuous *ex post facto* concoction. The gentlemen enjoyed their evil, so long as there was something to enjoy. One behaves differently after the party's over, of course. So much for today. I hope you really will write something about my Kabbalah book. As you may have noticed, I have packed a lot into it.

Sincerely,
Gerhard

LETTER 136 From Arendt

New York
August 18, 1963

Dear Gerhard,
Thank you for your long letter; I'll be answering it in detail soon. Today I'm writing in a hurry. Naturally, it never occurred to me to publish Golda Meir's name. When I wrote to you, I wasn't thinking about your suggestion to publish the letter. Your alterations are perfect.

As far as publishing the letters in the *Zürcher Zeitung*, though, I don't entirely agree with you. I assume that Dr. Streiff, whom I know from Jerusalem, will tell you that the dispute between us is of no interest to his readers. Maybe I'm wrong. If case you want, and are able, to publish the letters anyway, I'll have to ask for my text back so I can make some minor stylistic changes. I wrote very casually because I never took seriously the idea of presenting the letter to the public, while apparently from the beginning you wrote in order to publish. Of course, I would change nothing about the content, at most I'd add a sentence here or there, but not in the actual polemical part of the letter.

Give my warmest greetings to Streiff if you see him. I'm really grateful for the dazzling review he did of a chapter of my revolution book. I couldn't have done a better job.

In passing, I'm happy that I misunderstood what you said about my membership in the Jewish people. You mentioned the "anti-Semite" Tucholsky, and I naturally made a connection between that and what you said about me. In terms of Tucholsky, I don't share your opinion. An anti-Semite is an anti-Semite and not a Jew who occasionally expresses himself critically about Jewish things, irrespective of whether he is right or not. It's obvious why people marked by oppression tend to write off anyone who dares breathe even the slightest criticism as an enemy and oppressor. What isn't so obvious is that you would join them. But you aren't even consistent in this. For instance, in your attacks on me, and after everything you wrote, you didn't accuse me of "self-hatred."

I realize that you "brought" a lot of extraordinary things into your book on the Kabbalah. Which is precisely the reason I didn't want to say anything before I had the chance to read it thoroughly. I'm therefore eager to get at it! Many thanks for this "little bit of Jewish theology."[1] Take care!

Sincerely,
Your Hannah

P.S. By the way, this business with the post-Zionist assimilationism is new to me. We don't have such a thing here in this country. At the moment I'm reading in the *New York Times Magazine* that I belong to the American school of behaviorists and Darwinians. Which at least has the charm of something fresh.

LETTER 137 From Scholem

Copenhagen
[Undated]

Dear Hannah,
Thanks so much for your letter. I assume that the *Neue Zürcher Zeitung* will be publishing the letters in the next available literary supplement. The only sentence I changed was the one on Murmelstein. Meanwhile, yesterday I got a telegram from Mander[1] asking my permission to publish, and so we have voiced our opinions, as far as it was feasible. Perhaps there is something useful in this.

I have a different, minor concern: I had Suhrkamp Verlag send you my volume of essays *Judaica*,[2] which was published in Germany five weeks ago. That is to say, I put your name and address on a list of those set to receive author's copies. Since you haven't mentioned it, I'm doubtful whether you got the book in New York. Please write to me in Frankfurt at the Parkhotel, Wiesenhüttenplatz, where I'll be until October 8. I want to discuss with the publisher the printing of Walter Benjamin's letters, which are ready for press—if S. [Peter Suhrkamp][3] takes all of the pieces I selected, which will make for a larger volume than he had until now intended. I've worked on

3/4 or more of the letters, with Adorno doing the others. Possibly the volume will come out next year. You can just imagine how many fantastic things are in the letters.[4]

This evening is Yom Kippur—well! Warmest greetings

Your Gerhard

LETTER 138 From Arendt

370 Riverside Drive
New York 25, NY
September 14

Dear Gerhard,
Along with this letter I'm sending you copies of my letters to the *Zürcher Zeitung* and *ENCOUNTER*.[1] Naturally, I'm perfectly aware that you are going to be disappointed with me, but you'll also have to understand that I had no choice but to put forward my own viewpoint in this issue. You shouldn't forget how until now, during this entire dispute, I haven't uttered a word in public, even though I was literally swamped with opportunities to offer a reaction. I still don't know whether I will make a public comment or not; I certainly won't over the coming months.

Hence, the publication of our correspondence represents an exception that I didn't oppose so long as we remained within the "Jewish sector." The situation for me is entirely different once we turn to the non-Jewish world as well. There was nothing I could have done, or wanted to do, against the "Jewish establishment" intentionally and unintentionally misunderstanding and distorting my intentions in the letter. That said, you can't expect me to promote what I consider senseless distortion.

Now just a couple comments to your letter from August 12. I don't remember any longer what I said to you about the years before 1933 in Paris, but I must have told you how, through my first husband,[2] I knew a whole string of "leftist intellectuals," for instance Brecht, Hanns Eisler, and Korsch. This doesn't mean that I was one of them, and certainly not that I "came from them." Before 1933 I wrote two books and a series of articles; I believe you know most of them. Had I been among the leftist intellectuals it should show up in these writings, and you know perfectly well that it doesn't.

Concerning my "heartlessness" and so on, you really can't expect any kind of reaction from me on this point. I've responded only to the extent that your charge goes beyond personal invective, such as "love of the Jewish people," etc. I could approach the subject from a different direction, namely by looking at the role of the "heart" in politics, but right now I don't have the time. I would ask of you, however, when you get the chance, to take a look at the second chapter of my book on revolution. I discuss the issue there.

What I said about "non-participation"—here you misunderstood me—wasn't directed at the masses, it was directed rather at the individual members of the Jewish councils. I want to emphasize once again the different criteria of judgment for the Jewish councils on the one hand, and the Jewish people on the other. In my book I made this distinction crystal clear.

Once again you have misunderstood the "banality of evil." The point isn't to turn evil into something banal or harmless. The opposite is true. Evil is a surface phenomenon, the decisive issue being that completely average people, neither good nor evil by nature, were able to bring about such immense ruin.

My last point: I consider it a fairy tale that the death of Eichmann could "make it easier for the Germans to confront their past." Even if it weren't a fairy tale, it wouldn't be a valid argument. After all is said and done, a trial was held in Jerusalem; and once a trial starts, the rules of the legal system must be followed. The real question was: How useful are legal means in coming to grips with these issues? All political considerations, regardless of which side they relate to, could only be pernicious here. A trial does not set out to make history; it pronounces justice. Once the death sentence was read, it would have been impossible, in the pursuit of justice, not to carry it out. The only reason would have been a principled opposition to the death penalty, an argument that neither you nor the others made (even though Buber now gives this as his reason).

With best wishes for your trip to Europe.
Your Hannah

[Enclosure]

Dear Mr. Mander:
I thank you for your letter of September 5. There are not technical difficulties in granting you first serial English language rights for the correspondence between Professor Scholem and myself. My only technical condition would be that I must see and approve the English translation.

There are, however, other considerations. This correspondence concerns an aspect of the book which, it is true, has aroused a great deal of polemics but which I consider to be of only marginal importance. My report on the Eichmann trial does not deal with Jewish history, Jewish politics, Zionism, the State of Israel, etc.; it deals only with the trial itself, and I reported only on issues as they came up during the trial. The emphasis on the Jewish aspect in the Jewish press is understandable, but it nevertheless distorts the actual content of the book. I think I understand and appreciate why these purely Jewish issues are of paramount interest to Professor Scholem, but I should also like to make it clear that they never were of central concern to me.

There is one more consideration. You say—very kindly—that you found this correspondence "most interesting." I, however, have the feeling that this debate is not conducted in terms and on a level which could justify its publication in *Encounter*. I also must consider the fact that I have kept silent throughout the polemics my book has aroused. I think this was the only right and proper thing to do under the rather peculiar circumstances. But I must, of course, avoid the impression that this letter to Scholem (an old friend) is all or even a significant part of what I would have to say if I should ever choose to reply in public.

You will have noticed that this is not a clear-cut No. Copy of this letter is sent to Prof. Scholem. I shall wait with a final decision until I hear from you and from Scholem.

Sincerely,
Hannah Arendt

LETTER 139 From Scholem

Copenhagen
October 19, 1963

Dear Hannah,
Your letter that arrived today was more surprising than disappointing. Nothing in these letters of ours, and also nothing in your original agreement to publish them, was bound to the "Jewish sector," which came up for the first time in your letter. Proof of just how mistaken you are on this point can be seen in the unexpected willingness of the two editors of the *Neue Zürcher Zeitung* to publish the letters at once. On the one hand, you tell me that if the *NZZ* is willing to print the letters you'd like to reformulate some sloppy sentences of yours, and then on the other—as I see from your letter to Weber[1]—

you're trying to prevent the *NZZ* from publishing them altogether, and you do so with an entirely new justification. *That* is what surprises me. It is as if you've had second thoughts. What I should do about this, I still don't know, especially after the letter to Mr. Mander.[2] In this dispute of ours I am puzzled why you, as someone who wrote your book for the general public and not for Jews and not for Christians—why you would draw this distinction between the Jewish and the non-Jewish sectors. You should permit readers to form their own opinion of what you depict as the "senseless distortion" in my letter. By doing so, far from "encouraging" the distortion, you will be illuminating the issue from your own perspective.

While I am still in Europe I hope to hear if you are still planning to make the stylistic changes as you had planned, or whether you intend on pulling the plug altogether on the publication of the letters with the *NZZ* and *Encounter*. I'll be in Copenhagen, at Hotel Codan, until the end of September. From the first to the seventh of October I'll be at the Park Hotel in the Wisenhüttenplatz in Frankfurt, and finally in Zurich (Hotel Seidenhof) between October 8–14. I have no idea why your airmail letter took five days to reach Copenhagen. Is that the norm with the post office now?

With best regards for Rosh Hashanah
Your Gerhard

LETTER 140 From Arendt

[Undated]
Dear Gerhard, regarding your letter. From the above you can see that I sent back the galleys to the *Zürcher Zeitung*. Second thoughts? Well, not exactly. When you first asked to publish the letters I had thought only about the *Mitteilungsblatt*. What I consider a "distortion" is the way my book has been written off as a "book by a Jew about the Jews." My reservations are that our correspondence, which revolves around this Jewish angle, will only reinforce this approach to my book.

I'm about to travel to Chicago. You can reach me there until December 15, at Quadrangle Club, 1155 East 57th, Chicago 37, Ill.

Happy New Year,
Your Hannah

LETTER 141 From Scholem

July 27, 1964

Dear Hannah,
For ten days, between October 8 and the 22nd, I'll be in New York to deliver the annual Leo Baeck lecture. I'll be speaking on Walter Benjamin.[1] I don't know how to interpret your silence—I haven't heard from you since last fall. If we want to see one another again, this will be the opportune moment if you are in New York at the time.

On August 14 we will be setting out, so it makes no sense for you to send any news here. With the post you can reach me in Europe: until August 30 I'll be at Hotel Tamaro in Ascona. Until September 14 I'll be at the Park Hotel in Frankfurt, and until September 22 you can reach me at Hotel Carlton in Strasbourg. So perhaps we'll see one another again!

Warmest greetings,
Your Gerhard Scholem

PART TWO

Documents

Hannah Arendt

Five Reports from Germany

Editorial Note

In editing the documents originally written in English, minor formatting changes have been made to reflect the update from a typewritten document to a computerized one (such as italics instead of underscoring). Otherwise, the documents are reproduced exactly as they appeared in the original, including typos. Where possible, German words have been spelled with umlauts rather than with double vowels.

DOCUMENT 1 Field Report No. 12

JEWISH CULTURAL RECONSTRUCTION, INC.
1841 Broadway, New York 23, N.Y.

CONFIDENTIAL

Hannah Arendt
December 1949

I

A draft memorandum to be submitted to the Permanent Conference of the Ministers of Education in the German Federal Republic for its next meeting in Stuttgart on February 10, 1950, has been the outcome of my negotiations with German librarians and governmental authorities during the month of December. Copy of it was mailed to Mr. Ferencz of JRSO whom I tried to keep informed and with whom I discussed all problems connected with my activities. Mr. Ferencz will complete and revise the present text which I then shall submit to Minister Hundhammer in Munich for further action. The memo together with an accompanying letter should be in Munich by the middle of January.

Prof. Eppelsheimer of Frankfurt/M., Director of the Frankfurt Municipal and University Library and an important man in the Hesse-Government, suggested that I approach the President of the German Librarians' Association, Generaldirektor Dr. Gustav Hofmann of the Bavarian State Library in Munich. I discussed this suggestion in detail in Bonn with Dr. Gisela von Busse (in charge of the Reichsaustauschstelle of German libraries in the Notgemeinschaft der deutschen Wissenschaft in Bad Godesberg), former Staatssekretaer Prof. Brill of Frankfurt University (who spent 5 years in a prison and 2 years in Buchenwald), Dr. Weisweiler of the Bonn University Library and former head of Oriental Department of the Prussian State Library in Berlin, and also with Prof. Jaspers in Basel. All these people agreed that without active cooperation from the German librarians nothing can be achieved, that there will be people glad and ready to help in a number of places, but that, generally speaking, an appeal to the librarians may not be enough. Prof. Brill, closely connected with the Bonn Government, was the first to suggest action through the Ministers of Education.

Dr. Gustav Hofmann in Munich received me in the most cordial manner. He agreed at once to publish an appeal in his bulletin, asked me not to formulate this appeal, but to draft a few paragraphs stating what we expect them to do, and then told me in no uncertain words that he did not want to rely on voluntary cooperation alone but would need a government decree to follow up his appeal. He suggested that during the current absence of Minister Hundhammer in Rome, I get in touch with Staatssekretaer Dr. Sattler in Munich, a very important personality in the Bavarian Kultusministerium, and propose the issuance of a decree for all three Western zones. Since Hundhammer is the President of the Permanent Conference of the Kultusministerien of Western Germany (the Bonn Government has no ministry of Education), Munich seemed to be the right place to take this initiative.

Before seeing Dr. Sattler, I met Prof. Held of the Munich Municipal Library, a great friend of the Jews in a slightly mystical way, and discussed with him Hofmann's proposal. He, too, agreed that we shall need a regular decree.

Apart from all other reasons, such a decree appears necessary because Law 59 under which all libraries were asked to report their confiscated property has the serious shortcoming of limiting the obligation of such reports (not of restitution!) to property exceeding in value DM 1,000. Thus, the Munich Municipal Library, for instance, reporting the confiscated collections which they had found in their own stacks, to the Office of Military Government, Property Control, stated expressly that, according to Law 59 they were not obliged to report "insofar as the individual books or the value of books of a group belonging to the same owner does not exceed DM 1,000." (By the way, nowhere else have such books been more carefully segregated and prepared for restitution. See below.) From what I have seen, Jewish confiscated property has been widely scattered, not only through the Nazis but also through later incorporation from caches. Only a decree which rules that everything has to be reported independent of all monetary value (which is uncertain and open to interpretations anyhow) can be of use to us in the long run.

Another reason which makes a decree necessary are the present conditions of German libraries. Large quantities of books which have come back from caches are not yet unpacked and nobody knows what is in the cases. It is quite possible that Jewish property will turn up during a number of years.

Of the two million volumes of the Bavarian State Library, to give an example, only 800,000 are now on shelves, 3 to 4,000 are still in depots and the rest in the cellars. The same condition is true for museums (though apparently not for archives).

Before I went to the Kultusministerium, I also talked to Prof. Heydenreich of the Kunsthistorisches Institut of Munich. He told me at once that a similar action ought to be taken for the museums and that he would be glad to help. As soon as Dr. Hofmann has published this appeal, he would prepare a similar appeal for the museums' officers. He asked me spontaneously why I did not go to Heuss and ask him that the Bonn Government publish a law (as distinguished form a mere decree) for reparation in kind. He believed that this should be possible at this moment. He belongs with Gisela v. Busse and a few others to those people who suffer honestly and seriously from what has been done.

After these preliminaries and after having discussed the matter with Dr. Auerbach, who made the appointment with Dr. Sattler, I went to see Dr. Sattler and discussed with him the more general terms of the matter. He then introduced me to their legal adviser Dr. Eugene Mayer. Before I drafted the memorandum mentioned above, which is the result of my discussion with Dr. Mayer and Dr. Sattler, I went to Nuremberg to discuss the whole matter with Ferencz.

Our Tentative List of Jewish Cultural Treasures, which unfortunately was not known to the German librarians (and more unfortunately even not to JRSO), proved of great help. Dr. Hofmann asked for 30 copies in order to send them to all grater libraries and the people in Ministry wanted it as proof of former possession. JRSO, as you know, has claimed globally community property; but in the coming discussions of who is going to inherit cultural property, the communities or JCR-JRSO, it would have been by far better if they could have claimed according to our catalogue.

II. Caches

In addition to information which you received or will receive shortly from Bernstein, I shall enumerate in the following briefly pertinent information which I gathered in a non-systematic way:

1. Archives: Jewish archival material is in the following archives in Bavaria: Geheime Staatsarchiv—Munich

Staatsarchiv—Amberg
" —Neuburg
" —Nuernberg
" —Wuerzburg

Source: Dr. Winkler, Generaldirektor der Staatlichen Archive Bayern to JRSO

The Frankfurt and Hamburg Community Archives seem to be among the Gesamt-Archiv material in Berlin. For this Gesamtarchiv, Dr. Alex Bein is now negotiation in Berlin, as I reported previously.

Source: Lowenthal.

2. Libraries

a. At least two cases with Hebraica and Zionistica were among the material of a depot in the French zone, Neustadt a.d. Hardt, Haus der Industrie und Handelskammer (near Ludwigshafen). The depot consisted of Nazi state and party archives which had been shipped during the war to the Marienfestung in Wuerzburg.

Source: Dr. Rossmann, Philosophical Seminary of the University Heidelberg.

b. The library of the Munich Institut zur Erforschung der modernen deutschen Geschichte, Abt. Judenfrage, had been in a cache in the neighborhood of Passau. Part of this library is now in the Bavarian State Library. About 20 volumes with stamps of the Munich community were found and returned. The origin of the books is not yet certain, about 5 to 6,000 volumes. The greater part of this library was distributed by the American authorities to DP camps from the Freising Collecting Point. The DP camps were not Jewish; I shall try to trace the whereabouts of these books when I am again in Munich. This library should have been of almost equal importance with the Frankfurt/Rosenberg collection.

c. In the depot of the Munich Municipal Library where formerly confiscated material is being sorted and catalogued are 1,239 volumes bearing the stamp of the Munich Jewish Community and 23 volumes with stamps of the Jewish Communities in Aschaffenburg, Augsburg and smaller Jewish organizations. There are also about 5,000 volumes which are unidentifiable as to ownership, among them a certain number of Judaica which will be returned. I looked through a card catalogue and talked to the librarians—the depot is under the direct supervision of Dr. Seestaller—who seem to be very cooperative. The whole depot consists of about 13 to 14,000 volumes, and contains quite a number of political libraries, Trade Unions, Socialist and Communist party-organizations, etc. The whole depot was liberated by the Americans and then handed to the Municipal Library for trusteeship. 5,250 volumes are private identifiable property belonging to 890 owners. A number of these books are claimed, but I do not yet know how many and did not look into this material.

d. Fifty to a hundred cases with bocks are now under the trusteeship of the Bayrische Landesamt für Vermoegensverwaltung und Wiedergutmachung, Aussenstelle Muenchen Stadt. I talked to Mr. Gastiger who did not even know the exact number of cases. The depot is not in Munich and we could not visit it. Seven cases, however, had been catalogued and I looked through these lists. Not very interesting material, almost entirely non-Jewish but undoubtedly of Jewish ownership, since each case contained a certain number of' books which could be found only in Jewish libraries, such as prayerbooks, etc. Mr. Gastiger agreed that this was certainly Jewish-owned material and promised an exact count and possibly the opening of more cases for the end of January.

e. In Heidelberg in the library of the Jewish Community are some 200 books of more than ordinary interest, Judaica, which were returned to Mr. Sprecher, the librarian, (Sprecher is student at Heidelberg's medical school) through the librarian of the Municipal Library. Mr. Sprecher will return these books to JCR.

More important is that the Heidelberg University Library is still in possession of the Mombert Library, an important collection of first editions and religious literature. Alfred Mombert, a German-Jewish poet, was deported to Southern France together with all other Jews from Baden in the fall of 1940. At that moment, all private libraries of the Jews in Baden were confiscated and apparently sold in public auctions through the Gestapo. Mombert's library was saved through the personal intervention of some of his friends and later transferred to the Finanzamt. Several cases with manuscripts and correspondence with German and other poets from Liliencron to Hofmannsthal were sent to the Gestapo headquarters in Berlin. The Mombert library was sold by the Finanzamt to the Heidelberg University tor 3,000 DM—i.e. for an insignificant amount. The cases were not unpacked and remained in the cellar of the library. A niece of Mombert, Mrs. Clara Vogel, seems to have claimed this library in 1947; however, it seems that no action was taken because she finally did not know what to do with the books. When I am in Heidelberg, I shall try to clear this matter up through Dr. Preisendanz, the head of the manuscripts department.

f. The military authorities have handed about 130,000 non-Jewish books from the Offenbach Depot to Prof. Eppelsheimer in Frankfurt. The greater part of these books is identifiable as to ownership, and it seems beyond doubt that great parts of them did not belong to Jews. However, after my experiences in Munich where the Municipal Library has the trusteeship for similar material, I intend to look into this matter once more. It is probable that German Judaica (though not Hebraica) will be among them.

III. Leads and Other Pertinent Information

a. In Munich, one of the employees of the Municipal Library, an Austrian, told me of the existence of a two-million volumes depot in Carinthia; this depot was one of the Gestapo caches. According to his information, part of this material had been sold after the war and part had been transferred into state institutions. He gave me the addresses of persons who are likely to possess more information.

b. In the Eastern Zone:

1. The Library of the Zuchthaus Brandenburg possessed a rich collection of Judaica, Hebraica, ceremonial objects and Tora-scrolls, Source: Prof. Brill. More information when I am in Berlin.

2. 50,000 volumes bearing the stamp of the *Einsatzstab Rosenberg* with many Judaica and Hebraica were found in the printer shop Vogel in Poestneck, Saalfeld/Thueringen, where the SS had brought them to in fall 1944. In 1947, they seem to have been carried off by the Russians.

3. Confiscated private Jewish libraries in Berlin were offered to the Reichsaustauschstelle and bought for the reconstruction of German libraries shortly before the end of the war. These bocks were later dispersed in caches in Berlin. It seems that most of them were taken by the Russians.

4. Generally speaking, hundreds of thousands of books were brought back to Berlin after the catastrophe (Source: Dr. Weissweiler). Dr. Wolf Haenisch, present head of the Oriental Department of the Prussian State Library, should be contacted for information, for the State Library has incorporated the libraries of former Nazi Institutes and organizations.

5. A great quantity of books bearing the stamp of the Einsatzstab Rosenberg were found in a cache in the neighborhood of Halle and the incorporated into the University library in Halle. Source: Mrs. Hella Jaensch, former

librarian of the Halle Municipal Library, now with the American library in Frankfurt.

6. 80 cases with books of the Fraenkelsche Stiftung/Breslau as well as the archives of the Breslau community were in the Jewish Library in the Tlomackie Street in Warsaw in 1948.

The Warsaw National Library received many Judaica and Hebraica from Polish-Jewish libraries during 1939–1943.

A larger depot existed in Kladzko/Niederschlesien. At least one manuscript from the Viennese Community library was found there. Source: Bernstein.

IV

I finally succeeded in receiving the names and sometimes the addresses of people who bad been connected with libraries and archives during the last years of the Nazi regime.

I also received some leads for people in the Western zones who are in contact with the Eastern zone. However, this matter looks pretty hopeless.

Addresses of Nazis and SS people who have been or are still interned can be obtained from certain government departments.

V. Booksellers and Auctions

See the coming Bernstein report. I talked only to Dr. Karl of Karl & Faber, one of the biggest second-hand dealers in Germany. He told me that he has been trying for years to obtain a Hebrew incunablum for a client without success. He believes that such things are more likely to be offered outside of Germany or to smaller firms.

In this connection, the following item from the Herald Tribune may be of interest:

"Bamberg, Germany, Dec. 26, UP. Police here announced that they bad recovered a wash basket containing eighty-four silver objects which disappeared when the Nazis burned the local synagogue in 1938."

The original item in a German newspaper stated that this silver was found in the gold and silver-shop of a certain Barbara Wagner. According to the German police, this woman has hidden these objects ever since the synagogue fires of 1938.

VI. German-Jewish Communities

There is little doubt that this will be one of our most complicated problems. I talked repeatedly and at great length with Dr. Auerbach in Munich who was very helpful and cooperative. The needs of the communities are not much stressed, only their "rights" which after all look very dubious—and I am afraid even more dubious when one is in Germany. The secretary of the Central Committee for Liberated Jews (DPs) told me in Munich that they had had a library, chiefly from the Offenbach Depot through the DP camps. They had to close the library because there had been not a single reader in six months—and this with 7,000 Jews in Munich!

Dr. Auerbach proposed (and I agreed) to arrange two meetings in January, one in Munich on January 22 and the other in Stuttgart on January 29. The first meeting will be arranged by the Bavarian communities and the second by the Interessenvertretung with representatives of the other Länder. I must if at all possible try to see before January 29 certain key people in Frankfurt, Stuttgart and Freiburg. I shall propose that all distribution of books to German-Jewish communities should be handled by a central body which will be responsible for local distribution, because nobody seems to be aware of the fact that books were already distributed. However, this will be of little help. These communities, or rather these leaders, will probably demand that we give them a decisive voice in all our activities. I am now planning to see Leo Baeck; maybe he can help.

The danger is of course that all books which may turn up in the future will be returned to these communities. In order to get a more objective picture of what to expect, I went to see Dr. Enden, the President of the Bayrische Landesamt für Wiedergutmachung, and asked him what he intended to do with the identifiable books after all claims have been filed: He replied, he would invite the Jewish Community Munich, the Bavarian Landesverband and JRSO in order to come to a decision. I asked the same question of Professor Held of the Municipal Library and he replied: He would turn over the books to JRSO. Things, at any rate, will be handled differently in every city; but the temptation to return books with stamps simply to the former owner is very strong indeed and has already led to a very difficult situation. JRSO, though theoretically maintaining that Jewish communities are not rightful successors, practically does not want to interfere, once books or archives are in the possession of certain community leaders—as for instance in Bamberg, Regensburg, Augsburg and Karlsruhe (as far as the American zone is concerned).

DOCUMENT 2 Field Report No. 15

Hannah Arendt
February 10, 1950

I

In order to prepare my investigations in the French and British zones, I found it necessary to start my trip into these zones of Germany with a visit to London and Paris. Neither in the French nor in the British zone does a proper Jewish successor organization exist. However, it is likely that they will be established in the next few weeks. Steps were taken in London and Paris to assure that JCR concludes with these organizations agreements similar in form and content to that which we concluded between JCR and JRSO.

The British Trust Fund will probably be formed by the JDC, the Jewish Agency and the British Central Fund. Dr. Rabinowicz's Committee will be represented on its Board, as will probably the Board of Deputies, the Anglo-Jewish Association, and the Council of Jews from Germany. Dr. Rabinowicz will kindly act as our representative on the Board. A draft agreement, drafted along the lines of the agreement between JCR and JRSO, was sent to the Central British Fund and copies mailed to all British member organizations of JCR.

The formation of the British Trust Fund has been delayed time and again because of a certain opposition of the British Occupation Authorities which apparently were not too happy about the prospect of taking out of Germany all heirless and unclaimed Jewish property. The British Jewish agencies convinced the Foreign Office of the legitimate claims of the Jewish people to this inheritance: however, the ever repeated conflict between the German-Jewish communities which because of prestige and for less valid reasons have a tendency to establish themselves as successor organizations, and the international Jewish organizations have delayed the actual establishment even further, because only a united Jewish front is likely to overcome the British opposition. In the meantime, work in the British zone, especially with respect to cultural property, will be particularly difficult and delicate. I was asked to postpone my trip to the British zone to the second half of February. I'll start around February 20th but will first contact the United Restitution Office in Hannover (Mr. Schindler, a good man and in full sympathy with our efforts) and Mr. Norris of the British Monuments and Fine Arts Section.

The situation in the French Zone is worse. It seems as though a successor organization is now in the making, mainly due to the initiative of Mr Jerome Jacobson of the JDC. However, according to French restitution law, the German-Jewish Landesverbände are recognized as legal successors to property of extinct communities. The result can well be that a few Jews in Mainz will "inherit" the precious mss. archives, Thora-scrolls and silver of the Worms community (see below) as well as the cases with silver now stored in the Mainz Stadtmuseum and formerly belonging, not to the Mainz community but to the Verein zur Pflege der Jüdischen Altertuemer. How dangerous the lack of a proper successor organization is for our task can well be seen in the case of the Freiburg University Library which now admittedly possesses the private book collections of twenty Jews—and whose director told me quite frankly that, apart from 2 or 3 small units which were properly claimed by individuals, he intends to keep the rest! The trouble is that restitution in France herself is a very uncertain affair. The Consistoire has received some Judaica and Hebraica from the French authorities, all unidentifiable property. But this return was half illegal ("Ils voulaient faire plaisir") and on principle, the Jewish organizations and institutions have no claim whatsoever (nor apparently did they fight for such a claim) to unidentifiable or heirless Judaica and Hebraica.

LONDON: I visited the Council of Jews from Germany, the Board of Deputies, the Anglo-Jewish Association, the Jews' College, the Jewish Museum, the Wiener Library. Dr. Rabinowicz has kindly called a meeting of his Committee under the chairmanship of Prof. Cecil Roth. Present were Dr. Hyamson (Historical Society), and one representative each of the Council of Jews from Germany (Dr. Rosenstock), and the Jewish Museum, the Jews' College, the Wiener Library, and the Synagogue. We discussed the question of the two-year limitation on claims for recovery of identifiable property, and it was understood a) that the British members are at liberty to extend this time limit for Great Britain; b) that they have no right to bind JCR resolutions in this respect. The Committee furthermore welcomed the planned establishment or a Rabbinical Court and suggested that this Rabbinical Court should function even after the peaceful liquidation of JCR.—Ceremonial objects should be offered according to categories before shipment, if possible even with photographs. The Jewish Museum, with a very beautiful collection of its own, is not particularly interested; but new nuclei of collections are planned for Manchester, Leeds, Birmingham and Glasgow.—The Committee repeated its request for more Thora scrolls. The synagogue in London alone lost 25 out of its 36 scrolls through bombing. Prof. Roth and other members insisted that they were ready to pay for the scrolls, to some Jewish welfare organization, since they cannot pay directly to JCR. I suggested some donation to the JDC. (I talked already to Judah Shapiro about this request and it is likely that Great Britain will receive between 35 and 40 scrolls out of the Paris stock.)

My other visits in London, particularly also my visit to Brotman of the Board of Deputies, were all rather useful and yielded a certain amount of detailed information but do not warrant a detailed report.

PARIS: I visited the Alliance Israélite Universelle (Eugene Weil), the Consistoire (Sachs and Manuel), the Jewish Agency (Jarblum), JDC (Jerome Jacobson and Judah Shapiro and Mr. Stein), the World Jewish Congress (Kahn-Debreux), Monsieur Leon Meiss (the most influential jew right now, former president of the Consistoire and the Conseil Representatif des Juifs de France) and Gershom Epstein, French representative of Yivo. I received some help from Leon Meiss and the Consistoire—letters of introduction for the French zone, etc., and some valuable information from Jerome Jacobson for the legal situation in the French zone and from Epstein. The Alliance received all its books with the exception of the Genizah fragments, about 30 boxes, but the Library of the Fédération des Sociétés Juives en France (foreign and immigrant Jews) received only about 500 volumes of its former collection of several thousands. Only the Alliance made a specific request for periodicals.

Dr. Shapiro gave me the following account for Thora-scrolls: Of a total of 774 scrolls, 548 were shipped to Israel as usable but requiring repair, 98 were left in Paris for distribution in Europe, and 127 had to be buried.—Ceremonial objects are distributed; only about 25 pieces are left. I saw such objects from our collection somewhere in the Consistoire.

The following is the restitution procedure of Jewish unidentifiable property in France: all items are sold for the profit of the French authorities; every other procedure is exceptional. Specific claims from individuals are honored from the pool of unidentifiable property. (See my last report.)

II

When I came back to Germany, I had first to follow up on those pending matters which I had initiated during the month of December. I also spent one week in Wiesbaden to get a better idea of problems involving allocation and handling of individually owned books.

1. I sent the memorandum to the president of the Permanent Conference of the Kultusminister, Hundhammer in Munich, and copies of it to the Kultusministerien of Baden, Freiburg; Nordrhein-Westfalen, Duesseldorf; Hessen, Wiesbaden; and Rhineland Pfalz, Koblenz. I talked once more to Staatssekretaer Dr. Sattler in Munich who promised the formation of a special Library Committee which then would promptly issue a decree and who told me repeatedly that he liked the memorandum and thought that my propositions were reasonable and appropriate. I also saw Prof. Stein, Kultusminister of Hessen, who had called our office after having received copy of the memo: very friendly and interested. Stein, whom I saw about ten days after Sattler, told me that he had already been informed by Munich of the matter and formation of a library commission. I finally saw Dr. Clemens von Brentano in Freiburg, chief of the Staatskanzlei, in my opinion the best man, Catholic, anti-Nazi of old standing etc.

In Munich, I also saw Dr. Middendorf, editor of the Bulletin of the Librarians, who promised the draft of his appeal for the beginning of February. I did not see Dr. Hofmann.

2. Wiesbaden: We have some difficulties with Mr. Heinrich with regard to the individually owned books. Many claims were received, mostly phony, and many more are expected; the whole thing has received a kind of notoriety which makes him hesitate to give us the books. I outlined to him our proposition to search for owners of 6 or more books. He first agreed, but later raised more difficulties (obviously not his own, but from some superior authority) with respect to books in lots of 5 and less. He wanted all books treated as we want to treat those of 6 or more. I refused this, pointing out a) the technical difficulties, b) my lack of authority to go beyond our first proposition. But I showed him paragraph 4 of our agreement with recipient libraries and we then agreed that in the distribution of the individually owned books we would make reasonably sure that books belonging to the same owner would go to one institution and not be dispersed between several libraries.

In the meantime, the individually owned books are already processed (see Lowenthal's report). But the work is slow and difficult. I still fight tor a deadline of April 30 to close all present operations, but I am afraid I'll lose the fight. As to the other, i.e. the remainder of the institutional collections, it will be necessary, as I pointed out before, to pool all remaining Hebraica and Judaica from the various communities, including Koenigsberg and Frankfurt, in order to fill the needs of South American countries. But I think we can ship everything directly, only scientific material, periodicals, rare books (including those printed prior to 1790), some non-Jewish material and the pedagogical collection of the Frankfurt Religionslehrer are prepared for New York.

Mr. Heinrich, fortunately, agreed to put the collecting point at our disposal for material not collected by the military Authorities but by ourselves be it through claims by JRSO under Law 59 or through agreement with the communities. This is very important, as there is reasonable hope to receive quite a number of archives, some thousands of books and the important silver collection the Frankfurt Jewish museum in the near future.

III

Frankfurt: 18 cases and two golden cups of the 17th century are claimed and prepared for restitution. They had been saved and stored by the Historical Museum in Frankfurt. The collection of Thora curtains has been destroyed through an air raid on a Dominican monastery where they were hidden by Dr. Rapp, the present director of the Museum. The Jewish community in Frankfurt made no difficulties they would not know what to do with these things anyhow. Mr. Maier, President of the community, asked to receive a few objects if they are of no particular interest for his community.

Munich: 2,500 Judaica from the Municipal Library (which prepared an itemized list) and 25 cases with general material are claimed. There is a possibility that this claim may be contested by the Bayrische Landesverband even though Orenstein, the Rabbi of Munich, is definitely on our side and Dr. Auerbach promised to leave us alone.

I'd like to stress that in both cases no claims would have been made if we had not taken matters in hand and found out what where is what.

Schnaittach: The objects in the Heimatmuseum are now being claimed. Because of difficulties with the present director, I asked Dr. Lill of the Amt für Denkmalspflege (die vorgesetzte Behörde) to intervene.

Before I forget: The most helpful introductions in Germany are those of

Dr. Schoenberger who seems to be the best liked man in this country. Moreover, with very few exceptions, his friends are indeed the few "good" people whome one can meet here.

Archives are being claimed all over Bavaria and some in Württemberg.

Systematic searches are planned for the local museums into which ceremonial objects after 1938 may have been "saved." The Munich Amt für Denkmalspflege (Lill) and Prof. Martin of Karlsruhe and Freiburg will issue circular letters to Bavaria and Baden respectively.

We shall have to initiate a similar action for all monasteries; I contacted Prof. Hauser in Heidelberg who promised a list of the Bischöfliche Diözesen who should issue such circular letters.

A similar action will be undertaken for a number of central archival institutions in the different Länder. In the case of Bavaria, one letter to the General Director brought more information about archives in Bavaria than all our previous investigations.

French Zone. Mainz: I was promised, but did not yet receive, a list of the objects of the former museum, now stored in the Museum of the Municipality. There, something seems to be fishy, and we shall have more trouble, investigations, contacts, etc.

Moreover: the Jewish community in Mainz possesses as you know still its library which one can only *see* upon written request, several days before. The present librarian, moreover, thinks of emigration. The whole business is fantastic, but there is little we can do about it. Mr. Oppenheim of Mainz, a nice man, told me the only possibility would be some pressure from the Jews in the French occupation army. I went to see Rabbi Kalifa of Landau and his superior, Eischitzky, to whom I had an introduction from Meiss and the Consistoire. He had an infected throat and could not see me. His assistant promised quick reply. He should tell Kalifa that he should go with me and talk to the Mainz jews. To make things a little brighter, I also went to see Gustav Levy, President du Tribunal Supreme in Baden, who was extremely friendly, is an old Zionist and may be useful when we need French authorities.

Worms: The story of Dr. Illert is well known by now. He has exhibited the Mahsorim and an old scroll, as well as a few pieces of silver. He now wants to restore the synagogue, has already started, and will soon begin to dig in order to see if he can find more objects of the former museum. He also promised to try to find out who took the silver cups of the Chevra Kadishah out of the bank safe in 1939. In his opinion, Worms will get some Jews back, if he only holds on to what he has. He has photographed all the tombstones and saved all the splinters of the capitals (Kapitäle) of the pillars, in order to put them together again. The whole archives are safely in the Museum. He showed me everything and promised a list. The gentlemen from Mainz have already tried to get them, but he has told them, that with these objects 2,000 tombstones would roll to Mainz—and would they please tell him what they are going to do in this event. Whereupon they disappeared. For the time being, Worms has become, according to him, a "Wallfahrtsort" of the Jews; now they need a synagogue in order to be able to pray properly. He has asked the Bundesregierung for the necessary funds and I am not at all sure that he won't get them.

As long as we have no agreement with the Jewish communities in the French zone, I rather have these things with Illert than ship them around. The rights of the Landesverband, i.e. Mainz, to these things are out of question. Moreover, I think it will not be wise to make him angry right now because I do'nt know who else will got to the trouble of digging on the synagogue place.

Freiburg: Nathan Rosenberger, President of the Oberrat der Israeliten Badens is an extremely nice man; intelligent, idealistic, but rather old. There is hardly anything worth while our time, with the exception of the very suspicious University library (see above). I also saw there some bishop but without results.

IV

Microfilming: I still believe that we should think of investigation and microfilming as one operation, because the microfilming will give an access to the stacks. I talked to Eppelsheimer and then went to Soecken of the New Documentation Center in Frankfurt. Please insert here my former letters on the question of the budget. (I am too tired to copy the whole business once more.)

This is a matter of great importance. There will not be any difficulties for microfilming in German libraries,—manuscripts, documents, archive collection, whatever we want. In my opinion, the manuscripts of the Munich, Frankfurt, Berlin and Hamburg libraries should be microfilmed, as well as some important archival material.

For microfilming properly speaking, the following possibilities exist:

1. 10-page strip, used in Western Europe. Advantage: easy to find a given page. 2. Roll films as used by the Library of Congress. 3. Some new system to make the microfilms as usable as a book.

In my opinion, the mss. of the Munich, Frankfurt, Berlin and Hamburg liberaries should be microfilmed. In addition some important archival material.

All archival material which we get into our depot should be microfilmed. If and when the Gesamtarchiv will finally arrive, it should be microfilmed before being shipped to Palestine.

Other matters: The German Museum people plan the formation of a German restitution commission and a true search of their material. The important people in this commission will be: Prof. Martin, Karlsruhe; Holzinger, Frankfurt; Metternich, Bonn; Heidenreich, Munich. (All friends of Schoenberger.) We shall probably be able to work very closely together with them; up to now, they have not yet the okay of the occupation authorities and there are difficulties between the three zones.

Jewish communities: I attended two meetings, the meeting of the Bayr. Landesverband in Munich on January 22 and the meeting of the Interessenvertretung in Stuttgart on January 29. Both were not very pleasant. However, we arrived at a kind of agreement:

1. They will not hinder us in the recovery of scientific or otherwise valuable material which the community can't use.

2. They will inform us of the cultural needs of their communities, i.e. the Landesverbände, and the rabbis will be responsible for distribution of and requests for books for the communities of a given Landesverband.

3. They will hand over to us what they don't need.

None of these promises are binding or very reliable. It ist difficult to explain in such a report why that is so. But, unfortunately, it is a fact. It is quite typical that Augsburg is supposed to have had a library of 3,000 volumes which allegedly dwindled down to 300 or 500. But even this information needs not to be true. C'est comme ca.

The following items were formally promised us:

1. The ceremonial objects from Augsburg, now with Orenstein in Munich.

2. 360 volumes of archives in Regensburg, currently with Mr. E. Hermann.

3. The archives of the Straubinger community.

4. The archives now housed by the Karlsruhe community.

5. About 15 Thora-scrolls and some hundred books now in Freiburg.

6. The more important items in Heidelberg community.

The case of the sale of the Laemmle Klaus collection through the Mannheim community is interesting and unfortunate for two reasons: a. this is a precedent; we must insist on cultural property not being sold. Almost all communities are in the possession of other property though it is true that none of them has the possibility to take care of cultural property. The Frankfurt community admitted this very frankly when the question of the silver objects was being discussed. b) The Laemmle Klaus collection was never the property of the Community but was owned by a special foundation. This will be quite important for instance for the Mainz silver, which also was not the property of the Community, and in a number of other instances.

This is by far not all, but all for the moment. In order to give you some idea of the work in detail, I enclose copy of my last memo to Dr. Lowenthal in which I am asking him to follow up a number of things, which turned up during the last 10 days mostly, or which I had forgotten.

Respectfully submitted,
Hannah Arendt

P. S. Itinerary:
January 2–8: London
9–15: Paris
16–18: Wiesbaden
19: Mainz
20: Frankfurt
21: Wiesbaden
22–25: Munich
26–29: Stuttgart and Tübingen
30: Heidelberg
31: Karlsruhe
February 1: Worms and Landau
2: Wiesbaden—Mainz
3: Heidelberg
6: Basel and Freiburg
8: Baden-Baden, Rastatt
9: Wiesbaden
10: Wiesbaden

DOCUMENT 3 Field Report No. 16

If you want to circulate this report, please leave out all sentences in brackets.

Hannah Arendt
Report on Berlin, February 11–18, 1950

I

Generally speaking, conditions in Berlin are most unfavorable for us because all larger libraries as well as the main stocks of the Jewish Community are located in the eastern sector. (Transportation from the Russian into one of the western sectors is not impossible, but depends entirely upon good will of the Berlin community and is, indeed, a rather dangerous affair. Every office in the Eastern sector, Jewish or non-Jewish, is infested with agents.) The following cultural treasures are exceptions to this rule:

1. The collection of paintings of the Jewish Museum which is now being claimed by the new offices of JRSO in Berlin according to a specified JCR list. This collection seems to be complete and will eventually come into our possession.

2. More than 300 pounds of silverware (ceremonial objects) are now housed in the JDC warehouse of the Jewish Community building at Joachimsthalerstrasse 13. These are the remnants of an almost complete Gestapo collection in the Muenchener Strasse consisting of synagogue silver from all over Germany. There were originally more than 500 pounds of silver (the difference has been sold or stolen or what not). There is no doubt that the Berlin community has the right to these ceremonial objects, but, unfortunately, it is also beyond doubt that one will have considerable difficulty in persuading this community that it should give up its greatest treasure (in terms of money). Information on these objects was given to me by some people, Jews, who had worked in the Muenchener Strasse, and the story was confirmed by Rabbi Schwarzschild who told me about the present whereabouts of this huge collection.

3. A small amount of books and archival material in the Haupt-Archiv of Berlin, formerly belonging to the Reichs-Sippenamt. This material contains stray books from the Fraenkelsche Stiftung and the Viennese Community Library as well as some documents of Yivo, Vilna. This material Is now being claimed by JRSO und is awaiting restitution to JCR. (I talked to the Director, Bellee, as well as to other officers.)

4. It is possible that some material is still in the Volksbuechereien in the Western sectors of Berlin. The Berlin Municipality through the Volksbildungsamt (Mr. S. Link) and the Amt für Literatur (Dr. Moser) will initiate a systematic search.

II

The following collections are now in the eastern sector:

1. On the cemetery in Weissensee there are about 1,000 Torah-scrolls, kept in a small room in rather poor condition. It was already pretty difficult to be permitted into the room through a gardener, Schwarzwaelder, to whom I had a personal introduction and who is a nice and friendly fellow. As a rule, nobody is permitted to enter the room and it was quite impossible to examine anything. We did a rough count; the scrolls seem to be in pretty good condition, but handles are mostly broken und there are hardly any covers.

2. In the community building there are still an estimated 8–10,000 books as well as many archives, documents, etc. From this "library" a small staircase leads up to a room directly under the roof where I found mountains of paper which, upon closer inspection, turned out to be parts of the Gesamtarchiv—I don't know how great a part, impossible to estimate—unbound periodicals, books, loose documents, folders of the Reichsvereinigung up to 1943, books bearing the stamp of the Gesamtarchiv, possibly manuscripts, correspondence, etc. The so-called librarian, a certain Mr. Fink whose "catalogue" of the library defies description, did his best to prevent me from climbing the stairs and "soiling" my hands. I asked Rabbi Schwarzschild to give the good man specific instructions to forget his "catalogue" and start sorting the material and putting it on shelves in the library.

3. I worked in the library for many hours, but the conditions are such that it is almost impossible to say exactly what is there and what is not. However there are at least 70 bound volumes of *Ketuwoth* from Amsterdam, covering at least a period of 250 years or more as well as a great many unbound documents. Among the latter, I saw documents from Mantua, Germany, Bialystok, the correspondence of Caro, Posen 1810, apparently from the archives of the Lehranstalt, pinkassim of the 18th century from Breslau and Posen. About 1,500 good non-Jewish books, such as the complete set of Die Zukunft of Maximilian Harden, 5 volumes Aristoteles (Akademie Ausgabe), some nice modern bibliographical items.

There are not more than about 1,000 German Judaica, but a great many Hebrew and German-Jewish periodicals as well as non-Jewish periodicals (Magazin fürdie neue Historie und Geographie of 1769 etc.)

The following periodicals: Der Jude, 1916–1922, scattered, the Monatsschrift Israelitisches Familienblatt, CV Zeitung, Der Morgen, Neue jüdische Monatshefte, Jhb. f. Jüdische Geschichte u. Litteratur, Jüd. Zeitschrift

(A. Geiger), Jüd. Zeitschrift f. Wissenschaft und Leben I–IX, Allgemeine Zeitung d. Judentums, etc. etc.

A small collection of music literature (but not Arno Nadel).

A collection of about 700 volumes of legal literature.

Some good theological literature. About 200 Zionistica. And a few hundred Judaica in English, Russian and French.

There are thousands of prayerbooks and chumashim and some 800 Hebraica, mostly Talmud and Mishnayoth as far as I could find out.

About 500 Hebrew periodicals.

III

1. Our main source is still Prof. Grumach and the people with whom he has or had contact. It appears from what I learned that the German synagogue silver which we always thought had been smelted was on the contrary carefully preserved for the purpose of establishing an anti-Jewish museum. The people who worked there, i.e. under the Gestapo in the Muenchener Strasse, told me that they had seen silver from all over Germany and many items from abroad, for instance a Torah-scroll from Sloniki which was 500 years old.

2. Library of the *Hochschule*: Part of it has been destroyed through bombing in the Eisenacher Strasse, part of it was shipped to Theresienstadt, a few volumes are in the Oranienburgerstrasse, and part seems to have been sold in Jerusalem by the firm Bamberger and Wahrmann who apparently bought these volumes in Holland!

3. In 1945/1946 hundreds of thousands of books were spread all over Berlin. Even parts of the Jewish central collection in the Eisenacherstrasse were still there. The German libraries (especially the State library in this instance) took whatever they wanted. Some months later, the Bergungsgesellschaft stepped in and distributed books to the Staatsbibliothek, the Stadtbibliothek and the Ratsbibliothek as well as to a number of Volksbuechereien.

4. In 1947 the Oranienburgerstrasse still housed the following material which had been put there by the Nazis: (a) One room with archival material from the Reichssippenamt (which generally received Jewish archives everywhere in Germany) and (b) one room stacked with books to the roof. According to information from various sources, partly from Germans and partly from Jews who had worked there, the present president of the Community handed all this material over to the municipal authorities of the OstSector (a certain Mr. Reutti of the stadt. Bergungsgesellschaft) and retained only

the Jewish material. (Rabbi Schwarzschild claims to have selected this Jewish material; I am more than doubtful that he has done anything at all—and can understand that he preferred to leave this little matter alone. It seems, that Dr. Mayer adopted an openly threatening attitude.

In 1945/1946: Hundreds of thousands of books were all over Berlin. Even parts of the Jewish central collection in the Eisenacherstrasse was still there. The German library (esp. the State library in this instance) took whatever they wanted. Some months later the Bergungsgesellschaft stepped in and distributed books to the Staatsbibliothek, the Stadtbibliothek and the Ratsbibliothek as well as to a number of Volksbuechereien.

5. For reasons, unknown to everybody, the Mormones were the first to get permission from the Russians to have a look at caches. They seem to have taken a certain number of archives (for God knows which reason) and especially the films of the Gesamtarchiv and other Jewish archives which had been prepared by the Nazis and which partly are now in Duisburg-Hamborn in Westfalen. The photographer in Westfalen is also a Mormone and offers currently photostats or films to Jewish communities in the Western zone for money. Munich and Stuttgart have bought such material, whereas for instance Karlsruhe had no money. Parts of these films are now in the hands of Mr. Langheinrich, a photographer in the Staatsbibliothek. One probably could get them for a small amount of money. Mr. Langheinrich said he wanted to hand these films over to his colleague in Duisburg.

6. *Gesamtarchiv*: I wish Mr. Bein is right and that there is some hope to get this back. From what I heard in Berlin, I am not very hopeful. The Gesamtarchiv, originally in the cache in Schoenebeck, was transported years ago—to Halle?, to Merseburg?, to Potsdam?? Mr. Korfes of the Zentralarchiv in Potsdam knows probably where it is. (I am afraid this is not a proper matter for a report. But if Mr Bein gets it, he has achived a miracle.

IV

What can we do?

I did not even attempt to talk to the community people but talked and tried to arrange a little understanding with Rabbi Schwarzschild who will be back in the States around June 1. (Schwarzschild is a young and nice fellow, but whoever had the idea to put him in this most difficult position in all Germany—all right, I am not going finish.) Schwarzschild has a certain but limited influence in the community.

He might try to work out an agreement with us along the following lines:

1) We get the Torah-scrolls via western sector with the understanding that not more than 15% of the scrolls are returned in repaired condition to the community for distribution in Germany (this will give them some prestige), and that some high rabbinical authorities—let us say the chief rabbi of Palestine and Finkelstein and Glück and the President of Yeshiva University write them a letter felicitating them on their steadfastness and spirit of sacrifice and what not. (2) We get the more valuable parts of the library to be determined by Schwarzschild and one representative of JCR and all the archival material, as well as manuscripts etc. In return we give them what they need, and since we won't have it in Wiesbaden—textbooks and Einheitsgebetsbuch—we give them money as a contribution toward publication of text- and prayerbooks. A Tentative Agreement will be sent you in one of these days. Schwarzschild is supposed to fill in a draft which I prepared some exact figures as to how many books they want and how much money. He will then proceed to talk his community people into the deal and I am supposed to persuade you to accept it. (There is really no choice. We should not pay more than 4–5000 Marks or ab. 1000 $. The Thorascrolls alone are of course much more valuable than that.) 3) The silver In the Joachimsthaler Strasse should be claimed by JRSO, in my opinion. I don't know if they will succeed. But there is a chance since it is housed in a JDC warehouse (though in a community building) and it is doubtless not silver which ever belonged to the Berlin community. As far as I can see and from what Schwarzschild and others told me, there is no hope for getting it from the community through an agreement.

This is a pretty sad report, but we should try along these lines. There Is hardly an alternative left.

Considerable quantities of Judaica and Hebraica are now being offered through dealers from the eastern zones because of an acute lack of money everywhere in Eastern Germany. Schwarzschild told me that he buys everything he can afford to buy and showed me a few nice items, such as a set of Der Jude of 1771 (9 vols. the first missing), a Kessuva from Padua of 1680 and an illustrated Pessah Haggadah (Wolf) 1740. He'd like to have a fund of 1.000 Marks and buy for us certain special items. (To give you an instance of the general conditions: he offered me a sederplate from the collection of Paris Rothschild with inlaid Gold mosaic for 350.– Marks! This has been offered to him, but he had not the money. That the plate after all once belonged to M. de Rothschild and still bore his name did not bother anybody.)

Respectfully submitted
Hannah Arendt

DOCUMENT 4 Field Report No. 18

JEWISH CULTURAL RECONSTRUCTION, INC.
1841 Broadway, New York 23, N.Y.

STRICTLY CONFIDENTIAL *Not for Circulation*

Hannah Arendt
February 15–March 10, 1950

I had postponed my trip to the British zone in the hope that the negotiations between the British and international Jewish organizations on one side, and the German Jewish communities on the other, scheduled for the beginning of February, would have resulted in an agreement with respect to the succession to community property. (The chief difficulty for the establishment of a "British Trust Fund".—the successor organization in the British Zone—has been the current conflict between the claims of German Jewish communities to succession to the pre-Nazi community property and those of the International Jewish organizations.) However, these negotiations started only at the beginning of March. Things look considerably brighter now than when I visited the British zone, because, according to a news item in the Times of April 6, the Allied High Commissioners have nullified a German governmental decree which has recognized the Jewish communities of Rhineland-Westphalia—one of the Länder in the British zone—as legal successors to community property, stating explicitly (a) that this recognition was unfair because a majority of the surviving members are now living outside of Germany, and (b) that the German government had overstepped its competence. This is of general importance because the German Jewish communities frequently show a deplorable tendency to make common cause with the German government against the international Jewish organizations.

I started out on February 20, and went first to Hannover, in order to talk to Mr. Schindler, head of the United Restitution Office in the British zone. Because of the unsettled situation, he urged me to avoid contact with German political bodies, not to discuss any restitution problems and to explain that we are interested only in the centralization of information. The reason for this caution is that the British Occupation authorities, as distinguished from the Foreign Office in London, have shown a not too friendly attitude towards the claims of the Jewish organizations, and that even the London authorities were willing to recognize a Jewish successor organization only if they were confronted with a united Jewish front, which at that time had not yet been constituted.

This caution was even more important for cultural property than for real estate, bonds, etc. I saw at length Mr. Norris of the British Monument and Fine Arts Section at Bünde in Westphalen. Although Mr. Norris has not much love for the Germans, he also would be clearly opposed to shipping cultural objects out of Germany. This general opposition has been considerably strengthened through the IRO sale of cultural objects in New York. The French, as well as the British officials in Germany, felt that this sale was against all international agreements and constituted a kind of looting. Mr. Norris told me that he and his French colleagues have reported the matter to their governments and hoped for diplomatic intervention on the highest level. It is, therefore, very important for our work that we stress the fact that our organization does not sell.

Mr. Norris was on the whole very friendly and cooperative. He gave me introductions wherever I needed them, and in one instance, where I had to interview a librarian who had been a member of the Nazi party and to whom I had not been able to get an introduction, he made an appointment for me through the British authorities. In his opinion big SS caches exist still in the British zone in the neighborhood of Hamburg as well as in Westphalia, which the British have never been able to locate. He also drew my attention to a small collection of Torah scrolls in Berlin, American sector, for which in the meantime I contacted the proper municipal authorities and which will be claimed through the usual channels. He gave me also information about the *Ahnen Erbe*, a Bavarian Nazi outfit, whose president was a certain Professor Wüst, former Rector of the Munich University. This organization had many branches and sent looting missions into the Balkans. They had an agreement with the German military authorities according to which they could keep 10% of all looted material found its way into Munich University library, because of the connection between the *Ahnen Erbe* and the university through its president, and this matter is now under investigation.

Hannover:—The Jewish community of Hannover has a small library of not more than 1,000 volumes among which are a few interesting items—periodicals, broken sets, and some scholarly Hebrew and other material—which I asked them to send to the Wiesbaden depot. They also have a few folders with archives of the 18th century from smaller communities in the neighborhood. I hope that these documents also will be sent to the Wiesbaden depot.

While I was there, I went to the headquarters of the Social Democratic Party to which I had personal introductions from Berlin and other places. They promised to try to get us some information about the eastern zone and this information will be valuable even though it has hardly any practical consequences at this moment.

Hamburg: —The situation in Hamburg is somewhat different from any other city in Germany. The Hamburg municipal authorities under the Nazi regime and, of course, being Nazis themselves, were the only ones who succeeded in saving tangible and valuable material from the SS and Gestapo depots in Berlin, where all these things in general ware centralized. The following items have been saved:

1. The entire Hamburg community library was handed over to the Hamburg University library and put into the same caches which the University library had used for its own books in the neighborhood of Dresden. The numbers of the cases are 401–499. The greater part of these cases are now in the hands of the Dresden Jewish community and the remainder in the Albertinum in Dresden. Dresden is located in the Russian zone and all efforts of' the university library to get back its own material together with these cases, as well as the efforts or the Jewish community (relations are very good in Hamburg between Jews and Germans and all efforts were coordinated) have proved to be of no avail. Our only consolation is that this valuable library still exists in its entirety.

2. When the Hamburg Jews were forced to give up their household silver, a total of about 20,000 kilos, the Hamburg Museum people, and especially a certain Dr. Schellenberg, who is now with the Museum für Hamburgische Geschichte, were permitted to take out the most valuable objects, so that 2,000 kilos of silver were saved from smelting. These items, about 30,000 objects, among which, however, there are only few ceremonial objects (Schellenberg mentioned especially a beautiful Wand Menorah from Hamburg from the beginning of the 19th century) were bought by the municipality of Hamburg. 150 items were photographed and that photos are with Prof. Meyer of the Kunstgewerbe Museum, Hamburg. The whole material is now under the guardianship of the Hamburg municipality (Stadt-Kämmerei). The objects-are being listed by the municipality under the direction of Schellenberg, and the catalogue will be ready in about a year from now.

This is private property and there are a few claims to restitution. However, only in one case has property been returned. Schellenberg, upon my question as to what he thinks will ultimately be the fate of unclaimed objects, told me of his plans to establish with them a special division in his museum. He did not hide his sharp opposition to every attempt shipping "his" collection (which in fact is his selection) out of Hamburg. The British Trust Fund, however, will have no trouble of claiming this hoard as heirless private property.

3. The archives of the Hamburg Jewish community, which were previously reported to us and for which Shunami negotiated with Dr. Pardo, are now in the Hamburg State Archives, with the express agreement of Mr. Goldstein, President of the Hamburg Jewish Community. For the moment, there is no prospect whatsoever of getting this valuable material. Mr. Goldstein, by the way, a very decent man, has received considerable help from the Hamburg municipality for the restoration of the Jewish cemetery. In his opinion, the Jewish organizations have not done a thing for the Hamburg Jews and as long as the international Jewish organizations do not help in the reconstruction of Hamburg community life, Mr. Goldstein will oppose every attempt to get Jewish things out of Hamburg. In other words, he wants mainly help for the restoration of the cemetery. He is convinced, and probably rightly so, that the Jewish community archives are well cared for by the Hamburg State Archives. I did not press the matter, for the reasons mentioned above, but have the impression that it now should be possible to come to an agreement with Mr. Goldstein whose honesty is beyond doubt.

Dr. Prado, by the way, is without much influence in the Jewish community at present and negotiations for the archives should not be conducted with him. There is, however another personality involved: a certain Notar Hertz, a Jew or a half-Jew who simply happens to have a special interest in this material, loves to work with them, etc. Strange as it may sound, it seems to me quite obvious that if Dr. Hertz does not want to part with the things, which he finds very conveniently housed in the State Archives, we shall have trouble to get them. This is only one illustration among many that every cultural treasure to which German Jewish communities lay claim eventually becomes private property of some member of the community, and this not because of wickedness or dishonesty, but simply because of objective conditions.

4. What Dr. Schellenberg had done for private household silver was done by the Hamburg Völkerkundemuseum for synagogal silver. The more valuable items were bought by the Museum from the Nazi authorities. After the

war the Museum reported its treasures to the British authorities which in turn gave them *as a loan* to the Hamburg Jewish community.

5. The Jewish community in Hamburg has also interesting items in its library. The books are on shelves, but not used. There are about 400 Judaica with the stamp of the Talmud Torah Schule Hamburg, approximately 500 Hebraica with either ex-libris of private owners or unidentifiable as to ownership. Only a small percentage of private owners are Hamburg Jews. 200 more Hebraica bear Hebrew ex-libris. More than 100 Judaica bear the stamps of private owners, not necessarily from Hamburg, but from all over Germany, and about 100 non-Jewish items were the property of a missionary Catholic association called Fluss-Schiffer-Seelsorge.

6. Part of the ceremonial objects from the synagogues in Altona is now in the Altonaer Museum.

Other Interesting Information:—1) The collection of Hebrew manuscripts in the Hamburg State Library, and especially the collection of Levy, is saved and unpacked. I saw the collection myself. The Director, Dr. Tiemann, is friendly and cooperative.

2) I also saw Dr. Heise, Director of the Kunsthalle in Hamburg, with whom I discussed the situation in the Altona Museum, and who recommended a letter to the Ämter für Denkmalpflege in the British zone. He gave the names and addresses and agreed that we write "upon his suggestion."

3) I also visited the Voelkerkunde Museum in Hamburg, where I talked to Dr. Dittmer. The reason was my unfortunately fruitless attempt to find out what had happened to the Hamburg Museum für Jüdische Volkskunde. This museum had been on loan in the Voelkerkundemuseum until April 27, 1937. On that date Dr. Bamberger, as a representative of the Gesellschaft für Jüdische Volkskunde, received 60 books, 29 paintings, and 445 ethnographic objects. A list of this material is in the files of the museum. I have been asking Mr. Goldstein, President of the Hamburg Jewish Community, to help us find out what happened later, but so far without success.

Another item of interest is the following: Dr. Dittmer, moreover, who formerly was in Berlin, told me that his colleague, Dr. Neverman of the Berlin Voelkerkundemuseum, which is now in Dahlem in the American sector, received ceremonial objects from the Jewish communities in Galicia during the war "zu treuen Händen."[1] This matter is now under investigation.

Lübeck:—In Lübeck, I talked to Norbert Wollheim, who is the head of

1. "For safe keeping."

the so-called Central Committee, that is, the overall organization of Jews in the British zone. As distinguished from the other zones, Jewish DP's and German Jews are organized together. However, the German Jewish communities in Rheinland Westphalia have already broken away, and it is likely that this whole combination will dissolve in the near future. The reason that it could function so long and so well is the personal friendship between Norbert Wollheim of the German Jews and Jessel Rosensaft of the DP's. Wollheim as well as Rosensaft adopted a friendly attitude toward our claims.

In Lübeck, the Jewish community had received a number of ceremonial objects from the municipality at the end of the war. These objects were supposed to be from the local synagogues and given last year to some Israeli congregations. In Israel, however, where members of the former Lübeck community now live, it turned out that these objects had never belonged to any synagogue in Lübeck. Nobody has thus far been able to identify these items.

I saw Rosensaft later in Hamburg, and explained to him, as I had done to Wollheim, what our aims are. Both assured me that there is a considerable amount of cultural property in the hands of the communities now. They seem to be aware of the danger that this may be dispersed, or even sold, and at any rate be lost to Jewish scholars and the Jewish tradition in the world. Upon their request, I wrote them an official letter asking them to write to the Jewish communities in support of our purpose and get them to report at least what they hold now.

Cologne:—I spent several days in Cologne with very little result. I tried, without success, to find out what happened to the collection of the ceremonial objects from Deutz, and talked especially to the people of the Rheinisches Museum in Deutz, who had this collection, among other objects from the Rheinland, for their exhibition in 1928. Nobody seems to know what happened after 1929, when everything was returned.

I also tried to find out if any Jewish archives survived in the municipal archives, and was assured that there were none.

However, my main reason for going to Cologne was to interview Dr. Juchhoff of the University library, who, during the entire Nazi time, was chief of the so-called Gesamtkatalog, and who, therefore, should know almost offhand which libraries during the period in question acquired Hebraica for their Oriental departments. I made an appointment with Dr. Juchhoff through the British Occupation authorities—with the result that the reception was almost the worst which I ever got in Germany. Mr. Juchhoff, of course, knew nothing. However, my assumption that the Gesamtkatalog is lost or has been destroyed proved to be wrong. Only the card catalogue was found in a cache in the Russian zone and transported to Russia (two and a half million of cards!) The Gesamtkatalog exists in print until December 1944 under the title "Deutscher Gesamtkatalog, Neue Titel."

Up to 1939, volumes which cover 5-year periods were published; single unbound issues, covering three month periods, are available to the end of 1944. It may be worthwhile to go through this whole catalogue and see which are the oriental departments of the university libraries that acquired considerable quantities of Hebraica after 1933. I had a look at the matter and am pretty convinced that this will take up a lot of time, and the results, of course, are unsure. The Gesamtkatalog is available in many German libraries and probably also abroad.

To the treasures in the British zone now known to us must be added the following:

1. The 300 kilos of silver in Berlin which are now stored in the cellar of the Jewish community building, Joachimsthaler Strasse 13, in the British sector, which I reported previously. This is synagogue silver from all over Germany and came into the possession of the Berlin community only by accident.

2. Parts of the Koenigsberg community archives which had been incorporated into the Jewish Division of the Koenigsberg State Archives in 1934 and 1937 are now in Goslar in the *Zonales Archiv-Lager* under the custodianship of the Mayor of Goslar, Mr. Meyer. We shall receive a list of this material in the near future.

3. The Samsonschul-library is now, probably intact, in the Bibliotheca Augusta (also known as Lessing Library) in Wolfenbüttel. This collection has been handed over to the German Library in the early years of the Nazi regime for safekeeping. The acting librarian seems prepared to restitute to legal successors. The Samsonschule had been a Stiftung made by the Samson family.

4. A certain firm of photographers, Gatermann in Duisburg-Hamborn, possesses the microfilms of southern communities of which they have been trying to sell photostats to German Jewish communities in Bavaria, Württemberg and Baden. Part of these films seem to be in the hands of the photographer of the Berlin State Library in the eastern sector, a certain Mr. Langheinrich. We are now receiving photostatic copies of the lists of all films which are with Mr. Gatermann and received already those for Baden: A total of 1,021 films with 24,344 pages covers 92 communities in North Baden (American zone) and 450 films with 10,259 pages cover 33 communities in Süd-Baden (French Zone), mostly birth, marriage end death registers of the

19th century. These films were probably made from the *Gesamtarchiv*. The ownership question is complicated, because the *Gesamtarchiv* was confiscated Jewish property, but the films, made upon the initiative of the German Reich, are probably today German property.

The deadline for claims in the British zone expires on June 30, 1950. Since a successor organization does not yet exist in the British zone, we have brought all findings to the attention of Mr. Schindler of the United Restitution Office in Hannover. We also sent copies of the Tentative List to the Central British Fund in London, and to Mr. Schindler in Hannover, in order to make possible a specified list of claims to cultural community property. It should be borne in mind, however, that cultural treasures which now turn up in the British zone do not necessarily originate from the localities where they are found.

Addendum to My Previous Report on the French Zone:—We found out in the meantime that the more valuable part of the Jüdisches Altertumsmuseum in Buchau, Württemberg, French zone, is now in the Buchau Heimatmuseum. The cases are not unpacked; the museum officials intend to return these objects to the only Jew in Buchau, Mr. Siegfried Einstein.

I spent my last days in Germany in Wiesbaden, Frankfurt, and Nuremberg. In Wiesbaden I talked to Mr. Heinrich, who is now on vacation for two months and whose promises as to the availability of space at the Central Collecting Point for future incoming material unfortunately proved to be only tentative. The Occupation authorities are anxious to close their Monuments and Fine Arts Sections. There is, however, justified hope that we may keep some government facilities until the end of this year.

In Frankfurt I saw Prof. Eppelsheimer for the last time and talked to him about the considerable quantities of books which were turned over by the military authorities from the Offenbach depot to the German government in Hessen and which are now under his trusteeship. The large majority of these books are unclaimed private property of non-Jewish content. According to the agreement with the military authorities, unclaimed books were to go to German libraries. Prof. Eppelsheimer agreed that a majority of these books were formerly Jewish private property and assured me of his Intention to give us back a certain percentage. I proposed about 50%. This question, however, will come up only when restitution to claimants has been finished, i.e., at the end of the summer. Eppelsheimer then will need the okay of the Kultusminister of Hessen, Dr. Stein. Before I left Germany, I wrote to Stein explaining to him the situation and the tentative agreement which I had reached with Eppelsheimer.

DOCUMENT 5 Final Report to the JCR Commission

JEWISH CULTURAL RECONSTRUCTION; INC:
1841 Broadway, New York 23, N. Y.

CONFIDENTIAL

Hannah Arendt
Executive Secretary
Report of My Mission to Germany
respectfully submitted to the Board of Directors
for the meeting on April 12, 1950

My trip to Germany was based on the assumption that Nazi-confiscated Jewish cultural property must have found its way into German libraries, museums and archives and that it could be discovered only through active cooperation of the German personnel in charge of such institutions. My task therefore was (a) to get as much information as possible with respect to the whereabouts of Jewish communal cultural property, and (b) to try to enlist the cooperation of German librarians, museum-officials and archivists.

(a) Because of material conditions in Germany (destruction of buildings, return of large material from war-time caches, and great turn-over of personnel) it is impossible as yet to assess how much material will eventually turn up. The unpacking of cases will in many instances be a matter of years. However, it seems as though more archives and more ceremonial objects were saved than books, largely because the German-Jewish book collections were more strictly centralized in Berlin while synagogue silver and archival material more frequently found their way into local institutions. Discoveries which I made myself or which were made in connection with my trip have been reported in the field reports and will not be repeated here.

(b) Largely because of material conditions but also for other technical and psychological reasons, I am now even more convinced than I was before that we depend upon the good will of German personnel to a very large extent and that all other methods of investigation are impractical. To quote but two examples: (1) it took our library investigator more than four weeks of hard work to discover a few archives in Bavaria where Jewish confiscated material had been deposited during the Nazi regime. One single letter to the general director of Bavarian archives resulted in a reply which gave a probably complete list of such localities without omitting a singe "discovery" of the investigator. (2) I discovered the valuable Frankfurt art-collection through contacting the respective museum-directors and without using any detective methods.

I. Negotiations with German Librarians and Museum Officials

1. *Librarians.*—In order to establish contact with German librarians, I first visited Prof. Eppelsheimer in Frankfurt and Dr. Gustav Hofmann in Munich. The former enjoys the highest reputation in Germany today (he never was a Nazi), and the latter is the President of the German Librarians Association which covers the three western zones.

The outcome of these negotiations was an appeal to be published in the bulletin of the Librarians' Association, asking all librarians to search for confiscated Jewish material and to continue this search throughout the process of reorganization of the libraries. Special attention will be given to specific Nazi collections (special institutes which were or were not connected with the universities or seminars, which had been headed be outspoken members of the party, etc.) which in many instances were put into caches during the war together with the normal library material.

This appeal, for which I submitted a draft, asks only for centralization of information through Jewish Cultural Reconstruction; that is, every new discovered item should be reported of our office in Wiesbaden. The reason why restitution is not mentioned is that the restitution law is so different in the three western zones that we shall be confronted with a different situation in each of them. Moreover, centralization of information is a first and the most important step.

2. *Museums.*—I tried to achieve two different purposes: (a) to find out what had happened to outstanding Jewish art collections, and (b) to find out which part of the synagogue silver has survived. The results of these efforts have been reported in the field reports. We now know the whereabouts of the Frankfurt, Mainz, part of the Berlin, and the Buchau collections; synagogue silver as rule, was concentrated in Berlin, but important parts have survived, especially in Hamburg, Altona, and the British section of Berlin.

I saw a great many museum directors and officials of the German Monuments and Fine Arts Sections. Unfortunately, no over-all organization like the Association of German Librarians exists. In a number of cases, synagogue silver has gone to the local museums after the pogroms of 1938. This material can be located best through the Monuments and Fine Arts Sections, which are in charge of supervising local museums.

In Bavaria, the head of the Monuments and Fine Arts Section has issued a circular letter to all the local museums in Bavaria asking them to report what they have and to watch the unpacking of cases. The same is true for Baden. In a number of other instances we have been contacting these authorities ourselves, usually with reference to somebody who is either well known to them or has some authority over them.

As far as the Occupation authorities are concerned, the whole restitution process of art objects will come to an end in the very near future. A new, purely German body, is now in formation which will continue to search and to restitute art objects found in museums. I visited most of the professors, museum directors, etc. who will eventually sit on this body, and established a preliminary contact with them. Its president will probably be Staatssekretär Dr. Sattler of Munich, with whom we are in contact.

3. *Archives.*—Archives are a special problem, because they do not always fall under the authority of the Kultusministerium, but in most instances under the authority of the Ministry of the Interior. JRSO has claimed the Bavarian material, but we are not yet certain if we shall be able to ship archives out of the country. For this and other reasons, we decided to wait and see how restitution in these instances will be handled, to claim in the future only archives prior to 1870, and to restrict our activities to correspondence in which we ask for information. Such letters have been written to other Länder in the American zone, but it is generally agreed that the main bulk of surviving archives is located in Bavaria.

II. Negotiations with German Government Officials

Dr. Hofmann, President of the German Librarians' Association and General Director of the Bavarian State Library, pointed out to me at once that for operations on this scale the active support of the Kultusministerien would be needed. Western Germany is now divided into eleven Länder, and since the Bonn government does not have a Kultusministerium of its own, Dr. Hofmann's recommendation meant that we should contact eleven Länder Ministerien. Fortunately, the Kultusministerien are incorporated into a central body called "the Permanent Conference of the Kultusminsterien," which meets every two or three months. The President of this corporation is Dr. Hundhammer the Kultusminister of Bavaria.

After oral negotiations with several people in the Bavarian Kultusministerium, and especially Staatssekretär Dr. Sattler, I submitted a memo to Hundhammer in his capacity as President of the Permanent Länder Conference, in which I proposed the following steps:

> "1. To publish an appeal to all state and municipal libraries, university institutes, archives, and museums, to make a most careful examination of their stocks and constantly to keep this problem in mind while unpacking the material that comes back from the wartime relocation points.
>
> "2. To issue a decree of the Permanent Länder Conference of Kultusministerien, which would provide a legal basis for this voluntary action of the three western zones to submit periodic reports; a negative report in negative cases should be specifically required.
>
> "3. All information from the three western zones should be centralized by the German offices of Jewish Cultural Reconstruction in Wiesbaden."

I stressed moreover that

> The scattered bits of information which we have hitherto been able to gather indicate that there is justified hope to recover at least part of the cultural treasures of the German Jews and to make them accessible again for the Jewish educated and scholarly world. Particularly now that relocated stocks are flooding back into the German libraries and museums and that the libraries of former Party organizations and institutions are being incorporated by the German libraries, a systematic investigation of the German museums, archives, and libraries ought to become feasible.

I submitted copies of this memorandum to a number of other Kultusministerien, but not to all of them, and I paid personal visits to the Kultusminister of Hessen, Dr. Stein, and the chief of the Staatskanzlei in Freiburg, Baden, Clemens von Brentano.

During a second visit which I paid Dr. Sattler, he assured me of his sympathies for these demands which he thought to be very reasonable and practical. As a preliminary step he wanted to form a permanent library commission which then should have the power to issue a decree. Dr. Stein, whom I saw at some later date, was already informed of the formation of such a permanent library commission.

III. French and British Zones

With the exception of Freiburg, I avoided official German government contact in the French and British zones, because the question of restitution in these zones where no successor organizations exist is of a very dubious nature. This is also the reason why I asked in my memo addressed to the three zones only for centralization of information. I had been warned by the Jewish organizations in Germany, especially by those acquainted with conditions in the British and French zones, that even the discussion of restitution could be dangerous. The British and French authorities are generally opposed to handing over cultural items from Germany to international bodies which ship them out of the countries, and the German officials are only too well aware of this opposition.

Jewish cultural treasures are scattered all over Germany even though the bulk of them was found in the American zone. We should be aware, however, that through the confiscation and centralization policy of the Nazis and through war time conditions, hardly anything is being found in its former locality, i.e., books from Hanover may turn up in Munich, and vice versa, etc. It would be of great importance for our operation to enjoy equal status In all three zones.

In order to prepare the ground for future operations in the British and French zones, I got in contact with the British Central Fund in London and, after preliminary discussions with the Fund and with our British member organizations, presented to them a draft agreement which would assure that JCR becomes the cultural agent of the future British successor organization. Since the Central British Fund's memorandum for the Formation of a successor organization in the British zone has been drawn up along the lines of the by-laws of JRSO, I drafted a tentative agreement along the lines of our agreement with JRSO.

I also got in contact with Jerome Jacobson of the JDC Paris, who will be instrumental in setting up a successor organization in the French zone, if that ever comes to pass, and informally proposed to him a similar agreement.

IV. Russian Zone

It is impossible to get anything out of the Russian zone, it is difficult and dangerous to obtain precise information; but it is virtually certain that important parts of German-Jewish communal property are still in existence.

I tried to obtain as much information as I could and reported it in the field reports. Moreover, while I was in Hannover I contacted the headquarters of the Socialist party and asked them to pass information on to us and even to try to answer specific questions. We are now in current contact with them and every bit of information which we can get through them or other channels will be valuable even though it has hardly any practical consequences at this moment.

V. German Jewish Communities

Conditions in Germany are uncertain, chaotic and full of surprises; the same, unfortunately, holds true for conditions in the German Jewish communities. Throughout my stay in Germany, I have been trying to find a central body that enjoys enough authority to be able to enter into generally binding agreements. When this failed, I tried to come at least to agreements with the Landesverbände in order to avoid to have to negotiate with every single community. For this purpose I attended two meetings,—one of the Bavarian Landesverband In Munich, and the second of the Interessenvertretung in Stuttgart.

Unfortunately, I must admit that only negotiations carried out an a local level with the community leaders in a given city seem to have any chance to achieve results at the present moment. Promises made by larger bodies are not taken seriously, no matter how solemnly they are being pronounced.

These negotiations are important for three reasons: (a) German Jewish communities hold considerable material of Jewish cultural treasures, which in most instances are not used but allowed to deteriorate and which, moreover, in a majority of cases never belonged to that community, but were found by accident after the war in the neighborhood of the respective towns or cities.

(b) To this must be added the fact that the communities in many instances consist of a half-dozen people who do not care and a membership who cares even less. Communal property, therefore, has a deplorable tendency to be transformed into private property.

(c) Even in the American zone, where theoretically JRSO is recognized as successor to community property, the German Jewish communities are de facto in a position to interfere with every single claim which we submit. In the French zone they have even the Occupation law on their side. But law or no law, what actually happens time and again is that the municipal authorities, whenever they find any Jewish property, no matter what its nature or its former owner, go directly to the Jewish community leaders whom they know personally and turn the material over to them. Once this has happened, there is no way left but the very uncertain way of negotiations which in a number of cases have led to the desired results.

VI. Future Operation in Germany

Present operations in our Wiesbaden depot, concerning the distribution of the remainders of the German-Jewish institutional collections and the processing of the individually-owned books which have not yet been turned over to JCR, should be terminated on July 1st. The extent of future operations in Germany will depend to a large extent on the outcome of current negotiations for the establishment of successor organizations in the British and French zones where we know even now of the existence of important cultural material and where a thorough search for material has not yet started.

But even if we consider our future activities only within the framework of present conditions, it seems obvious that the results of my negotiations and the attempt at centralizing all information through our German offices can bring fruits only if we decide to keep a skeleton apparatus until the end of this current year. Moreover, in the American zone important material has been claimed by JRSO during my stay in Germany, especially in Bavaria, Frankfurt and the American sector of Berlin, and a number of German-Jewish communities are beginning to hand their more valuable material over to us. For the orderly reception of this material alone it will be necessary to keep JCR offices alive for the next nine months.

EDITORIAL REMARKS

At the beginning of the 1960s, in connection with Arendt's book on the Eichmann trial, two letters (Letters 132 and 133) from the Arendt–Scholem correspondence appeared in published form (see Letter 132, note 589). For the textual basis for the letters' publication, Scholem supplied newspapers with a copy of his draft letter to Arendt, as well as Arendt's original reply. Since his draft diverges by a few words from the final version of the letter found in the Arendt archives at the Library of Congress in Washington, the letter printed here deviates slightly from the familiar version.

In the middle of the 1990s, Itta Schedletzky and Thomas Sparr, editors of the multivolume Scholem correspondence, made public additional letters from the Arendt–Scholem correspondence. Moreover, various other excerpts from the Arendt–Scholem letters appeared in Schöttker and Wizisla's *Arendt und Benjamin*. This present volume brings together all letters, telegrams, and postcards Arendt and Scholem wrote to each other. The majority of these documents have been preserved as originals. Many of the official letters Scholem addressed to Arendt at Schocken Books or to the JCR central office in New York do not exist as originals, since few of the files from the New York publishing house were preserved. The archives of JCR have likewise vanished (they were presumably destroyed). For this reason, alongside Arendt's original letters found in the Scholem archives in Jerusalem (NLI), and Scholem's found in the Arendt archives in Washington, DC (LoC), the textual basis for this present volume comes from carbon copies and other copies of letters found in the Scholem archives. Additional letters we used are copies of originals sent to other people and which are now found in the JCR division of the JNUL Archives (more specifically, the Salo Baron archives) at Stanford University Library. Other such letters were found in the archives of the National Library in Jerusalem.

Many of the textual supplements Arendt mentioned in her JCR letters were not preserved among the letters, though they could be reconstructed through the JCR section of the JNUL archives. In the second half of the correspondence, information on documents (such as Arendt's review of Scholem's *Major Trends in Jewish Mysticism* and her reports from Germany for the JCR central office—the "Field Reports") can be gleaned from their respective introductory remarks.

The last page of Arendt's review of *Major Trends*, which appears in this volume for the first time and which Itta Schedletzky first mentioned in her edition of Scholem's letters, is included as part of the comments Arendt sent to Scholem on his *Major Trends*. Arendt's Field Reports are also published here for the first time.

In the annotations, special attention has been paid to the intellectual dialogue manifested in the letters, a dialogue in which Arendt and Scholem read and commented on each other's works. Examples of such dialogue are provided through references to works and, when applicable, to exact citations in those works. Annotations are especially essential for the official correspondence during the time period of the JCR. As key members of a far-flung communications network, Arendt and Scholem shared information that does not appear directly in the letters, and which cannot be assumed to belong to general knowledge today. The annotations therefore add essential information to illuminate Arendt and Scholem's common efforts at saving the cultural heritage of European Jewry. As with the Field Reports, these letters offer new insight into postwar German history.

In the annotations, critical information is provided in the pertinent place in the letters. Later reference to this material is given only when it appears two or more letters earlier and when it is not available in the index. To avoid any unnecessary break in the flow of the text, we have largely avoided employing the phrase "Information is unavailable."

ACKNOWLEDGMENTS

We would like to extend special thanks to Margot Cohn and Rachel Misrati (both work at the manuscript department of the National Library in Jerusalem); Alice Birney (at the manuscript department of the Library of Congress); Jeff Katz (Arendt Library, Bard College); Jerome Kohn and Jessica Reifer (both are at the Hannah Arendt Trust in New York); Esther Liebes (Scholem Library, Jerusalem); Zachary Baker (Stanford University Library); the Siegfried Unseld Foundation; as well as Frank Mecklenburg (Leo Baeck Institute, New York).

In addition, we want to give special thanks to Elisabeth Matthias (Frankfurt, Germany), Regina Nörtemann, and Petra Schreyer (both in Berlin) for their essential assistance in the completion of this manuscript; and to Yael Maagan (Jerusalem) and William Viestenz (Stanford) for their great help in archival research. For their frequent advice, we thank Steven Aschheim (Hebrew University, Jerusalem), Christiane Böhler (Berlin), Yvonne Domhardt (Israelite Cultural Community, Zurich), Sophie Freud (Massachusetts), Elisabeth Gallas (Simon Dubnow Institute, Leipzig), Anita Grossmann (Cooper Union, NY), Dana Hermann (American Jewish Archives, Cincinnati), Rachel Heuberger (Municipal and University Library, Frankfurt), Cilly Kugelmann (Jewish Museum, Berlin), Andreas Lehnardt (Johannes Gutenberg Institute, Mainz), Ursula Ludz (Munich), Ursula Marx (Walter Benjamin Archive, Berlin), Nadine Meyer (Frankfurt), Aubrey Pomerance (Jewish Museum, Berlin), Andy Rabinbach (Princeton University), Edith Raim (Institute for Contemporary History, Munich), Benjamin Richler (NLI, Jerusalem), Gudrun

Schwarz (Walter Benjamin Archive), Hermann Simon (Centrum Judaicum, Berlin), Natan Sznaider (Academic College, Tel Aviv), Claudia Wedepohl (Warburg Institute, London), Yfaat Weiss (Hebrew University, Jerusalem), Christian Wiese (Johann Wolfgang Goethe University, Frankfurt), and Erdmut Wizisla (Walter Benjamin Archive, Berlin).

NOTES

Introduction

1. Steven Aschheim, "The Metaphysical Psychologist: On Life and Letters from Gershom Scholem," in *Journal of Modern History* 76 (December 2004): 905.

2. As she wrote in a letter to her friend Erwin Loewenson, DLA, Loewenson Papers, 76.955/2.

3. Letter to Shalom Spiegel, 17 July 1941, NLI, Scholem Papers.

4. Letter to Arendt, 28 January 1945; see Letter 19.

5. Arendt writes about Eichmann, for instance, that he "had no authority to say who would die and who would live; he could not even know.... The prosecution, unable to understand a mass murderer who had never killed (and who in this particular instance probably did not even have the guts to kill), was constantly trying to prove individual murder." *Eichmann in Jerusalem: A Report on the Banality of Evil* (New York: Viking, 1963), 196.

6. Letter exchange with Hilde Fränkel, LoC, Manuscript Division, Hannah Arendt Papers.

7. Walter Benjamin and Gershom Scholem, *Briefwechsel* (Frankfurt: Suhrkamp Verlag, 1997), 265.

8. Hannah Arendt, *Rahel Varnhagen* (New York: Harcourt Brace Jovanovich, 1974), 214. Also quoted in Julia Kristeva, *Hannah Arendt* (New York: Columbia University Press, 2001), 128.

9. *The Correspondence of Walter Benjamin and Gershom Scholem*, trans. Gary Smith and André Lefevere (New York: Schocken, 1989), 244.

10. Benjamin, *Illuminations*, ed. Hannah Arendt, trans. Harry Zorn (New York: Schocken, 1969), 255.

11. Scholem, *The Messianic Idea in Judaism and Other Essays on Jewish Spirituality*, trans. Michael Meyer (New York: Schocken, 1972), 10.

12. Letter from Arendt to Jaspers on 7 September 1952, in *Hannah Arendt/Karl Jaspers Correspondence*, eds. Lotte Kohler and Hans Saner (New York: Harcourt Brace, 1992), 200.

13. See *The Correspondence of Walter Benjamin and Gershom Scholem*, 254.

14. Gershom Scholem, "On the Social Psychology of the Jews in Germany: 1900–1933," in *Jews and Germans: The Problematic Symbiosis*, ed. David Bronsen (Heidelberg: Universitätsverlag, 1979), 26.

15. See Letter 28.

16. Benjamin, *Illuminations*, 36.

17. Benjamin, *Illuminations*, 264.

18. "Creating a Cultural Atmosphere," in Arendt, *Jewish Writings* (2007), 310.

19. Ibid., *Jewish Writings*, 303.

20. "Jewish History Revised," in Arendt, *Jewish Writings*, 300.

21. Cecil Roth, in his "Opening Address at the Conference on Restoration of Continental Jewish Museums, Libraries and Archives," London, 11 April 1943, Wiener Library Microfilms, Roll 26.

22. There can be no precise accounting of these irreplaceable losses. An eyewitness cited in the *Frankfurter Zeitung* (28 March 1941), for instance, expressed pride and malice when recounting the arson attack of the most illustrious Jewish library in Poland, the Chachmei yeshiva in Lublin: "The fire lasted twenty hours. The Lublin Jews assembled around and wept bitterly, almost silencing us with their cries. We summoned the military band, and with joyful shouts the soldiers drowned out the sounds of the Jewish cries." Cited in Philip Friedman, "The Fate of the Jewish Books during the Nazi Era," *Jewish Book Annual* 15 (1957–1958): 5–6.

23. See the footnotes to Letter 51.

24. Letter from 26 December 1949.

25. See Arendt, *Fragwürdige Traditionsbestände im politischen Denken der Gegenwart* (Frankfurt: Europäische Verlagsanstalt, 1957).

26. Quoted in Hans Sluga, *Politics and the Search for the Common Good* (Cambridge University Press, 2014), 147. Elisabeth Young-Bruel quotes the same passage in *Hannah Arendt: For Love of the World* (New Haven, CT: Yale University Press, 2004), 323.

27. David Biale, "Gershom Scholem's Ten Unhistorical Aphorisms," *Modern Judaism* 5(1) (February 1985): 67–94.

The following notes have been abridged from the German edition.

Letter 1

1. Neither of the two letters is in the archives.

2. Arendt fled to Prague after 1933, and from there she sent a friend back to Germany to take her mother to Paris. Together with her mother, in Paris Arendt and her second husband, Heinrich Blücher, lived in a hotel—the Principeautés Unies—ten minutes from Benjamin's apartment on 10 rue Dombasle. In early 1939 she

began work directing the office for the Jewish Agency's Central Bureau for the Settlement of German Jews.

3. Arendt finished her biography of Rahel Varnhagen in Paris and sent the manuscript to Scholem. Scholem, after reading it, made comments in a letter that later went missing. Benjamin had already announced Arendt's work to Scholem in his letter of February 20, 1939, and wrote that the book had "made a great impression" on him. Arendt swims "with powerful strokes against the current of edifying and apologetic Judaic studies. You know best of all that everything one could read about 'the Jews in German literature' up to now has allowed itself to be swept along on precisely this current" (*Benjamin/Scholem Briefwechsel*, p. 295). Scholem replied to Benjamin on June 30, 1939: "The [book] of Arendt on Rahel has ... pleased me *very* much although I probably read it with a different accent than she wrote it in. It is an excellent analysis of what took place at that time, and shows that an association built on lies like this could not be sent from the German Jews with their 'German-ness' without misfortune. In lies—namely on the assumption that everything only comes from one side and the other always self-sacrificing (in the strictest sense) and likely taking joy in it. Too bad, I do not see how the book should ever be released" (*Benjamin/Scholem Briefwechsel*, p. 309).

4. The titles Arendt gave these final two chapters are "Between Pariah and Parvenu" (1815–1819) and "There Is No Leaving Judaism" (1820–1833).

5. The German-Jewish publisher, collector, and bibliophile Salman Schocken (1877–1959) had a large collection of first editions, manuscripts, letters, and papers from the time of Rahel Varnhagen.

6. Arendt had sent Scholem a draft manuscript of the book.

7. Walter Benjamin.

8. For several years Benjamin had depended on a stipend from the Institute for Social Research headed by Max Horkheimer. In February 1939 Horkheimer informed Benjamin that due to a shortage of funds the Institute might be forced to stop their support, which would have left Benjamin bereft of an income. Arendt, upon hearing about his financial troubles, offered to help find him new sources of support. See Benjamin's letter to Scholem from April 8, 1939.

9. In the mid-1930s Arendt had worked for Youth Aliyah, a Zionist organization that at the time was bringing German-Jewish youth to Palestine. She accompanied one such group, and it was during this visit that she met Scholem.

Letter 2

1. The Nazi regime stripped German Jews living abroad of their citizenship, making them stateless. Most German Jews in France had just a temporary residence permit. The French government refused to grant these German Jews exit visas.

2. Benjamin's sister, Dora, lived for a time with Benjamin in France. In 1942 she fled from France to Switzerland.

Letter 3

1. In the spring semester of 1938 Scholem was invited as a guest professor to deliver the Hilda Stich Stroock Lectures at the Jewish Institute of Religion in New York. On his way from Palestine to New York, he visited Benjamin in Paris. Fanja, his second wife, accompanied Scholem to Paris only on his return trip. At the time, Benjamin was in Denmark with the German playwright Bertolt Brecht. Fanja met Arendt and Blücher in Paris, but not Walter Benjamin, who was still with Brecht in Denmark.

2. Arendt and Hans Jonas met at the University of Marburg. They both studied under Martin Heidegger. In 1940, at the beginning of the Second World War, Jonas volunteered to serve in a Palestinian military unit and later with the Jewish Brigade, which was attached to the British Army.

3. Kurt Blumenfeld (1884–1963) and Arendt, both from Königsberg, were close friends. The older Blumenfeld, who had been the president of the German Zionist organization, had asked her in 1933 to do work for the organization by researching anti-Semitic propaganda. The Gestapo arrested her for a week. She and Blumenfeld remained friends after he immigrated to Palestine. In 1942 he lived in New York, where he worked for the Zionist organization Keren Hayessod.

4. Marianne Zittau (1901–1972) was a friend of both Arendt's and Scholem's. She fled Germany for France. Later she immigrated to Palestine.

5. Shalom Spiegel (1899–1984) was a professor of medieval Hebrew literature at the Jewish Theological Seminary in New York.

6. On the same day Scholem wrote in a letter to Shalom Spiegel: "One of my good female friends, Mrs. Hannah Arendt-Blücher, has arrived in New York from Paris. I wrote to her that she should pay you a visit. She is a wonderful woman and an excellent Zionist. I'm sure you'll find her most interesting."

Letter 4

1. Theodor Wiesengrund Adorno (1903–1969) was a German-Jewish philosopher. On October 8, 1940, Adorno wrote to Scholem and began the letter with the line "Walter Benjamin has taken his life." In a later letter from November 19, Adorno described to Scholem what he knew of the details of Benjamin's death.

2. In July 1939 Benjamin completed his essay "On Some Motifs in Baudelaire." The essay appeared in the January 1940 edition of *Zeitschrift für Sozial Forschung*. The essay was part of his uncompleted book on Baudelaire.

3. Heinrich Blücher.

4. Benjamin was interned in a French holding camp at Nevers.

5. The handwritten copy of "Theses on the Philosophy of History," sent by Benjamin to Scholem, was probably lost in the mail. Arendt had another copy, which she gave to Adorno, Benjamin's literary executor, after her arrival in New York.

6. The Institute for Social Research, as the Institut für Sozialforschung, was

founded in 1923 in Frankfurt. After 1933 Max Horkheimer and Theodor Adorno rebuilt the Institute in New York.

7. See above, note 8.

8. Probably meant here is the draughtsman and caricaturist Augustus Hamburger.

9. In the 1920s the United States introduced a national-origin quota system, which pegged the number of immigrants allowed into the United States to the ethnic makeup of the American population. In 1939 the immigration quota for the United States for Germans and Austrians was 27,350.

10. In May–June 1940, Arendt spent five weeks at the women's internment camp in Gurs. She got out due to the chaos caused by the German victory over France.

11. The armistice agreement, signed in June 1940, required the French government to repeal its law granting right of asylum and to release from prison all German prisoners, both military and civilian. In addition, it required the French government, "upon demand," to hand over to Germany all former German citizens.

12. On July 15, 1940, Adorno sent Benjamin a letter of support, and then on July 17 a formal declaration stating that the Institute was prepared to employ Benjamin as editor of the Institute's journal.

13. In Benjamin's final letter to Arendt, from July 17, 1940, he writes about his fears about the fate of his manuscripts. Meanwhile, the Gestapo, armed with addresses of German Jews and socialists, confiscated all of the material Benjamin had left in his apartment on rue Dombasle. Arendt learned at the end of 1941 that two suitcases filled with Benjamin's writings had arrived in New York, and were with Adorno. Benjamin's sister, Dora, had asked one of his acquaintances to get the materials to Adorno. Other writings, mainly the work he did in Paris in the 1930s and which would be published later as the Arcades Project, were hidden in the Bibliothèque Nationale, which Arendt did not know at the time she wrote the letter.

14. In August 1940 Benjamin traveled to Marseilles, where there was a visa awaiting him at the American consulate.

15. After 1940, the Institute's journal appeared in English, as *Studies in Philosophy and Social Science*.

16. In the 1930s Salman Schocken, the department store entrepreneur and publisher, established a branch of his German publishing house in Tel Aviv, later in New York.

17. Kurt Blumenfeld's wife, Jenny (1889–1962), remained in Palestine during her husband's US trip.

Letter 5

1. In a letter he wrote in November 1940, Adorno asked Scholem's assistance in bringing together all of Benjamin's writings, the ultimate aim being the publication

of his collected works. In the same letter, he announced that the Institute was planning a special edition of its journal that would be devoted to Benjamin.

2. In the November letter, Adorno wrote to Scholem, "in all truth, after Benjamin's death you are about the only one from the old world whose survival means a lot to me personally. Forgive me this clumsy confession, but the world no longer permits us to speak in hints and allusions. There must be some way for you to come here" (Adorno, *Blätter* 5, pp. 150–53).

3. Shortly after writing this letter, Scholem received a letter from Adorno in which he informed him that a number of letters from 1941 had been lost in the mail. In this letter Adorno also described the situation with Benjamin's literary estate: that two suitcases filled with manuscripts and books had arrived in New York and that Adorno had made an inventory of the contents. Few of the manuscripts were entirely new to Adorno. "The most important ones," he wrote, "are a selection of exceedingly bold notes bearing the title Zentralpark (a double entendre referring to the importance of these notes as well as to his plans to come to New York) which evidently should be the nucleus for the last big section of the Baudelaire book which never was written. There are also the historico-philosophical theses from spring 1940 which you probably know. There is, however, not a single trace of the huge body of material comprising the Arcades Project which doubtless exists somewhere. There are rumors that he deposited this material at the Bibliothèque Nationale in Paris ... The whole question of an edition of Walter's work can be approached only after the war."

4. Arthur Koestler (1905–1983) lived in the same house as Benjamin in Paris. After escaping from France, he settled in England. In 1940 he published his book on the Stalin trials of the 1930s, *Darkness at Noon*.

5. *Major Trends in Jewish Mysticism* grew out of Scholem's 1938 Hilda Stich Stroock Lectures. The first of the lectures, "Philosophy and Jewish Mysticism," appeared in the *Review of Religion* (May 1938), pp. 385–402.

6. Scholem's dedication to Benjamin is this: "To the memory of Walter Benjamin (1892–1940). The friend of a lifetime, whose genius united the insight of the metaphysician and the interpretive power of the critic and the erudition of the scholar, died at Portbout (Spain) on his way to freedom." (Scholem wrote these words in uppercase.)

7. Paul Tillich (1886–1965) was a Protestant theologian. He and Arendt met in Frankfurt and then, after the Nazis barred him from teaching at German universities, he left for the United States.

Letter 6

1. *Major Trends in Jewish Mysticism* (Tel Aviv: Schocken Books, 1941).

2. In his book *Story of a Friendship* (New York: New York Review Books Classics, 2003), Scholem writes about Arendt's highly critical sentiments toward Adorno and Horkheimer.

3. "Monsieur," Arendt's husband Heinrich Blücher, was not Jewish.

4. Blücher worked as a German expert for the study *German Psychological Warfare* (edited by Ladislas Farago), supported by the American government.

5. Arendt's essay "From the Dreyfus Affair to France Today" appeared in *Jewish Social Studies*, 4, 1942, pp. 195–240. The other essays Arendt wrote at the time are "Why the Cremieux Decree Was Abrogated" (*Contemporary Jewish Record* 6, no. 2 [1943]: 115–23), reprinted in *Jewish Writings*, eds. Jerome Kohn and Ron Feldman (New York: Schocken, 2007), pp. 244–53; "Concerning Minorities" (*Contemporary Jewish Record*, no. 4 [1944]: 353–68), also in *Jewish Writings* (pp. 125–33); and "Race Thinking Before Racism" (*Review of Politics*, no. 1 [1944]: 36–73).

6. Between March and October 1939, Arendt published a column in the weekly Jewish-German journal *Aufbau*. Her column "This Means You" called on all Jews, both in and outside Palestine, to support the creation of a "Jewish army" against Hitler.

7. The French interned German nationals in the internment camp in Gurs.

8. "Zion" refers here to the Zionist project in Palestine.

Letter 7

1. *Walter Benjamin zum Gedächtnis* (In Memory of Walter Benjamin) appeared in early 1942. Along with Benjamin's essay on history, there was a comprehensive bibliography of Benjamin's writings.

2. In January 1942, German and Italian troops approached the Suez Canal in Egypt. In July, Allied troops surrendered to Rommel's army in the Libyan port city of Tobruk.

Letter 8

1. Arendt's letter went missing.

2. In his article in *Aufbau* (4 July 1942), Emil Ludwig, aka Emil Cohn (1881–1948), a German-Jewish author living in the United States, countered the "wrong and dangerous" notion that the war was being fought against the German government, and not the German people. "Germany is Hitler and Hitler is Germany." The article initiated a heated debate in *Aufbau*. The Protestant theologian Paul Tillich, also writing in *Aufbau* (17 July 1942), disputed this approach to the war, and accused Ludwig of practicing a manner of thinking akin to anti-Semitism. Arendt defended Tillich in her *Aufbau* article (31 July 1942). "Jews," she wrote, "have no right whatsoever to spread a manner of thinking that has caused them so much terrible suffering." See "The Jewish War That Isn't Happening, Articles from *Aufbau*," in *Jewish Writings*, pp. 134–85.

3. In July 1942, in the battle of Al-Alamein in Egypt, Allied forces prevented Rommel from taking Alexandria. The Allied counteroffensive from October and

November defeated Rommel and was the turning point in the North Africa campaign.

4. The seventeenth-century Sabbatian movement developed in Asia Minor around the charismatic false messiah Sabbatai Zvi. Scholem wrote about the movement long frowned on by Jewish historians in *Major Trends* (1941) and in his magnum opus, *Sabbatai Sevi, the Mystical Messiah* (Princeton, NJ: Princeton University Press, 1973).

Letter 9

1. *Major Trends in Jewish Mysticism.*

2. An abridged version of these notes was finally published in 1948 under the title "Jewish History, Revised," in *Jewish Frontier* 15, no. 3 (1948): 34–38. These notes are to be found, in English, in Arendt's *Jewish Writings*. The last part of her notes, which she sent Scholem but which were not published, can be found in the Scholem library in the NLI. They are also reproduced here:

> The story is not ended, it has not yet become history, and the secret life it holds can breakout tomorrow in you or in me. Under what aspects this invisible stream of Jewish mysticism will again come to the surface we cannot tell ... To speak of the mystical course which, in the great cataclysm now stirring the Jewish people more deeply perhaps than in the entire history of Exile, destiny may still have in store for us—and I for one believe that there is such a course—is the task of prophets, not of professors.
>
> With this confession of faith Scholem concludes his book. Having told the "story of how it was done" he seems to cling to the old mystical hope that story-telling may have somehow the "same effect as the actions."
>
> He illustrates his belief very clearly by a Hasidic story in which the miraculous performation finally is done by the word alone: "We cannot light the fire, we cannot speak the prayers, we do not know the place, but we can tell the story how it was done. And, the story-teller adds, the story which he told had the same effect as the actions of the other three." (345) In this tale, indeed, the two main pillars upon which the grandiose construction of Jewish mystical thought rested, the more general doctrine that the WORD *is* action and the more specific Jewish insistence on the all-importance of tradition are combined in a unique simple way.
>
> Whether one shares belief and hope of these story-tellers—Scholem too is a story-teller in the clothes of a professor, and therefore knows more about the great story which is history than many a professor—is not so much a matter of opinion as he would like us to believe. Nor is it the task of prophets to decide upon our ultimate political will. There always were and may be false prophets and the catastrophical course of the Sabbatian movement can hardly be explained by the conversion of the Sabbatai Zvi alone, but ought to be seen as the inherent logic of

mysticism put into action. What the "enlightened" professors of nineteenth century history did not know was the fact that mysticism can work. What we, fascinated though we may be by the fact that all will to action and political realization of our history has been nourished and formulated in mystical thought, ought not forget is the fact that, in the last instance it is up to man to decide upon his political fate—and not to the "invisible stream" whose catastrophical course Scholem has revealed.

3. The American Jewish Committee, an organization founded in 1906 to defend Jewish civil rights in the United States, funded a study of anti-Semitism undertaken by the Institute together with the Berkeley Public Opinion Study Group. See "Research Project on Anti-Semitism," in *Theodor W. Adorno: The Stars Down to Earth and Other Essays on the Irrational in Culture*, ed. Stephen Crook (London: Routledge, 1994), pp. 181–218.

4. The German novelist Thomas Mann lived in California, close to Adorno.

5. Arendt's plan for a book on anti-Semitism culminated in the second part of her *Origins of Totalitarianism*. See also her "Anti-Semitism," in *Jewish Writings*, pp. 46–121.

6. In *Major Trends*, Scholem investigated the role played by the Sabbatian movement in modern Jewish history, more specifically in the reform efforts within nineteenth-century European Jewry. Arendt regarded Scholem's work as a fundamentally new and welcome interpretation of the Jewish Reform movement. See Arendt's essay on Scholem, "Jewish History Revised," in *Jewish Writings*, p. 203.

Letter 10

1. In the last letter Scholem received from Adorno (February 19, 1942), Adorno asked Scholem to send him a copy of *Major Trends*. The letter from Gretel Adorno, in which she thanks Scholem for the book, is not extant.

2. Leo Strauss (1899–1973), a philosopher, met Arendt, Benjamin, and Scholem in Berlin. He left Germany in 1932 and taught at the New School in New York, and eventually at the University of Chicago.

3. Abraham Heschel (1907–1972) taught at the Institute for the Wissenschaft des Judentums in Berlin. After his expulsion from Germany, he eventually moved to New York and taught at the Jewish Theological Seminary.

4. Scholem taught Jewish mysticism at the Institute for Jewish Studies at the Hebrew University.

5. The original edition of *Major Trends* had nine chapters. In the new edition—it would appear in 1946 from the Schocken Publishing House in New York—Scholem planned to add an additional chapter on the historical beginnings of the Kabbalah.

6. Horkheimer and Scholem first met in 1938 in New York. To Benjamin, Scho-

lem described in a letter, which did not survive, the reasons for his strong objections to Horkheimer's essay "The Jews and Europe." See *Benjamin/Scholem Briefwechsel*, p. 235.

7. "Things thus standing."

8. Horace, "Lightning always strikes the peaks." The letter from Scholem to Schocken is not extant.

9. Here Scholem refers to disagreements with the New York–based organization American Friends of the Hebrew University.

Letter 11

1. Adolph Sigmund Oko, the chief editor of the journal *Contemporary Jewish Record*, had asked historian Hans Kohn (1891–1971) to write a review of *Major Trends*. Scholem objected vehemently, and suggested to Oko that he turn to Arendt for the review. "She is one of the best minds who have come over from Europe," Scholem wrote. "She has sent me one of the two most intelligent criticisms of my book that I have seen, and heaven knows why she has not printed them" (Scholem to Oko, 26 March 1944, in Scholem, *Briefe* 1 [Frankfurt: Suhrkamp, 1996], p. 292). In his answer from May 25, 1944, Oko wrote, "I know Hannah Blücher as Hannah Arendt. I fully share your opinion of her, both as to mind and personality. She is a truly civilized being indeed. It may amuse you to know that my first real talk with her was about the Spinozist, Count de Boulainvillier—and G. Scholem ("For the mouth speaks what the heart is full of." [Matthew 12:34]). Yes, Hannah Arendt has a true comprehension of your great book."

2. Scholem's comment on "challenge" and "response" refers to his aforementioned letter to Oko: "I was stupid enough to think my book a challenge to Jewish scholars who have written so many everlasting idiotic statements about Jewish mysticism, and I thought somebody would feel obliged to answer that challenge, but all the wise men kept their peace." In Scholem, *Briefe* 1, p. 292.

3. The "political shenanigans" Arendt refers to here were Tillich's involvement in the Council for a Democratic Germany.

4. On February 14, 1944, Arendt sent a copy of her notes on *Major Trends* to Henry Hurwitz at the *Menorah Journal*. The attached note reads "I enclose a few pages of commentary on the book of Gerhard Scholem about Jewish mysticism which might interest you. They were written originally only for Scholem himself, who asked for my opinion. After having followed rather carefully the reviews of the book, I began to wonder if it would not be a good idea to have them published."

5. On December 13, 1943, Oko had written to Scholem asking him if he was interested in writing an article on Jewish mysticism for his journal. Scholem agreed to write the article. Scholem, *Briefe* 1, p. 438.

6. The NBC radio program was called *We Fight Back*.

7. The quarrel between Arendt and Blumenfeld revolved around her criticism

of Zionist politics, and in particular the tendency among Zionists to question the value of the Jewish diaspora.

8. Jakob Klatzkin (1882–1948) was a philosopher and Zionist intellectual. He was a leader of the movement to revive the Hebrew language.

9. This remark may refer to a stamp of the postal censure.

Letter 12

1. Scholem is most likely referring to Arendt's essays "The Jew as Pariah—A Hidden Tradition" (*Jewish Social Studies*, no. 2 [1944]: 99–122). Reprinted in Arendt, *Jewish Writings*, pp. 275–97.

2. Rashi, or Rabbi Shlomo ben Isaak (1040–1105), a commentator on the Bible and Talmud. Here, Scholem means "according to my interpretation."

3. In her essay "Jew as Pariah," Arendt interprets the central character in Kafka's *The Castle* as a stranger who seeks only his basic "rights as a human being." This, Arendt argues, is the drama of Jewish assimilation. See Arendt, *Jewish Writings*, p. 291.

4. As an implicit criticism of Martin Buber's understanding of Hasidism, Scholem treats Hasidism in *Major Trends* as part of the Kabbalah, that is, as the "final phase of the Kabbalah," the phase that "neutralizes messianism." In 1961 Scholem published a direct attack on Buber's notion of Hasidism. See "Martin Buber's Chassidism: A Critique," *Commentary* (October 1961): 305–16.

5. In 1938 Steven Wise, from the Jewish Institute of Religion in New York, had invited Scholem to deliver lectures at the Institute.

6. Saul Lieberman (1898–1983) was a rabbi and scholar of Talmud.

7. The Jewish Theological Seminary in New York was inspired and led by Salomon Schechter.

8. Tefillin are a set of small black leather boxes containing scrolls of parchment inscribed with verses from the Torah. They are worn by observant male Jews during weekday morning prayers.

Letter 13

1. The American Jewish Committee was the publisher of the *Contemporary Jewish Record*.

2. Arendt is probably referring to her article in the journal, "Privileged Jews," *Contemporary Jewish Record*, no. 1 [1946]: 3–30.

3. See Letter 9.

4. On October 23, 1944, the new editor, Clement Greenberg, wrote to Scholem: "One of the first things Dr. Oko spoke of was the pleasurable anticipation with which he was looking forward to the article on the Cabbala or Jewish Mysticism that you had expressed your intention of writing for us. I want you to know that we are carrying on in the same direction as Dr. Oko. We wish very much to publish your

essay and hope we shall not have to wait long before receiving it" (NLI, archive 4, file 1599).

5. This is a reference to the following line in Jaroslav Hasek's antiwar novel *The Good Soldier Schweik*: "When Švejk said goodbye to Vodička and each of them was taken off to his unit he said: 'When the war's over come and see me. You'll find me every evening from six o'clock onwards in The Chalice at Na Bojišti.'"

6. Siegfried Moses (1887–1974), a lawyer, was in New York to discuss questions of postwar compensation and restitution.

7. The Alijah Hadasha, or "New Immigrants," was a political party created by German-speaking Jews. The party opposed the idea of a Jewish state and promoted instead a future joint Arab-Jewish confederation. For Arendt's views on the group, see "The Crisis in Zionism" (1943), reprinted in *Jewish Writings*, p. 337.

8. The League for Arab-Jewish Rapprochement and Cooperation, founded in 1939, called for a binational Arab-Jewish state. The Alijah Hadasha was a member of the organization.

9. Arendt's "Zionism Reconsidered" appeared in *Menorah*, no. 2 [1945]: 162–96. Arendt asked the editor, Henry Hurwitz, to send the essay to her friends, though she added, "I am afraid of my Zionist friends, that is the truth and not a brave one. But they are the kind of people I never wanted to hurt. It is the old story of *amicus Plato, amicus Socrates sed magis estimanda veritas*. Brrr period!"

10. Arendt was writing her book *Origins of Totalitarianism* (New York: Harcourt, Brace & Co., 1951).

Letter 14

1. Arendt, "Franz Kafka: A Reevaluation. On the Occasion of the Twentieth Anniversary of His Death," *Partisan Review*, no. 4 [1944]: 412–22.

2. American Jewish Committee.

3. In 1937 the British proposed to partition Palestine into Jewish and Arab states, with British control maintained in Jerusalem.

4. Robert Weltsch (1891–1982), a journalist from Prague and a member of Martin Buber's circle and the Alijah Hadasha, argued against both a partition and the creation of a Jewish state.

5. "Official policy" refers to Ben-Gurion's position that a Jewish state should be established on the entire territory west of the Jordan River.

6. In "Franz Kafka," Arendt critiques the desire by many to interpret religiosity or the Kabbalah into Kafka's writings, calling such interpretations "errors."

Letter 15

1. Arendt's dissertation was titled *Augustine's Concept of Love*. It was later published as *Love and Saint Augustine* (Chicago: University of Chicago Press, 1996).

2. *Contemporary Jewish Record.*

3. At the end of 1945, the leadership of the American Jewish Committee founded *Commentary* magazine as the successor to the *Contemporary Jewish Record*. The chief editor was Elliot Cohen.

4. By this Arendt refers to Scholem's comment that during the war many of his letters to and from Adorno were lost.

5. Arendt and Salman Schocken first met in August 1945.

6. Max Strauss was a German-Jewish translator.

7. The Schocken Verlag in prewar Germany published a series of short works of Jewish fiction and nonfiction.

8. Mordechai Bentov (1900–1985) was a Zionist politician and leader of the socialist Hashomer Hazair movement.

9. The Hashomer Hazair, or "Young Guards," was a left-wing Zionist organization that grew out of the youth and kibbutz movements.

10. "Haluz," or "pioneer," was mainly associated with the kibbutz movement.

11. The German expression (ja bitte, wo käma man denn da hin?) is, literally, "where would one be if . . ."

12. Jewish World Congress. See Arendt, "Concerning Minorities," *Contemporary Jewish Record*, 353–68.

Letter 16

1. On the Jewish Brigade, see above, note 13.

2. Hans Lewy (1901–1945) taught ancient philology at the Hebrew University.

3. Abba P. Lerner was the author of *The Economies of Control: Principles of Welfare Economies* (New York: Macmillan, 1944).

4. Stefan George (1868–1933) was a German poet. For more on the memorial volume and Adorno's essay, see Stefan Muller-Doohm, *Adorno: A Biography* (London: Polity, 2005), p. 281.

5. Benjamin's sister, Dora, lived in Zurich. She died in 1946.

6. Arthur Koestler, *Darkness at Noon* (London: Jonathan Cape, 1940). It was first published in England (Macmillan) in German as *Sonnenfinsternis*.

7. On Scholem's plan for an expanded second edition of *Major Trends*, see Letter 10.

8. Under Greenberg's editorial direction, *Commentary* was the successor publication to the *Contemporary Jewish Record*.

9. George Lichtheim translated *Major Trends* from Hebrew into English. The "new translator" Scholem refers to is unknown.

10. Scholem first met Max Strauss in 1917, in Berlin.

Letter 17

1. Hans Lewy.

2. Rabbi Joachim Prinz: Rabbi and leader of the American Federation of Jews from Central Europe; Max Gruenewald; there is no information on Tischel.

3. Arendt first met Hans Lewy during her trip to Palestine in 1935.

4. Maxwell Alan Lerner was a well-known leftist journalist who wrote for the *New Republic* and *Partisan Review*. In the 1940s he taught at the New School for Social Research in New York.

5. Georg Benjamin (1895–1942), Walter's brother.

6. Arendt was mistaken. On the materials in the Bibliothèque Nationale, see above, note 30.

7. Max Strauss.

8. Arthur Koestler, *Scum of the Earth* (London: Left Book Club Edition, 1941).

9. Karl Jaspers gave his talk, "Renewal of the University," during a ceremony marking the reinstitution of the course's medical school at the University of Heidelberg.

10. She meant the essay "Organized Guilt and Universal Responsibility," and probably "Approaches to the German Problem," *Partisan Review*, no. 1 [1945]: 93–106.

Letter 18

1. The essay on the two Hölderlin poems is found in *Gesammelte Schriften* (GS) 11-1, pp. 104–26. The essay on Kafka was first published in 1934 in the German-Jewish newspaper *Jüdische Rundschau*. See Benjamin, *Illuminations*, pp. 11–140.

2. Gustav Glück (1902–1973), an Austrian banker, was a friend of Benjamin's and his inspiration for the essay "The Destructive Character."

3. Ernst Schoen (1894–1960), German musician, poet, and translator, was a close friend of Benjamin's.

4. The second edition of *Major Trends* appeared in 1946 (Schocken Books). Scholem did not include in this edition his planned extra chapter.

5. The essay "Beginnings of the Kabbalah" appeared in Hebrew.

6. The final sentence of Arendt's review is "What we, fascinated though we may be by the fact that all will to action and political realization of our history has been nourished and formulated in mystical thought, ought not to forget is the fact that, in the last instance, it is up to man to decide upon his political fate and (sic) not to the 'invisible stream,' whose catastrophic course Scholem has revealed." This final part of Arendt's review, which was not published, can be found in the Scholem library in the NLI.

7. The final passage of Scholem's book is "In the end all that remained of the mystery was the tale. That is the position in which we find ourselves today, or in which Jewish Mysticism finds itself. The story is not ended, it has not yet become history, and the secret life it holds can break out tomorrow in you or in me. Under what aspects this invisible stream of Jewish Mysticism will again come to the surface we cannot tell. But I have come here to speak to you of the main tendencies of Jewish Mysticism as we know them. To speak of the mystical course which, in the great cataclysm now stirring the Jewish people more deeply perhaps, than in the

entire history of Exile, destiny may still have in store for us—and I for one believe that there is such a course—is the task of prophets, not of professors" (*Major Trends*, 1941, p. 345).

8. Anger at British immigration policies led to terror attacks against British installations and personnel by Jewish underground groups. In December 1946 the situation turned temporarily calmer.

9. See Letter 14.

10. US president Harry Truman proposed that the British permit 100,000 Jewish survivors to emigrate from Europe. The British rejected the proposal.

11. Beginning in 1940, Salman Schocken supported financially the Institute for Jewish Mysticism, headed by Scholem. Schocken continued his support until 1950. Salman Schocken made his fortune through a chain of department stores based in Zwickau, Germany.

12. Hans Jonas married Eleonore Weiner.

13. Jonas was working on a philosophical biology.

14. In the 1930s Arendt worked for Youth Aliyah in Paris.

15. Hans Jonas added this salutation.

Letter 19

1. It is unclear which articles Scholem meant. Arendt published "Zionism Reconsidered" in the *Menorah Journal*.

2. The article begins with an overview of political developments within the Zionist movement, and more specifically the decision of the World Zionist Organization in 1944 to declare as its goal "a free and democratic Jewish commonwealth . . . which shall embrace the whole of Palestine, undivided and undiminished." This, she continues, had long been the aim of the right-wing Revisionist movement, and now was accepted by the mainstream Zionists as well. See Arendt, *Jewish Writings*, p. 343.

3. Scholem's comment on the moon is in response to Arendt's assertion about the socialist Zionists, that "They escaped to Palestine as one might wish to escape to the moon, to a region beyond the wickedness of the world. True to their ideals, they established themselves on the moon; and with the extraordinary strength of their faith they were able to create small islands of perfection." See Arendt, *Jewish Writings*, p. 349.

4. See *Jewish Writings*, p. 337.

5. Latin, "pardon the expression."

6. Arendt rejected both a Jewish state and a binational one. Instead, she promoted the idea of a federal system based on local and regional governments.

7. Brit Shalom (Covenant of Peace) was formed by intellectuals mostly at the Hebrew University. They called for a Jewish-Arab understanding and for a binational Jewish-Arab state.

8. Arendt writes about the Zionist socialists that they "shut themselves off from

the destiny of the Jews all over the world." They had "ideologically placed the center of the Jewish people's existence outside the pale of European peoples and outside the destiny of the European continent." See *Jewish Writings*, pp. 361 and 366. They developed a "dismissive attitude toward the world around them and a kind of self-centeredness [Selbstbezogenheit]."

9. Scholem was referring to the following passage in Arendt's essay: "A third political consequence of a fundamentally unpolitical attitude was the place which Palestine itself was assigned in the philosophy of Zionism. Its clearest expression may be found in Weizmann's dictum during the thirties that 'the upbuilding of Palestine is our answer to anti-Semitism'—the absurdity of which was to be shown only a few years later, when Rommel's army threatened Palestine Jewry with exactly the same fate as in European countries. Since antisemitism was taken to be a natural corollary of nationalism, it could not be fomented, it was supposed, against that part of world Jewry established as a nation. In other words, Palestine was conceived as the place, the only place, where Jews could escape from Jew-hatred. There, in Palestine, they would be safe from their enemies; nay, their very enemies would miraculously change into their friends" (*Jewish Writings*, pp. 360–61).

10. The Haavara Agreement, signed in 1933 by the Zionist leadership (ZVfD and Anglo-Palestine Band) and the Nazi government, promoted Jewish immigration from Germany to Palestine by enabling an indirect transfer of wealth.

11. The Revisionists, which opposed Ben-Gurion and the Labor Party, were founded by Vladimir Jabotinsky in 1925. The Revisionists, voting for a boycott against Nazi Germany, were sharp critics of the Haavara Agreement.

12. The American Jewish Joint Distribution Committee.

13. Arendt believed that the Zionist leadership's attitude regarding a Jewish army reflected "that old mentality of enslaved peoples, the belief that it does not pay to fight back, that one must dodge and escape in order to survive. How deep-rooted is this conviction could be seen during the first years of the war, when only through the pressure of Jews throughout the world was the Zionist organization driven to ask for a Jewish army—which, indeed, was the only important issue in a war against Hitler. Weizmann, however, always refused to make this a major political issue, spoke deprecatingly of a 'so-called Jewish army,' and, after five years of war, accepted the 'Jewish Brigade,' which another spokesman of the Jewish Agency hastened to diminish in importance. The whole matter apparently was, for them, a question of prestige for Palestine Jewry. That an early, distinct, and demonstrable participation of Jews as Jews in this war would have been the decisive way to prevent the antisemitic slogan which, even before victory was won, already represented Jews as its parasites, apparently never entered their heads" (*Jewish Writings*, p. 361).

14. The Jewish Agency was a body that represented the Jews in pre-1948 Palestine.

15. Scholem's article "What Is the Quarrel About" appeared in Hebrew in 1930. His letter to Benjamin was from 1 August 1931.

16. For Scholem's attitude regarding the American Jewish Committee, see Letter 14.

17. Scholem received an invitation to return to the Jewish Institute of Religion to deliver a new set of lectures. He asked to postpone the lectures due to his work in Europe for the Hebrew University and the Jewish National Library in Jerusalem.

Letter 20

1. Eric Bentley, one of the translators of Brecht into English, never carried out these plans. Benjamin's "Notes on Brecht's Epic Theatre" first appeared, in English, in *Western Review* 12, no. 1 (1948): 167–73, trans. Edward Landberg.

2. *Yishuv* was the Hebrew term for the pre-state Jewish community in Palestine.

3. The president of the Zionist organization, Chaim Weizmann, spoke disparagingly about the "so-called Jewish army" during the Zionist Conference at the Biltmore Hotel in New York in 1942.

4. The JVA (Jordan Valley Authority) was a plan drawn up by American experts to develop the region of Palestine and Transjordan through irrigation and electricity production. As this was supposed to accelerate Jewish immigration, the Zionists supported the plan.

Letter 21

1. "Past days" refers to the days Scholem spent with Benjamin, Arendt, and Blücher in Paris in 1938.

2. In the regions around Frankfurt, the US military had found large collections of Jewish property partly stolen by the Nazi organization of Alfred Rosenberg for their future "Gegnermuseum" (Museum of Enemies). The United States stored the looted property at the former I. G. Farben factory in Offenbach.

Letter 22

1. The letterhead was from the New York–based Conference on Jewish Relations, which was founded by American academics in 1936 to counter Nazism. In summer 1944 the Council founded the Commission on European Jewish Cultural Reconstruction (CEJRC), under the leadership of Salo Baron (1895–1989). A central goal of the group was to work with the Allies to recover stolen Jewish property and return it to their owners, or if the owners were dead or murdered, to Jewish organizations all over the world.

2. Arendt headed the research department for the Commission on European Jewish Cultural Reconstruction. While she worked with them, the CEJRC published the "Tentative List of Jewish Cultural Treasures in Axis-Occupied Countries" with *Jewish Social Studies* in 1946, the basis for the work of the later Jewish Cultural Reconstruction, Inc. (JCR).

3. Scholem did not have the required documents to travel from Paris to Frankfurt. He traveled instead to Prague and Vienna.

4. Anne Weil, née Mendelssohn. Käte Mendelssohn was her sister.

5. Dolf Sternberger (1907–1989), later editor of the *Neue Rundschau*, edited together with Karl Jaspers the German journal *Die Wandlung* (1945–1949).

6. Ernst Grumach (1902–1967), Germanist and librarian, was forced by the Nazi regime to catalogue stolen books stored in the Eisenacherstrasse in Berlin.

7. See enclosure to Letter 22.

8. Werner Senator (1896–1953), Zionist administrator. Ben-Gurion (1886–1973). Judah Magnes (1877–1948) was the first president of the Hebrew University. Magnes and CEJCR negotiated with the American government in the creation of an international body representing Jewish organizations that would act as a trustee for Jewish property whose owners or heirs were no longer alive.

9. Koppel S. Pinson (1904–1961) was the secretary of CEJCR. In Germany he directed between October 1945 and September 1946 the Joint's education program for displaced persons. Scholem met Pinson in Frankfurt.

10. Supreme Headquarters Allied Expeditionary Force.

Letter 23

1. The telegram is not in the Scholem archives.

2. Scholem and Salman Schocken quarreled over the continued financing of the Institute of Jewish Mysticism in Jerusalem. Due to their disagreement, Scholem canceled his planned trip to New York.

3. On 29 August 1946 Arendt wrote to Salo Baron that she hadn't heard from Scholem. "I suppose you will meet him in Paris. I am personally very much disturbed because Schocken told me that Scholem does not plan to come to America. Could you try to exert a little pressure? I confess—personal reasons" (Arendt to Baron, SUL, Box 39, Folder 2).

4. The American journalist Marie Syrkin (1900–1989) met Scholem on her trip to Jerusalem where she made her field research for *Blessed Is the Match: The Story of Jewish Resistance* (A. A. Knopf, 1947).

5. In July 1946 Arendt began working as an editor for Schocken Books in New York.

Letter 24

1. For details on Scholem's planned book, see Letter 8.

2. Hilde Benjamin (1902–1989). She would become the minister of justice in communist East Germany. Hilde and Georg's son was named Michael.

3. The article "Expansion and Philosophy of Power" appeared in *Sewanee Review* 54 (1946): 601–16.

4. Berl Katznelson (1887–1944) was a leader of the Zionist labor movement.

5. See Berl Katznelson, "Talks to Youth," *Jewish Frontier*, no. 9 (September 1945): 20–24. In the article Katznelson, reflecting on the growing worship of power in the Zionist movement, asks, "Do we, the bitter enemies of fascism, not share in so greatly exaggerating the value of force and placing it at the very heart of our scale of values?"

6. This was the wave of Jewish immigrants from Eastern Europe that arrived in Palestine between 1904 and 1914.

7. Kurt Blumenfeld.

Letter 25

1. Arendt's greeting for the Jewish New Year.

2. For Arendt's views of the DP camps in Haifa and Cyprus, see her letter to Karl Jaspers, in *Hannah Arendt/Karl Jaspers Correspondence, 1926–1969*, edited by Lotte Kohler and Hans Saner (New York: Harcourt Brace Jovanovich, 1992), p. 53.

3. Most of these essays Arendt later published in Benjamin, *Illuminations*.

4. See *The Correspondence of Walter Benjamin and Gershom Scholem*, trans. Gary Smith and Andre LeFevere (Cambridge, MA: Harvard University Press, 1980), p. 220.

5. Fritz Lieb edited *Orient und Occident*, a Swiss journal of theology and sociology.

6. The German-born rabbi and historian Kurt Wilhelm (1900–1965) worked for Schocken Books. S. J. Agnon, the Hebrew novelist, put together a memorial volume for Berl Katznelson. It was published in Hebrew in 1944.

7. Arendt is referring to the second edition of *Major Trends in Jewish Mysticism*, which was published with Schocken Books in New York.

Letter 26

1. Karl Jaspers, *The Question of German Guilt* (New York: Doubleday, 1948).

2. During the war the Nazis hid vast numbers of cultural objects in then-occupied Czechoslovakia, among them a large number of Jewish books and Jewish ceremonial objects from the KZ Theresienstadt.

3. Hannah Arendt, "The Jewish State: 50 Years After, Where Have Herzl's Politics Led?," in *Commentary* 1 (1945–1946): 1–8.

4. This was an agreement made in the summer of 1945 between the United States, Britain, and the Soviet Union on postwar German occupation.

5. See Arendt's request, Letter 24.

6. Benjamin wrote essays on the literary works of Gottfried Keller (1819–1890) and the French Catholic novelist Julien Green (1900–1998).

7. For Benjamin's critique on Max Brod, see *Benjamin/Scholem Briefwechsel*, pp. 220–23.

8. Scholem wrote to Benjamin about Horkheimer. See *Benjamin/Scholem Briefwechsel*, p. 235.

9. This was probably Benjamin's friend Pierre Missac (1910–1986). Georges Bataille gave over part of Benjamin's papers to Missac in 1945 that had survived in the Bibliothèque Nationale.

10. This refers to Arendt's question about a book with essays by Berl Katznelson; see Letter 24.

Letter 27

1. This letter may have crossed with Scholem's letter of November 6. When and why Arendt heard of an ostensible affliction is unknown.

Letter 28

1. Benjamin's article was scheduled to appear in *View* (*Through the Eyes of Poets* 7 [1946–1947]), but *View* stopped its publication. The article was first published in *Western Review* 12 (1947):167–73.

2. Kurt and Jenny Blumenfeld.

3. Lilli Mendelssohn was Blumenfeld's great love in the 1920s.

Letter 29

Original letter written in English.

1. Alfred Cohn (1892–1954) was a childhood friend of Benjamin's. Ernst Schoen (1894–1960), German musician, poet, and translator, was also a close friend of Benjamin's.

2. Arendt had only the French translation of the essay.

Letter 30

1. See above, note 37.

2. Alfred Cohn believed that Scholem had a large number of photographs of Benjamin's writings.

3. Kurt Wilhelm.

4. Salman Schocken's son Gustav (1912–1990) was the owner and editor of the Hebrew newspaper *Haaretz*. He also ran the Hebrew publishing house Schocken Books in Tel Aviv.

5. See Max Weinreich, *Hitler's Professors* (New York, Yiddish Scientific Institute, 1946). Arendt wrote that "Dr. Weinreich's main thesis is that 'German scholarship provided the ideas and techniques that led to and justified unparalleled slaughter' … In its implications and honest presentation of the facts [this book] constitutes the best guide to the nature of Nazi terror that I have read so far." Arendt, "The Image of Hell," a review of *The Black Book: The Nazi Crime Against the Jewish People* (New York: Duell, Sloan & Pierce, 1946). The review appeared in *Commentary* 2 (1946): 291–95.

6. Unterkätig—Scholem's variation of "unterkötig," an expression of disgust with reference to excrement.

Letter 31

1. The letters from Max Brod (the Kafka editor) are not in the Arendt archive.

2. Arendt reviewed Hermann Broch's *Death of Virgil*. The review, "The Achievement of Hermann Broch," appeared in *Kenyon Review* 11, no. 3 (Summer 1949): 476–83.

Letter 32

Original letter written in English.

1. The full title to Benjamin's essay is "The Storyteller: Reflections on the Works of Nikolai Leskov."

2. This was probably Scholem's article "What's the Dispute All About," which he wrote during his Brit Shalom time in 1930–1931.

Letter 33

Original letter written in English.

1. Scholem's letter and the Benjamin materials referred to by Arendt are not in the archives.

2. See Letter 30: Scholem's letter from December 25, 1946.

3. On the essay, "Conversations with Brecht," see above, note 168.

4. Benjamin's first essays were on Hölderlin's poems "Dichtermut" and "Blodigkeit."

5. This is not in the Scholem archive.

Letter 34

Original letter written in English.

1. On March 1, 1947, Adorno offered to contribute to the Benjamin edition planned by Schocken Books. Arendt sent a copy of Adorno's letter to Scholem.

2. Unknown letter.

Letter 35

1. Arendt refers to an unknown letter from Scholem.

2. Arendt sent review copies of Scholem's book *Major Trends* (New York, 1946) to various possible reviewers in Europe.

3. The literary editor of *The Nation* was the poet and novelist Randall Jarrell (1914–1965), a friend of Arendt's and Heinrich Blücher's.

4. Hans-Joachim Schoeps (1909–1980), a German-Jewish historian of religion, wanted to publish a collection of Kafka's short prose, in Germany.

5. Arendt's notes on *Major Trends*; see note 57.

6. For the picture of Benjamin, see fig. 2.

7. Before 1932 Benjamin published a number of literary essays in the journal *Die Gesellschaft*, whose editor at the time was Albert Salomon.

Letter 36

1. In early 1947 the British Mandate government introduced a series of roadblocks and curfews in the Jewish quarters of Jerusalem because of armed Jewish militant groups fighting against the British and the Arabs.

2. Gottfried Keller (1819–1890) was a Swiss-German writer best known for his novel *Green Henry*.

3. Germaine Krull (1897–1985) was a Polish-German photographer who lived in Paris in the 1930s.

4. In 1932 Scholem wrote a public letter in response to Schoep's book *Jüdischer Glaube in dieser Zeit*. The letter was published August 15, 1932, in *Bayische israelitische Gemeindezeitung*.

5. In 1933 Schoeps formed a political organization that advocated a German-Jewish nationalism against Zionism and Eastern European Jews, and which attempted to come to terms with the Nazis. He called the group Deutscher Vortrupp: Gefolgschaft deutscher Juden, or the German Vanguard.

6. Joshua Trachtenberg wrote the review of the first (Palestinian) edition in *Jewish Frontier* (September 1943): 28–34.

7. Letter not in the Scholem archive.

8. Between 1938 and 1950 Scholem stopped publishing articles and books in German; after 1950, he published again in German, first in Switzerland.

9. Scholem's article on the Wissenschaft des Judentums appeared in the *Yearbook* of the Hebrew newspaper *Haaretz* in 1944, pp. 94–112.

10. Scholem's book on the origins of the Kabbalah was published, in Hebrew, by Schocken Books in Tel Aviv in 1948.

11. The book is *The Sabbatian Book of Songs and Exaltation* (Hebrew, 1947–1948).

12. *Ha-Adon* is Hebrew for "Mr."

Letter 37

1. The letter from Bultmann is not in the Scholem archive.

2. Schocken's son Gideon (1919–1981).

Letter 38

1. David de Sola Pool, "The Mystic's Contribution to Judah," *New York Times*, 8 June 1947.

Letter 39

Original letter written in English.

1. Scholem probably spoke with the zoologist Ulrich Carl Friedrich Gerhardt (1875–1950) and his son, Dietrich Gerhardt.

Letter 40

1. In Bultmann's letter from May 1947 he thanked his former student Arendt for her articles in *Die Wandlung* and expressed gratitude that, following the war, "scholarly exchange is once again possible, and across boundaries," and that "intellectual community, once established, can continue to exist" (LoC, Box 9). Rudolf Bultmann (1884–1976) was a German Protestant theologian.

2. Hans Schrader (1869–1948) was a German classical archeologist and art historian.

3. Richard Harder (1896–1957) taught Arendt classical Greek. During the Nazi period he remained in Germany and was a supporter of the government.

Letter 41

Original letter written in English.

1. Alexander Koyré (1892–1964) was a historian of religion, science, and philosophy. Arendt first met him in Paris after 1933.

2. Georges Vajda (1908–1981) was a Hungarian-born Orientalist who worked in Paris. He was the editor of the *Revue des Etudes Juives*. "Précisions sur la Kabbale," Vajda's review of *Major Trends*, appeared in *Critique* (June–July 1947).

Letter 42

Original letter written in English.

1. Edmund Fleg (1874–1963) was a historian of religion and a writer.

Letter 43

Original letter written in English.

1. Ernst Simon (1899–1988) was a philosopher of religion and an educator living in Jerusalem.

2. Kurt Blumenfeld.

Letter 44

1. Blumenfeld's letter to Schocken is not in the archives.

2. Rioting broke out following the decision by the UN in October 1947 to partition Palestine into Jewish and Arab states.

3. Jacob Taubes (1923–1987) was a philosopher of religion. He taught at universities in Switzerland, Israel, and Berlin.

Letter 45

1. The abridged version of Arendt's comments on *Major Trends* finally appeared in *Jewish Frontier* 15, no. 3 (1948): 34–38. See note 57.

Letter 46

1. Arendt was probably referring to Scholem's essay on the Wissenschaft des Judentums that appeared in the *Yearbook* of *Haaretz*. Reflections on the Wissenschaft des Judentums (in Hebrew), in *Haaretz Yearbook* (Tel Aviv, 1944), pp. 94–112. Also in *Judaica* 6, pp. 7–52. See Letter 36.

2. Scholem apparently showed Schocken his and Arendt's letters regarding her essay "Zionism Reconsidered." See Letters 19 and 20.

Letter 47

1. *Zohar, the Book of Splendor*, selected and edited by Gershom G. Scholem (New York: Schocken, 1949).

2. Schocken Books published Max Brod's biography of Kafka in 1947.

3. Trachtenberg's review appeared in the September 1943 edition of *Jewish Frontier*.

Letter 48

1. Arendt is referring to the ongoing civil war that broke out in late 1947.

2. Arendt wrote about the shift in Jewish-American public opinion in "To Save the Jewish Homeland, There Is Still Time," *Commentary* 5, no. 5 (1948): 398–406. Reprinted in Arendt, *Jewish Writings*, pp. 388–404.

3. Arendt is referring to the chapters "Anti-Semitism" and "Imperialism."

4. "The Concentration Camp" appeared in *Partisan Review* 15, no. 7 (1948): 743–63.

5. At the time, Arendt contacted Waldemar Gurian at Notre Dame University to invite Scholem as guest lecturer. The plan failed.

6. Ernst Simon was a supporter of plans for a federal Arab-Jewish government for Palestine. He was in New York to raise money and support for a political group in Jerusalem whose name was Ihud.

Letter 49

Original letter written in English.

1. The Jewish Civil Guard, or Mishmar Ma'am, worked to distribute food and medicine in the Jewish neighborhoods under siege by Arab armies.

2. On April 13, 1948, an Arab militia group attacked a convoy carrying professors and students of the Hebrew University, killing seventy-eight, one of them a close friend of Scholem's, Abraham Chaim Freimann.

3. In April the British discontinued mail service in Palestine.

Letter 50

1. Scholem is referring to Arendt's book *Sechs Essays*. Some of the essays he had already received separately.

2. Scholem traveled to New York in early 1949. "Devekuth, or Communion with God," an essay based on a lecture he gave there, appeared in *Review of Religion* 14 (1949–1950): 115–39.

3. Arendt ended her work with Schocken Books in spring 1948.

Letter 51

Original letter written in English.

1. A number of Jewish organizations in Palestine, Great Britain, and the United States banded together in April 1947 with the goal of establishing a mechanism for finding, protecting, and distributing Jewish cultural objects and properties that survived the war but whose owners could not be identified. Beginning in the spring of 1949, JCR brought under its control, according to its own estimate, approximately 250,000 books, 10,000 ceremonial objects, and 700 Torah scrolls. Most of these objects had been seized by the Nazis during the war, in part with the intention to create a "Museum of Enemies" following their supposed final victory. The Allies after the war attempted to find the original owners, and to return the property to them. Arendt worked under Salo Baron and managed the daily affairs of JCR. Between November 1949 and April 1950, she traveled on behalf of the organization back to Germany. Beginning in 1949, Scholem represented the Hebrew University and was a vice president of JCR. With regard to the divvying up of the ownerless property, in February 1949 the following formula was adopted: the Hebrew University and the Jewish National University Library (JNUL) had first priority for books not found in the JNUL. Non-Jewish books that had belonged to Jews would also be given over to the university library. For all other objects, 40 percent would go to Israel, 40 percent to the United States, and 20 percent to the rest of the world.

2. From the United States, Scholem traveled to Switzerland in the summer of 1950 to attend a conference of the Eranos-Circle.

3. This letter is not in the archive.

4. Bernard Heller (1896–1976) was a rabbi and scholar. He was the field coordinator for JCR in Germany. He was replaced by Ernst Gottfried Lowenthal (1904–1994) in 1951.

5. Hermann Cohen (1842–1918) was a prominent Jewish philosopher in Germany. His library contained 5,000 books and after his death had been moved as

a separate collection to the Israelitische Gemeindebibliothek in Frankfurt. What remained of this collection in 1945 was deposited in Offenbach.

6. Scholem proposed that what remained of the collection be sent to Jerusalem. "The reason for this is that it is not only a collection actually preserved intact but is predominantly a philosophical library of non-Jewish character. This collection should fittingly honor the memory of this great Jewish thinker in the philosophical seminar of the Hebrew University" (Scholem to Baron, 31 May 1949, NLI archive 4, file 793). The Advisory Committee of JCR supported Scholem's proposal during their meeting on September 19, 1949. Today the catalogued part of the remnants of the Cohen Collection are found under separate call numbers in the NLI.

7. According to military authorities, the priority was to return books and ceremonial objects to living owners or heirs. Only cultural objects with no owner or heirs were to go to JCR.

8. The Jewish seminary in Breslau had 40,000 volumes when the Nazis took power in 1933. In November 1938 the library was destroyed, and in 1939 about 28,000 volumes were transported to SS headquarters in Berlin. In 1945, 12,000 volumes turned up in Offenbach. Other parts were found in Bohemia and in Warschau (see Field Report 12, p. 231.

9. A US military law in 1947 required German institutions to report all stolen property in their possession.

10. One of Benjamin's cousins was married to William Stern (1871–1938), a founder of child psychology. William and his wife Clara's son Gunther was Arendt's first husband.

Letter 52

Original letter written in English.

1. The Jewish organization in Prague agreed to send all Jewish books found in Czechoslovakia, which did not belong to Czech citizens and which could not be returned to their countries of origin, to Israel. Representatives of the Hebrew University selected over 16,000 books from the concentration camp Theresienstadt, and 45,000 books that were found in a Bohemian chateau. The Czech authorities demanded payment of a million krona before the Theresienstadt books could be transported. Not willing to pay what was their due proper heritage, a way was found to bring the most important parts secretly out of the country.

2. Shlomo Shunami (1897–1984) was the Hebrew University's representative working in the depots at Offenbach and Wiesbaden.

3. Rabbi Steven Samuel Schwarzschild (1924–1989) was a German rabbi and chief rabbi in postwar Berlin. Scholem agreed to take into account the needs of the Berlin Jewish community in the HU's request for books.

4. US military government.

5. Mordechai Bernstein (1905–1966) was a librarian and writer. In postwar

Germany he worked for YIVO as a librarian and investigator concentrating his detective work on finding the prewar archives of the Jewish communities.

Letter 53

Original letter written in English.

1. Alexander Marx (1878–1953), from the Jewish Theological Seminary, and Isaac Edward Kiev (1905–1975), from the Jewish Institute of Religion, both requested rare books for their institutions' libraries.

2. The project, created by Leo Baeck and CJG, was not without controversy. In his letter to Salo Baron, Scholem wrote on May 31, 1949: "Should JCR encourage the allocation of quantities of books to institutions founded effectively only in the post-war II period and which propose to utilise mainly JCR material as a nucleus? . . . Moreover, it is open to question whether German émigré academic groups are not of a too transitory character to ensure us of their continued development" (NLI, archive 4, files 793/288). The German Jewish Memorial Library was never established. In 1955 CJG founded the Leo Baeck Institute.

3. The "Gesamtarchiv der deutschen Juden" was established in 1905 with the aim to collect, preserve, and evaluate systematically all documents from the Jewish communities in Germany (including birth and death records, protocol books, and community newspapers, but also archives of Jewish organizations and private estates). The archives, mainly membership lists, served the Nazis in identifying the Jewish background of German citizens. Soviet troops seized the archive in 1945 and deposited it in what became East Germany.

Letter 55

Original letter written in English.

1. Kurt Wormann (1900–1991) was a librarian in Tel Aviv and the director of the Jewish National Library.

Letter 56

Original letter written in English.

1. Arendt's letter, from 7 November 1949, argues against keeping the Breslau collection intact and sending it to Switzerland.

2. Shunami mistakenly thought that all Jewish collections would be preserved intact.

3. The Minutes BoD from 17 October 1949, NLI, archive 4, files 793/288.

4. Before it was seized by the Nazi regime, the library of Raphael Kirchheim (1804–1899) was housed partly in the Religionsschule der israelitischen Gemeinde in Frankfurt, partly in the library of the Frankfurt Jewish community.

5. JRSO was the Jewish Restitution Successor Organization. On Military Law 59, see Letter 51, note 7, above.

6. According to Arendt, the JRSO did not recognize the postwar Jewish communities in Germany as the legal successors to prewar communities. A Memorandum to Salo Baron and Jerome Michael Arendt on 11 November 1949 stated: "JRSO does not recognize the present Jewish communities as legal successors to property owned by German Jewish communities and institutions." She added that "JRSO is, of course, anxious to avoid lawsuits. In the case of Jewish communities in Germany, they try to give them what they need and even leave them real estate and other property on the basis of usufruct" (CAHJP JRSO files 923 b). The JRSO, however, worked with the communities to find compromises to conflicting property claims.

Letter 57

Original letter written in English.

1. Scholem had not yet received Arendt's November 7 letter and argues against shipping the entire Breslau collection to the Swiss Jewish communities.

2. On the Kirchheim collection, see Letter 56, note 324. Scholem knew the large collection of around 64,000 volumes—he had used it as a young scholar (see *Von Berlin nach Jerusalem*, p. 40). The Kirchheim collection was confiscated in 1939 for the library of the RSHA. After 1945, only 7,000 books and periodicals remained.

Letter 59

Original letter written in English.

1. High Salpeter (1911–1969) was the vice president of the Friends of the Hebrew University in New York. He was a member of the board of JCR.

2. Scholem is referring to the Brecht volume in the journal *Sinn und Form*. Sonderheft Bertolt Brecht [1], Potsdam, 1949. A contribution by Brecht on poetry was not found.

Letter 60

1. Dolf Sternberger (1907–1989) was editor of the *Neue Rundschau* and cofounded the German journal *Die Wandlung*. In his letter to Scholem he asked Scholem's assistance in his plan to publish some of Benjamin's writings, referring to his earlier correspondence with Arendt. In 1950 he published Benjamin's text on philosophy of history. On Benjamin's accusation, see *Benjamin/Scholem Briefwechsel*, p. 241.

2. Benjamin wrote the letter to Scholem on February 4, 1939.

3. Henny Gurland belonged to the group Benjamin joined in an effort to cross the French-Spanish border. Scholem writes about the letter in his book *Walter Benjamin: The Story of a Friendship* (New York: Schocken, 1981), p. 224.

4. *The Story of a Friendship*, p. 226.

5. In 1932 Benjamin made Scholem his literary executor, but later he orally

made Adorno the executor. In 1950 Stefan Benjamin, the son of Walter Benjamin, confirmed Adorno's position.

Letter 62

1. Arendt wrote regular Field Reports during her trip to Germany for JCR.

2. On 19 December 1949 the Board of Directors (BOD) of JCR agreed to send the Hebrew University a part of the Breslau collection (BoD, 12. 4. 1950, NLI, archive 4, files 493/288).

3. In January 1950 the members of the board of JCR voted per mail on a measure to transfer to Jerusalem some of the books and periodicals originally from the Berlin community and which were found in the Wiesbaden depot to Jerusalem.

4. During the civil war of 1947 and 1948, fighting and terror attacks made the road impassable that led to Mount Scopus, where the university was. After the armistice of 1949, the Jordanians prevented Israelis from using the road.

5. See Arendt's Field Report 12, Document 1, pp. 225–32. In April 1950 the "Verein deutscher Bibliothekare" published an appeal to all librarians to report on properties of Jewish origin found in public libraries (Nachricht für wissenschaftliche Bibliotheken 3 [1950]: 62).

6. Hanns Wilhelm Eppelsheimer (1889–1972) was a librarian. He was dismissed from his position as librarian in 1933 because he was married to a Jewish woman. In 1946 he became the director of the Frankfurt Municipal and University Library.

7. Wolf Hänisch (1908–1978) was the director of the Oriental section of the Prussian State Library. See Arendt's Field Report, pp. 225–32.

8. The general director of the Prussian State Library until his suicide in 1945 was Hugo Andres Krüss (1879–1945).

9. The Munich-based Institute for the Study of the Jewish Question was led by Walter Frank. Approximately 35,000 stolen Jewish books ended up in the Institute.

10. The project sponsored by the Library of Congress gathered confiscated Nazi writings for the sake of historical documentation.

11. Hans Ludwig Held (1885–1954) was a librarian. He was dismissed from his position by the Nazis. Scholem, who knew Held from his time as a student, wrote in a letter to the Hebrew University on July 29, 1946: "Prof. Held in Munich, who could act for us, is an outstanding anti-Nazi and one of the few people in Germany with a deep knowledge of Jewish things, whom I have known for many years and whom I was glad to find holding a high position" (Scholem, *Briefe* 1, pp. 320 ff.). See also Arendt's Field Report 12.

12. To finish its engagement, the JRSO signed a "global agreement" with Bavaria in July 1952.

13. The Codex Hebraicus 95, a manuscript with main parts of the Babylonian Talmud from 1342, remains in the Bavarian State Library.

14. Alex Bein (1903–1988) was the vice director of the Central Zionist Archives

in Jerusalem. Bein conducted negotiations with the East Berlin Jewish community and East German officials.

15. In response to Benjamin's earlier plagiarism charge against him, Sternberger wrote a letter to Scholem on 14 December 1949. He also notified Scholem that his German publisher had sent Scholem the book, so that he could judge himself (NLI archive 4, file 1599, Arendt Corr.).

Letter 63

1. Arendt was visiting Karl Jaspers. Her line comes from Friedrich Schiller's poem "The Walk," trans. Marianna Wertz:

> Brooding, the sage is in search, stalking the creative mind.
> Matter's power he tests, the hatreds and loves of the magnet,
> Follows the sound through the air, follows through ether the ray.
> Seeks the familiar law in the awful wonders of hazard,
> Seeks the immobile pole in the occurrence of flight.

2. The Christian Hebraist August Wünsche (1839–1913) built a collection that was sold to the Jewish community of Dresden in 1911. During the Nazi period the collection ended up in a library run by the SS.

3. Werner Senator (1896–1953) was the vice president of the Hebrew University.

4. The former Nazi Party administrative building was used by the Americans as a Central Art Collecting Point for stolen art and other objects.

5. See the Field Report from 10 February 1950, pp. 233–41.

6. In 1938, following the Kristallnacht pogrom, the Historical Museum of Frankfurt saved numerous ceremonial objects from destroyed Jewish synagogues and museums.

7. Frequently, the original members of Jewish communities were either no longer alive or no longer in Germany. Those that claimed to represent the prewar communities were often from elsewhere.

8. See Arendt's Field Report 15, in Document 2, p. 234.

9. The Laemmle Klaus Library contained Hebrew incunabula and early prints as well as illuminated manuscripts from the early sixteenth century, two of which were Bible commentaries by the famous exegete Rabbi Shlomo ben Isaak (Rashi). There was also a 1505 print from Eleasar ben Juda of Worms's *Book of the Perfumer* (Sefer ha Rokeah). See Field Report 15, Document 2, pp. 238–39.

Letter 65

1. See Field Report 16, Document 3, pp. 241–46.

2. A large number of books contained in the SS's Jewish Central Library in Berlin burned during the wartime air raids. Several hundred thousand items, mostly

newspapers, survived. Many of these were stolen after the war. The US Army transported what remained to Offenbach.

3. See Field Report 16, Document 3, p. 244.

4. See Field Report 16, pp. 243 and 245.

5. See Field Report 16, pp. 244–46.

6. *Die Zukunft* was a weekly avant-garde cultural and political journal that appeared between 1892 and 1922.

7. Pinkas are bound volumes of Jewish community records with information on electing local authorities, and records referring to financial and various religious matters.

8. Arendt writes about the Berlin Torah scrolls in Field Report 16, p. 246.

9. Decree 2 from 1 February 1945 ordered the confiscation of all enemy property. Included in the decree was Jewish property stolen by the Nazis inside and outside Czechoslovakia.

10. Isaac Leo Seeligmann was heir to a collection of over 18,000 books. The collection was stolen by the Nazis in 1941 and transported to Czech territory.

11. Scholem is referring to the Jerusalem book dealer Bamberger & Wahrmann.

Letter 66

Original letter written in English.

1. Arendt is probably referring to a report by the Jewish Telegraphic Agency regarding the planned microfilm program in Israel.

2. The Cosman-Werner Library belonged to the Israelite Community of Munich, and contained 2,500 Hebrew and other Jewish books. Only a small percentage of the books survived by being hidden in the old Jewish cemetery. Rescued books included 13 incunabula and old prints.

Letter 67

Original letter written in English.

1. Salo Baron (1895–1989).

2. The archives of the Jewish community of Darmstadt.

3. JCR established several committees, among others the Allocation Committee. Only representatives of American Jewish institutions were members of the committee.

4. See Letters 64 and 65.

5. Parts of the Gesamtarchiv were stored at a depot in Merseburg in the eastern German state of Saxony.

Letter 68

1. Jewish Telegraphic Agency.

2. Simcha Assaf (1889–1953) was a professor of rabbinical literature at the Hebrew University.

3. Siegmund Katznelson (1893–1959) was the owner of the Jüdischer Verlag in Berlin, and founder of the Jewish Publishing House in Palestine. Fearing that a flood of books from Germany could undermine his sales of German-language books in Israel, Katznelson disputed the JCR's ownership rights of books confiscated by the Nazis in Germany. "Possession derived from a confiscation of the books from the Nazis is not 'lawfully' obtained" (letter to Shunami, 18 January 1950, NLI, archive 4, files 793/288).

4. See "Report of My Mission to Germany," Document 5, pp. 255–61.

Letter 70

Original letter written in English.

1. See enclosure to Letter 70.

2. Gerlin's letter is not in the archive. Heinz Gerling (1904) worked for the Jewish Agency on reparations.

3. See Field Report 18, see, Document 4, pp. 247–55.

4. "Believe it or not."

5. In 1945–1946, Jewish survivors in DP camps founded the Central Historical Commission to gather evidence of persecution and mass murder at the hands of the Nazis, as well as historical materials on destroyed Jewish communities. The State Archives of Bamberg had handed over to the Commission the archives of several Jewish communities from the Region of Bamberg and Bayreuth that had been confiscated by the Nazis.

Letter 71

Original letter written in English.

1. Eliahu Livneh.

2. In 1946 the Jewish leadership in Palestine formed a committee to build a research and memorial center for Jews murdered in the Holocaust. The center is called Yad Vashem.

3. See Field Report 18, Document 4, pp. 247–55.

4. The US military authorities gave the state of Hesse between 100,000 and 150,000 books of non-identified provenance with non-Jewish topics. Eppelsheimer, director of the Frankfurt Municipal Library, agreed to give JCR half of these volumes.

5. "Jewish Books and Religious Articles Found in the Hand of Nazis," in *Forverts* 12 (February 1950): 8.

6. US military officials gave JCR 20,000 books from the so-called "Baltic Collection," books that originated from the Baltic countries. From the collection over 12,000 books were sent to Israel.

7. Arendt submitted her memorandum on microfilming documents in Germany to the Board of Directors Meeting on April 12, 1950.

8. Mordechai Bernstein; see Letter 52.

9. Heinz Gerling worked for the Jewish Agency for Israel.

10. Arendt, "Der Dichter Bertolt Brecht," *Die neue Rundschau* 61, no. 1 (1950): 53–67.

Letter 72

1. Alfred Mombert (1872–1942) was a lawyer and writer. See Field Report 12, p. 229.

Letter 73

Original letter written in English.

1. Friedrich Gundolf (1880–1931) was a poet and member of the George Circle in Munich.

2. Walter Benjamin, "Über einige Motive bei Baudelaire," *Sinn und Form* 4 (1949): 5–47.

Letter 75

Original letter written in English.

1. Meir Ben-Horin (1918–1988) was the field director for JCR in Western Europe.

2. Arendt was referring to the Jewish manuscript collection of the Prussian State Library. After the war, most of the surviving manuscripts ended up in Marburg. Hebrew manuscripts were in the university library in Tübingen.

3. The Levy Collection was built by H. B. Levy, a lawyer from Hamburg. The collection included 177 manuscripts.

4. Moritz Steinschneider (1816–1907) was a bibliographer and Orientalist. In 1878 he created a bibliography of Hebrew manuscripts for the Municipal Library of Hamburg.

5. The Varnhagen collection is now at the University Library of Krakau.

Letter 76

Original letter written in English.

1. In the summer of 1950 Scholem held his first lecture at the ten-day Eranos conference, which was organized by Gustav Jung as an interdisciplinary forum for questions related to religion, spirituality, and anthropology.

Letter 78

1. This probably refers to the letter Arendt sent on July 7, 1950 (Letter 77).

Letter 79

Original letter written in English.

1. See Field Report 16, p. 243. A letter from Heinz Galinski, a leader of the Jewish community of Berlin, appealed to JCR to provide the community with cultural materials. "Our people here hunger for spiritual things and we urgently ask for your help in fulfilling our responsibilities to the members of our community by also in this spiritual direction" (NLI, JCR Archives).

2. In 1950 the Jewish Trust Corporation for Germany was founded in the British Zone to negotiate with the German government over heirless and unclaimed Jewish property.

3. The Committee on Restoration of Continental Jewish Museums, Libraries, and Archives, cofounded by the historian Cecil Roth and the author Oscar Rabinovicz, was established in 1943.

4. Arendt is referring to objects originating from the Jewish Museum in Frankfurt. The Bavarian archives were the archives from the Bavarian Jewish community. Philip Auerbach, the head of the Jewish community in Bavaria, pushed to keep the archives in Bavaria. He believed strongly in rebuilding Jewish life in postwar Germany and, as such, wanted cultural objects and books to remain in the country to assist German Jewish life.

5. That is, invalid.

Letter 80

Original letter written in English.

1. In a letter written to Wormann on September 8, 1950, Arendt sent legal documents related to Katznelson's legal challenges. In a letter she wrote the following day, Arendt expressed skepticism on finding additional libraries in Germany in the little time remaining, as the JCR planned to wind up its work by the end of the year.

Letter 81

Original letter written in English.

1. Moritz Freier (1889–1969) was a Swiss rabbi who served as rabbi in postwar Berlin.

Letter 82

1. These books were those of unidentified owners held by the Municipal and University Library of Frankfurt.

Letter 83

1. The previous day, on September 19, Julius Meyer, president of the Organization of Jewish Communities in the DDR, wrote the following to the minister of the interior: "The National Federation of Jewish Communities in the Democratic Republic (Berlin N 4) requests permission to transfer the Gesamtarchiv of the German Jews to the university in Jerusalem. In justifying this request we would like to add that most of the few surviving Jews live in that country. Furthermore, our local community is not able to do the scholarly analysis and make use of this archive. This is possible only with the academically trained and motivated manpower available in the land of Israel. The Archive is of exclusively inner-Jewish interest, and there is not the slightest German political interest" (Meyer to Korfes, 19 September 1950, NLI, archive 4, files 793/288).

In clarification, Scholem wrote on the following day to Alex Bein, the archivist at the Central Zionist Archive:

> Julius Meyer didn't want to write the request in such a way that the State of Israel appeared in it, nor did he want to mention your archive directly because of the word "Zionist." The reason for this is that he needs Russian permission in order to export anything abroad. In the application, which has already been submitted, we used the harmless address of the university as the recipient.
>
> . . . It is of utmost importance to the government of the German Democratic Republic that the transfer to the corresponding Jewish entities in Israel, in whichever form it takes, be combined with an official act.
>
> I had two long telephone conversations with Livneh (the Israeli consul in Munich), a man who both Julius Meyer and I assumed would eventually, once we are at that point, be prepared to travel to Berlin simply as the representative of the Jewish receiving office in Israel.
>
> Unfortunately, this is where politics begins.
>
> Dr. Livneh doubts highly that the Foreign Ministry will allow him to participate in such an official act, due to reasons of which you are well aware: mainly, because of possible repercussions in the Western Zone. He is going to send a telegraph to Tel Aviv and suggest that in case from our side the permission isn't granted for him to appear as the representative of the university or of the Archive, that when the time comes you, dear Dr. Bein, will come from Jerusalem. (Scholem to Bein, 20. September 1950, NLI, archive 4, files 793/288)

2. Lazarus Goldschmidt (1871–1950) translated the Babylonian Talmud into German for Katznelson's Jüdischer Verlag in Berlin (1930–1936).

3. On the same day, Scholem wrote a letter to Heinz Galinski from the Jewish community in Berlin: "I don't believe there are any difficulties from the side of JCR in providing your community necessary categories of books." Scholem suggested a

swap: JCR could provide the books needed by the community in exchange for books the community has no use for but which were wanted by JCR. These books included scholarly Judaica; modern Hebrew literature; old rabbinical literature; Hebrew- and German-language periodicals; and non-Jewish scientific literature.

4. See Letter 62.

Letter 84

1. This eight-page letter is a fragment, with only the final page in the archive. The missing pages apparently deal with a meeting between Scholem and Adorno in 1950 in Frankfurt. They discussed Benjamin's literary estate.

2. In 1950 Adorno and the German publisher Peter Suhrkamp discussed the publication of Benjamin's writings. The first volume was Benjamin's *Berlin Childhood Around 1900*.

3. His ironic nickname for Horkheimer.

4. The Frankfurt Municipal Library had one of the most important collections of Hebrew manuscripts and Judaica in Europe. The Nazis seized the entire collection and transported it to Alfred Rosenberg's Institute for the Study of the Jewish Question. During the war much of the Hebrew collection was destroyed, while the Judaica survived intact.

5. On the Hebrew collection of Frankfurt, see Letter 75. Abraham Merzbacher (1812–1885) was a banker and collector. Six thousand books in the collection were destroyed during the war; 156 manuscripts survived.

Letter 85

Original letter written in English.

1. Dr. Lowenthal's report dealt with the question of microfilming collections in Austria.

2. The Nazis in Austria stored many of the stolen books in the Castle Tanzenberg. After the war the British discovered 500,000 books.

3. Following negotiations in 1951, 23,000 of the 230,000 books with "unknown owners" were set aside for purposes of restitution. According to Lowenthal's report, most of the 230,000 books had been expropriated from Jews by the Nazis. In a later decision, in 1954, the Austrians decided to send to the Hebrew University 60 percent of ownerless books found in the Austrian National Library, and 70 percent in the University Library.

Letter 86

Original letter written in English.

1. JCR had decided to suspend its work in Germany by the end of 1950.

Letter 87

Original letter written in English.

1. During the meeting Arendt pushed to send the Judaica archives directly to Israel, while Rabbi Kiev wanted to transport them to Cincinnati with the argument that, given the precarious political situation in Israel, the archives would be more accessible to scholars in Cincinnati.

2. Benjamin Halpern (1912–1990) and High Salpeter were the Hebrew University's representatives within the board of JCR.

3. Negotiations with the Jewish community of Mainz were inconclusive, and no agreement was reached regarding their ownership of books and manuscripts that had belonged to the prewar community of Worms. The objects are now in the Johannes-Gutenberg University Library.

Letter 88

Original letter written in English.

1. Arendt notified Scholem about the forthcoming annual board meeting of JCR on December 21, 1950. Her memorandum included a series of suggested topics of discussion.

2. In Arendt's memorandum for the annual gathering of JCR, she addressed the question of the Bavarian community archives, which JCR was attempting to receive. If JCR were to receive the archives, she suggested not to divide them up but to pass them on in their entirety to an organization. In her memorandum Arendt also suggested to the directors of JCR to consider that if the Gesamtarchiv were to go to Israel, the other community archives should be brought to the United States.

3. Arendt asked the board about the continuation of her efforts to convince the various ministries of culture in the German states to demand that cultural institutions identify Jewish property. "This may again involve quite a bit of work and you may therefore decide to let it drop altogether" (Memorandum, NLI, archive 4, files 793/288).

4. In her memorandum Arendt raises the question about pressing the Jewish community to hand over ownerless property to JCR. Scholem responded that "I can not visualize that there will be any results in Berlin following legal steps except such things the Jewish Community will give on its own accord in accordance with amicable agreements. It should be taken into account that much material was actually destroyed through fire, etc. and that there are no caches. For this reason I do not recommend that JCR should make a new effort next year" (NLI, archive 4, file 1599, Arendt Corr.).

5. Point 7a deals with the remaining newspapers and journals in the JCR depot.

6. Point 8 in the memorandum deals with over 30,000 books held at a depot in Paris. Arendt's suggestion was that the books whose owners were known but

couldn't be located be held until the middle of 1951 in case of potential restitution claims.

7. Judah Shapiro (1912–1980) was responsible for the depot in Paris.

8. Point 9 of the memorandum concerns the files of JCR and what should happen to them once its work is concluded.

9. Hannah Arendt, "The Aftermath of Nazi-Rule: Report from Germany," *Commentary* 4 (1950): 342–53.

Letter 89

Original letter written in English.

1. The historian Selma Stern-Täubler (1890–1981) worked as an archivist. Her husband, Eugen Täubler (1879–1953), taught at the Hebrew Union College in Cincinnati.

2. The state of Hesse issued a decree requiring all German institutions to identify Jewish cultural property acquired during the Nazi regime.

3. "Kabbalah und Mythus," *Eranos-Jahrbuch* 17 (1949): 287–334.

4. Walter Benjamin, *Berliner Kindheit um neunzehnhundert* (Frankfurt: Suhrkamp, 1950).

Letter 90

Original letter written in English.

1. Annual Meeting of the Corporation, 21 December 1950.

2. Representatives from the British Committee on Restoration of Continental Jewish Museums, Libraries, and Archives proposed that objects from the former Jewish museum in Frankfurt be given to the Tel Aviv Art Museum.

Letter 91

Original letter written in English.

1. Judah Leib Maimon (1875–1962).

2. In the letter from February 12, 1951, Arendt wrote to Wormann, the director of the Jewish National Library. She reported to him about her discussion with Baron and the Israeli minister of religious affairs, Judah Maimon. She discussed the need to document the Hebrew University's distribution of the JCR books to other institutions in Israel, documentation that had hitherto been unsatisfactory (NLI, archive 4, files 793/288).

Letter 92

Original letter written in English.

1. The letter concerns the publication of lists of 1,000 names of private owners of books and other valuable objects. In a letter to Wormann (March 13, 1951),

Arendt proposed to publish the list in *Haaretz* and the *Palestine Post* following its publication with *Aufbau*, in the United States, and the *Jewish Chronicle*, in Great Britain (NLI, archive 4, files 793/288).

2. Gustav Schocken (1912–1990) was the owner and editor of the Hebrew newspaper *Haaretz*.

Letter 93

1. Arendt, *Origins of Totalitarianism*.

2. The title of part 1 of *Origins* is "Anti-Semitism."

3. Scholem's lecture was published as "Tradition und Neuschöpfung im Ritus der Kabbalisten," *Eranos-Jahrbuch* (1950), pp. 121–80.

4. On the microfilm project, see Letter 80.

Letter 94

1. Arendt writes about her book on totalitarianism, "Elements by themselves never cause anything. They become origins of and when they suddenly crystallized into fixed and definite forms. Then, and only then, can we trace their history backwards. The event illuminates its own past but it never can be deduced from it." Found on pp. 6 and 7, Arendt archive, LoC, Box 76.

2. See Arendt, "The Ex-Communists," *The Commonwealth* 57 (March 1953): 595–99.

3. In 1952 Arendt applied for a Guggenheim research fellowship to examine the "totalitarian elements within Marxism."

4. The Jewish Restitutions Successor Organization had its main office in Nuremberg.

5. The decree from January 16, 1951, issued by the Hessen Ministry of Education and Volksbildung called for the "return of all cultural objects formerly in Jewish possession."

Letter 95

1. Alex Bein, from the Central Zionist Archive in Jerusalem, represented Israeli and university interests in Berlin. He sought to bring the Gesamtarchiv to Israel. In 1951 he succeeded in getting 35 boxes of materials out of East Germany and transporting them to Israel.

2. See Letter 66.

3. Bruno Bauer (1809–1882) was a German philosopher, theologian, and historian.

4. Nathan Rotenstreich, "For and Against Emancipation: The Bruno Bauer Controversy," in *Leo Baeck Year Book* 1959, pp. 3–36.

5. Theodor Adorno, *Minima Moralia: Reflections on a Damaged Life* (New York: Verso, 2005).

Letter 96

Original letter written in English.

1. Scholem is probably referring to a memo Arendt wrote on the JCR's annual meeting of the Board of Directors, 10 December 1951.

Letter 97

1. Scholem's lecture was "Tradition und Neuschöpfung im Ritus der Kabbalisten" (Tradition and New Creation in the Rites of the Kabbalists), *Eranos-Jahrbuch.*

2. In his letter to Rabbi Kiev, Scholem wrote about Arendt, "I am proud to think how lucky JCR has been in having her service as head of the staff. I am an old friend and admirer of Miss Arendt as an engaging personality and masterly intellect, but in this latest phase of her career she has revealed even greater qualities: her sensitiveness and understanding, her energy that knew no bounds, and her devotion to the task have been of highest value. I shall always remember with the greatest pleasure this period of our common work. We have shared the excitement of digging for the lost treasures of the Jewish cultural heritage, we have shared the hopes and disappointments involved and also the joy of discovery and recovery. It is our hope that one fine day Miss Arendt will come to Israel and discover in many places the results and fruits of her endeavors and her diligence."

3. Hans Jonas (1903–1993) was a philosopher and historian of Gnosticism.

4. Philip Auerbach (1906–1952) was president of the Bavarian Jewish community. In August 1952, convicted of fraud and sentenced to two years in prison, he committed suicide in prison.

Letter 99

1. The article based on his lecture is titled "Zur Entwickelungsgeschichte der kabbalistischen Konzeption der Shechinah," *Eranos-Jahrbuch* 21 (1952), pp. 45–107.

2. The philosopher and religious thinker Martin Buber (1878–1956) spent several months in the United States, where he gave lectures.

Letter 100

1. Rabbi Haim Zvi Taubes (1900–1966), rabbi in Zurich.

2. Paul Bredo (1880–1957), director of the Jewish library in Zurich.

3. Most of these manuscripts remained in Poland.

4. At the Hague Conference in 1952, the West German government negotiated with the State of Israel along with the Conference on Jewish Material Claims against Germany (JCC), a group of twenty-two Jewish organizations under the chairmanship of Nahum Goldmann (1895–1982), the president of the World Jewish Congress. The object of the conference was legally to regulate the process of com-

pensation and return of property, and to arrive at a comprehensive compensation payment the Federal Republic of Germany would pay to Israel and to the JCC. In a letter to Goldmann, Baron suggested, within the negotiations, to take up again the old demand for a restitution-in-kind of lost cultural property, a demand that JCR during its founding had dropped in 1947 at the request of the United States. Baron argued that due to measures by the German government, unique cultural treasures that had been lost should be compensated through comparable cultural treasures found in public German institutions, treasures that frequently had ended up in public institutions thanks to Jewish patrons. These objects, for which no one had any use any longer, he argued, should be transferred to Israel as compensation (letter from Baron to Goldmann on 21 March 1952; copy SUL, Paron Papers, Box 59, Folder 1).

As reported by Arendt, Scholem, on behalf of the Israeli government, similarly suggested the following mechanism for compensation:

1. German scientific literature from 1933 to the present, selected by the HUL.
2. Current German literature for the next ten years.
3. Hebrew mss. 100 to 200 as restitution in kind, chosen by the HUL. He asked specifically of the Munich Talmud.
4. Photocopies of all mss.
5. Photocopies of microfilms . . . of Archival material, selected by HUL or rather the National Archives.
6. Law (and not only decrees) for restitution of Jewish cultural properties (Arendt to Baron, 24 April 1952, SUL, Baron Papers, Box 59, Folder 1).

The restitution-in-kind did not figure into the "Luxembourg Agreement" between the Federal Republic of Germany, the State of Israel, and the JCC. According to the September 10, 1952, agreement, Germany was to pay 3.5 billion marks to Israel and the JCC. (On the parallel initiative with the German Book Association, see Letter 104, note 512.)

5. Moses Aron Leavitt (1894–1965) worked for the Joint Distribution Committee.

Letter 101

1. The "lovely letter" is not in the archives. Arendt wrote to Blücher on April 11, 1952, "In Basel I received a pathetic letter from Scholem—with a . . . invitation for Passover dinner. My God, me at one of these national-religious ceremonies! I guess since I got myself into this mess, I'll have to get myself out. What a jackass I am."

Letter 102

1. Arendt traveled to Paris, Zurich, London, Heidelberg, and Mainz. In Paris, where she spent four weeks, she wrote to Baron, "Paris is simply wonderful. I work

in the libraries and at the Centre de la Documentation Juive. . . . I am very glad to have this opportunity. I'll have to correct and to add quite a few things when my book [*Origins of Totalitarianism*] comes out in German or in a second edition" (letter on 24 April 1952). In addition, Arendt undertook research funded by the Guggenheim Foundation on leftist totalitarianism (see Letter 94, note 481). She also delivered lectures (among other places, in Heidelberg, Berlin, and Tübingen); wrote her contribution to a Festschrift for Jaspers (see Letter 106, note 1); and wrote the article "The Secret Police," in *Der Monat* 4, no. 46 (1952): 370–88.

2. Scholem wrote to Baron on June 12, 1952, and asked for a stipend from JCR.

3. Hermann Broch died in 1951. As his literary executor, Arendt went to Lugano to edit two collections of his essays, *Dichten und Erkennen* as well as *Erkennen und Handeln* (Zürich, 1955).

4. On efforts to secure the archives from Jewish communities in Germany, see Letter 79. Negotiations continued until 1954, when the archives arrived in Israel.

5. This is a reference to Philip Auerbach. See Letter 97.

Letter 103

1. Arendt and Scholem made plans to meet in Zurich. Scholem suggested these dates in a letter missing from the archive.

2. On behalf of JCR, Arendt traveled to Paris, Zurich, London, Heidelberg, and Mainz.

3. George Lichtheim (1912–1973) was a journalist and translator living in London. He translated *Major Trends* from Hebrew into English.

Letter 104

1. The federation representing the German book industry agreed after consultations with the JNUL to make an annual donation of books directly to the Hebrew University as a sort of reparation.

2. The other option, made unnecessary by the agreement, was for the German book industry to make the donation indirectly to Israel by transferring the donation first to JCR.

3. Mordichai Narkiss was an Israeli art historian (1898–1957).

4. Luise von Schwartzkoppen (1902–1986) was a lawyer and librarian working in the "Tauschstelle" of the Berlin Prussian State Library. Later she was a leading figure in building the American Gedenkbibliothek and the library at the Freie Universität in Berlin. Arendt discussed with her the status of Jewish book collections in East Germany.

5. Fritz Moser (1908–1988) was a librarian. For the Berlin Senate he was responsible for matters pertaining to libraries and archives.

6. Benjamin Barell Ferencz (1920–) was a lawyer who led the JRSO in Nuremberg.

7. Erich Katzenstein (1893–1963) was a Swiss neurologist. He and Scholem met at the Eranos conference in 1949.

Letter 106

1. Arendt's article is "Ideology and Terror." The Jaspers Festschrift appeared in 1953 (Munich: Klaus Piper).

2. Shmuel Samburski (1900–1990) was a physicist. In a letter to Scholem, Samburski praised the Americans for being wealthy enough to be friendly and generous (NLI, archive 4, file 1599, Corr Samburski).

3. Mapam was the socialist labor party that sought to orient Israeli politics on the Soviet Union. There was a crisis in the party because of a wave of anti-Semitic attacks in the Soviet Union, and after the Soviet government broke off diplomatic relations with Israel in February 1953 following an attack on the Russian embassy in Tel Aviv.

4. Jacob Taubes settled in the United States, following a rupture with Scholem. He eventually taught at the Free University of Berlin.

5. Louis Finkelstein (1895–1991) was the president of JTS. The conference was on "moral standards."

Letter 107

1. In 1947 the Jewish Theological Seminary in New York opened up a branch in Los Angeles, the University of Judaism.

2. Scholem's essay was "Zur Entwickelungsgeschichte der kabbalistischen Konzeption der Shechinah" (The Historical Development of the Kabbalistic Conception of the Shechina).

3. "Sabra" is a native-born Israeli Jew.

4. *The Joshua Starr Memorial Volume: Studies in History and Philology* (New York: Conference of Jewish Relations, 1953).

Letter 108

1. Louis Finkelstein.

2. Arendt's Princeton lecture was on Karl Marx and the Western tradition.

3. For Arendt's attitude toward McCarthy, see "The Eggs Speak Up," *Essays in Understanding, 1930–1954: Formation, Exile, and Totalitarianism*, edited by Jerome Kohn (New York: Harcourt Brace & Co., 1994), pp. 270–84. See also her essay "The Ex-Communists," *The Commonwealth* (March 20, 1953), 595–98.

4. Arendt never made the trip to India.

5. This is a reference to the decrees regarding stolen Jewish property. See Letter 89.

Letter 109

1. Scholem's essay on the Golem appeared in the 1953 *Eranos-Jahrbuch* as "Die Vorstellung des Golem in ihren tellurischen und magischen Beziehungen." "Zur Geschichte der Anfänge der christlichen Kabbala," the essay on the history of the Christian Kabbalah, came out in *Essays Presented to Leo Baeck* (London: Leo Baeck Institute, 1954), pp. 158–93. The article in the *Revue de l'histoire des religions* was on the Sabbatian movement in Poland.

Letter 110

1. Arendt is referring to the Golem essay in the *Eranos-Jahrbuch*. The letter mentioned is not in the archive.

2. The proposal was for microfilming Jewish archives.

3. Arendt used the expression "Interpretaster."

4. "Tradition and the Modern Age," *Partisan Review* (1954): 53–75. The title of the lecture series was "Karl Marx and the Tradition of Western Political Thought."

5. Jacob Taubes, "From Cult to Culture," *Partisan Review* (1954): 387–400.

6. The Bollinger Foundation in New York funded the Eranos conferences in Switzerland as well as offered stipends for writers and scholars. In December 1953 Scholem had a grant in support of his research on Sabbatianism.

7. Scholem writes in his lecture on the Golem, "The idea of the Golem as a magical servant of his master does not appear in any of the older traditions. It was first in the late Middle Ages when a group of German Hasidim developed a ritual around their hero that the Golem emerged as a folk legend."

8. For Arendt's discussion of the Garden of Eden and work, see *The Human Condition* (Chicago: University of Chicago Press, 1958), chapter 4, note 3.

Letter 111

1. In 1954 Scholem was in London working on his book on Sabbatianism.

2. This was the lecture series he held in New York at the Jewish Institute of Religion. See Letter 50.

3. See Scholem's letters to Taubes, in *Gershom Scholem: A Life in Letters* (Cambridge, MA: Harvard University Press), pp. 467–68.

4. Scholem was at the Warburg Institute in London.

Letter 112

1. Undated letter. It was sent May 22, 1955.

2. The lecture series took place in 1955. Scholem's lecture appeared as "The Meaning of the Torah in Jewish Mysticism," in *Diogenes* 14, pp. 36–47.

Letter 113

1. At Berkeley, Arendt had three seminars in spring 1955: History of Political Theory, Political Theory of Kant, and Ideologies.

2. Secretly financed in part by the CIA, the Congress for Cultural Freedom was based in Paris and brought together liberal intellectuals who were committed to democratic and humanistic values. Arendt gave a lecture on the development of totalitarianism.

Letter 114

1. In July 1953 the Congress for Cultural Freedom held a conference in Milan on science and freedom.

Letter 115

1. Arendt was working on the book *The Human Condition*.

2. Literally, "the beautiful, twice and three times."

Letter 116

1. Arendt spent the last days of her trip to Israel in Jerusalem, and left on October 28.

Letter 117

1. Hermann Broch.

2. See Arendt's "Hermann Broch: 1886–1951," in *Men in Dark Times* (New York: Harcourt, Brace & World, 1968), pp. 111–53.

Letter 118

1. "The die has been cast."

2. Scholem's biography of Sabbatai Zvi was published in Tel Aviv, in Hebrew, in 1957.

3. Scholem planned a second volume to explore the history of the Sabbatian movement, with a focus on the work of Jakob Frank (1726–1791).

4. The Leo Baeck Institute published Arendt's manuscript as *Rahel Varnhagen: The Life of a Jewess*, translated from German by Richard and Clara Winston (London: East and West Library, 1957).

5. This is a reference to the Sinai War that broke out in October 1956.

6. Scholem and Arendt met in New York. Arendt wrote to her friend Blumen-

feld about their encounter: "You know that Scholem was here.... Both of us gave it our best effort but nothing came of it."

Letter 119

1. In 1958 Jaspers received the Peace Prize given annually by the German book industry. Arendt gave the laudation. Both her speech and Jaspers's appeared in the *Börsenblatt für den Deutschen Buchhandel* 14, no. 79 (1958): 1313–22, later reprinted separately with Piper Verlag, Munich.

2. On 8 October 1958 in Zurich, Scholem gave a lecture on the Messianic idea in rabbinical Judaism titled "Die messianische Idee im rabbinischen Judentum und ihre Spannungen" (The Messianic Idea in Rabbinic Judaism and Its Tensions).

Letter 120

1. The letter has no exact date. It was presumably written in 1958.

2. One publication was her laudation for Jaspers, reprinted in *Men in Dark Times* (New York: Harvest, 1995), pp. 71–81. The other was a book, in German, on the Hungarian revolution and totalitarianism, *Die ungarische Revolution und der totalitäre Imperialismus* (Munich: Piper, 1958). Arendt was named guest professor at Princeton.

Letter 121

1. "Ten Unhistorical Aphorisms on Kabbalah," in *Gershom Scholem*, ed. Harold Bloom (New York: Chelsea House, 1987).

2. Arthur Cohen (1928–1986) was a writer and historian and cofounder of Noonday Press and Meridian Books. Cohen, after reading from the German edition of Benjamin's *Schriften*, suggested to Arendt that he publish an edition of Benjamin's essays. Arendt agreed and suggested that Scholem should write the introduction. The book project never materialized. Cohen left Meridian Books in 1960.

3. Siegfried Moses (1887–1974) was a lawyer and Zionist leader. He was cofounder and president of the Leo Baeck Institute in Israel.

4. Arendt received the Lessing Prize bestowed to her by the city of Hamburg. The lecture she delivered on the occasion was "Von der Menschlichkeit in finsteren Zeiten. Gedanken zu Lessing" (On Humanity in Dark Times: Thoughts on Lessing).

Letter 122

1. Alan Stroock (1907–1987) was chairman of the board of directors at JTS.

Letter 123

1. This refers to writings by the followers of Jacob Frank (1726–1791).

2. Chaim Nachman Bialik (1973–1934) was a lyricist, author, publisher, and translator.

Letter 124

1. A German edition of Arendt's biography on Rahel Varnhagen appeared in 1959.

2. Karl August Varnhagen von Ense (1785–1858) was a German Protestant historian, writer, and biographer. In 1814 he married Rahel Levin. His memoirs appeared in nine volumes between 1837 and 1858.

3. The archives are in Krakau.

Letter 125

1. The German expression "Lebenslüge" is a lie people tell themselves.

2. The board meeting of the Leo Baeck Institute in London.

3. Rudolf Borchardt (1877–1945) was a German-Jewish writer. Scholem supported the publication of a book on Borchardt because he was an example of "radical assimilation," of a Jewish intellectual who became a German nationalist.

Letter 126

1. The essay is found in *On the Kabbalah and Its Symbolism*, trans. Ralph Manheim (New York: Schocken, 1976).

2. Ruth Nanda Anshen (1900–2003) was a philosopher, writer, and publisher. She was in charge of the Religious Perspectives book series at Harper & Row, where she wanted to collect essays from Karl Barth, Paul Ricoeur, W. H. Auden, Jens Muilenberg, Hans Jonas, and Alexandre Koyré.

3. Adolf Eichmann (1906–1962) was kidnapped by the Israeli Mossad agency in May 1960. The *New Yorker* sent Arendt to Jerusalem to cover the trial.

Letter 128

1. Erich Neumann (1905–1960) was a psychoanalyst in Tel Aviv. Arendt first met him at the University of Heidelberg in the 1920s.

2. Benjamin wrote his "Kafka letter" on June 12, 1938, from Paris. See *The Correspondence of Walter Benjamin and Gershom Scholem, 1932–1940*, p. 220.

Letter 131

1. Arendt, *Between Past and Future* (New York: Harcourt Brace, 1962).

2. Scholem, *On the Mystical Shape of the Godhead: Basic Concepts in the Kabbalah*, ed. Jonathan Chipman, trans. Joachim Neugroschel (New York: Schocken, 1991).

3. Greek for "good spirit."

4. "Martin Buber's Chassidism: A Critique," *Commentary* (October 1961): 305–16.

Letter 132

1. This letter with Arendt's response appeared, with few changes, in the journal *Encounter*, on January 31, 1964.

2. Arendt's *Eichmann in Jerusalem: A Report on the Banality of Evil* (New York: Viking, 1963).

3. The persecution of Spanish Jews began with the burning of the Jewish quarter in Seville in 1391.

4. Arendt cites Raul Hilberg's *The Destruction of the European Jews*. See Arendt, *Eichmann in Jerusalem*, p. 104.

5. *Eichmann in Jerusalem*, p. 105. This expression was removed from later editions of the book.

6. H. G. Adler, ed., *Die verheimlichte Wahrheit: Theresienstädter Dokumente* (Tübingen: Mohr, 1958).

7. Benjamin Murmelstein (1905–1989) was a rabbi. The SS designated him to be leader in Theresienstadt. Following the war, fellow survivors accused him of collaboration. He was never charged, and he immigrated to Rome.

8. Paul Eppstein (1902–1944), a German-Jewish sociologist, was shot by the Nazis in 1944.

9. Emil Utitz (1883–1956) was a philosopher and the librarian at Theresienstadt. Otto Muneles (1894–1967) was a Hebrew scholar.

10. "Logical fallacy."

11. Moses Chaim Lau (1892–1943) was a Polish rabbi. Shortly before being deported to Treblinka, where he was murdered, Lau wrote the book (in Hebrew) *The Sanctification of the Name*.

12. Kurt Tucholsky (1890–1935) was a German-Jewish writer and publicist. Scholem is referring to Tucholsky's *Ausgewählte Brief* (1913–1935), ed. Mary Gerold-Tucholsky (Hamburg, 1962).

13. Arendt's final statement in *Eichmann* is "And just as you supported and carried out a policy of not wanting to share the earth with the Jewish people and the people of a number of other nations—as though you and your superiors had any right to determine who should and who should not inhabit the world—we find that no one, that is, no member of the human race, can be expected to want to share the

earth with you. This is the reason, and the only reason, you must hang." *Eichmann in Jerusalem*, p. 256.

14. See Scholem, "Eichmann," *Amoth* (August–September 1962), p. 10.

15. After reading Herzl's *The Jewish State*, writes Arendt, Eichmann was "converted promptly and forever to Zionism. From then on he thought of hardly anything but a 'political solution' (as opposed to the later physical solution, the first meaning expulsion and the second extermination) and how to 'get some firm ground under the feet of Jews.'" See *Eichmann in Jerusalem*, p. 36.

Letter 133

1. On 8 May 1961, Arendt wrote to fellow historian Leni Jachil, who had arranged for her to meet Golda Meir during Arendt's visit to Jerusalem, "What horrifies me is simply this: that this nation which for thousands of years had believed in the God of justice is now starting to cling to that aspect of their religion that Heine rightly dubbed the 'unhealthy ancient Egyptian belief'; and they do so because it helps them to 'believe in the Jewish people,' that is to say, to believe in themselves. Pardon me for saying so, but this is true idolatry. If only all the idol worshippers could be as sympathetic as your friend was and is."

2. Gideon Hausner (1915–1919) was the Israeli attorney general who led the prosecution against Eichmann.

3. "Simple."

4. Zindel Grynspan (1886–1992) was the father of Herschel Grynspan, who assassinated a German official in Paris in 1938. In response the Nazis launched the Kristallnacht pogroms. Arendt was impressed with Zindel's honesty and integrity. See *Eichmann*, p. 227.

5. As Abba Kovner reported during the Eichmann trial, Anton Schmid (1900–1942) was a German soldier executed by the Germans for helping Jews. See *Eichmann*, p. 230.

Letter 134

1. The editor of the *Neue Zürcher Zeitung*, Eric Streiff (1901–1988), wrote the review "Eichmann in Jerusalem: 'Eine kritische Darstellung des Kriegsverbrecherprozesses,'" in *Neue Zürcher Zeitung* (22 June 1963), p. 3.

Letter 135

1. "Olej Germania" was the group that published the *Mitteilungsblatt*.

Letter 136

1. Scholem wrote this as dedication to Arendt on an offprint of his essay "Tradition und Kommentar als religiöse Kategorie im Judentum" (Tradition and

Commentary as Religious Categories in Judaism). The essay appeared in *Eranos-Jahrbuch* (1963), pp. 19–48.

Letter 137

1. John Mander wrote for *Encounter* magazine.
2. Gershom Scholem, *Judaica* (Frankfurt: Suhrkamp, 1963).
3. Peter Suhrkamp (1891–1959) founded the publishing house Suhrkamp in 1950.
4. The two-volume edition of Benjamin's letters appeared in 1966.

Letter 138

1. Like the Congress for Cultural Freedom, the British cultural journal *Encounter* was subsidized by the CIA.
2. Arendt's first husband was Günther Anders (1902–1992), a German-Jewish philosopher who, like Arendt, had studied with Martin Heidegger. Anders (he had changed his name from Stern) was also Benjamin's cousin.

Letter 139

1. Werner Weber (1919–2005) was chief editor of the cultural section of the *Neuen Zürcher Zeitung*.
2. See enclosure to Letter 138.

Letter 141

1. The lecture was published as "Walter Benjamin," *Leo Baeck Year Book* (1965), pp. 117–36.

BIBLIOGRAPHY

1. Works by Hannah Arendt

1.1. Monographs and Edited Editions

Between Past and Future, New York 1962.

Eichmann in Jerusalem: A Report on the Banality of Evil, New York 1963; Ger. *Eichmann in Jerusalem. Ein Bericht von der Banalität des Bösen*, Hamburg 1964.

Elemente und Ursprünge totaler Herrschaft, Munich 2005; Eng. *The Origins of Totalitarianism*, New York 1951.

Fragwürdige Traditionsbestände im politischen Denken der Gegenwart, Hamburg 1957.

The Human Condition, Chicago 1958; Ger. *Vita activa oder vom tätigen Leben*, Munich 1967.

Ich will verstehen. Selbstauskünfte zu Leben und Werk, Munich 2005.

The Jewish Writings, eds. Jerome Kohn and Ron H. Feldman, New York 2007.

Karl Jaspers. Rede zur Verleihung des Friedenspreises des deutschen Buchhandels, Munich 1958; also in the *Börsenblatt für den Deutschen Buchhandel*, 1958, no. 79.

Die Krise des Zionismus, trans. and ed. Eike Geisel, Berlin 1989.

Der Liebesbegriff bei Augustin. Versuch einer philosophischen Interpretation, Berlin 1929; reissued with an afterword by Ludger Lütkehaus, Berlin/Vienna 2003.

Men in Dark Times, New York 1968; Ger. *Menschen in finsteren Zeiten*, essays and other texts 1955–1975, ed. Ursula Ludz, Munich 2001.

On Revolution, New York 1963; Ger. *Über die Revolution*, Munich 1963.

Rahel Varnhagen. Lebensgeschichte einer deutschen Jüdin aus der Romantik, Munich 1981; Eng. *The Life of a Jewess*, trans. Richard and Clara Winston, London 1957.

Sechs Essays, Heidelberg 1948.
Die ungarische Revolution und der totalitäre Imperialismus, Munich 1958.
Verborgene Tradition, Frankfurt am Main 2007.
Von der Menschlichkeit in finsteren Zeiten. Gedanken zu Lessing, Hamburg 1960.
Vor Antisemitismus ist man nur noch auf dem Monde sicher, ed. Marie Luise Knott, Munich 2001.
Was ist Politik? Fragmente aus dem Nachlaß, ed. Ursula Ludz, with a foreword by Kurt Sontheimer, Munich 1993.
Zur Zeit, ed. Marie Luise Knott, Berlin 1986.
Arendt, Hannah/Heinrich Blücher, *Briefe 1936–1968*, ed. L. Köhler, Munich 1996.
Arendt, Hannah/Kurt Blumenfeld, *In keinem Besitz verwurzelt*, Berlin 1995.
Arendt, Hannah/Hermann Broch, *Briefwechsel 1946 bis 1951*, ed. Paul Lützeler, Frankfurt am Main 1996.
Arendt, Hannah/Karl Jaspers, *Briefwechsel 1926–1969*, Munich 2001.

1.2. Articles and Essays

"The Aftermath of Nazi Rule," in *Commentary*, 4, 1950, pp. 342–353.
"Approaches to the German Problem," in *Partisan Review*, 1945, no. 1, pp. 93–106.
"The Concentration Camps," in *Partisan Review*, 15, 1948, no. 7, pp. 743–763; Ger. in *Die Wandlung* 3, 1948, no. 4, pp. 309–330.
"Concerning Minorities," in *Contemporary Jewish Record*, 4, 1944, pp. 353–368.
"Creating a Cultural Atmosphere," in *Commentary*, 4, 1947, no. 5, pp. 424–426.
"Der Dichter Bertolt Brecht," in *Neue Rundschau*, 61, 1950, no. 1, pp. 53–67.
"Eric Voegelin (A Reply)," in *Review of Politics*, 1953, no. 1, pp. 76–84.
"The Ex-Communists," in *The Commonwealth*, 57, 20 March 1953, no. 24, pp. 595–599.
"Expansion and the Philosophy of Power," in *Sewanee Review*, 54, 1946, no. 4, pp. 601–616.
"From the Dreyfus Affair to France today," in *Jewish Social Studies*, 4, 1942, no. 3, pp. 195–240.
"Für und gegen Paul Tillich," in *Aufbau*, 31 July 1942, p. 6.
"Die Geheimpolizei," in *Der Monat*, 4, 1952, no. 46, pp. 370–388.
"Gestern waren sie noch Kommunisten," in *Aufbau*, 19, 1953, no. 31, p. 19; and no. 32, pp. 13, 16.
"Hermann Broch und der moderne Roman," in *Der Monat*, 1, 1948–1949, no. 8–9, pp. 147–151.
"Ideologie und Terror," in *Offener Horizont. Festschrift für Karl Jaspers*, ed. Klaus Piper, Munich 1953, pp. 229–254.
"The Image of Hell," in *Commentary*, 2, 1946, pp. 291–295.
"In Memoriam Adolf S. Oko," in *Aufbau*, 13 October 1944, p. 9.
"The Jew as Pariah—A Hidden Tradition," in *Jewish Social Studies*, 1944, no. 2, pp. 99–122; Ger. "Die verborgene Tradition," in *Sechs Essays*, Heidelberg 1948.

"Jewish History Revised," in *Jewish Frontier*, 1948, no. 3, pp. 34–38.
"The Jewish State—50 Years After," in *Commentary*, 1, 1945/46, no. 7, pp. 1–8; Ger. "Der Judenstaat—Wohin hat uns Herzls Politik geführt," in *Die Krise des Zionismus*, pp. 61–81.
"Karl Marx and the Tradition of Western Political Thought," lecture from 1953; excerpted in *Social Research*, Summer 2002.
"No Longer and Not Yet," in *The Nation*, 163, 14 September 1946, no. 11, pp. 300–302.
"Organised Guilt and Universal Responsibility," in *Jewish Frontier*, 12, 1945, no. 1, pp. 19–23.
"Das Phänomen der Revolution," in *Politische Vierteljahresschrift*, Cologne and Opladen, no. 2, pp. 116–149.
"Privileged Jews," in *Jewish Social Studies*, 8, 1946, 1, pp. 3–30.
"Race Thinking before Racism," in *Review of Politics*, 1, 1945, pp. 36–43.
"Die sogenannte jüdische Armee," in *Aufbau*, 22 May 1942.
"To Save the Jewish Homeland There Is Still Time," in *Commentary*, 5, 1948, no. 5, pp. 398–406.
"Tradition and the Modern Age," in *Partisan Review*, 1954, no. 1, pp. 53–75.
"Why the Cremieux Decree Was Abrogated," in *Contemporary Jewish Record*, 6, 1943, no. 2, pp. 115–122.
"Zionism Reconsidered," in *Menorah*, 2, 1945, pp. 162–196; Ger. "Der Zionismus aus heutiger Sicht," trans. Friedrich Griese, in *Die verborgene Tradition. Acht Essays*, Frankfurt am Main 1976, pp. 127–168.

2. Works by Gershom Scholem

2.1. Monographs and Edited Editions

Anfänge der Kabbala (Hebr.), Jerusalem and Tel Aviv 1948.
Briefe I, Frankfurt am Main1996.
Briefe II, Frankfurt am Main 1995.
Die Geheimnisse der Tora. Ein Kapitel aus dem Sohar, Berlin 1936.
Judaica 1–6, Frankfurt am Main 1968–1997.
Major Trends in Jewish Mysticism, New York 1941.
Sabbatai Zwi und die sabbatianische Bewegung zu seinen Lebzeiten (Hebr.), Tel Aviv 1957 (Ger. *Sabbatei Zwi. Der mystische Messias*, trans. Angelika Schweikhart, Frankfurt am Main 1992).
Ursprung und Anfänge der Kabbala, Berlin 1962 (Studia Judaica, Forschungen zur Wissenschaft des Judentums 3) (Eng. *The Origins of the Kabbalah*, Princeton 1987).
Von Berlin nach Jerusalem, expanded edition, Frankfurt am Main 1997.
Von der mystischen Gestalt der Gottheit. Studien zu Grundbegriffen der Kabbala, Zurich 1962.

Walter Benjamin—die Geschichte einer Freundschaft, Frankfurt am Main 1997.
Walter Benjamin und sein Engel. Vierzehn Aufsätze und kleine Beiträge, Frankfurt am Main 1983.
Zur Kabbala und ihrer Symbolik, Zurich 1960.
Benjamin, Walter/Scholem, Gershom, *Briefwechsel 1933–1940*, Frankfurt am Main 1980.

2.2. Articles and Essays

"Anfänge der Kabbala" (Hebr.), in *Buchreihe im Gedenken an Bialik* (Hebr.), 10, 1946/1947, pp. 179–228.
"Devekuth, or Communion with God," in *Review of Religion*, 14, 1949/1950, pp. 115–139.
"Eichmann," in *Amoth*, August/September 1962, pp. 10 f.
"Identifizierung und Distanz. Ein Rückblick," in *Eranos-Jahrbuch*, 48, 1979, pp. 463–467.
"Juden und Deutsche," in *Neue Rundschau*, 77, 1966, pp. 547–572; reprinted in *Judaica*, 2, pp. 20–46.
"Kabbalah und Mythos," in *Eranos-Jahrbuch*, 17, 1949, pp. 287–334.
"Die Lehre vom 'Gerechten' in der jüdischen Mystik," in *Eranos-Jahrbuch*, 27, 1958, pp. 237–297.
"Martin Buber's Chassidism: A Critique," in *Commentary*, October 1961, pp. 305–316.
"The Meaning of the Torah in Jewish Mysticism," in *Diogenes*, 1956, no. 14, pp. 36–47; no. 15, pp. 65–94; Ger. "Der Sinn der Tora in der jüdischen Mystik," in *Zur Kabbala und ihrer Symbolik*, Zurich 1960, pp. 49–116.
"Die Metamorphose des häretischen Messianismus der Sabbatianer im religiösen Nihilismus im 18. Jahrhundert," in *Zeugnisse. Theodor W. Adorno zum sechzigsten Geburtstag*, Frankfurt am Main 1963, pp. 20–32; reprinted in *Judaica*, 3, Frankfurt am Main 1973, pp. 198–217.
"Le mouvement sabbataïste en Pologne," in *Revue de l'histoire des religions*, 1953, pp. 42–77.
"Tradition und Kommentar als religiöse Kategorie im Judentum," *Sonderdruck aus Eranos-Jahrbuch*, 31, 1962.
"Tradition und Neuschöpfung im Ritus der Kabbalisten," in *Eranos-Jahrbuch*, 19, 1950, pp. 121–180.
"Um was geht der Streit," in *Scheifotenu*, 2, 1931/1932, no. 6, pp. 191–203; also *Informationsblatt*, ed. *Hechaluz, Deutscher Landesverband*, 4, 1931, no. 39, pp. 15–19.
"Die Vorstellung des Golem in ihren tellurischen und magischen Beziehungen," in *Eranos-Jahrbuch*, 22, 1953, pp. 235–289.
"Walter Benjamin," in *Leo Baeck Yearbook*, 10, 1965, 117–136; Ger. "Walter Benjamin," in *Neue Rundschau*, 76, 1965, pp. 1–21; reprinted in *Judaica*, 2, Frankfurt

am Main 1970 and *Walter Benjamin und sein Engel. Vierzehn Aufsätze und kleine Beiträge*, Frankfurt am Main 1983.
"Die Wissenschaft vom Judentum," in *Judaica*, 6, Frankfurt am Main 1997, pp. 7–52.
"Zehn unhistorische Sätze über Kabbala," in *Geist und Werk. Festschrift zum 75. Geburtstag von Dr. Daniel Brody*, Zurich 1958, pp. 209–215. Slightly expanded version reprinted in *Judaica*, 3, Frankfurt am Main 1973, pp. 264–271.
"Zum Verständnis der messianischen Idee im Judentum," in *Eranos-Jahrbuch*, 28, 1959, pp. 193–239; reprinted in *Judaica*, 1, Frankfurt am Main 1963, pp. 7–74.
"Zur Entwicklungsgeschichte der kabbalistischen Konzeption der Schechinah," in *Eranos-Jahrbuch*, 11, 1952, pp. 45–207.
"Zur Geschichte der Anfänge der christlichen Kabbala," in *Essays Presented to Leo Baeck*, London 1954.

3. Additional Authors and Works

3.1. Monographs and Edited Editions

Adler, Hans Günther, *Theresienstadt 1941–1945. Das Antlitz einer Zwangsgemeinschaft*, Tübingen 1955, 2nd revised and expanded edition 1960.
Adorno, Theodor W., *Minima Moralia*, Frankfurt am Main 1950.
Althaus, Claudia, *Erfahrung Denken. Hannah Arendts Weg von der Zeitgeschichte zur politischen Theorie*, Göttingen 2000.
Baron, Salo, *A Social and Religious History of the Jews*, 3 volumes, New York 1937.
Benjamin, Walter, *Berliner Kindheit um neunzehnhundert*, Frankfurt am Main 2000.
Benjamin, Walter, *Gesammelte Schriften*, Frankfurt am Main 1977 ff.
Benjamin, Walter, *Illuminationen*, Frankfurt am Main 2006.
Benjamin, Walter, *Illuminations*, ed. Hannah Arendt, New York 1967.
Benjamin, Walter, *Schriften I und II*, eds. Theodor W. Adorno and Gretel Adorno in collaboration with Friedrich Podszus, 2 volumes, Frankfurt am Main 1955.
Benjamin, Walter, *Versuche über Brecht*, ed. and with an afterword by Rolf Tiedemann, Frankfurt am Main 1966.
Benjamin, Walter/Scholem, Gershom, *Briefwechsel 1933–1940*, Frankfurt am Main 1980.
The Black Book: The Nazi Crime Against the Jewish People, comp. and ed. World Jewish Congress et al., New York 1946.
Blumenfeld, Kurt, *Erlebte Judenfrage. Ein Vierteljahrhundert deutscher Zionismus*, Stuttgart 1962.
Blumenfeld, Kurt, *Im Kampf um den Zionismus*, Stuttgart 1976.
Broch, Hermann, *Der Tod des Vergil*, New York 1945.
Broch, Hermann, *Dichten und Erkennen*, ed. and with an introduction by Hannah Arendt, Zurich 1955.

Broch, Hermann, *Erkennen und Handeln*, ed. Hannah Arendt, Zurich 1955.

Dawidowicz, Lucy, *From That Place and Time: A Memoir, 1938–1947*, Rutgers, NJ, 1989.

Elbogen, Ismar/Klatzkin, Jakob, *Encyclopaedia Judaica: das Judentum in Geschichte und Gegenwart*, Berlin 1928–1934.

Frankfurter Adorno Blätter 5, Frankfurt am Main 1998.

German Psychological Warfare, ed. Ladislas Farago, New York 1942.

Gershom Scholem. Zwischen den Disziplinen, eds. Peter Schäfer and Gary Smith, Frankfurt am Main 1995.

Hahn, Barbara/Knott, Marie Luise, *Hannah Arendt—Von den Dichtern erwarten wir Wahrheit*, publication series of the Literaturhaus Berlin, vol. 17, Berlin 2007.

Hannah Arendt in Jerusalem, ed. Steven Aschheim, Los Angeles 2001.

Hannah Arendt Revisited: "Eichmann in Jerusalem" und die Folgen, ed. Gary Smith, Frankfurt am Main 2000.

Herzl, Theodor, *Der Judenstaat*, Vienna 1896.

Honigmann, Barbara, *Roman von einem Kinde*, Darmstadt/Neuwied 1987.

Jaspers, Karl, *Die Schuldfrage*, Heidelberg/Zurich 1946.

Jonas, Hans, *Erinnerungen*, Frankfurt am Main 2005.

Jonas, Hans, *Organismus und Freiheit. Ansätze zu einer philosophischen Biologie*, Göttingen 1973.

The Joshua Starr Memorial Volume: Studies in History and Philology, ed. Conference on Jewish Relations, New York 1953.

Jüdischer Almanach 2001, Frankfurt am Main 2000.

Klatzkin, Jakob, *Thesaurus Philosophiens Linguae Hebraicae*, Berlin 1926.

Koestler, Arthur, *Darkness at Noon* (Ger. *Sonnenfinsternis*), London 1940.

Koestler, Arthur, *Scum of the Earth* (Ger. *Abschaum der Erde*), New York 1941.

Lau, Moses Chaim, *Ha-derech lekidusch ha-schem* (The Path to Healing the Name), Tel Aviv 1963.

Lüscher, Rudolf M./Schweizer, Werner, *Amalie und Theo Pinkus-De Sassi. Leben im Widerspruch*, Zurich 1987.

Moses, Siegfried, *Jüdische Nachkriegsforderungen*, Tel Aviv 1944.

Mosès, Stephane, *Der Engel der Geschichte*, Frankfurt am Main 1994.

Nach dem Eichmann-Prozess—Zu einer Kontroverse über die Haltung der Juden, ed. Council of Jews from Germany, Tel Aviv 1963.

Offener Horizont, Festschrift für Karl Jaspers, ed. Klaus Piper, Munich 1953.

Sahl, Hans, *Das Exil im Exil. Memoiren eines Moralisten II*, Darmstadt and Neuwied 1985.

Sahl, Hans, "Walter Benjamin im Lager," in *Zur Aktualität Walter Benjamins*, ed. Siegfried Unseld, Frankfurt am Main 1972.

Schoeps, Hans-Joachim, *Ja—Nein—und Trotzdem. Erinnerungen—Begegnungen—Erfahrungen*, Mainz 1974.

Schopf, Wolfgang (ed.), *"So müsste ich ein Engel und kein Autor sein." Adorno und seine Frankfurter Verleger, Der Briefwechsel mit Peter Suhrkamp und Siegfried Unseld*, Frankfurt am Main 2003.

Sinn und Form. Sonderheft Bertolt Brecht [I], Potsdam 1949.

Steinschneider, Moritz, *Catalog der Hebräischen Handschriften in der Stadtbibliothek zu Hamburg*, Hamburg 1878.

Sternberger, Dolf, *Panorama oder Ansichten vom 19. Jahrhundert*, Hamburg 1938.

Syrkin, Marie, *Blessed Is the Match: The Story of Jewish Resistance*, Philadelphia 1947.

Taubes, Jacob, *Der Preis des Messianismus: Briefe von Jacob Taubes an Gershom Scholem und andere Materialien*, ed. Elettra Stimilli, Würzburg 2006.

Tishby, Isaiah, *Torat ha-Ra ve-ha-Qelippa be-Kabbalat ha-Ari* (Teaching of Evil and Vessels/OR Shells in Lurianic Kabbalah), Jerusalem 1942.

Varnhagen von Ense, Karl August, *Denkwürdigkeiten des eigenen Lebens*, 3 volumes, Frankfurt am Main 1988.

Vierzig Jahre Flaschenpost: Dialektik der Aufklärung, 1947–1987, eds. Willem van Reijen and Gunzelin Schmid Noerr, Frankfurt am Main 1987.

"Von Walter Benjamins Archiven zum Walter Benjamin Archiv," comps. U. Marx, G. Schwarz, M. Schwarz, and E. Wizisla, in *Text und Kritik* 31/32, new edition, Göttingen 2009, pp. 134–210.

Walter Benjamin 1892–1940. Eine Ausstellung des Theodor W. Adorno Archivs Frankfurt am Main in Verbindung mit dem Deutschen Literaturarchiv Marbach am Neckar, eds. Rolf Tiedemann, Christoph Gödde, and Henri Lonitz, Marbach am Neckar 1990 (Marbacher Magazin 55).

Walter Benjamin zum Gedächtnis, special publication of the Institut für Sozialforschung, New York 1942.

Was übrig blieb. Das Museum jüdischer Altertümer in Frankfurt 1922–1938, exhibition (1988–1989) of the Jewish Museum Frankfurt, Frankfurt am Main 1988.

Weinreich, Max, *Hitler's Professors*, New York 1946.

Wiedebach, Hartwig, *Die Hermann-Cohen-Bibliothek* (Hermann Cohen, *Werke*, Supplement 2), Hildesheim 2000.

Wizisla, Erdmut, *Benjamin und Brecht*, Frankfurt am Main 2004.

Wizisla, Erdmut/Schöttker, Detlev (eds.), *Arendt und Benjamin*, Frankfurt am Main 2006.

Zadoff, Noam, "Reise in die Vergangenheit, Entwurf einer neuen Zukunft. Gershom Scholems Reise nach Deutschland im Jahre 1946," in *Münchner Beiträge zur Jüdischen Geschichte und Kultur* 2007, no. 2, pp. 67–80.

Zohar, the Book of Splendor, selected and ed. Gershom G. Scholem, New York 1949.

Zur Aktualität Walter Benjamins, ed. Siegfried Unseld, Frankfurt am Main 1972.

3.2. Articles and Essays

Adorno, Theodor W., "Charakteristik Walter Benjamins," in *Neue Rundschau*, 1950, no. 4, pp. 571–584.

Auras, Christiane, "Das Zuhause im Exil—Hannah Arendt und Hans Jonas. Eine Lebens-Freundschaft im Schatten des Nationalsozialismus," in *Mensch—Gott—Welt. Philosophie des Lebens, Religionsphilosophie und Metaphysik im Werk von Hans Jonas*, eds. Dieter Böhler, Horst Gronke, and Bernadette Herrmann, Freiburg 2008.

Baron, Salo, "Ghetto and Emancipation. Shall we Revise the Traditional View," in *Menorah Journal*, 14, 1928, no. 6, pp. 515–526.

Benjamin, Walter, "Notes on Brecht's Epic Theatre," in *Western Review*, 12, 1948, no. 1, pp. 167–173.

Benjamin, Walter, "Über den Begriff der Geschichte," in *Sonderheft des Instituts für Sozialforschung*, 1942; "Sur le concept d'histoire," Fr. first in *Les temps modernes*, 2, 1947, no. 25, pp. 623–634 (trans. Pierre Missac); Ger. reprinted in *Neue Rundschau*, 4, 1950, pp. 560–570.

Benjamin, Walter, "Über einige Motive bei Baudelaire," in *Zeitschrift für Sozialforschung*, 8, 1939, appeared 1940, no. 1–2, pp. 50–89; reprinted in *Sinn und Form*, no. 4, first volume, 1949.

"Eichmann Tells His Own Damning Story," in *Life*, 28 November and 5 December 1960.

Fleg, Edmond, "Les grands courants de la mystique juive de G.-G. Scholem," in *Revue de la pensée juive*, 1950, no. 1/3, pp. 134–137.

Heller, Bernard, "Jewish Books and Religious Articles Found in the Hand of Nazis," in *Forward, Forverts*, 12 February 1950, p. 8.

Horkheimer, Max, "Die Juden in Europa," in *SPSS*, 8, 1939, pp. 136 ff.

Jaspers, Karl, "Erneuerung der Universität," in *Die Wandlung*, 1945/1946, pp. 66–74.

Knott, Marie Luise, "Aus einer Totenpost. Wie das erste Schreibwerk von Walter Benjamin die Jahrzehnte überlebt hat," in *Frankfurter Allgemeine Zeitung*, 2 January 2010, pp. Z1 and 2.

Rosenstreich, Nathan, "For and against Emanzipation. The Bruno Bauer Controversy," in *Leo Baeck Yearbook*, 4, 1959, pp. 3–36.

Schidorsky, Dov, "Confiscation of Libraries and Assignments to Forced Labor: Two Documents of the Holocaust," in *Libraries & Culture*, 33, 1998, no. 4, pp. 347–388.

Suchoff, David, "Gershom Scholem, Hannah Arendt and the Scandal of Jewish Particularity," in *Germanic Review*, 72, Winter 1997, no. 1, pp. 57 ff.

Taubes, Jacob, "From Cult to Culture," in *Partisan Review*, 21, 1954, pp. 387–400.

Vajda, Georges, "Précisions sur la Kabbale," in *Critique*, June/July 1947.

INDEX OF PERSONS

ABBREVIATIONS

AJA	American Jewish Archives
AJC	American Jewish Committee
BN	Bibliothèque Nationale de France
BoD	Board of Directors
CAHJP	Central Archives for the History of the Jewish People
CEJCR	Commission on European Jewish Cultural Reconstruction
CJG	Council (for the Protection of Rights and Interests) of Jews from Germany
CJR	*Contemporary Jewish Record*
ConfJR	Conference on Jewish Relations
CRCJM	Committee on Restoration of Continental Jewish Museums, Libraries, and Archives
CV	Central Association for German Citizens of Jewish Belief
FR	Field Reports
HMEV	Hessen Minister of Education and Popular Education
HU	Hebrew University of Jerusalem
HUC	Hebrew Union College
IfS	Institute for Social Research
IKG	Israelite Cultural Community Vienna
IOME	Organization of Central European Immigrants (Irgun Olej Merkasz Europa)
JA	Jewish Agency
JCC	Conference on Jewish Material Claims against Germany
JCR	Jewish Cultural Reconstruction, Inc.
JDC	*See* Joint
JHGA	Jewish Historical General Archives
JIR	Jewish Institute of Religion
JNL	Jewish National Library (from 1924: JNUL)

	Joint American Jewish Joint Distribution Committee
JPS	Jewish Publication Society
JRSO	Jewish Restitution Successor Organization
JSS	*Jewish Social Studies*
JTA	Jewish Telegraphic Agency
JTC	Jewish Trust Corporation
JTS	Jewish Theological Seminary of America
KPD	Communist Party of Germany
LBI	Leo Baeck Institute
LBYB	Leo Baeck Year Book
LoC	Library of Congress
MB	Mitteilungsblatt of the IOME
NLI	National Library of Israel
NZZ	*Neue Zürcher Zeitung*
ÖWB	Public Scientific Library (former Prussian State Library, 1946–1954)
PR	*Partisan Review*
RSHA	Reichssicherheitshauptamt
SED	Socialist Unity Party of Germany
SPSS	*Studies in Philosophy and Social Science* (from 1940)
UTS	Union Theological Seminary
WIZO	Women's International Zionist Organization
WJC	World Jewish Congress
ZfS	*Zeitschrift für Sozialforschung* (until 1940)
ZVfD	Zionist Federation of Germany